# THE GREATEST STORY EVER REVEALED;

# THE GOSPEL ACCORDING TO ANDREW

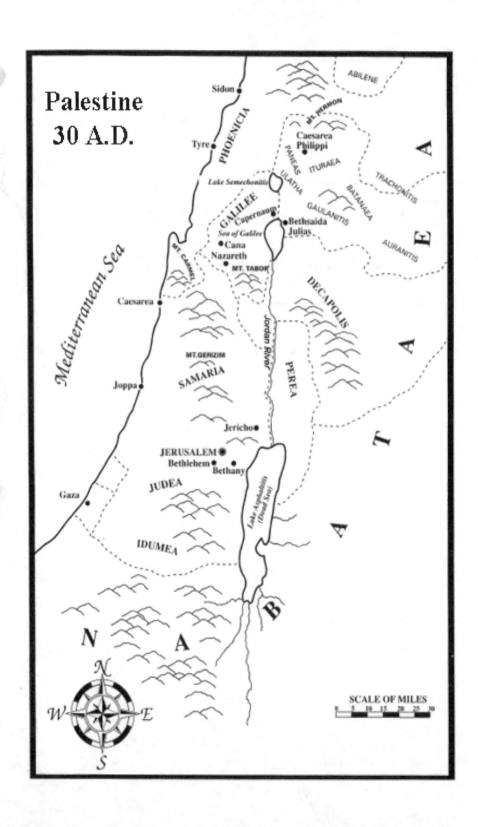

# THE GREATEST STORY EVER REVEALED;

# THE GOSPEL ACCORDING TO ANDREW

Edited by Steve Hart

**Hart-Burn Press, Inc.**
PO Box 99
Newton Jct, New Hampshire 03859

First Hart-Burn Press Edition, January 2004

FIRST EDITION

10 9 8 7 6 5 4 3 2 1

Published in 2004 in the United States by
Hart-Burn Press, Inc., PO Box 99,
Newton Jct., New Hampshire 03859

www.stevehartbooks.com
Hart-Burn ISBN 0-9740318-3-6

**Cataloging in Publication Data**:
Hart, Steve
The Greatest Story Ever Revealed;
The Gospel According to Andrew-1st ed. p.432 cm.
1-Christianity
2- Christianity- origin
3-Bible N.T.- criticism, interpretation, etc.

ATTENTION CORPORATIONS, UNIVERSITIES, COLLEGES,
AND PROFESSIONAL ORGANIZATIONS:

Quantity discounts are available on bulk purchases of this book
for educational, gift purposes, or as premiums for increasing maga-
zine subscriptions or renewals.
For information contact info@stevehartbooks.com

*For all of us*

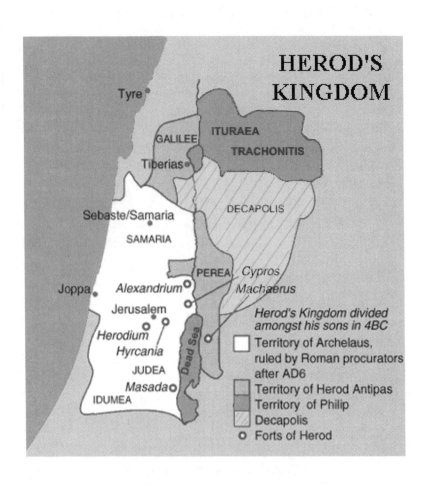

# Contents

## Part Two

# PART
# TWO

# THE PUBLIC MINISTRY

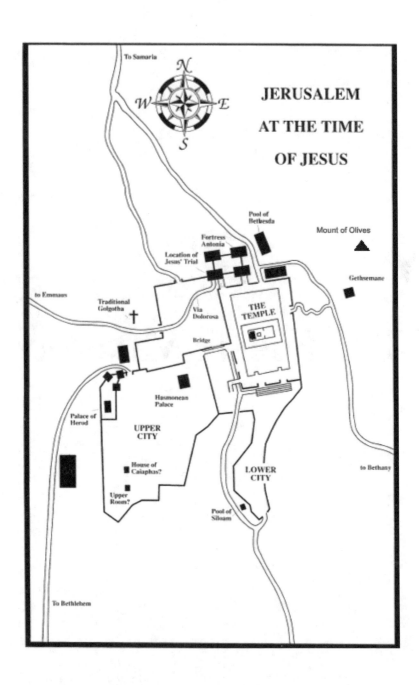

JERUSALEM

AT THE TIME

OF JESUS

## TARRYING TIME IN GALILEE

**E**ARLY ON Saturday morning, February 23, A.D. 26, Jesus came down from the hills to rejoin John's company encamped at Pella. All that day Jesus mingled with the multitude. He ministered to a lad who had injured himself in a fall and journeyed to the nearby village of Pella to deliver the boy safely into the hands of his parents.

**D**uring this Sabbath two of John's leading disciples spent much time with Jesus. Of all John's followers one named Andrew was the most profoundly impressed with Jesus; he accompanied him on the trip to Pella with the injured boy. On the way back to John's rendezvous Andrew asked Jesus many questions, and just before reaching their destination, they paused for a short talk, during which Andrew said, "I have observed you ever since you came to Capernaum, and I believe you are the new Teacher, and though I do not understand all your teaching, I have fully made up my mind to follow you; I would sit at your feet and learn the whole truth about the new kingdom." And Jesus, with hearty assurance, welcomed Andrew as the first of his apostles, that group of twelve who were to labor with him in the work of establishing the new kingdom of God in the hearts of men.

Andrew was a silent observer of, and sincere believer in, John's work, and he had a very able and enthusiastic brother, named Simon, who was one of John's foremost disciples. It would not be amiss to say that Simon was one of John's chief supporters.

Soon after Jesus and Andrew returned to the camp, Andrew sought out his brother, Simon, and taking him aside, informed him that he had settled in his own mind that Jesus was the great Teacher, and that he had pledged himself as a disciple. He went on to say that Jesus had accepted his proffer of service and suggested that he (Simon) likewise go to Jesus and offer himself for fellowship in the service of the new kingdom.

Said Simon, "Ever since this man came to work in Zebedee's shop, I have believed he was sent by God, but what about John? Are we to forsake him? Is this the right thing to do?" Whereupon they agreed to go at once to consult John.

John was saddened by the thought of losing two of his able advisers and most promising disciples, but he bravely answered their inquiries, saying, "This is but the beginning; presently will my work end, and we shall all become his disciples." Then Andrew beckoned to Jesus to draw aside while he announced that his brother desired to join himself to the service of the New Kingdom.

And in welcoming Simon as his second apostle, Jesus said, "Simon, your enthusiasm is commendable, but it is dangerous to the work of the kingdom. I admonish you to become more thoughtful in your speech. I would change your name to Peter."

The parents of the injured lad who lived at Pella had besought Jesus to spend the night with them, to make their house his home, and he had promised. Before leaving Andrew and his brother, Jesus said, "Early on the morrow we go into Galilee."

After Jesus had returned to Pella for the night, and while Andrew and Simon were yet discussing the nature of their service in the establishment of the forthcoming kingdom, James and John the sons of Zebedee arrived upon the scene, having just returned from their long and futile searching in the hills for Jesus. When they heard Simon Peter tell how he and his brother, Andrew, had become the first accepted counselors of the New Kingdom, and that they were to leave with their new Master on the morrow for Galilee, both James and John were sad. They had known Jesus for some time, and they loved him. They had searched for him many days in the hills, and now they returned to learn that others had been preferred before them. They inquired where Jesus had gone and made haste to find him.

Jesus was asleep when they reached his abode, but they awakened him. "How is it," they asked, "that while we who have so long lived with you are searching in the hills for you, you prefer others before us and choose Andrew and Simon as your first associates in the new kingdom?"

Jesus answered them, "Be calm in your hearts and ask yourselves, `who directed that you should search for the Son of Man when he was about his Father's business?'" After they had recited the details of their long search in the hills, Jesus further instructed them. "You should learn to search for the secret of the New Kingdom in your hearts and not in the hills. That which you sought was already present in your souls. You are indeed my brethren; you needed not to be received by me, already were you of the kingdom, and you should be of good cheer, making ready also to go with us tomorrow into Galilee."

John then made bold to ask, "But, Master, will James and I be associates with you in the New Kingdom, even as Andrew and Simon?"

And Jesus, laying a hand on the shoulder of each of them, said, "My brethren, you were already with me in the spirit of the kingdom, even before these others made request to be received. You, my brethren, have no need to make request for entrance into the kingdom; you have been with me in the kingdom from the beginning. Before men, others may take precedence over you, but in my heart did I also number you in the councils of the kingdom, even before you thought to make this request of me. And even so might you have been first before men had you not been absent engaged in a well-intentioned but self-appointed task of seeking for one who was not lost. In the coming kingdom, be not mindful of those things which foster your anxiety but rather at all times concern yourselves only with doing the will of the Father who is in heaven."

James and John received the rebuke in good grace; never more were they envious of Andrew and Simon. And they made ready, with their two associate apostles, to depart for Galilee the next morning. From this day on the term apostle was employed to distinguish the chosen family of Jesus' advisers from the vast multitude of believing disciples who subsequently followed him.

Late that evening, James, John, Andrew, and Simon held converse with John the Baptist, and with tearful eye but steady voice the stalwart Judean prophet surrendered two of his leading disciples to become the apostles of the Galilean Prince of the coming kingdom.

Sunday morning, February 24, A.D. 26, Jesus took leave of John the Baptist by the river near Pella, never again to see him in the flesh.

That day, as Jesus and his four apostles departed for Galilee, there was a great tumult in the camp of John's followers. The first great division was about to take place. The day before, John had made his positive pronouncement to Andrew and Ezra that Jesus was the Deliverer. Andrew decided to follow Jesus, but Ezra rejected the mild-mannered carpenter of Nazareth, proclaiming to his associates, "The Prophet Daniel declares that the Son of Man will come with the clouds of heaven, in power and great glory. This Galilean carpenter, this Capernaum boatbuilder, cannot be the Deliverer. Can such a gift of God come out of Nazareth? This Jesus is a relative of John, and through much kindness of heart has our teacher been deceived. Let us remain aloof from this false Messiah."

When John rebuked Ezra for these utterances, he drew away with many disciples and hastened south. And this group continued to baptize in John's name and eventually founded a sect of those who believed in John but refused to accept Jesus. A remnant of this group persists in Mesopotamia even to this day.

While this trouble was brewing among John's followers, Jesus and his four apostles were well on their way toward Galilee. Before they crossed the Jordan, to go by way of Nain to Nazareth, Jesus, looking ahead and up the road, saw one Philip of Bethsaida with a friend coming toward them. Jesus had known Philip aforetime, and he was also well known to all four of the new apostles. He was on his way with his friend Nathaniel to visit John at Pella to learn more about the reported coming of the kingdom of God, and he was delighted to greet Jesus. Philip had been an admirer of Jesus ever since he first came to Capernaum. But Nathaniel, who lived at Cana of Galilee, did not know Jesus. Philip went forward to greet his friends while Nathaniel rested under the shade of a tree by the roadside.

Peter took Philip to one side and proceeded to explain that they, referring to himself, Andrew, James, and John, had all become associates of Jesus in the New Kingdom and strongly urged Philip to volunteer for service. Philip was in a quandary. What should he do? Here, without a moment's warning, on the roadside near the Jordan, there had come up for immediate decision the most momentous question of a lifetime. By this time he was in earnest converse with Peter, Andrew, and John while Jesus was outlining to James the trip through Galilee and on to Capernaum. Finally, Andrew suggested to Philip, "Why not ask the Teacher?"

It suddenly dawned on Philip that Jesus was a really great man, possibly the Messiah, and he decided to abide by Jesus' decision in this matter; and he went straight to him, asking, "Teacher, shall I go down to John or shall I join my friends who follow you?"

And Jesus answered, "Follow me."

Philip was thrilled with the assurance that he had found the Deliverer.

Philip now motioned to the group to remain where they were while he hurried back to break the news of his decision to his friend Nathaniel, who still tarried behind under the mulberry tree, turning over in his mind the many things which he had heard concerning John the Baptist, the coming kingdom, and the expected Messiah. Philip broke in upon these meditations, exclaiming, "I have found the Deliverer, him of whom Moses and the prophets wrote and whom John has proclaimed."

Nathaniel, looking up, inquired, "Whence comes this teacher?"

And Philip replied, "He is Jesus of Nazareth, the son of Joseph, the carpenter, more recently residing at Capernaum."

And then, somewhat shocked, Nathaniel asked, "Can any such good thing come out of Nazareth?"

But Philip, taking him by the arm, said, "Come and see."

Philip led Nathaniel to Jesus, who, looking benignly into the face of the sincere doubter, said, "Behold a genuine Israelite, in whom there is no deceit. Follow me."

And Nathaniel, turning to Philip, said: "You are right. He is indeed a master of men. I will also follow, if I am worthy."

And Jesus nodded to Nathaniel, again saying, "Follow me."

Jesus had now assembled one half of his future corps of intimate associates, five who had for some time known him and one stranger, Nathaniel. Without further delay they crossed the Jordan and, going by the village of Nain, reached Nazareth late that evening.

They all remained overnight with Joseph in Jesus' boyhood home. The associates of Jesus little understood why their new-found teacher was so concerned with completely destroying every vestige of his writing which remained about the home in the form of the Ten Commandments and other mottoes and sayings. But this proceeding, together with the fact that they never saw him subsequently write, except upon the dust or in the sand, made a deep impression upon their minds.

The next day Jesus sent his apostles on to Cana, since all of them were invited to the wedding of a prominent young woman of that town, while he prepared to pay a hurried visit to his mother at Capernaum, stopping at Magdala to see his brother Jude.

Before leaving Nazareth, the new associates of Jesus told Joseph and other members of Jesus' family about the wonderful events of the then recent past and gave free expression to their belief that Jesus was the long-expected deliverer.

And these members of Jesus' family talked all this over, and Joseph said, "Maybe, after all, Mother was right; maybe our strange brother is the coming king."

(Editor's Note: See "The Gospel According to Andrew Part I" for a recitation of Jesus' early years, from birth to his baptism under John and the momentous decisions he made at that time.)

Jude was present at Jesus' baptism and, with his brother James, had become a firm believer in Jesus' mission on earth. Although both James and Jude were much perplexed as to the nature of their brother's mission, their mother had resurrected all her early hopes of Jesus as the Messiah, the son of David, and she encouraged her sons to have faith in their brother as the deliverer of Israel.

Jesus arrived in Capernaum Monday night, but he did not go to his own home, where lived James and his mother; he went directly to the home of Zebedee. All his friends at Capernaum saw a great and pleasant change in him. Once more he seemed to be comparatively cheerful and more like himself as he was during the earlier years at Nazareth. For years previous to his baptism and the isolation periods just before and just after, he had grown increasingly serious and self-contained. Now he seemed quite like his old self to all of them. There was about him something of majestic import and exalted aspect, but he was once again light-hearted and joyful.

Mary was thrilled with expectation. She anticipated that the promise of Gabriel was nearing fulfillment. She expected all Palestine soon to be startled and stunned by the miraculous revelation of her son as the supernatural king of the Jews. But to all of the many questions which his mother, James, Jude, and Zebedee asked, Jesus only smilingly replied: "It is better that I tarry here for a while; I must do the will of my Father who is in heaven."

On the next day, Tuesday, they all journeyed over to Cana for the wedding of Naomi, which was to take place on the following day. And in spite of Jesus' repeated warnings that they tell no man about him "until the Father's hour shall come," they insisted on quietly spreading the news abroad that they had found the Deliverer. They each confidently expected that Jesus would inaugurate his assumption of Messianic authority at the forthcoming wedding at Cana, and that he would do so with great power and sublime grandeur. They remembered what had been told them about the phenomena attendant upon his baptism, and they believed that increasing manifestations of supernatural wonders and miraculous demonstrations would mark his future course on earth. Accordingly, the entire countryside was preparing to gather together at Cana for the wedding feast of Naomi and Johab the son of Nathan.

Mary had not been so joyous in years. She journeyed to Cana in the spirit of the queen mother on the way to witness the coronation of her son. Not since he was thirteen years old had Jesus' family and friends seen him so carefree and happy, so thoughtful and understanding of the wishes and desires of his associates, so touchingly sympathetic. And so they all whispered among themselves, in small groups, wondering what was going to happen. What would this strange person do next? How would he usher in the glory of the coming kingdom? And they were all thrilled with the thought that they were to be present to see the revelation of the might and power of Israel's God.

By noon on Wednesday almost a thousand guests had arrived in Cana, more than four times the number bidden to the wedding feast. It was a Jewish custom to celebrate weddings on Wednesday, and the invitations had been sent abroad for the wedding one month previously. In the forenoon and early afternoon it appeared more like a public reception for Jesus than a wedding. Everybody wanted to greet this near-famous Galilean, and he was most cordial to all, young and old, Jew and gentile. And everybody rejoiced when Jesus consented to lead the preliminary wedding procession.

Jesus was now thoroughly self-conscious regarding his human existence, his divine pre-existence, and the status of his combined, or fused, human and divine natures. With perfect poise he could at one moment enact the human role or immediately assume the personality prerogatives of the divine nature.

As the day wore on, Jesus became increasingly conscious that the people were expecting him to perform some wonder; more especially he recognized that his family and his six disciple-apostles were looking for him appropriately to announce his forthcoming kingdom by some startling and supernatural manifestation.

Early in the afternoon Mary summoned James, and together they made bold to approach Jesus to inquire if he would admit them to his confidence to the extent of informing them at what hour and at what point in connection with the wedding ceremonies he had planned to manifest himself as the "supernatural one."

No sooner had they spoken of these matters to Jesus than they saw they had aroused his characteristic indignation. He said only, "If you love me, then be willing to tarry with me while I wait upon the will of my Father who is in heaven." But the eloquence of his rebuke lay in the expression of his face.

This move of his mother was a great disappointment to the human Jesus, and he was much sobered by his reaction to her suggestive proposal that he permit himself to indulge in some outward demonstration of his divinity. That was one of the very things he had decided not to do when so recently isolated in the hills.

(Editor's Note: See "The Gospel According to Andrew Part I")

For several hours Mary was much depressed. She said to James, "I cannot understand him; what can it all mean? Is there no end to his strange conduct?"

James and Jude tried to comfort their mother, while Jesus withdrew for an hour's solitude, after which he returned to the gathering and was once more lighthearted and joyous.

The wedding proceeded with a hush of expectancy, but the entire ceremony was finished and not a move, not a word, from the honored guest. Then it was whispered about that the carpenter and boatbuilder, announced by John as "the Deliverer," would show his hand during the evening festivities, perhaps at the wedding supper.

But all expectance of such a demonstration was effectually removed from the minds of his six disciple-apostles when he called them together just before the wedding supper. In great earnestness, he said, "Think not that I have come to this place to work some wonder for the gratification of the curious or for the conviction of those who doubt. Rather are we here to wait upon the will of our Father who is in heaven."

But when Mary and the others saw him in consultation with his associates, they were fully persuaded in their own minds that something extraordinary was about to happen. And they all sat down to enjoy the wedding supper and the evening of festive good fellowship.

The father of the bridegroom had provided plenty of wine for all the guests bidden to the marriage feast, but how was he to know that the marriage of his son was to become an event so closely associated with the expected manifestation of Jesus as the Messianic deliverer? He was delighted to have the honor of numbering the celebrated Galilean among his guests, but before the wedding supper was over, the servants brought him the disconcerting news that the wine was running short. By the time the formal supper had ended and the guests were strolling about in the garden, the mother of the bridegroom confided to Mary that the supply of wine was exhausted.

Mary confidently said, "Have no worry; I will speak to my son. He will help us." And thus did she presume to speak, notwithstanding the rebuke of but a few hours before.

Throughout a period of many years, Mary had always turned to Jesus for help in every crisis of their home life at Nazareth so that it was only natural for her to think of him at this time. But this ambitious mother had still other motives for appealing to her eldest son on this occasion. As Jesus was standing alone in a corner of the garden, his mother approached him, saying, "My son, they have no wine."

Jesus answered, "My good woman, what have I to do with that?"

Said Mary, "But I believe your hour has come; cannot you help us?"

Jesus replied, "Again I declare that I have not come to do things in this wise. Why do you trouble me again with these matters?"

And then, breaking down in tears, Mary entreated him, "But, my son, I promised them that you would help us; won't you please do something for me?"

And then spoke Jesus, "Woman, what have you to do with making such promises? See that you do it not again. We must in all things wait upon the will of the Father in heaven."

Mary the mother of Jesus was crushed; she was stunned! As she stood there before him motionless, with the tears streaming down her face, the human heart of Jesus was overcome with compassion for the woman who had borne him in the flesh; and bending forward, he laid his hand tenderly upon her head, saying, "Now, now, Mother Mary, grieve not over my apparently hard sayings, for have I not many times told you that I have come only to do the will of my heavenly Father? Most gladly would I do what you ask of me if it were a part of the Father's will..." and Jesus stopped short, he hesitated.

Mary seemed to sense that something was happening. Leaping up, she threw her arms around Jesus' neck, kissed him, and rushed off to the servants' quarters, saying, "Whatever my son says, that do."

But Jesus said nothing. He now realized that he had already said, or rather desirefully thought, too much.

Mary was dancing with glee. She did not know how the wine would be produced, but she confidently believed that she had finally persuaded her first-born son to assert his authority, to dare to step forth and claim his position and exhibit his Messianic power.

And, because of the presence and association of certain universe powers and personalities, of which all those present, save Jesus, were wholly ignorant, she was not to be disappointed. The wine Mary desired and which Jesus, the God-man, humanly and sympathetically wished for, was forthcoming.

Near at hand stood six waterpots of stone, filled with water, holding about twenty gallons apiece. This water was intended for subsequent use in the final purification ceremonies of the wedding celebration. The commotion of the servants about these huge stone vessels, under the busy direction of his mother, attracted Jesus' attention, and going over, he observed that they were drawing wine out of them by the pitcherful.

It was gradually dawning upon Jesus what had happened. Of all persons present at the marriage feast of Cana, Jesus was the most surprised. Others had expected him to work a wonder, but that was just what he had purposed not to do. And then the Son of Man recalled the admonition of his Personalized Thought Adjuster in the hills. He recounted how the Adjuster had warned him about the inability of any power or personality to deprive him of the creator prerogative of independence of time.

(Editor's Note: See The Gospel According to Andrew Part I; this will be the last interjection of this reminder.)

On this occasion power transformers, midwayers, and all other required personalities were assembled near the water and other necessary elements, and in the face of the expressed wish of the Universe Creator Sovereign, there was no escaping the instantaneous appearance of *wine.* And this occurrence was made doubly certain since the Personalized Adjuster had signified that the execution of the Son's desire was in no way a contravention of the Father's will.

But this was in no sense a miracle. No law of nature was modified, abrogated, or even transcended. Nothing happened but the abrogation of *time* in association with the celestial assembly of the chemical elements requisite for the elaboration of the wine. At Cana on this occasion the agents of the Creator made wine just as they do by the ordinary natural processes *except* that they did it independently of time and with the intervention of superhuman agencies in the matter of the space assembly of the necessary chemical ingredients.

Furthermore it was evident that the enactment of this so-called miracle was not contrary to the will of the Paradise Father, else it would not have transpired, since Jesus had already subjected himself in all things to the Father's will.

The servants drew this new wine and carried it to the best man, the "ruler of the feast," and when he had tasted it, he called to the bridegroom, saying, "It is the custom to set out first the good wine and, when the guests have well drunk, to bring forth the inferior fruit of the vine; but you have kept the best of the wine until the last of the feast."

Mary and the disciples of Jesus were greatly rejoiced at the supposed miracle which they thought Jesus had intentionally performed, but Jesus withdrew to a sheltered nook of the garden and engaged in serious thought for a few brief moments. He finally decided that the episode was beyond his personal control under the circumstances and, not being adverse to his Father's will, was inevitable. When he returned to the people, they regarded him with awe; they all believed in him as the Messiah. But Jesus was sorely perplexed, knowing that they believed in him only because of the unusual occurrence that they had just inadvertently beheld. Again Jesus retired for a season to the housetop that he might think it all over.

Jesus now fully comprehended that he must constantly be on guard lest his indulgence of sympathy and pity become responsible for repeated episodes of this sort. Nevertheless, many similar events occurred before the Son of Man took final leave of his mortal life in the flesh.

Though many of the guests remained for the full week of wedding festivities, Jesus, with his newly chosen apostles; James, John, Andrew, Peter, Philip, and Nathaniel, departed very early the next morning for Capernaum, going away without taking leave of anyone. Jesus' family and all his friends in Cana were much distressed because he so suddenly left them, and Jude, Jesus' youngest brother, set out in search of him. Jesus and his apostles went directly to the home of Zebedee at Bethsaida. On this journey Jesus talked over many things of importance to the coming kingdom with his newly chosen associates and especially warned them to make no mention of the turning of the water into wine. He also advised them to avoid the cities of Sepphoris and Tiberias in their future work.

After supper that evening, in this home of Zebedee and Salome, there was held one of the most important conferences of all Jesus' earthly career. Only the six apostles were present at this meeting; Jude arrived as they were about to separate. These six chosen men had journeyed from Cana to Bethsaida with Jesus, walking, as it were, on air. They were alive with expectancy and thrilled with the thought of having been selected as close associates of the Son of Man. But when Jesus set out to make clear to them who he was and what was to be his mission on earth and how it might possibly end, they were stunned. They could not grasp what he was telling them. They were speechless; even Peter was crushed beyond expression.

Only Andrew dared to make reply to Jesus' words of counsel. When Jesus perceived that they did not comprehend his message, when he saw that their ideas of the Jewish Messiah were so completely crystallized, he sent them to their rest while he walked and talked with his brother Jude.

And before Jude took leave of Jesus, he said with much feeling, "My father-brother, I never have understood you. I do not know of a certainty whether you are what my mother has taught us, and I do not fully comprehend the coming kingdom, but I do know you are a mighty man of God. I heard the voice at the Jordan, and I am a believer in you, no matter who you are." And when he had spoken, he departed, going to his own home at Magdala.

That night Jesus did not sleep. Donning his evening wraps, he sat out on the lakeshore thinking, thinking until the dawn of the next day. In the long hours of that night of meditation Jesus came clearly to comprehend that he never would be able to make his followers see him in any other light than as the long-expected Messiah. At last he recognized that there was no way to launch his message of the kingdom except as the fulfillment of John's prediction and as the one for whom the Jews were looking. After all, though he was not the Davidic type of Messiah, he was truly the fulfillment of the prophetic utterances of the more spiritually minded of the olden seers. Never again did he wholly deny that he was the Messiah. He decided to leave the final untangling of this complicated situation to the outworking of the Father's will.

The next morning Jesus joined his friends at breakfast, but they were a cheerless group. He visited with them and at the end of the meal gathered them about him, saying, "It is my Father's will that we tarry hereabouts for a season. You have heard John say that he came to prepare the way for the kingdom; therefore it behooves us to await the completion of John's preaching. When the forerunner of the Son of Man shall have finished his work, we will begin the proclamation of the good tidings of the kingdom." He directed his apostles to return to their nets while he made ready to go with Zebedee to the boatshop, promising to see them the next day at the synagogue, where he was to speak, and appointing a conference with them that Sabbath afternoon.

Jesus' first public appearance following his baptism was in the Capernaum synagogue on Sabbath, March 2, A.D. 26. The synagogue was crowded to overflowing. The story of the baptism in the Jordan was now augmented by the fresh news from Cana about the water and the wine. Jesus gave seats of honor to his six apostles, and seated with them were his brothers in the flesh, James and Jude. His mother, having returned to Capernaum with James the evening before, was also present, being seated in the women's section of the synagogue. The entire audience was on edge; they expected to behold some extraordinary manifestation of supernatural power that would be a fitting testimony to the nature and authority of him who was that day to speak to them. But they were destined to be disappointed.

When Jesus stood up, the ruler of the synagogue handed him the Scripture roll, and he read from the Prophet Isaiah: "Thus says the Lord: 'The heaven is my throne, and the earth is my footstool. Where is the house that you built for me? And where is the place of my dwelling? All these things have my hands made,' says the Lord. 'But to this man will I look, even to him who is poor and of a contrite spirit, and who trembles at my word.' Hear the word of the Lord, you who tremble and fear: 'Your brethren hated you and cast you out for my name's sake.' But let the Lord be glorified. He shall appear to you in joy, and all others shall be ashamed. A voice from the city, a voice from the temple, a voice from the Lord says: 'Before she travailed, she brought forth; before her pain came, she was delivered of a man child.' Who has heard such a thing? Shall the earth be made to bring forth in one day? Or can a nation be born at once? But thus says the Lord: 'Behold I will extend peace like a river, and the glory of even the gentiles shall be like a flowing stream. As one whom his mother comforts, so will I comfort you. And you shall be comforted even in Jerusalem. And when you see these things, your heart shall rejoice.'"

When he had finished this reading, Jesus handed the roll back to its keeper. Before sitting down, he simply said, "Be patient and you shall see the glory of God; even so shall it be with all those who tarry with me and thus learn to do the will of my Father who is in heaven." And the people went to their homes, wondering what was the meaning of all this.

That afternoon Jesus and his apostles, with James and Jude, entered a boat and pulled down the shore a little way, where they anchored while he talked to them about the coming kingdom. And they understood more than they had on Thursday night.

Jesus instructed them to take up their regular duties until "the hour of the kingdom comes." And to encourage them, he set an example by going back regularly to work in the boatshop. In explaining that they should spend three hours every evening in study and preparation for their future work, Jesus further said, "We will all remain hereabout until the Father bids me call you. Each of you must now return to his accustomed work just as if nothing had happened. Tell no man about me and remember that my kingdom is not to come with noise and glamour, but rather must it come through the great change which my Father will have wrought in your hearts and in the hearts of those who shall be called to join you in the councils of the kingdom. You are now my friends; I trust you and I love you; you are soon to become my personal associates. Be patient, be gentle. Be ever obedient to the Father's will. Make yourselves ready for the call of the kingdom. While you will experience great joy in the service of my Father, you should also be prepared for trouble, for I warn you that it will be only through much tribulation that many will enter the kingdom. But those who have found the kingdom, their joy will be full, and they shall be called the blest of all the earth.

"But do not entertain false hope; the world will stumble at my words. Even you, my friends, do not fully perceive what I am unfolding to your confused minds. Make no mistake; we go forth to labor for a generation of sign seekers. They will demand wonderworking as the proof that I am sent by my Father, and they will be slow to recognize in the revelation of my Father's *love* the credentials of my mission."

That evening, when they had returned to the land, before they went their way, Jesus, standing by the water's edge, prayed. "My Father, I thank you for these little ones who, in spite of their doubts, even now believe. And for their sakes have I set myself apart to do your will. And now may they learn to be one, even as we are one."

For four long months; March, April, May, and June, this tarrying time continued. Jesus held over one hundred long and earnest, though cheerful and joyous, sessions with these six associates and his own brother James. Owing to sickness in his family, Jude seldom was able to attend these classes.

James, Jesus' brother, did not lose faith in him, but during these months of delay and inaction Mary nearly despaired of her son. Her faith, raised to such heights at Cana, now sank to new low levels. She could only fall back on her so oft-repeated exclamation: "I cannot understand him. I cannot figure out what it all means." But James's wife did much to bolster Mary's courage.

Throughout these four months these seven believers - one his own brother in the flesh - were getting acquainted with Jesus; they were getting used to the idea of living with this God-man. Though they called him Rabbi, they were learning not to be afraid of him. Jesus possessed that matchless grace of personality that enabled him so to live among them that they were not dismayed by his divinity. They found it really easy to be "friends with God," God incarnate in the likeness of mortal flesh. This time of waiting severely tested the entire group of believers. Nothing, absolutely nothing, miraculous happened. Day by day they went about their ordinary work, while night after night they sat at Jesus' feet. And they were held together by his matchless personality and by the gracious words that he spoke to them evening upon evening.

This period of waiting and teaching was especially hard on Simon Peter. He repeatedly sought to persuade Jesus to launch forth with the preaching of the kingdom in Galilee while John continued to preach in Judea. But Jesus' reply to Peter ever was: "Be patient, Simon. Make progress. We shall be none too ready when the Father calls."

And Andrew would calm Peter now and then with his more seasoned and philosophic counsel. Andrew was tremendously impressed with the human naturalness of Jesus. He never grew weary of contemplating how one who could live so near God could be so friendly and considerate of men.

Throughout this entire period Jesus spoke in the synagogue but twice. By the end of these many weeks of waiting the reports about his baptism and the wine of Cana had begun to quiet down. And Jesus saw to it that no more apparent miracles happened during this time. But even though they lived so quietly at Bethsaida, reports of the strange doings of Jesus had been carried to Herod Antipas, who in turn sent spies to ascertain what he was about. But Herod was more concerned about the preaching of John. He decided not to molest Jesus, whose work continued along so quietly at Capernaum.

In this time of waiting Jesus endeavored to teach his associates what their attitude should be toward the various religious groups and the political parties of Palestine. Jesus' words always were, "We are seeking to win all of them, but we are not *of* any of them."

The scribes and rabbis, taken together, were called Pharisees. They referred to themselves as the "associates." In many ways they were the progressive group among the Jews, having adopted many teachings not clearly found in the Hebrew scriptures, such as belief in the resurrection of the dead, a doctrine only mentioned by a later prophet, Daniel.

The Sadducees consisted of the priesthood and certain wealthy Jews. They were not such sticklers for the details of law enforcement. The Pharisees and Sadducees were really religious parties, rather than sects.

The Essenes were a true religious sect, originating during the Maccabean revolt, whose requirements were in some respects more exacting than those of the Pharisees. They had adopted many Persian beliefs and practices, lived as a brotherhood in monasteries, refrained from marriage, and had all things in common. They specialized in teachings about angels.

The Zealots were a group of intense Jewish patriots. They advocated that any and all methods were justified in the struggle to escape the bondage of the Roman yoke.

The Herodians were a purely political party that advocated emancipation from the direct Roman rule by a restoration of the Herodian dynasty.

In the very midst of Palestine there lived the Samaritans, with whom "the Jews had no dealings," notwithstanding that they held many views similar to the Jewish teachings.

All of these parties and sects, including the smaller Nazarite brotherhood, believed in the sometime coming of the Messiah. They all looked for a national deliverer. But Jesus was very positive in making it clear that he and his disciples would not become allied to any of these schools of thought or practice. The Son of Man was to be neither a Nazarite nor an Essene.

While Jesus later directed that the apostles should go forth, as John had, preaching the gospel and instructing believers, he laid emphasis on the proclamation of the "good tidings of the kingdom of heaven." He unfailingly impressed upon his associates that they must "show forth love, compassion, and sympathy." He early taught his followers that the kingdom of heaven was a spiritual experience having to do with the enthronement of God in the hearts of men.

As they thus tarried before embarking on their active public preaching, Jesus and the seven spent two evenings each week at the synagogue in the study of the Hebrew scriptures. In later years after seasons of intense public work, the apostles looked back upon these four months as the most precious and profitable of all their association with the Master. Jesus taught these men all they could assimilate. He did not make the mistake of over-teaching them. He did not precipitate confusion by the presentation of truth too far beyond their capacity to comprehend.

On Sabbath, June 22, shortly before they went out on their first preaching tour and about ten days after John's imprisonment, Jesus occupied the synagogue pulpit for the second time since bringing his apostles to Capernaum.

A few days before the preaching of this sermon on "The Kingdom," as Jesus was at work in the boatshop, Peter brought him the news of John's arrest. Jesus laid down his tools once more, removed his apron, and said to Peter, "The Father's hour has come. Let us make ready to proclaim the gospel of the kingdom."

Jesus did his last work at the carpenter bench on this Tuesday, June 18, A.D. 26. Peter rushed out of the shop and by mid-afternoon had rounded up all of his associates, and leaving them in a grove by the shore, he went in quest of Jesus. But he could not find him, for the Master had gone to a different grove to pray. And they did not see him until late that evening when he returned to Zebedee's house and asked for food. The next day he sent his brother James to ask for the privilege of speaking in the synagogue the coming Sabbath day. And the ruler of the synagogue was much pleased that Jesus was again willing to conduct the service.

Before Jesus preached this memorable sermon on the kingdom of God, the first ambitious effort of his public career, he read from the Scriptures these passages: "You shall be to me a kingdom of priests, a holy people. Yahweh is our judge, Yahweh is our lawgiver, Yahweh is our king; He will save us. Yahweh is my king and my God. He is a great king over all the earth. Loving-kindness is upon Israel in this kingdom. Blessed be the glory of the Lord for He is our King."

When he had finished reading, Jesus said, "I have come to proclaim the establishment of the Father's kingdom. And this kingdom shall include the worshiping souls of Jew and gentile, rich and poor, free and bond, for my Father is no respecter of persons; His love and His mercy are over all.

"The Father in heaven sends His spirit to indwell the minds of men, and when I shall have finished my work on earth, likewise shall the Spirit of Truth be poured out upon all flesh. And the spirit of my Father and the Spirit of Truth shall establish you in the coming kingdom of spiritual understanding and divine righteousness.

My kingdom is not of this world. The Son of Man will not lead forth armies in battle for the establishment of a throne of power or a kingdom of worldly glory. When my kingdom shall have come, you shall know the Son of Man as the Prince of Peace, the revelation of the everlasting Father. The children of this world fight for the establishment and enlargement of the kingdoms of this world, but my disciples shall enter the kingdom of heaven by their moral decisions and by their spirit victories; and when they once enter therein, they shall find joy, righteousness, and eternal life.

"Those who first seek to enter the kingdom, thus beginning to strive for a nobility of character like that of my Father, shall presently possess all else that is needful. But I say to you in all sincerity: Unless you seek entrance into the kingdom with the faith and trusting dependence of a little child, you shall in no wise gain admission.

"Be not deceived by those who come saying here is the kingdom or there is the kingdom, for my Father's kingdom concerns not things visible and material. And this kingdom is even now among you, for where the spirit of God teaches and leads the soul of man, there in reality is the kingdom of heaven. And this kingdom of God is righteousness, peace, and joy in the Holy Spirit.

"John did indeed baptize you in token of repentance and for the remission of your sins, but when you enter the heavenly kingdom, you will be baptized with the Holy Spirit.

"In my Father's kingdom there shall be neither Jew nor gentile, only those who seek perfection through service, for I declare that he who would be great in my Father's kingdom must first become server of all. If you are willing to serve your fellows, you shall sit down with me in my kingdom, even as, by serving in the similitude of the creature, I shall presently sit down with my Father in his kingdom.

"This new kingdom is like a seed growing in the good soil of a field. It does not attain full fruit quickly. There is an interval of time between the establishment of the kingdom in the soul of man and that hour when the kingdom ripens into the full fruit of everlasting righteousness and eternal salvation.

"And this kingdom which I declare to you is not a reign of power and plenty. The kingdom of heaven is not a matter of meat and drink but rather a life of progressive righteousness and increasing joy in the perfecting service of my Father who is in heaven. For has not the Father said of his children of the world, 'It is my will that they should eventually be perfect, even as I am perfect.'

"I have come to preach the glad tidings of the kingdom. I have not come to add to the heavy burdens of those who would enter this kingdom. I proclaim the new and better way, and those who are able to enter the coming kingdom shall enjoy the divine rest. And whatever it shall cost you in the things of the world, no matter what price you may pay to enter the kingdom of heaven, you shall receive manyfold more of joy and spiritual progress in this world, and in the age to come eternal life.

"Entrance into the Father's kingdom waits not upon marching armies, upon overturned kingdoms of this world, nor upon the breaking of captive yokes. The kingdom of heaven is at hand, and all who enter therein shall find abundant liberty and joyous salvation.

"This kingdom is an everlasting dominion. Those who enter the kingdom shall ascend to my Father; they will certainly attain the right hand of His glory in Paradise. And all who enter the kingdom of heaven shall become the sons and daughters of God, and in the age to come so shall they ascend to the Father. And I have not come to call the would-be righteous, but sinners and all who hunger and thirst for the righteousness of divine perfection.

"John came preaching repentance to prepare you for the kingdom; now have I come proclaiming faith, the gift of God, as the price of entrance into the kingdom of heaven. If you would but believe that my Father loves you with an infinite love, then you are in the kingdom of God."

When he had thus spoken, he sat down. All who heard him were astonished at his words. His disciples marveled. But the people were not prepared to receive the good news from the lips of this God-man. About one third who heard him believed the message even though they could not fully comprehend it; about one third prepared in their hearts to reject such a purely spiritual concept of the expected kingdom, while the remaining one third could not grasp his teaching, many truly believing that he "was beside himself."

# TRAINING THE KINGDOM'S MESSENGERS

**A**FTER PREACHING the sermon on "The Kingdom," Jesus called the six apostles together that afternoon and began to disclose his plans for visiting the cities around and about the Sea of Galilee. His brothers James and Jude were very much hurt because they were not called to this conference. Up to this time they had regarded themselves as belonging to Jesus' inner circle of associates. But Jesus planned to have no close relatives as members of this corps of apostolic directors of the kingdom. This failure to include James and Jude among the chosen few, together with his apparent aloofness from his mother ever since the experience at Cana, was the starting point of an ever-widening gulf between Jesus and his family. This situation continued throughout his public ministry; they very nearly rejected him, and these differences were not fully removed until after his death and resurrection. His mother constantly wavered between attitudes of fluctuating faith and hope, and increasing emotions of disappointment, humiliation, and despair. Only Ruth, the youngest, remained unswervingly loyal to her father-brother.

Until after the resurrection, Jesus' entire family had very little to do with his ministry. If a prophet is not without honor save in his own country, he is not without understanding appreciation save in his own family.

**T**he next day, Sunday, June 23, A.D. 26, Jesus imparted his final instructions to the six. He directed them to go forth, two and two, to teach the glad tidings of the kingdom. He forbade them to baptize and advised against public preaching. He went on to explain that later he would permit them to preach in public, but that for a season, and for many reasons, he desired them to acquire practical experience in dealing personally with their fellow men. Jesus purposed to make their first tour entirely one of *personal work*. Although this announcement was something of a disappointment to the apostles, still they saw, at least in part, Jesus' reason for thus beginning the proclamation of the kingdom, and they started out in good heart and with confident enthusiasm. He sent them forth by twos, James and John going to Kheresa, Andrew and Peter to Capernaum, while Philip and Nathaniel went to Tarichea.

Before they began this first two weeks of service, Jesus announced to them that he desired to ordain twelve apostles to continue the work of the kingdom after his departure and authorized each of them to choose one man from among his early converts for membership in the projected corps of apostles.

John spoke up, asking, "But, Master, will these six men come into our midst and share all things equally with us who have been with you since the Jordan and have heard all your teaching in preparation for this, our first labor for the kingdom?"

And Jesus replied, "Yes, John, the men you choose shall become one with us, and you will teach them all that pertains to the kingdom, even as I have taught you." After thus speaking, Jesus left them.

The six did not separate to go to their work until they had exchanged many words in discussion of Jesus' instruction that each of them should choose a new apostle. Andrew's counsel finally prevailed, and they went forth to their labors. In substance Andrew said, "The Master is right; we are too few to encompass this work. There is need for more teachers, and the Master has manifested great confidence in us inasmuch as he has entrusted us with the choosing of these six new apostles."

This morning, as they separated to go to their work, there was a bit of concealed depression in each heart. They knew they were going to miss Jesus, and besides their fear and timidity, this was not the way they had pictured the kingdom of heaven being inaugurated.

It had been arranged that the six were to labor for two weeks, after which they were to return to the home of Zebedee for a conference. Meantime Jesus went over to Nazareth to visit with Joseph and Simon and other members of his family living in that vicinity. Jesus did everything humanly possible, consistent with his dedication to the doing of his Father's will, to retain the confidence and affection of his family. In this matter he did his full duty and more.

While the apostles were out on this mission, Jesus thought much about John, now in prison. It was a great temptation to use his potential powers to release him, but once more he resigned himself to "wait upon the Father's will."

This first missionary tour of the six was eminently successful. They all discovered the great value of direct and personal contact with men. They returned to Jesus more fully realizing that, after all, religion is purely and wholly a matter of *personal experience*. They began to sense how hungry were the common people to hear words of religious comfort and spiritual good cheer. When they assembled about Jesus, they all wanted to talk at once, but Andrew assumed charge, and as he called upon them one by one, they made their formal reports to the Master and presented their nominations for the six new apostles.

Jesus, after each man had presented his selection for the new apostleships, asked all the others to vote upon the nomination; thus all six of the new apostles were formally accepted by all of the older six. Then Jesus announced that they would all visit these candidates and give them the call to service.

The newly selected apostles were:

1. *Matthew Levi,* the customs collector of Capernaum, who had his office just to the east of the city, near the borders of Batanea. He was selected by Andrew.

2. *Thomas Didymus,* a fisherman of Tarichea and onetime carpenter and stone mason of Gadara. He was selected by Philip.

3. *James Alpheus,* a fisherman and farmer of Kheresa, was selected by James Zebedee.

4. *Judas Alpheus,* the twin brother of James Alpheus, also a fisherman, was selected by John Zebedee.

5. *Simon Zelotes* was a high officer in the patriotic organization of the Zealots, a position which he gave up to join Jesus' apostles. Before joining the Zealots, Simon had been a merchant. He was selected by Peter.

6. *Judas Iscariot* was an only son of wealthy Jewish parents living in Jericho. He had become attached to John the Baptist, and his Sadducee parents had disowned him. He was looking for employment in these regions when Jesus' apostles found him, and chiefly because of his experience with finances, Nathaniel invited him to join their ranks. Judas Iscariot was the only Judean among the twelve apostles.

Jesus spent a full day with the six, answering their questions and listening to the details of their reports, for they had many interesting and profitable experiences to relate. They now saw the wisdom of the Master's plan of sending them out to labor in a quiet and personal manner before the launching of their more ambitious public efforts.

The next day Jesus and the six went to call upon Matthew, the customs collector. Matthew was awaiting them, having balanced his books and made ready to turn the affairs of his office over to his brother. As they approached the tollhouse, Andrew stepped forward with Jesus, who, looking into Matthew's face, said, "Follow me." And he arose and went to his house with Jesus and the apostles.

Matthew told Jesus of the banquet he had arranged for that evening, at least that he wished to give such a dinner to his family and friends if Jesus would approve and consent to be the guest of honor. And Jesus nodded his consent. Peter then took Matthew aside and explained that he had invited one Simon to join the apostles and secured his consent that Simon be also bidden to this feast.

After a noontide luncheon at Matthew's house they all went with Peter to call upon Simon the Zealot, whom they found at his old place of business, which was now being conducted by his nephew. When Peter led Jesus up to Simon, the Master greeted the fiery patriot and only said, "Follow me."

They all returned to Matthew's home, where they talked much about politics and religion until the hour of the evening meal. The Levi family had long been engaged in business and tax gathering; therefore many of the guests bidden to this banquet by Matthew would have been denominated "publicans and sinners" by the Pharisees.

In those days, when a reception-banquet of this sort was tendered a prominent individual, it was the custom for all interested persons to linger about the banquet room to observe the guests at meat and to listen to the conversation and speeches of the men of honor. Accordingly, most of the Capernaum Pharisees were present on this occasion to observe Jesus' conduct at this unusual social gathering.

As the dinner progressed, the joy of the diners mounted to heights of good cheer, and everybody was having such a splendid time that the onlooking Pharisees began, in their hearts, to criticize Jesus for his participation in such a lighthearted and carefree affair.

Later in the evening, when they were making speeches, one of the more malignant of the Pharisees went so far as to criticize Jesus' conduct to Peter, saying, "How dare you to teach that this man is righteous when he eats with publicans and sinners and thus lends his presence to such scenes of careless pleasure making." Peter whispered this criticism to Jesus before he spoke the parting blessing upon those assembled.

When Jesus began to speak, he said, "In coming here tonight to welcome Matthew and Simon to our fellowship, I am glad to witness your lightheartedness and social good cheer, but you should rejoice still more because many of you will find entrance into the coming kingdom of the spirit, wherein you shall more abundantly enjoy the good things of the kingdom of heaven. And to you who stand about criticizing me in your hearts because I have come here to make merry with these friends, let me say that I have come to proclaim joy to the socially downtrodden and spiritual liberty to the moral captives. Need I remind you that they who are whole need not a physician, but rather those who are sick? I have come, not to call the righteous, but sinners."

And truly this was a strange sight in all Jewry; to see a man of righteous character and noble sentiments mingling freely and joyously with the common people, even with an irreligious and pleasure-seeking throng of publicans and reputed sinners.

Simon Zelotes desired to make a speech at this gathering in Matthew's house, but Andrew, knowing that Jesus did not want the coming kingdom to become confused with the Zealots' movement, prevailed upon him to refrain from making any public remarks.

Jesus and the apostles remained that night in Matthew's house, and as the people went to their homes, they spoke of but one thing, the goodness and friendliness of Jesus.

On the morrow all nine of them went by boat over to Kheresa to execute the formal calling of the next two apostles, James and Judas the twin sons of Alpheus, the nominees of James and John Zebedee. The fisherman twins were expecting Jesus and his apostles and were therefore awaiting them on the shore. James Zebedee presented the Master to the Kheresa fishermen, and Jesus, gazing on them, nodded and said, "Follow me."

That afternoon, which they spent together, Jesus fully instructed them concerning attendance upon festive gatherings, concluding his remarks by saying, "All men are my brothers. My Father in heaven does not despise any creature of our making. The kingdom of heaven is open to all men and women. No man may close the door of mercy in the face of any hungry soul who may seek to gain an entrance thereto. We will sit at meat with all who desire to hear of the kingdom. As our Father in heaven looks down upon men, they are all alike. Refuse not therefore to break bread with Pharisee or sinner, Sadducee or publican, Roman or Jew, rich or poor, free or bond. The door of the kingdom is wide open for all who desire to know the truth and to find God."

That night at a simple supper at the Alpheus home, the twin brothers were received into the apostolic family. Later in the evening Jesus gave his apostles their first lesson dealing with the origin, nature, and destiny of unclean spirits, but they could not comprehend the import of what he told them. They found it very easy to love and admire Jesus but very difficult to understand many of his teachings.

After a night of rest the entire party, now numbering eleven, went by boat over to Tarichea.

Thomas the fisherman and Judas the wanderer met Jesus and the apostles at the fisher-boat landing at Tarichea, and Thomas led the party to his near-by home. Philip now presented Thomas as his nominee for apostleship and Nathaniel presented Judas Iscariot, the Judean, for similar honors. Jesus looked upon Thomas and said, "Thomas, you lack faith; nevertheless, I receive you. Follow me."

To Judas Iscariot the Master said, "Judas, we are all of one flesh, and as I receive you into our midst, I pray that you will always be loyal to your Galilean brethren. Follow me."

When they had refreshed themselves, Jesus took the twelve apart for a season to pray with them and to instruct them in the nature and work of the Holy Spirit, but again did they largely fail to comprehend the meaning of those wonderful truths which he endeavored to teach them. One would grasp one point and one would comprehend another, but none of them could encompass the whole of his teaching. Always would they make the mistake of trying to fit Jesus' new gospel into their old forms of religious belief. They could not grasp the idea that Jesus had come to proclaim a new gospel of salvation and to establish a new way of finding God; they did not perceive that he *was* a new revelation of the Father in heaven.

The next day Jesus left his twelve apostles quite alone; he wanted them to become acquainted and desired that they be alone to talk over what he had taught them. The Master returned for the evening meal, and during the after-supper hours he talked to them about the ministry of seraphim, and some of the apostles comprehended his teaching. They rested for a night and the next day departed by boat for Capernaum.

Zebedee and Salome had gone to live with their son David so that their large home could be turned over to Jesus and his twelve apostles. Here Jesus spent a quiet Sabbath with his chosen messengers. He carefully outlined the plans for proclaiming the kingdom and fully explained the importance of avoiding any clash with the civil authorities, saying, "If the civil rulers are to be rebuked, leave that task to me. See that you make no denunciations of Caesar or his servants."

It was this same evening that Judas Iscariot took Jesus aside to inquire why nothing was done to get John out of prison. And Judas was not wholly satisfied with Jesus' attitude.

The next week was devoted to a program of intense training. Each day the six new apostles were put in the hands of their respective nominators for a thoroughgoing review of all they had learned and experienced in preparation for the work of the kingdom. The older apostles carefully reviewed, for the benefit of the younger six, Jesus' teachings up to that hour. Evenings they all assembled in Zebedee's garden to receive Jesus' instruction.

It was at this time that Jesus established the mid-week holiday for rest and recreation. And they pursued this plan of relaxation for one day each week throughout the remainder of his material life. As a general rule, they never prosecuted their regular activities on Wednesday. On this weekly holiday Jesus would usually take himself away from them, saying, "My children, go for a day of play. Rest yourselves from the arduous labors of the kingdom and enjoy the refreshment that comes from reverting to your former vocations or from discovering new sorts of recreational activity." While Jesus, at this period of his earth life, did not actually require this day of rest, he conformed to this plan because he knew it was best for his human associates. Jesus was the teacher - the Master; his associates were his pupils - disciples.

Jesus endeavored to make clear to his apostles the difference between his teachings and his *life among them* and the teachings that might subsequently spring up *about* him. Said Jesus, "My kingdom and the gospel related thereto shall be the burden of your message. Be not sidetracked into preaching *about* me and *about* my teachings. Proclaim the gospel of the kingdom and portray my revelation of the Father in heaven but do not be misled into the bypaths of creating legends and building up a cult having to do with beliefs and teachings *about* my beliefs and teachings." But again they did not understand why he thus spoke, and no man dared to ask why he so taught them.

In these early teachings Jesus sought to avoid controversies with his apostles as far as possible excepting those involving wrong concepts of his Father in heaven. In all such matters he never hesitated to correct erroneous beliefs. There was just *one* motive in Jesus' post-baptismal life on Earth, and that was a better and truer revelation of his Paradise Father; he was the pioneer of the new and better way to God, the way of faith and love. Ever his exhortation to the apostles was: "Go seek for the sinners; find the downhearted and comfort the anxious."

Jesus had a perfect grasp of the situation; he possessed unlimited power, which might have been utilized in the furtherance of his mission, but he was wholly content with means and personalities which most people would have regarded as inadequate and would have looked upon as insignificant. He was engaged in a mission of enormous dramatic possibilities, but he insisted on going about his Father's business in the most quiet and undramatic manner; he studiously avoided all display of power. And he now planned to work quietly, at least for several months, with his twelve apostles around about the Sea of Galilee.

J esus had planned for a quiet missionary campaign of five months' personal work. He did not tell the apostles how long this was to last; they worked from week to week. And early on this first day of the week, just as he was about to announce this to his twelve apostles, Simon Peter, James Zebedee, and Judas Iscariot came to have private converse with him. Taking Jesus aside, Peter made bold to say: "Master, we come at the behest of our associates to inquire whether the time is not now ripe to enter into the kingdom. And will you proclaim the kingdom at Capernaum, or are we to move on to Jerusalem? And when shall we learn, each of us, the positions we are to occupy with you in the establishment of the kingdom..." and Peter would have gone on asking further questions, but Jesus raised an admonitory hand and stopped him.

And beckoning the other apostles standing near by to join them, Jesus said, "My little children, how long shall I bear with you! Have I not made it plain to you that my kingdom is not of this world? I have told you many times that I have not come to sit on David's throne, and now how is it that you are inquiring which place each of you will occupy in the Father's kingdom? Can you not perceive that I have called you as ambassadors of a spiritual kingdom? Do you not understand that soon, very soon, you are to represent me in the world and in the proclamation of the kingdom, even as I now represent my Father who is in heaven? Can it be that I have chosen you and instructed you as messengers of the kingdom, and yet you do not comprehend the nature and significance of this coming kingdom of divine preeminence in the hearts of men?

"My friends, hear me once more. Banish from your minds this idea that my kingdom is a rule of power or a reign of glory. Indeed, all power in heaven and on earth will presently be given into my hands, but it is not the Father's will that we use this divine endowment to glorify ourselves during this age. In another age you shall indeed sit with me in power and glory, but it behooves us now to submit to the will of the Father and to go forth in humble obedience to execute his bidding on earth."

Once more were his associates shocked, stunned. Jesus sent them away two and two to pray, asking them to return to him at noontime. On this crucial forenoon they each sought to find God, and each endeavored to cheer and strengthen the other, and they returned to Jesus as he had bidden them.

Jesus now recounted for them the coming of John, the baptism in the Jordan, the marriage feast at Cana, the recent choosing of the six, and the withdrawal from them of his own brothers in the flesh, and warned them that the enemy of the kingdom would seek also to draw them away.

After this short but earnest talk the apostles all arose, under Peter's leadership, to declare their undying devotion to their Master and to pledge their unswerving loyalty to the kingdom, as Thomas expressed it, "To this coming kingdom, no matter what it is and even if I do not fully understand it." They all truly *believed in Jesus,* even though they did not fully comprehend his teaching.

Jesus now asked them how much money they had among them; he also inquired as to what provision had been made for their families. When it developed that they had hardly sufficient funds to maintain themselves for two weeks, he said: "It is not the will of my Father that we begin our work in this way. We will remain here by the sea two weeks and fish or do whatever our hands find to do; and in the meantime, under the guidance of Andrew, the first chosen apostle, you shall so organize yourselves as to provide for everything needful in your future work, both for the present personal ministry and also when I shall subsequently ordain you to preach the gospel and instruct believers."

They were all greatly cheered by these words; this was their first clear-cut and positive intimation that Jesus designed later on to enter upon more aggressive and ambitious public efforts.

The apostles spent the remainder of the day perfecting their organization and completing arrangements for boats and nets for embarking on the morrow's fishing as they had all decided to devote themselves to fishing; most of them had been fishermen, even Jesus was an experienced boatman and fisherman. Many of the boats that they used the next few years had been built by Jesus' own hands. And they were good and trustworthy boats.

Jesus enjoined them to devote themselves to fishing for two weeks, adding, "And then will you go forth to become fishers of men." They fished in three groups, Jesus going out with a different group each night. And they all so much enjoyed Jesus. He was a good fisherman, a cheerful companion, and an inspiring friend; the more they worked with him, the more they loved him.

Said Matthew one day, "The more you understand some people, the less you admire them, but of this man, even the less I comprehend him, the more I love him."

This plan of fishing two weeks and going out to do personal work in behalf of the kingdom for two weeks was followed for more than five months, even to the end of this year of A.D. 26, until after the cessation of those special persecutions which had been directed against John's disciples subsequent to his imprisonment.

After disposing of the fish catches of two weeks, Judas Iscariot, the one chosen to act as treasurer of the twelve, divided the apostolic funds into six equal portions, funds for the care of dependent families having been already provided. And then near the middle of August, in the year A.D. 26, they went forth two and two to the fields of work assigned by Andrew. The first two weeks Jesus went out with Andrew and Peter, the second two weeks with James and John, and so on with the other couples in the order of their choosing. In this way he was able to go out at least once with each couple before he called them together for the beginning of their public ministry.

Jesus taught them to preach the forgiveness of sin through *faith in God* without penance or sacrifice, and that the Father in heaven loves all his children with the same eternal love. He enjoined his apostles to refrain from discussing:

1. The work and imprisonment of John the Baptist.

2. The voice at the baptism. Said Jesus, "Only those who heard the voice may refer to it. Speak only that which you have heard from me; speak not hearsay."

3. The turning of the water into wine at Cana. Jesus seriously charged them, saying, "Tell no man about the water and the wine."

They had wonderful times throughout these five or six months during which they worked as fishermen every alternate two weeks, thereby earning enough money to support themselves in the field for each succeeding two weeks of missionary work for the kingdom.

The common people marveled at the teaching and ministry of Jesus and his apostles. The rabbis had long taught the Jews that the ignorant could not be pious or righteous. But Jesus' apostles were both pious and righteous; yet they were cheerfully ignorant of much of the learning of the rabbis and the wisdom of the world.

Jesus made plain to his apostles the difference between the repentance of so-called good works as taught by the Jews and the change of mind by faith (the new birth) which he required as the price of admission to the kingdom. He taught his apostles that *faith* was the only requisite to entering the Father's kingdom. John had taught them "repentance; to flee from the wrath to come." Jesus taught, "Faith is the open door for entering into the present, perfect, and eternal love of God."

Jesus did not speak like a prophet, one who comes to declare the word of God. He seemed to speak of himself as one having authority. Jesus sought to divert their minds from miracle seeking to the finding of a real and personal experience in the satisfaction and assurance of the indwelling of God's spirit of love and saving grace.

The disciples early learned that the Master had a profound respect and sympathetic regard for *every* human being he met, and they were tremendously impressed by this uniform and unvarying consideration which he so consistently gave to all sorts of men, women, and children. He would pause in the midst of a profound discourse that he might go out in the road to speak good cheer to a passing woman laden with her burden of body and soul. He would interrupt a serious conference with his apostles to fraternize with an intruding child. Nothing ever seemed so important to Jesus as the *individual human* who chanced to be in his immediate presence. He was master and teacher, but he was more; he was also a friend and neighbor, an understanding comrade.

Though Jesus' public teaching mainly consisted in parables and short discourses, he invariably taught his apostles by questions and answers. He would always pause to answer sincere questions during his later public discourses.

The apostles were at first shocked by, but early became accustomed to, Jesus' treatment of women; he made it very clear to them that women were to be accorded equal rights with men in the kingdom.

This somewhat monotonous period of alternate fishing and personal work proved to be a grueling experience for the twelve apostles, but they endured the test. With all of their grumblings, doubts, and transient dissatisfactions they remained true to their vows of devotion and loyalty to the Master. It was their personal association with Jesus during these months of testing that so endeared him to them that they all (save Judas Iscariot) remained loyal and true to him even in the dark hours of the trial and crucifixion. Real men simply could not actually desert a revered teacher who had lived so close to them and had been so devoted to them as had Jesus. Through the dark hours of the Master's death, in the hearts of these apostles all reason, judgment, and logic were set aside in deference to just one extraordinary human emotion, the supreme sentiment of friendship-loyalty. These five months of work with Jesus led these apostles, each one of them, to regard him as the best *friend* he had in the entire world. And it was this human sentiment, and not his superb teachings or marvelous doings, that held them together until after the resurrection and the renewal of the proclamation of the gospel of the kingdom.

Not only were these months of quiet work a great test to the apostles, a test which they survived, but this season of public inactivity was a great trial to Jesus' family. By the time Jesus was prepared to launch forth on his public work, his entire family (except Ruth) had practically deserted him. On only a few occasions did they attempt to make subsequent contact with him, and then it was to persuade him to return home with them, for they came near to believing that he was beside himself. They simply could not fathom his philosophy nor grasp his teaching; it was all too much for those of his own flesh and blood.

The apostles carried on their personal work in Capernaum, Bethsaida-Julias, Chorazin, Gerasa, Hippos, Magdala, Cana, Bethlehem of Galilee, Jotapata, Ramah, Safed, Gischala, Gadara, and Abila. Besides these towns they labored in many villages as well as in the countryside. By the end of this period the twelve had worked out fairly satisfactory plans for the care of their respective families. Most of the apostles were married, some had several children, but they had made such arrangements for the support of their home folks that, with some little assistance from the apostolic funds, they could devote their entire energies to the Master's work without having to worry about the financial welfare of their families.

The apostles early organized themselves in the following manner:

1. Andrew, the first chosen apostle, was designated chairman and director general of the twelve.
2. Peter, James, and John were appointed personal companions of Jesus. They were to attend him day and night, to minister to his physical and sundry needs, and to accompany him on those night vigils of prayer and mysterious communion with the Father in heaven.
3. Philip was made steward of the group. It was his duty to provide food and to see that visitors, and even the multitude of listeners at times, had something to eat.
4. Nathaniel watched over the needs of the families of the twelve. He received regular reports as to the requirements of each apostle's family

and, making requisition on Judas, the treasurer, would send funds each week to those in need.

5. Matthew was the fiscal agent of the apostolic corps. It was his duty to see that the budget was balanced, the treasury replenished. If the funds for mutual support were not forthcoming, if donations sufficient to maintain the party were not received, Matthew was empowered to order the twelve back to their nets for a season. But this was never necessary after they began their public work; he always had sufficient funds in the treasurer's hands to finance their activities.

6. Thomas was manager of the itinerary. It devolved upon him to arrange lodgings and in a general way select places for teaching and preaching, thereby insuring a smooth and expeditious travel schedule.

7. James and Judas the twin sons of Alpheus were assigned to the management of the multitudes. It was their task to deputize a sufficient number of assistant ushers to enable them to maintain order among the crowds during the preaching.

8. Simon Zelotes was given charge of recreation and play. He managed the Wednesday programs and also sought to provide for a few hours of relaxation and diversion each day.

9. Judas Iscariot was appointed treasurer. He carried the bag. He paid all expenses and kept the books. He made budget estimates for Matthew from week to week and also made weekly reports to Andrew. Judas paid out funds on Andrew's authorization.

In this way the twelve functioned from their early organization up to the time of the reorganization made necessary by the desertion of Judas, the betrayer. The Master and his disciple-apostles went on in this simple manner until Sunday, January 12, A.D. 27, when he called them together and formally ordained them as ambassadors of the kingdom and preachers of its glad tidings. And soon thereafter they prepared to start for Jerusalem and Judea on their first public preaching tour.

# THE TWELVE APOSTLES

I T IS an eloquent testimony to the charm and righteousness of Jesus' earth life that, although he repeatedly dashed to pieces the hopes of his apostles and tore to shreds their every ambition for personal exaltation, only one deserted him.

The apostles learned from Jesus about the kingdom of heaven, and Jesus learned much from them about the kingdom of men, human nature as it lives on Earth and on the other evolutionary worlds of time and space. These twelve men represented many different types of human temperament, and they had not been made *alike* by schooling. Many of these Galilean fishermen carried heavy strains of gentile blood as a result of the forcible conversion of the gentile population of Galilee one hundred years previously.

Do not make the mistake of regarding the apostles as being altogether ignorant and unlearned. All of them, except the Alpheus twins, were graduates of the synagogue schools, having been thoroughly trained in the Hebrew scriptures and in much of the current knowledge of that day. Seven were graduates of the Capernaum synagogue schools, and there were no better Jewish schools in all Galilee.

When your records refer to these messengers of the kingdom as being "ignorant and unlearned," it was intended to convey the idea that they were laymen, unlearned in the lore of the rabbis and untrained in the methods of rabbinical interpretation of the Scriptures. They were lacking in so-called higher education. In modern times they would certainly be considered uneducated, and in some circles of society even uncultured. One thing is certain. They had not all been put through the same rigid and stereotyped educational curriculum. From adolescence on they had enjoyed separate experiences of learning how to live.

✫ ✫ ✫

Andrew, chairman of the apostolic corps of the kingdom, was born in Capernaum. He was the oldest child in a family of five — himself, his brother Simon, and three sisters. His father, now dead, had been a partner of Zebedee in the fish-drying business at Bethsaida, the fishing harbor of Capernaum. When he became an apostle, Andrew was unmarried but made his home with his married brother, Simon Peter. Both were fishermen and partners of James and John the sons of Zebedee.

In A.D. 26, the year he was chosen as an apostle, Andrew was 33, a full year older than Jesus and the oldest of the apostles. He sprang from an excellent line of ancestors and was the ablest man of the twelve. Excepting oratory, he was the peer of his associates in almost every imaginable ability. Jesus never gave Andrew a nickname, a fraternal designation. But even as the apostles soon began to call Jesus Master, so they also designated Andrew by a term the equivalent of Chief.

Andrew was a good organizer but a better administrator. He was one of the inner circle of four apostles, but his appointment by Jesus as the head of the apostolic group made it necessary for him to remain on duty with his brethren while the other three enjoyed very close communion with the Master. To the very end Andrew remained dean of the apostolic corps.

Although Andrew was never an effective preacher, he was an efficient personal worker, being the pioneer missionary of the kingdom in that, as the first chosen apostle, he immediately brought to Jesus his brother, Simon, who subsequently became one of the greatest preachers of the kingdom. Andrew was the chief supporter of Jesus' policy of utilizing the program of personal work as a means of training the twelve as messengers of the kingdom.

Whether Jesus privately taught the apostles or preached to the multitude, Andrew was usually conversant with what was going on; he was an understanding executive and an efficient administrator. He rendered a prompt decision on every matter brought to his notice unless he deemed the problem one beyond the domain of his authority, in which event he would take it straight to Jesus.

Andrew and Peter were very unlike in character and temperament, but it must be recorded everlastingly to their credit that they got along together splendidly. Andrew was never jealous of Peter's oratorical ability. Not often will an older man of Andrew's type be observed exerting such a profound influence over a younger and talented brother. Andrew and Peter never seemed to be in the least jealous of each other's abilities or achievements. Late on the evening of the day of Pentecost, when, largely through the energetic and inspiring preaching of Peter, two thousand souls were added to the kingdom, Andrew said to his brother: "I could not do that, but I am glad I have a brother who could."

To which Peter replied, "And but for your bringing me to the Master and by your steadfastness *keeping* me with him, I should not have been here to do this."

Andrew and Peter were the exceptions to the rule, proving that even brothers can live together peaceably and work together effectively.

After Pentecost Peter was famous, but it never irritated the older Andrew to spend the rest of his life being introduced as "Simon Peter's brother."

Of all the apostles, Andrew was the best judge of men. He knew that trouble was brewing in the heart of Judas Iscariot even when none of the others suspected that anything was wrong with their treasurer; but he told none of them his fears. Andrew's great service to the kingdom was in advising Peter, James, and John concerning the choice of the first missionaries who were sent out to proclaim the gospel, and also in counseling these early leaders about the organization of the administrative affairs of the kingdom. Andrew had a great gift for discovering the hidden resources and latent talents of young people.

Very soon after Jesus' ascension on high, Andrew began the writing of a personal record of many of the sayings and doings of his departed Master. After Andrew's death other copies of this private record were made and circulated freely among the early teachers of the Christian church. These informal notes of Andrew's were subsequently edited, amended, altered, and added to until they made up a fairly consecutive narrative of the Master's life on earth, and latterly became called by some, "The Book of Light," or simply, "Q." The last of these few altered and amended copies was destroyed by fire at Alexandria about one hundred years after the original was written by the first chosen of the twelve apostles.

Andrew was a man of clear insight, logical thought, and firm decision, whose great strength of character consisted in his superb stability. His temperamental handicap was his lack of enthusiasm; he many times failed to encourage his associates by judicious commendation. And this reticence to praise the worthy accomplishments of his friends grew out of his abhorrence of flattery and insincerity. Andrew was one of those all-round, even-tempered, self-made, and successful men of modest affairs.

Every one of the apostles loved Jesus, but it remains true that each of the twelve was drawn toward him because of some certain trait of personality that made a special appeal to the individual apostle. Andrew admired Jesus because of his consistent sincerity, his unaffected dignity. When men once knew Jesus, they were possessed with the urge to share him with their friends; they really wanted all the world to know him.

When the later persecutions finally scattered the apostles from Jerusalem, Andrew journeyed through Armenia, Asia Minor, and Macedonia and, after bringing many thousands into the kingdom, was finally apprehended and crucified in Patrae in Achaia. It was two full days before this robust man expired on the cross, and throughout these tragic hours he continued effectively to proclaim the glad tidings of the salvation of the kingdom of heaven.

★ ★ ★

When Simon joined the apostles, he was thirty years of age. He was married, had three children, and lived at Bethsaida, near Capernaum. His brother, Andrew, and his wife's mother lived with him. Both Peter and Andrew were fisher partners of the sons of Zebedee.

The Master had known Simon for some time before Andrew presented him as the second of the apostles. When Jesus gave Simon the name Peter, he did it with a smile; it was to be a sort of nickname. Simon was well known to all his friends as an erratic and impulsive fellow. True, later on, Jesus did attach a new and significant import to this lightly bestowed nickname.

Simon Peter was a man of impulse, an optimist. He had grown up permitting himself freely to indulge strong feelings; he was constantly getting into difficulties because he persisted in speaking without thinking. This sort of thoughtlessness also made incessant trouble for all of his friends and associates and was the cause of his receiving many mild rebukes from his Master. The only reason Peter did not get into more trouble because of his thoughtless speaking was that he very early learned to talk over many of his plans and schemes with his brother, Andrew, before he ventured to make public proposals.

Peter was a fluent speaker, eloquent and dramatic. He was also a natural and inspirational leader of men, a quick thinker but not a deep reasoner. He asked many questions, more than all the apostles put together, and while the majority of these questions were good and relevant, many of them were thoughtless and foolish. Peter did not have a deep mind, but he knew his mind fairly well. He was therefore a man of quick decision and sudden action. While others talked in their astonishment at seeing Jesus on the beach, Peter jumped in and swam ashore to meet the Master.

The one trait that Peter most admired in Jesus was his supernal tenderness. Peter never grew weary of contemplating Jesus' forbearance. He never forgot the lesson about forgiving the wrongdoer, not only seven times but seventy times and seven. He thought much about these impressions of the Master's forgiving character during those dark and dismal days immediately following his thoughtless and unintended denial of Jesus in the high priest's courtyard.

Simon Peter was distressingly vacillating; he would suddenly swing from one extreme to the other. First he refused to let Jesus wash his feet and then, on hearing the Master's reply, begged to be washed all over. But, after all, Jesus knew that Peter's faults were of the head and not of the heart. He was one of the most inexplicable combinations of courage and cowardice that ever lived on earth. His great strength of character was loyalty, friendship. Peter really and truly loved Jesus. And yet despite this towering strength of devotion he was so unstable and inconstant that he permitted a servant girl to tease him into denying his Lord and Master. Peter could withstand persecution and any other form of direct assault, but he withered and shrank before ridicule. He was a brave soldier when facing a frontal attack, but he was a fear-cringing coward when surprised with an assault from the rear.

Peter was the first of Jesus' apostles to come forward to defend the work of Philip among the Samaritans and Paul among the gentiles; yet later on at Antioch he reversed himself when confronted by ridiculing Judaizers, temporarily withdrawing from the gentiles only to bring down upon his head the fearless denunciation of Paul.

He was the first one of the apostles to make wholehearted confession of Jesus' combined humanity and divinity and the first - save Judas - to deny him. Peter was not so much of a dreamer, but he disliked descending from the clouds of ecstasy and the enthusiasm of dramatic indulgence to the plain and matter-of-fact world of reality.

In following Jesus, literally and figuratively, he was either leading the procession or else trailing behind - "following afar off." But he was the outstanding preacher of the twelve; he did more than any other one man, aside from Paul, to establish the kingdom and send its messengers to the four corners of the earth in one generation.

After his rash denials of the Master he found himself, and with Andrew's sympathetic and understanding guidance he again led the way back to the fish nets while the apostles tarried to find out what was to happen after the crucifixion. When he was fully assured that Jesus had forgiven him and knew he had been received back into the Master's fold, the fires of the kingdom burned so brightly within his soul that he became a great and saving light to thousands who sat in darkness.

After leaving Jerusalem and before Paul became the leading spirit among the gentile Christian churches, Peter traveled extensively, visiting all the churches from Babylon to Corinth. He even visited and ministered to many of the churches that had been raised up by Paul. Although Peter and Paul differed much in temperament and education, even in theology, they worked together harmoniously for the upbuilding of the churches during their later years.

Something of Peter's style and teaching is shown in the sermons partially recorded by Luke and in the Gospel of Mark. His vigorous style was better shown in his letter known as the First Epistle of Peter; at least this was true before it was subsequently altered by a disciple of Paul.

But Peter persisted in making the mistake of trying to convince the Jews that Jesus was, after all, really and truly the Jewish Messiah. Right up to the day of his death, Simon Peter continued to suffer confusion in his mind between the concepts of Jesus as the Jewish Messiah, Christ as the world's redeemer, and the Son of Man as the revelation of God, the loving Father of all mankind.

Peter's wife was a very able woman. For years she labored acceptably as a member of the women's corps, and when Peter was driven out of Jerusalem, she accompanied him upon all his journeys to the churches as well as on all his missionary excursions. And the day her illustrious husband yielded up his life, she was thrown to the wild beasts in the arena at Rome.

And so this man Peter, an intimate of Jesus, one of the inner circle, went forth from Jerusalem proclaiming the glad tidings of the kingdom with power and glory until the fullness of his ministry had been accomplished; and he regarded himself as the recipient of high honors when his captors informed him that he must die as his Master had died - on the cross. And thus was Simon Peter crucified in Rome.

James, the older of the two apostle sons of Zebedee, whom Jesus nicknamed "sons of thunder," was thirty years old when he became an apostle. He was married, had four children, and lived near his parents in the outskirts of Capernaum, Bethsaida. He was a fisherman, plying his calling in company with his younger brother John and in association with Andrew and Simon. James and his brother John enjoyed the advantage of having known Jesus longer than any of the other apostles.

This able apostle was a temperamental contradiction; he seemed really to possess two natures, both of which were actuated by strong feelings. He was particularly vehement when his indignation was once fully aroused. He had a fiery temper when once it was adequately provoked, and when the storm was over, he was always wont to justify and excuse his anger under the pretense that it was wholly a manifestation of righteous indignation. Except for these periodic upheavals of wrath, James's personality was much like that of Andrew. He did not have Andrew's discretion or insight into human nature, but he was a much better public speaker. Next to Peter, unless it was Matthew, James was the best public orator among the twelve.

Though James was in no sense moody, he could be quiet and taciturn one day and a very good talker and storyteller the next. He usually talked freely with Jesus, but among the twelve, for days at a time he was the silent man. His one great weakness was these spells of unaccountable silence.

The outstanding feature of James's personality was his ability to see all sides of a proposition. Of all the twelve, he came the nearest to grasping the real import and significance of Jesus' teaching. He, too, was slow at first to comprehend the Master's meaning, but ere they had finished their training, he had acquired a superior concept of Jesus' message. James was able to understand a wide range of human nature; he got along well with the versatile Andrew, the impetuous Peter, and his self-contained brother John.

Though James and John had their troubles trying to work together, it was inspiring to observe how well they got along. They did not succeed quite so well as

Andrew and Peter, but they did much better than would ordinarily be expected of two brothers, especially such headstrong and determined brothers. But, strange as it may seem, these two sons of Zebedee were much more tolerant of each other than they were of strangers. They had great affection for one another; they had always been happy playmates. It was these "sons of thunder" who wanted to call fire down from heaven to destroy the Samaritans who presumed to show disrespect for their Master. But the untimely death of James greatly modified the vehement temperament of his younger brother John.

That characteristic of Jesus which James most admired was the Master's sympathetic affection. Jesus' understanding interest in the small and the great, the rich and the poor, made a great appeal to him.

James Zebedee was a well-balanced thinker and planner. Along with Andrew, he was one of the more levelheaded of the apostolic group. He was a vigorous individual but was never in a hurry. He was an excellent balance wheel for Peter.

He was modest and undramatic, a daily server, an unpretentious worker, seeking no special reward when he once grasped something of the real meaning of the kingdom. And even in the story about the mother of James and John, who asked that her sons be granted places on the right hand and the left hand of Jesus, it should be remembered that it was the mother who made this request. And when they signified that they were ready to assume such responsibilities, it should be recognized that they were cognizant of the dangers accompanying the Master's supposed revolt against the Roman power, and that they were also willing to pay the price. When Jesus asked if they were ready to drink the cup, they replied that they were. And as concerns James, it was literally true - he did drink the cup with the Master, seeing that he was the first of the apostles to experience martyrdom, being early put to death with the sword by Herod Agrippa. James was thus the first of the twelve to sacrifice his life upon the new battle line of the kingdom. Herod Agrippa feared James above all the other apostles. He was indeed often quiet and silent, but he was brave and determined when his convictions were aroused and challenged.

James lived his life to the full, and when the end came, he bore himself with such grace and fortitude that even his accuser and informer, who attended his trial and execution, was so touched that he rushed away from the scene of James's death to join himself to the disciples of Jesus.

When he became an apostle, John was twenty-four years old and was the youngest of the twelve. He was unmarried and lived with his parents at Bethsaida; he was a fisherman and worked with his brother James in partnership with Andrew and Peter. Both before and after becoming an apostle, John functioned as the personal agent of Jesus in dealing with the Master's family, and he continued to bear this responsibility as long as Mary the mother of Jesus lived.

Since John was the youngest of the twelve and so closely associated with Jesus in his family affairs, he was very dear to the Master, but it cannot be truthfully said that he was "the disciple whom Jesus loved." You would hardly suspect such a magnanimous personality as Jesus to be guilty of showing favoritism, of loving one of his apostles more than the others. The fact that John was one of the three personal aides of Jesus lent further color to this mistaken idea, not to mention that John, along with his brother James, had known Jesus longer than the others.

Peter, James, and John were assigned as personal aides to Jesus soon after they became apostles. Shortly after the selection of the twelve and at the time Jesus appointed Andrew to act as director of the group, he said to him, "And now I desire that you assign two or three of your associates to be with me and to remain by my side, to comfort me and to minister to my daily needs." And Andrew thought best to select for this special duty the next three first-chosen apostles. He would have liked to volunteer for such a blessed service himself, but the Master had already given him his commission; so he immediately directed that Peter, James, and John attach themselves to Jesus.

John Zebedee had many lovely traits of character, but one that was not so lovely was his inordinate but usually well-concealed conceit. His long association with Jesus made many and great changes in his character. This conceit was greatly lessened, but after growing old and becoming more or less childish, this self-esteem reappeared to a certain extent, so that, when engaged in directing Nathan in the writing of the Gospel which now bears his name, the aged apostle did not hesitate repeatedly to refer to himself as the "disciple whom Jesus loved." In view of the fact that John came nearer to being the chum of Jesus than any other earth mortal, that he was his chosen personal representative in so many matters, it is not strange that he should have come to regard himself as the "disciple whom Jesus loved" since he most certainly knew he was the disciple whom Jesus so frequently trusted.

The strongest trait in John's character was his dependability; he was prompt and courageous, faithful and devoted. His greatest weakness was this characteristic conceit. He was the youngest member of his father's family and the youngest of the apostolic group. Perhaps he was just a bit spoiled; maybe he had been humored slightly too much. But the John of after years was a very different type of person than the self-admiring and arbitrary young man who joined the ranks of Jesus' apostles when he was twenty-four.

Those characteristics of Jesus that John most appreciated were the Master's love and unselfishness; these traits made such an impression on him that his whole subsequent life became dominated by the sentiment of love and brotherly devotion. He talked about love and wrote about love. This "son of thunder" became the "apostle of love"; and at Ephesus, when the aged bishop was no longer able to stand in the pulpit and preach but had to be carried to church in a chair, and when at the close of the service he was asked to say a few words to the believers, for years his only utterance was, "My little children, love one another."

John was a man of few words except when his temper was aroused. He thought much but said little. As he grew older, his temper became more subdued, better controlled, but he never overcame his disinclination to talk; he never fully mastered this reticence. But he was gifted with a remarkable and creative imagination.

There was another side to John that one would not expect to find in this quiet and introspective type. He was somewhat bigoted and inordinately intolerant. In this respect he and James were much alike; they both wanted to call down fire from heaven on the heads of the disrespectful Samaritans. When John encountered some strangers teaching in Jesus' name, he promptly forbade them. But he was not the only one of the twelve who was tainted with this kind of self-esteem and superiority consciousness.

John's life was tremendously influenced by the sight of Jesus' going about without a home as he knew how faithfully he had made provision for the care of his mother and family. John also deeply sympathized with Jesus because of his family's failure to understand him, being aware that they were gradually withdrawing from him. This entire situation, together with Jesus' ever deferring his slightest wish to the will of the Father in heaven and his daily life of implicit trust, made such a profound impression on John that it produced marked and permanent changes in his character, changes which manifested themselves throughout his entire subsequent life.

John had a cool and daring courage which few of the other apostles possessed. He was the one apostle who followed right along with Jesus the night of his arrest and dared to accompany his Master into the very jaws of death. He was present and near at hand right up to the last earthly hour and was found faithfully carrying out his trust with regard to Jesus' mother and ready to receive such additional instructions as might be given during the last moments of the Master's mortal existence. One thing is certain, John was thoroughly dependable. John usually sat on Jesus' right hand when the twelve were at meat. He was the first of the twelve really and fully to believe in the resurrection, and he was the first to recognize the Master when he came to them on the seashore after his resurrection.

This son of Zebedee was very closely associated with Peter in the early activities of the Christian movement, becoming one of the chief supporters of the Jerusalem church. He was the right-hand support of Peter on the day of Pentecost.

Several years after the martyrdom of James, John married his brother's widow. The last twenty years of his life he was cared for by a loving granddaughter.

John was in prison several times and was banished to the Isle of Patmos for a period of four years until another emperor came to power in Rome. Had not John been tactful and sagacious, he would undoubtedly have been killed as was his more outspoken brother James. As the years passed, John, together with James the Lord's brother, learned to practice wise conciliation when they appeared before the civil magistrates. They found that a "soft answer turns away wrath." They also learned to represent the church as a "spiritual brotherhood devoted to the social service of mankind" rather than as "the kingdom of heaven." They taught loving service rather than ruling power - kingdom and king.

When in temporary exile on Patmos, John wrote the Book of Revelation, which you now have in greatly abridged and distorted form. This Book of Revelation contains the surviving fragments of a great revelation, large portions of which were lost, other portions of which were removed, subsequent to John's writing. It is preserved in only fragmentary and adulterated form.

John traveled much, labored incessantly, and after becoming bishop of the Asia churches, settled down at Ephesus. He directed his associate, Nathan, in the writing of the so-called "Gospel according to John," at Ephesus, when he was ninety-nine years old. Of all the twelve apostles, John Zebedee eventually became the outstanding theologian. He died a natural death at Ephesus in A.D. 103 when he was one hundred and one years of age.

Philip was the fifth apostle to be chosen, being called when Jesus and his first four apostles were on their way from John's rendezvous on the Jordan to Cana of Galilee. Since he lived at Bethsaida, Philip had for some time known of Jesus, but it had not occurred to him that Jesus was a really great man until that day in the Jordan valley when he said, "Follow me." Philip was also somewhat influenced by the fact that Andrew, Peter, James, and John had accepted Jesus as the Deliverer.

Philip was twenty-seven years of age when he joined the apostles; he had recently been married, but he had no children at this time. The nickname which the apostles gave him signified "curiosity." Philip was always wanting to be shown. He never seemed to see very far into any proposition. He was not necessarily dull, but he lacked imagination. This lack of imagination was the great weakness of his character. He was a commonplace and matter-of-fact individual.

When the apostles were organized for service, Philip was made steward; it was his duty to see that they were at all times supplied with provisions. And he was a good steward. His strongest characteristic was his methodical thoroughness; he was both mathematical and systematic.

Philip came from a family of seven, three boys and four girls. He was next to the oldest, and after the resurrection he baptized his entire family into the kingdom. Philip's people were fisherfolk. His father was a very able man, a deep thinker, but his mother was of a very mediocre family. Philip was not a man who could be expected to do big things, but he was a man who could do little things in a big way, do them well and acceptably. Only a few times in four years did he fail to have food on hand to satisfy the needs of all. Even the many emergency demands attendant upon the life they lived seldom found him unprepared. The commissary department of the apostolic family was intelligently and efficiently managed.

The strong point about Philip was his methodical reliability; the weak point in his make-up was his utter lack of imagination, the absence of the ability to put two and two together to obtain four. He was mathematical in the abstract but not constructive in his imagination. He was almost entirely lacking in certain types of imagination. He was the typical everyday and commonplace average man. There were a great many such men and women among the multitudes who came to hear Jesus teach and preach, and they derived great comfort from observing one like themselves elevated to an honored position in the councils of the Master; they derived courage from the fact that one like themselves had already found a high place in the affairs of the kingdom. And Jesus learned much about the way some human minds function as he so patiently listened to Philip's foolish questions and so many times complied with his steward's request to "be shown."

The one quality about Jesus that Philip so continuously admired was the Master's unfailing generosity. Never could Philip find anything in Jesus that was small, stingy, or miserly, and he worshiped this ever-present and unfailing liberality.

There was little about Philip's personality that was impressive. He was often spoken of as "Philip of Bethsaida, the town where Andrew and Peter live." He was almost without discerning vision; he was unable to grasp the dramatic possibilities of a given situation. He was not pessimistic; he was simply prosaic. He was also greatly lacking in spiritual insight. He would not hesitate to interrupt Jesus in the midst of one of the Master's most profound discourses to ask an apparently foolish question. But Jesus never reprimanded him for such thoughtlessness; he was patient with him and considerate of his inability to grasp the deeper meanings of the teaching. Jesus well knew that, if he once rebuked Philip for asking these annoying questions, he would not only wound this honest soul, but such a reprimand would so hurt Philip that he would never again feel free to ask questions. Jesus knew that on his worlds of space there were untold billions of similar slow-thinking mortals, and he wanted to encourage them all to look to him and always to feel free to come to him with their questions and problems. After all, Jesus was really more interested in Philip's foolish questions than in the sermon he might be preaching. Jesus was supremely interested in *men and women* of all kinds and types.

The apostolic steward was not a good public speaker, but he was a very persuasive and successful personal worker. He was not easily discouraged; he was a plodder and very tenacious in anything he undertook. He had that great and rare gift of saying, "Come." When his first convert, Nathaniel, wanted to argue about the merits and demerits of Jesus and Nazareth, Philip's effective reply was, "Come and see." He was not a dogmatic preacher who exhorted his hearers to "Go" - do this and do that. He met all situations as they arose in his work with "Come" "come with me; I will show you the way." And that is always the effective technique in all forms and phases of teaching. Even parents may learn from Philip the better way of saying to their children *not* "Go do this and go do that," but rather, "Come with us while we show and share with you the better way."

The inability of Philip to adapt himself to a new situation was well shown when the Greeks came to him at Jerusalem, saying, "Sir, we desire to see Jesus." Now Philip would have said to any Jew asking such a question, "Come." But these men were foreigners, and Philip could remember no instructions from his superiors regarding such matters; so the only thing he could think to do was to consult the chief, Andrew, and then they both escorted the inquiring Greeks to Jesus. Likewise, when he went into Samaria preaching and baptizing believers, as he had been instructed by his Master, he refrained from laying hands on his converts in token of their having received the Spirit of Truth. This was done by Peter and John, who presently came down from Jerusalem to observe his work in behalf of the mother church.

Philip went on through the trying times of the Master's death, participated in the reorganization of the twelve, and was the first to go forth to win souls for the kingdom outside of the immediate Jewish ranks, being most successful in his work for the Samaritans and in all his subsequent labors in behalf of the gospel.

Philip's wife, who was an efficient member of the women's corps, became actively associated with her husband in his evangelistic work after their flight from the Jerusalem persecutions. His wife was a fearless woman. She stood at the foot of Philip's cross encouraging him to proclaim the glad tidings even to his murderers, and when his strength failed, she began the recital of the story of salvation by faith in Jesus and was silenced only when the irate Jews rushed upon her and stoned her to death. Their eldest daughter, Leah, continued their work, later on becoming the renowned prophetess of Hierapolis.

Philip, the onetime steward of the twelve, was a mighty man in the kingdom, winning souls wherever he went; and he was finally crucified for his faith and buried at Hierapolis.

Nathaniel, the sixth and last of the apostles to be chosen by the Master himself, was brought to Jesus by his friend Philip. He had been associated in several business enterprises with Philip and, with him, was on the way down to see John the Baptist when they encountered Jesus.

When Nathaniel joined the apostles, he was twenty-five years old and was the next to the youngest of the group. He was the youngest of a family of seven, was unmarried, and the only support of aged and infirm parents, with whom he lived at Cana; his brothers and sister were either married or deceased, and none lived there. Nathaniel and Judas Iscariot were the two best-educated men among the twelve. Nathaniel had thought to become a merchant.

Jesus did not himself give Nathaniel a nickname, but the twelve soon began to speak of him in terms that signified honesty, sincerity. He was "without guile." And this was his great virtue; he was both honest and sincere. The weakness of his character was his pride; he was very proud of his family, his city, his reputation, and his nation, all of which is commendable if it is not carried too far. But Nathaniel was inclined to go to extremes with his personal prejudices. He was disposed to prejudge individuals in accordance with his personal opinions. He was not slow to ask the question, even before he had met Jesus, "Can any good thing come out of Nazareth?" But Nathaniel was not obstinate, even if he was proud. He was quick to reverse himself when he once looked into Jesus' face.

In many respects Nathaniel was the odd genius of the twelve. He was the apostolic philosopher and dreamer, but he was a very practical sort of dreamer. He alternated between seasons of profound philosophy and periods of rare and droll humor; when in the proper mood, he was probably the best storyteller among the twelve. Jesus greatly enjoyed hearing Nathaniel discourse on things both serious and frivolous. Nathaniel progressively took Jesus and the kingdom more seriously, but never did he take himself seriously.

The apostles all loved and respected Nathaniel, and he got along with them splendidly, excepting Judas Iscariot. Judas did not think Nathaniel took his apostleship sufficiently seriously and once had the temerity to go secretly to Jesus and lodge complaint against him. Said Jesus, "Judas, watch carefully your steps; do not overmagnify your office. Who of us is competent to judge his brother? It is not the Father's will that his children should partake only of the serious things of life. Let me repeat; I have come that my brethren in the flesh may have joy, gladness, and life more abundantly. Go then, Judas, and do well that which has been entrusted to you but leave Nathaniel, your brother, to give account of himself to God." And the memory of this, with that of many similar experiences, long lived in the self-deceiving heart of Judas Iscariot.

Many times, when Jesus was away on the mountain with Peter, James, and John, and things were becoming tense and tangled among the apostles, when even Andrew was in doubt about what to say to his disconsolate brethren, Nathaniel would relieve the tension by a bit of philosophy or a flash of humor; good humor, too.

Nathaniel's duty was to look after the families of the twelve. He was often absent from the apostolic councils, for when he heard that sickness or anything out of the ordinary had happened to one of his charges, he lost no time in getting to that home. The twelve rested securely in the knowledge that their families' welfare was safe in the hands of Nathaniel.

Nathaniel most revered Jesus for his tolerance. He never grew weary of contemplating the broadmindedness and generous sympathy of the Son of Man.

Nathaniel's father (Bartholomew) died shortly after Pentecost, after which this apostle went into Mesopotamia and India proclaiming the glad tidings of the kingdom and baptizing believers. His brethren never knew what became of their onetime philosopher, poet, and humorist. But he also was a great man in the kingdom and did much to spread his Master's teachings, even though he did not participate in the organization of the subsequent Christian church. Nathaniel died in India.

Matthew, the seventh apostle, was chosen by Andrew. Matthew belonged to a family of tax gatherers, or publicans, but was himself a customs collector in Capernaum, where he lived. He was thirty-one years old and married and had four children. He was a man of moderate wealth, the only one of any means belonging to the apostolic corps. He was a good business man, a good social mixer, and was gifted with the ability to make friends and to get along smoothly with a great variety of people.

Andrew appointed Matthew the financial representative of the apostles. In a way he was the fiscal agent and publicity spokesman for the apostolic organization. He was a keen judge of human nature and a very efficient propagandist. His is a personality difficult to visualize, but he was a very earnest disciple and an increasing believer in the mission of Jesus and in the certainty of the kingdom. Jesus never gave Levi a nickname, but his fellow apostles commonly referred to him as the "money-getter."

Levi's strong point was his wholehearted devotion to the cause. That he, a publican, had been taken in by Jesus and his apostles was the cause for overwhelming gratitude on the part of the former revenue collector. However, it required some little time for the rest of the apostles, especially Simon Zelotes and Judas Iscariot, to become reconciled to the publican's presence in their midst. Matthew's weakness was his shortsighted and materialistic viewpoint of life. But in all these matters he made great progress as the months went by. He, of course, had to be absent from many of the most precious seasons of instruction as it was his duty to keep the treasury replenished.

It was the Master's forgiving disposition that Matthew most appreciated. He would never cease to recount that faith only was necessary in the business of finding God. He always liked to speak of the kingdom as "this business of finding God."

Though Matthew was a man with a past, he gave an excellent account of himself, and as time went on, his associates became proud of the publican's performances. He was one of the apostles who made extensive notes on the sayings of Jesus, and these notes were used as the basis of Isador's subsequent narrative of the sayings and doings of Jesus, which has become known as the Gospel according to Matthew.

The great and useful life of Matthew, the business man and customs collector of Capernaum, has been the means of leading thousands upon thousands of other business men, public officials, and politicians, down through the subsequent ages, also to hear that engaging voice of the Master saying, "Follow me." Matthew really was a shrewd politician, but he was intensely loyal to Jesus and supremely devoted to the task of seeing that the messengers of the coming kingdom were adequately financed.

The presence of Matthew among the twelve was the means of keeping the doors of the kingdom wide open to hosts of downhearted and outcast souls who had regarded themselves as long since without the bounds of religious consolation. Outcast and despairing men and women flocked to hear Jesus, and he never turned one away.

Matthew received freely tendered offerings from believing disciples and the immediate auditors of the Master's teachings, but he never openly solicited funds from the multitudes. He did all his financial work in a quiet and personal way and raised most of the money among the more substantial class of interested believers. He gave practically the whole of his modest fortune to the work of the Master and his apostles, but they never knew of this generosity, save Jesus, who knew all about it. Matthew hesitated openly to contribute to the apostolic funds for fear that Jesus and his associates might regard his money as being tainted; so he gave much in the names of other believers. During the earlier months, when Matthew knew his presence among them was more or less of a trial, he was strongly tempted to let them know that his funds often supplied them with their daily bread, but he did not yield. When evidence of the disdain of the publican would become manifest, Levi would burn to reveal to them his generosity, but always he managed to keep still.

When the funds for the week were short of the estimated requirements, Levi would often draw heavily upon his own personal resources. Also, sometimes when he became greatly interested in Jesus' teaching, he preferred to remain and hear the instruction, even though he knew he must personally make up for his failure to solicit the necessary funds. But Levi did so wish that Jesus might know that much of the money came from his pocket! He little realized that the Master knew all about it. The apostles all died without knowing that Matthew was their benefactor to such an extent that, when he went forth to proclaim the gospel of the kingdom after the beginning of the persecutions, he was practically penniless.

When these persecutions caused the believers to forsake Jerusalem, Matthew journeyed north, preaching the gospel of the kingdom and baptizing believers. He was lost to the knowledge of his former apostolic associates, but on he went, preaching and baptizing, through Syria, Cappadocia, Galatia, Bithynia, and Thrace. And it was in Thrace, at Lysimachia, that certain unbelieving Jews conspired with the Roman soldiers to encompass his death. And this regenerated publican died triumphant in the faith of a salvation he had so surely learned from the teachings of the Master during his recent sojourn on earth.

Thomas was the eighth apostle, and he was chosen by Philip. In later times he has become known as "doubting Thomas," but his fellow apostles hardly looked upon him as a chronic doubter. True, his was a logical, skeptical type of mind, but he had a form of courageous loyalty which forbade those who knew him intimately to regard him as a trifling skeptic.

When Thomas joined the apostles, he was twenty-nine years old, was married, and had four children. Formerly he had been a carpenter and stone mason, but latterly he had become a fisherman and resided at Tarichea, situated on the west bank of the Jordan where it flows out of the Sea of Galilee, and he was regarded as the leading citizen of this little village. He had little education, but he possessed a keen, reasoning mind and was the son of excellent parents, who lived at Tiberias. Thomas had the one truly analytical mind of the twelve; he was the real scientist of the apostolic group.

The early home life of Thomas had been unfortunate; his parents were not altogether happy in their married life, and this was reflected in Thomas's adult experience. He grew up having a very disagreeable and quarrelsome disposition. Even his wife was glad to see him join the apostles; she was relieved by the thought that her pessimistic husband would be away from home most of the time. Thomas also had a streak of suspicion that made it very difficult to get along peaceably with him. Peter was very much upset by Thomas at first, complaining to his brother, Andrew, that Thomas was "mean, ugly, and always suspicious." But the better his associates knew Thomas, the more they liked him. They found he was superbly honest and unflinchingly loyal. He was perfectly sincere and unquestionably truthful, but he was a natural-born faultfinder and had grown up to become a real pessimist. His analytical mind had become cursed with suspicion. He was rapidly losing faith in his fellow men when he became associated with the twelve and thus came in contact with the noble character of Jesus. This association with the Master began at once to transform Thomas's whole disposition and to effect great changes in his mental reactions to his fellow men.

Thomas's great strength was his superb analytical mind coupled with his unflinching courage - when he had once made up his mind. His great weakness was his suspicious doubting, which he never fully overcame throughout his whole lifetime in the flesh.

In the organization of the twelve Thomas was assigned to arrange and manage the itinerary, and he was an able director of the work and movements of the apostolic corps. He was a good executive, an excellent businessman, but he was handicapped by his many moods; he was one man one day and another man the next. He was inclined toward melancholic brooding when he joined the apostles, but contact with Jesus and the apostles largely cured him of this morbid introspection.

Jesus enjoyed Thomas very much and had many long, personal talks with him. His presence among the apostles was a great comfort to all honest doubters and encouraged many troubled minds to come into the kingdom, even if they could not wholly understand everything about the spiritual and philosophic phases of the teachings of Jesus. Thomas's membership in the twelve was a standing declaration that Jesus loved even honest doubters.

The other apostles held Jesus in reverence because of some special and outstanding trait of his replete personality, but Thomas revered his Master because of his superbly balanced character. Increasingly Thomas admired and honored one who was so lovingly merciful yet so inflexibly just and fair; so firm but never obstinate; so calm but never indifferent; so helpful and so sympathetic but never meddlesome or dictatorial; so strong but at the same time so gentle; so positive but never rough or rude; so tender but never vacillating; so pure and innocent but at the same time so virile, aggressive, and forceful; so truly courageous but never rash or foolhardy; such a lover of nature but so free from all tendency to revere nature; so humorous and so playful, but so free from levity and frivolity. It was this matchless symmetry of personality that so charmed Thomas. He probably enjoyed the highest intellectual understanding and personality appreciation of Jesus of any of the twelve.

In the councils of the twelve Thomas was always cautious, advocating a policy of safety first, but if his conservatism was voted down or overruled, he was always the first fearlessly to move out in execution of the program decided upon. Again and again would he stand out against some project as being foolhardy and presumptuous; he would debate to the bitter end, but when Andrew would put the proposition to a vote, and after the twelve would elect to do that which he had so strenuously opposed, Thomas was the first to say, "Let's go!" He was a good loser. He did not hold grudges nor nurse wounded feelings. Time and again did he oppose letting Jesus expose himself to danger, but when the Master would decide to take such risks, always was it Thomas who rallied the apostles with his courageous words, "Come on, comrades, let's go and die with him."

Thomas was in some respects like Philip; he also wanted "to be shown," but his outward expressions of doubt were based on entirely different intellectual operations. Thomas was analytical, not merely skeptical. As far as personal physical courage was concerned, he was one of the bravest among the twelve.

Thomas had some very bad days; he was blue and downcast at times. The loss of his twin sister when he was nine years old had occasioned him much youthful sorrow and had added to his temperamental problems of later life. When Thomas would become despondent, sometimes it was Nathaniel who helped him to recover, sometimes Peter, and not infrequently one of the Alpheus twins. When he was most depressed, unfortunately he always tried to avoid coming in direct contact with Jesus. But the Master knew all about this and had an understanding sympathy for his apostle when he was thus afflicted with depression and harassed by doubts.

Sometimes Thomas would get permission from Andrew to go off by himself for a day or two. But he soon learned that such a course was not wise; he early found that it was best, when he was downhearted, to stick close to his work and to remain near his associates. But no matter what happened in his emotional life, he kept right on being an apostle. When the time actually came to move forward, it was always Thomas who said, "Let's go!"

Thomas is the great example of a human being who has doubts, faces them, and wins. He had a great mind; he was no carping critic. He was a logical thinker; he was the acid test of Jesus and his fellow apostles. If Jesus and his work had not been genuine, it could not have held a man like Thomas from the start to the finish. He had a keen and sure sense of *fact*. At the first appearance of fraud or deception Thomas would have forsaken them all. Scientists may not fully understand all about Jesus and his work on earth, but there lived and worked with the Master and his human associates a man whose mind was that of a true scientist - Thomas Didymus - and he believed in Jesus of Nazareth.

Thomas had a trying time during the days of the trial and crucifixion. He was for a season in the depths of despair, but he rallied his courage, stuck to the apostles, and was present with them to welcome Jesus on the Sea of Galilee. For a while he succumbed to his doubting depression but eventually rallied his faith and courage. He gave wise counsel to the apostles after Pentecost and, when persecution scattered the believers, went to Cyprus, Crete, the North African coast, and Sicily, preaching the glad tidings of the kingdom and baptizing believers. And Thomas continued preaching and baptizing until he was apprehended by the agents of the Roman government and was put to death in Malta. Just a few weeks before his death he had begun the writing of the life and teachings of Jesus.

James and Judas the sons of Alpheus, the twin fishermen living near Kheresa, were the ninth and tenth apostles and were chosen by James and John Zebedee. They were twenty-six years old and married, James having three children, Judas two.

There is not much to be said about these two commonplace fisherfolk. They loved their Master and Jesus loved them, but they never interrupted his discourses with questions. They understood very little about the philosophical discussions or the theological debates of their fellow apostles, but they rejoiced to find themselves numbered among such a group of mighty men. These two men were almost identical in personal appearance, mental characteristics, and extent of spiritual perception. What may be said of one should be recorded of the other.

Andrew assigned them to the work of policing the multitudes. They were the chief ushers of the preaching hours and, in fact, the general servants and errand boys of the twelve. They helped Philip with the supplies, they carried money to the families for Nathaniel, and always were they ready to lend a helping hand to any one of the apostles.

The multitudes of the common people were greatly encouraged to find two like themselves honored with places among the apostles. By their very acceptance as apostles these mediocre twins were the means of bringing a host of fainthearted believers into the kingdom. And, too, the common people took more kindly to the idea of being directed and managed by official ushers who were very much like themselves.

James and Judas, who were also called Thaddeus and Lebbeus, had neither strong points nor weak points. The nicknames given them by the disciples were good-natured designations of mediocrity. They were "the least of all the apostles"; they knew it and felt cheerful about it.

James Alpheus especially loved Jesus because of the Master's simplicity. These twins could not comprehend the mind of Jesus, but they did grasp the sympathetic bond between themselves and the heart of their Master. Their minds were not of a high order; they might even reverently be called stupid, but they had a real experience in their spiritual natures. They believed in Jesus; they were sons of God and fellows of the kingdom.

Judas Alpheus was drawn toward Jesus because of the Master's unostentatious humility. Such humility linked with such personal dignity made a great appeal to Judas. The fact that Jesus would always enjoin silence regarding his unusual acts made a great impression on this simple child of nature.

The twins were good-natured, simple-minded helpers, and everybody loved them. Jesus welcomed these young men of one talent to positions of honor on his personal staff in the kingdom because there are untold millions of other such simple and fear-ridden souls on the worlds of space whom he likewise wishes to welcome into active and believing fellowship with himself and his outpoured Spirit of Truth. Jesus does not look down upon littleness, only upon evil and sin. James and Judas were *little,* but they were also *faithful.* They were simple and ignorant, but they were also bighearted, kind, and generous.

And how gratefully proud were these humble men on that day when the Master refused to accept a certain rich man as an evangelist unless he would sell his goods and help the poor. When the people heard this and beheld the twins among his counselors, they knew of a certainty that Jesus was no respecter of persons. But only a divine institution - the kingdom of heaven - could ever have been built upon such a mediocre human foundation!

Only once or twice in all their association with Jesus did the twins venture to ask questions in public. Judas was once intrigued into asking Jesus a question when the Master had talked about revealing himself openly to the world. He felt a little disappointed that there were to be no more secrets among the twelve, and he made bold to ask, "But, Master, when you do thus declare yourself to the world, how will you favor us with special manifestations of your goodness?"

The twins served faithfully until the end, until the dark days of trial, crucifixion, and despair. They never lost their heart faith in Jesus, and (save John) they were the first to believe in his resurrection. But they could not comprehend the establishment of the kingdom. Soon after their Master was crucified, they returned to their families and nets; their work was done. They had not the ability to go on in the more complex battles of the kingdom. But they lived and died conscious of having been honored and blessed with four years of close and personal association with a Son of God, the sovereign maker of a universe.

Simon Zelotes, the eleventh apostle, was chosen by Simon Peter. He was an able man of good ancestry and lived with his family at Capernaum. He was twenty-eight years old when he became attached to the apostles. He was a fiery agitator and was also a man who spoke much without thinking. He had been a merchant in Capernaum before he turned his entire attention to the patriotic organization of the Zealots.

Simon Zelotes was given charge of the diversions and relaxation of the apostolic group, and he was a very efficient organizer of the play life and recreational activities of the twelve.

Simon's strength was his inspirational loyalty. When the apostles found a man or woman who floundered in indecision about entering the kingdom, they would send for Simon. It usually required only about fifteen minutes for this enthusiastic advocate of salvation through faith in God to settle all doubts and remove all indecision, to see a new soul born into the "liberty of faith and the joy of salvation."

Simon's great weakness was his material-mindedness. He could not quickly change himself from a Jewish nationalist to a spiritually minded internationalist. Four years was too short a time in which to make such an intellectual and emotional transformation, but Jesus was always patient with him.

The one thing about Jesus that Simon so much admired was the Master's calmness, his assurance, poise, and inexplicable composure.

Although Simon was a rabid revolutionist, a fearless firebrand of agitation, he gradually subdued his fiery nature until he became a powerful and effective preacher of "Peace on earth and good will among men." Simon was a great debater; he did like to argue. And when it came to dealing with the legalistic minds of the educated Jews or the intellectual quibblings of the Greeks, the task was always assigned to Simon.

He was a rebel by nature and an iconoclast by training, but Jesus won him for the higher concepts of the kingdom of heaven. He had always identified himself with the party of protest, but he now joined the party of progress, unlimited and eternal progression of spirit and truth. Simon was a man of intense loyalties and warm personal devotions, and he did profoundly love Jesus.

Jesus was not afraid to identify himself with business men, laboring men, optimists, pessimists, philosophers, skeptics, publicans, politicians, and patriots.

The Master had many talks with Simon, but he never fully succeeded in making an internationalist out of this ardent Jewish nationalist. Jesus often told Simon that it was proper to want to see the social, economic, and political orders improved, but he would always add, "That is not the business of the kingdom of heaven. We must be dedicated to the doing of the Father's will. Our business is to be ambassadors of a spiritual government on high, and we must not immediately concern ourselves with aught but the representation of the will and character of the divine Father who stands at the head of the government whose credentials we bear." It was all difficult for Simon to comprehend, but gradually he began to grasp something of the meaning of the Master's teaching.

After the dispersion because of the Jerusalem persecutions, Simon went into temporary retirement. He was literally crushed. As a nationalist patriot he had surrendered in deference to Jesus' teachings; now all was lost. He was in despair, but in a few years he rallied his hopes and went forth to proclaim the gospel of the kingdom.

He went to Alexandria and, after working up the Nile, penetrated into the heart of Africa, everywhere preaching the gospel of Jesus and baptizing believers. Thus he labored until he was an old man and feeble. And he died and was buried in the heart of Africa.

Judas Iscariot, the twelfth apostle, was chosen by Nathaniel. He was born in Kerioth, a small town in southern Judea. When he was a lad, his parents moved to Jericho, where he lived and had been employed in his father's various business enterprises until he became interested in the preaching and work of John the Baptist. Judas's parents were Sadducees, and when their son joined John's disciples, they disowned him.

When Nathaniel met Judas at Tarichea, he was seeking employment with a fish-drying enterprise at the lower end of the Sea of Galilee. He was thirty years of age and unmarried when he joined the apostles. He was probably the best-educated man among the twelve and the only Judean in the Master's apostolic family. Judas had no outstanding trait of personal strength, though he had many outwardly appearing traits of culture and habits of training. He was a good thinker but not always a truly *honest* thinker. Judas did not really understand himself; he was not really sincere in dealing with himself.

Andrew appointed Judas treasurer of the twelve, a position which he was eminently fitted to hold, and up to the time of the betrayal of his Master he discharged the responsibilities of his office honestly, faithfully, and most efficiently.

There was no special trait about Jesus that Judas admired above the generally attractive and exquisitely charming personality of the Master. Judas was never able to rise above his Judean prejudices against his Galilean associates; he would even criticize in his mind many things about Jesus. Him whom eleven of the apostles looked upon as the perfect man, as the "one altogether lovely and the chiefest among ten thousand," this self-satisfied Judean often dared to criticize in his own heart. He really entertained the notion that Jesus was timid and somewhat afraid to assert his own power and authority.

Judas was a good businessman. It required tact, ability, and patience, as well as painstaking devotion, to manage the financial affairs of such an idealist as Jesus, to say nothing of wrestling with the helter-skelter business methods of some of his apostles. Judas really was a great executive, a farseeing and able financier. And he was a stickler for organization. None of the twelve ever criticized Judas. As far as they could see, Judas Iscariot was a matchless treasurer, a learned man, a loyal (though sometimes critical) apostle, and in every sense of the word a great success. The apostles loved Judas; he was really one of them. He must have *believed* in Jesus, but it is doubtful whether he really *loved* the Master with a whole heart. The case of Judas illustrates the truthfulness of that saying: "There is a way that seems right to a man, but the end thereof is death." It is altogether possible to fall victim to the peaceful deception of pleasant adjustment to the paths of sin and death. Be assured that Judas was always financially loyal to his Master and his fellow apostles. Money could never have been the motive for his betrayal of the Master.

Judas was an only son of unwise parents. When very young, he was pampered and petted; he was a spoiled child. As he grew up, he had exaggerated ideas about his self-importance. He was a poor loser. He had loose and distorted ideas about fairness; he was given to the indulgence of hate and suspicion. He was an expert at misinterpretation of the words and acts of his friends. All through his life Judas had cultivated the habit of getting even with those whom he fancied had mistreated him. His sense of values and loyalties was defective.

To Jesus, Judas was a faith adventure. From the beginning the Master fully understood the weakness of this apostle and well knew the dangers of admitting him to fellowship. But it is the nature of the Sons of God to give every created being a full and equal chance for salvation and survival. Jesus wanted not only the mortals of this world but the onlookers of innumerable other worlds to know that, when doubts exist as to the sincerity and wholeheartedness of a creature's devotion to the kingdom, it is the invariable practice of the Judges of men fully to receive the doubtful candidate. The door of eternal life is wide open to all; "whosoever will may come"; there are no restrictions or qualifications save the *faith* of the one who comes.

This is just the reason why Jesus permitted Judas to go on to the very end, always doing everything possible to transform and save this weak and confused apostle. But when light is not honestly received and lived up to, it tends to become darkness within the soul. Judas grew intellectually regarding Jesus' teachings about the kingdom, but he did not make progress in the acquirement of spiritual character, as did the other apostles. He failed to make satisfactory personal progress in spiritual experience.

Judas became increasingly a brooder over personal disappointment, and finally he became a victim of resentment. His feelings had been many times hurt, and he grew abnormally suspicious of his best friends, even of the Master. Presently he became obsessed with the idea of getting even, anything to avenge himself, yes, even betrayal of his associates and his Master.

But these wicked and dangerous ideas did not take definite shape until the day when a grateful woman broke an expensive box of incense at Jesus' feet. This seemed wasteful to Judas, and when his public protest was so sweepingly disallowed by Jesus right there in the hearing of all, it was too much. That event determined the mobilization of all the accumulated hate, hurt, malice, prejudice, jealousy, and revenge of a lifetime, and he made up his mind to get even with he knew not whom; but he crystallized all the evil of his nature upon the *one* innocent person in all the sordid drama of his unfortunate life just because Jesus happened to be the chief actor in the episode which marked his passing from the progressive kingdom of light into that self-chosen domain of darkness.

The Master many times, both privately and publicly, had warned Judas that he was slipping, but divine warnings are all-too-often useless in dealing with embittered human nature. Jesus did everything possible, consistent with man's moral freedom, to prevent Judas's choosing to go the wrong way. The great test finally came. The son of resentment failed; he yielded to the sour and sordid dictates of a proud and vengeful mind of exaggerated self-importance and swiftly plunged on down into confusion, despair, and depravity.

Judas then entered into the base and shameful intrigue to betray his Lord and Master and quickly carried the nefarious scheme into effect. During the outworking of his anger-conceived plans of traitorous betrayal, he experienced moments of regret and shame, and in these lucid intervals he faintheartedly conceived, as a defense in his own mind, the idea that Jesus might possibly exert his power and deliver himself at the last moment.

When the sordid and sinful business was all over, this renegade mortal, who thought lightly of selling his friend for thirty pieces of silver to satisfy his long-nursed craving for revenge, rushed out and committed the final act in the drama of fleeing from the realities of mortal existence - suicide.

The eleven apostles were horrified, stunned. Jesus regarded the betrayer only with pity. The worlds have found it difficult to forgive Judas, and his name has become eschewed throughout a far-flung universe.

# THE ORDINATION OF THE TWELVE

JUST BEFORE noon on Sunday, January 12, A.D. 27, Jesus called the apostles together for their ordination as public preachers of the gospel of the kingdom. The twelve were expecting to be called almost any day; so this morning they did not go out far from the shore to fish. Several of them were lingering near the shore repairing their nets and tinkering with their fishing paraphernalia.

As Jesus started down the seashore calling the apostles, he first hailed Andrew and Peter, who were fishing near the shore; next he signaled to James and John, who were in a boat near by, visiting with their father, Zebedee, and mending their nets. Two by two he gathered up the other apostles, and when he had assembled all twelve, he journeyed with them to the highlands north of Capernaum, where he proceeded to instruct them in preparation for their formal ordination.

For once all twelve of the apostles were silent; even Peter was in a reflective mood. At last the long-waited-for hour had come! They were going apart with the Master to participate in some sort of solemn ceremony of personal consecration and collective dedication to the sacred work of representing their Master in the proclamation of the coming of his Father's kingdom.

Before the formal ordination service Jesus spoke to the twelve as they were seated about him. "My brethren, this hour of the kingdom has come. I have brought you apart here with me to present you to the Father as ambassadors of the kingdom. Some of you heard me speak of this kingdom in the synagogue when you first were called. Each of you has learned more about the Father's kingdom since you have been with me working in the cities around about the Sea of Galilee. But just now I have something more to tell you concerning this kingdom.

"The New Kingdom which my Father is about to set up in the hearts of his earth children is to be an everlasting dominion. There shall be no end of this rule of my Father in the hearts of those who desire to do his divine will. I declare to you that my Father is not the God of Jew or gentile. Many shall come from the east and from the west to sit down with us in the Father's kingdom, while many of the children of Abraham will refuse to enter this new brotherhood of the rule of the Father's spirit in the hearts of the children of men.

"The power of this kingdom shall consist, not in the strength of armies nor in the might of riches, but rather in the glory of the divine spirit that shall come to teach the minds and rule the hearts of the reborn citizens of this heavenly kingdom, the sons and daughters of God. This is the brotherhood of love wherein righteousness reigns, and whose battle cry shall be: Peace on earth and good will to all men. This kingdom, which you are so soon to go forth proclaiming, is the desire of the good men of all ages, the hope of all the earth, and the fulfillment of the wise promises of all the prophets.

"But for you, my children, and for all others who would follow you into this kingdom, there is set a severe test. Faith alone will pass you through its portals, but you must bring forth the fruits of my Father's spirit if you would continue to ascend in the progressive life of the divine fellowship. Verily, verily, I say to you, not every one who says, 'Lord, Lord,' shall enter the kingdom of heaven; but rather he who does the will of my Father who is in heaven.

"Your message to the world shall be: Seek first the kingdom of God and his righteousness, and in finding these, all other things essential to eternal survival shall be secured therewith. And now would I make it plain to you that this kingdom of my Father will not come with an outward show of power or with unseemly demonstration. You are not to go hence in the proclamation of the kingdom, saying, 'it is here' or 'it is there,' for this kingdom of which you preach is God within you.

"Whosoever would become great in my Father's kingdom shall become a minister to all; and whosoever would be first among you, let him become the server of his brethren. But when you are once truly received as citizens in the heavenly kingdom, you are no longer servants but sons, sons of the living God. And so shall this kingdom progress in the world until it shall break down every barrier and bring all men and women to know my Father and believe in the saving truth which I have come to declare. Even now is the kingdom at hand, and some of you will not die until you have seen the reign of God come in great power.

"And this which your eyes now behold, this small beginning of twelve commonplace men, shall multiply and grow until eventually the whole earth shall be filled with the praise of my Father. And it will not be so much by the words you speak as by the lives you live that men will know you have been with me and have learned of the realities of the kingdom. And while I would lay no grievous burdens upon your minds, I am about to put upon your souls the solemn responsibility of representing me in the world when I shall presently leave you as I now represent my Father in this life which I am living in the flesh." And when he had finished speaking, he stood up.

Jesus now instructed the twelve mortals who had just listened to his declaration concerning the kingdom to kneel in a circle about him. Then the Master placed his hands upon the head of each apostle, beginning with Judas Iscariot and ending with Andrew. When he had blessed them, he extended his hands and prayed. "My Father, I now bring to you these men, my messengers. From among our children on earth I have chosen these twelve to go forth to represent me as I came forth to represent you. Love them and be with them as you have loved and been with me. And now, my Father, give these men wisdom as I place all the affairs of the coming kingdom in their hands. And I would, if it is your will, tarry on earth a time to help them in their labors for the kingdom. And again, my Father, I thank you for these men, and I commit them to your keeping while I go on to finish the work you have given me to do."

When Jesus had finished praying, the apostles remained still, each man bowed in his place. And it was many minutes before even Peter dared lift up his eyes to look upon the Master. One by one they embraced Jesus, but no man said aught. A great silence pervaded the place while a host of celestial beings looked down upon this solemn and sacred scene; the Creator of a universe placing the affairs of the divine brotherhood of man under the direction of human minds.

Then Jesus spoke, "Now that you are ambassadors of my Father's kingdom, you have thereby become a class of men separate and distinct from all other men on earth. You are not now as men among men but as the enlightened citizens of another and heavenly country among the ignorant creatures of this dark world. It is not enough that you live as you were before this hour, but henceforth must you live as those who have tasted the glories of a better life and have been sent back to earth as ambassadors of the Sovereign of that new and better world. Of the teacher more is expected than of the pupil; of the master more is exacted than of the servant. Of the citizens of the heavenly kingdom more is required than of the citizens of the earthly rule.

"Some of the things which I am about to say to you may seem hard, but you have elected to represent me in the world even as I now represent the Father; and as my agents on earth you will be obligated to abide by those teachings and practices which are reflective of my ideals of mortal living on the worlds of space, and which I exemplify in my earth life of revealing the Father who is in heaven.

"I send you forth to proclaim liberty to the spiritual captives, joy to those in the bondage of fear, and to heal the sick in accordance with the will of my Father in heaven. When you find my children in distress, speak encouragingly to them, saying:

"Happy are the poor in spirit, the humble, for theirs are the treasures of the kingdom of heaven.

"Happy are they who hunger and thirst for righteousness, for they shall be filled.

"Happy are the meek, for they shall inherit the earth.

"Happy are the pure in heart, for they shall see God.

"And even so speak to my children these further words of spiritual comfort and promise:

"Happy are they who mourn, for they shall be comforted. Happy are they who weep, for they shall receive the spirit of rejoicing.

"Happy are the merciful, for they shall obtain mercy.

"Happy are the peacemakers, for they shall be called the sons and daughters of God.

"Happy are they who are persecuted for righteousness' sake, for theirs is the kingdom of heaven. Happy are you when men shall revile you and persecute you and shall say all manner of evil against you falsely. Rejoice and be exceedingly glad, for great is your reward in heaven.

"My brethren, as I send you forth, you are the salt of the earth, salt with a saving savor. But if this salt has lost its savor, wherewith shall it be salted? It is henceforth good for nothing but to be cast out and trodden under foot of men.

"You are the light of the world. A city set upon a hill cannot be hid. Neither do men light a candle and put it under a bushel, but on a candlestick; and it gives light to all who are in the house. Let your light so shine before men that they may see your good works and be led to glorify your Father who is in heaven.

"I am sending you out into the world to represent me and to act as ambassadors of my Father's kingdom, and as you go forth to proclaim the glad tidings, put your trust in the Father whose messengers you are. Do not forcibly resist injustice; put not your trust in the arm of the flesh. If your neighbor smites you on the right cheek, turn to him the other also. Be willing to suffer injustice rather than to go to law among yourselves. In kindness and with mercy minister to all who are in distress and in need.

"I say to you: Love your enemies, do good to those who hate you, bless those who curse you, and pray for those who despitefully use you. And whatsoever you believe that I would do to men, do you also to them.

"Your Father in heaven makes the sun to shine on the evil as well as upon the good; likewise he sends rain on the just and the unjust. You are the sons of God; even more, you are now the ambassadors of my Father's kingdom. Be merciful, even as God is merciful, and in the eternal future of the kingdom you shall be perfect, even as your heavenly Father is perfect.

"You are commissioned to save men, not to judge them. At the end of your earth life you will all expect mercy; therefore do I require of you during your mortal life that you show mercy to all of your brethren in the flesh. Make not the mistake of trying to pluck a mote out of your brother's eye when there is a beam in your own eye. Having first cast the beam out of your own eye, you can the better see to cast the mote out of your brother's eye.

"Discern the truth clearly; live the righteous life fearlessly; and so shall you be my apostles and my Father's ambassadors. You have heard it said: 'If the blind lead the blind, they both shall fall into the pit.' If you would guide others into the kingdom, you must yourselves walk in the clear light of living truth. In all the business of the kingdom I exhort you to show just judgment and keen wisdom. Present not that which is holy to dogs, neither cast your pearls before swine, lest they trample your gems under foot and turn to rend you.

"I warn you against false prophets who will come to you in sheep's clothing, while on the inside they are as ravening wolves. By their fruits you shall know them. Do men gather grapes from thorns or figs from thistles? Even so, every good tree brings forth good fruit, but the corrupt tree bears evil fruit. A good tree cannot yield evil fruit; neither can a corrupt tree produce good fruit. Every tree that does not bring forth good fruit is presently hewn down and cast into the fire. In gaining an entrance into the kingdom of heaven, it is the motive that counts. My Father looks into the hearts of men and judges by their inner longings and their sincere intentions.

"In the great day of the kingdom judgment, many will say to me, 'Did we not prophesy in your name and by your name do many wonderful works?' But I will be compelled to say to them, EpI never knew you; depart from me you who are false teachers.' But every one who hears this charge and sincerely executes his commission to represent me before men even as I have represented my Father to you, shall find an abundant entrance into my service and into the kingdom of the heavenly Father."

Never before had the apostles heard Jesus speak in this way, for he had talked to them as one having supreme authority. They came down from the mountain about sundown, but no man asked Jesus a question.

The so-called "Sermon on the Mount" is not the gospel of Jesus. It does contain much helpful instruction, but it was Jesus' ordination charge to the twelve apostles. It was the Master's personal commission to those who were to go on preaching the gospel and aspiring to represent him in the world of men even as he was so eloquently and perfectly representative of his Father.

*"You are the salt of the earth, salt with a saving savor. But if this salt has lost its savor, wherewith shall it be salted? It is henceforth good for nothing but to be cast out and trodden under foot of men."*

In Jesus' time salt was precious. It was even used for money. The modern word "salary" is derived from salt. Salt not only flavors food, but it is also a preservative. It makes other things more tasty, and thus it serves by being spent.

*"You are the light of the world. A city set on a hill cannot be hid. Neither do men light a candle and put it under a bushel, but on a candlestick; and it gives light to all who are in the house. Let your light so shine before men that they may see your good works and be led to glorify your Father who is in heaven."*

While light dispels darkness, it can also be so "blinding" as to confuse and frustrate. We are admonished to let our light *so* shine that our fellows will be guided into new and godly paths of enhanced living. Our light should so shine as not to attract attention to self. Even one's vocation can be utilized as an effective "reflector" for the dissemination of this light of life.

Strong characters are not derived from *not* doing wrong but rather from actually doing right. Unselfishness is the badge of human greatness. The highest levels of self-realization are attained by worship and service. The happy and effective person is motivated, not by fear of wrongdoing, but by love of right doing.

*"By their fruits you shall know them."* Personality is basically changeless; that which changes (grows) is the moral character. The major error of modern religions is negativism. The tree which bears no fruit is "hewn down and cast into the fire." Moral worth cannot be derived from mere repression; obeying the injunction "Thou shalt not." Fear and shame are unworthy motivations for religious living. Religion is valid only when it reveals the fatherhood of God and enhances the brotherhood of mankind.

An effective philosophy of living is formed by a combination of cosmic insight and the total of one's emotional reactions to the social and economic environment. Remember: While inherited urges cannot be fundamentally modified, emotional responses to such urges can be changed; therefore the moral nature can be modified, character can be improved. In the strong character emotional responses are integrated and coordinated, and thus is produced a unified personality. Deficient unification weakens the moral nature and engenders unhappiness.

Without a worthy goal, life becomes aimless and unprofitable, and much unhappiness results. Jesus' discourse at the ordination of the twelve constitutes a master philosophy of life. Jesus exhorted his followers to exercise experiential faith. He admonished them not to depend on mere intellectual assent, credulity, and established authority.

Education should be a technique of learning (discovering) the better methods of gratifying our natural and inherited urges, and happiness is the resulting total of these enhanced techniques of emotional satisfactions. Happiness is little dependent on environment, though pleasing surroundings may greatly contribute thereto.

Every mortal really craves to be a complete person, to be perfect even as the Father in heaven is perfect, and such attainment is possible because in the last analysis the "universe is truly fatherly."

From the Sermon on the Mount to the discourse of the Last Supper, Jesus taught his followers to manifest *fatherly* love rather than *brotherly* love. Brotherly love would love your neighbor as you love yourself, and that would be adequate fulfillment of the "golden rule." But fatherly affection would require that you should love your fellow mortals as Jesus loves you.

Jesus loves mankind with a dual affection. He lived on earth as a twofold personality, human and divine. As the Son of God he loves man with a fatherly love; he is man's Creator, his universe Father. As the Son of Man, Jesus loves mortals as a brother; he was truly a man among men.

Jesus did not expect his followers to achieve an impossible manifestation of brotherly love, but he did expect them to so strive to be like God - to be perfect even as the Father in heaven is perfect - that they could begin to look upon man as God looks upon his creatures and therefore could begin to love men as God loves them, to show forth the beginnings of a fatherly affection. In the course of these exhortations to the twelve apostles, Jesus sought to reveal this new concept of *fatherly love* as it is related to certain emotional attitudes concerned in making numerous environmental social adjustments.

The Master introduced this momentous discourse by calling attention to four *faith* attitudes as the prelude to the subsequent portrayal of his four transcendent and supreme reactions of fatherly love in contrast to the limitations of mere brotherly love.

He first talked about those who were poor in spirit, hungered after righteousness, endured meekness, and who were pure in heart. Such spirit-discerning mortals could be expected to attain such levels of divine selflessness as to be able to attempt the amazing exercise of *fatherly* affection; that even as mourners they would be empowered to show mercy, promote peace, and endure persecutions, and throughout all of these trying situations to love even unlovely mankind with a fatherly love. A father's affection can attain levels of devotion that immeasurably transcend a brother's affection.

The faith and the love of these beatitudes strengthen moral character and create happiness. Fear and anger weaken character and destroy happiness. This momentous sermon started out upon the note of happiness.

1. *"Happy are the poor in spirit - the humble.* "To a child, happiness is the satisfaction of immediate pleasure craving. The adult is willing to sow

seeds of self-denial in order to reap subsequent harvests of augmented happiness. In Jesus' times and since, happiness has all too often been associated with the idea of the possession of wealth. In the story of the Pharisee and the publican praying in the temple, the one felt rich in spirit - egotistical; the other felt "poor in spirit" - humble. One was self-sufficient; the other was teachable and truth-seeking. The poor in spirit seek for goals of spiritual wealth - for God. And such seekers after truth do not have to wait for rewards in a distant future; they are rewarded *now*. They find the kingdom of heaven within their own hearts, and they experience such happiness *now*.

2. *"Happy are they who hunger and thirst for righteousness, for they shall be filled."* Only those who feel poor in spirit will ever hunger for righteousness. Only the humble seek for divine strength and crave spiritual power. But it is most dangerous to knowingly engage in spiritual fasting in order to improve one's appetite for spiritual endowments. Physical fasting becomes dangerous after four or five days; one is apt to lose all desire for food. Prolonged fasting, either physical or spiritual, tends to destroy hunger.

Experiential righteousness is a pleasure, not a duty. Jesus' righteousness is a dynamic love - fatherly-brotherly affection. It is not the negative or thou-shalt-not type of righteousness. How could one ever hunger for something negative; something "not to do"?

It is not so easy to teach a child mind these first two of the beatitudes, but the mature mind should grasp their significance.

3. *"Happy are the meek, for they shall inherit the earth."* Genuine meekness has no relation to fear. It is rather an attitude of man co-operating with God; "Your will be done." It embraces patience and forbearance and is motivated by an unshakable faith in a lawful and friendly universe. It masters all temptations to rebel against the divine leading. Jesus was the ideal meek man of Earth, and he inherited a vast universe.

4. *"Happy are the pure in heart, for they shall see God."* Spiritual purity is not a negative quality, except that it does lack suspicion and revenge. In discussing purity, Jesus did not intend to deal exclusively with human sex attitudes. He referred more to that faith which men and women should have in their fellows; that faith which parents have in their children, and which enables them to love their brothers and sisters even as a father would love them. A father's love need not pamper, and it does not condone evil, but it is always anticynical. Fatherly love has singleness of purpose, and it always looks for the best in humanity; that is the attitude of a true parent.

To see God (by faith) means to acquire true spiritual insight. And spiritual insight enhances Adjuster guidance, and these in the end augment God-consciousness. And when you know the Father, you are confirmed in the assurance of divine sonship, and you can increasingly love each of your brothers and sisters in the flesh, not only as a brother/sister - with brotherly/sisterly love - but also as a parent - with parental affection.

It is easy to teach this admonition even to a child. Children are naturally trustful, and parents should see to it that they do not lose that simple faith. In dealing with children, avoid all deception and refrain from suggesting suspicion. Wisely help them to choose their heroes and select their lifework.

And then Jesus went on to instruct his followers in the realization of the chief purpose of all human struggling - perfection - even divine attainment. Always he admonished them: "Be you perfect, even as your Father in heaven is perfect." He did not exhort the twelve to love their neighbors as they loved themselves. That would have been a worthy achievement; it would have indicated the achievement of brotherly love. He rather admonished his apostles to love men as he had loved them - to love with a *fatherly* as well as a brotherly affection. And he illustrated this by pointing out four supreme reactions of fatherly love:

1. *"Happy are they who mourn, for they shall be comforted."* So-called common sense or the best of logic would never suggest that happiness could be derived from mourning. But Jesus did not refer to outward or ostentatious mourning. He alluded to an emotional attitude of tenderheartedness. It is a great error to teach boys and young men that it is unmanly to show tenderness or otherwise to give evidence of emotional feeling or physical suffering. Sympathy is a worthy attribute of the male as well as the female. It is not necessary to be calloused in order to be manly. This is the wrong way to create courageous men. The world's great men have not been afraid to mourn. Moses, the mourner, was a greater man than either Samson or Goliath. Moses was a superb leader, but he was also a man of meekness. Being sensitive and responsive to human need creates genuine and lasting happiness, while such kindly attitudes safeguard the soul from the destructive influences of anger, hate, and suspicion.

2. *"Happy are the merciful, for they shall obtain mercy."* Mercy here denotes the height and depth and breadth of the truest friendship - loving-kindness. Mercy sometimes may be passive, but here it is active and dynamic - supreme fatherliness. A loving parent experiences little difficulty in forgiving his child, even many times. And in an unspoiled child the urge to relieve suffering is natural. Children are normally kind and sympathetic when old enough to appreciate actual conditions.

3. *"Happy are the peacemakers, for they shall be called the sons of God."* Jesus' hearers were longing for military deliverance, not for peacemakers. But Jesus' peace is not of the pacific and negative kind. In the face of trials and persecutions he said, "My peace I leave with you." "Let not your heart be troubled, neither let it be afraid." This is the peace that prevents ruinous conflicts. Personal peace integrates personality. Social peace prevents fear, greed, and anger. Political peace prevents race antagonisms, national suspicions, and war. Peacemaking is the cure of distrust and suspicion. And let it ever be understood that "sonship" has no gender connotations, both men and women aspire to sonship.

Children can easily be taught to function as peacemakers. They enjoy team activities; they like to play together. Said the Master at another time: "Whosoever will save his life shall lose it, but whosoever will lose his life shall find it."

4. *"Happy are they who are persecuted for righteousness' sake, for theirs is the kingdom of heaven. Happy are you when men shall revile you and persecute you and shall say all manner of evil against you falsely. Rejoice and be exceedingly glad, for great is your reward in heaven."*

So often persecution does follow peace. But young people and brave adults never shun difficulty or danger. "Greater love has no man than to lay down his life for his friends." And a fatherly love can freely do all these things - things which brotherly love can hardly encompass. And progress has always been the final harvest of persecution. Children always respond to the challenge of courage. Youth is ever willing to "take a dare." And every child should early learn to sacrifice.

And so it is revealed that the beatitudes of the Sermon on the Mount are based on faith and love and not on law - ethics and duty.

Fatherly love delights in returning good for evil - doing good in retaliation for injustice.

Sunday evening, on reaching the home of Zebedee from the highlands north of Capernaum, Jesus and the twelve partook of a simple meal. Afterward, while Jesus went for a walk along the beach, the twelve talked among themselves. After a brief conference, while the twins built a small fire to give them warmth and more light, Andrew went out to find Jesus, and when he had overtaken him, he said, "Master, my brethren are unable to comprehend what you have said about the kingdom. We do not feel able to begin this work until you have given us further instruction. I have come to ask you to join us in the garden and help us to understand the meaning of your words." And Jesus went with Andrew to meet with the apostles.

When he had entered the garden, he gathered the apostles around him and taught them further, saying, "You find it difficult to receive my message because you would build the new teaching directly upon the old, but I declare that you must be reborn. You must start out afresh as little children and be willing to trust my teaching and believe in God. The new gospel of the kingdom cannot be made to conform to that which is. You have wrong ideas of the Son of Man and his mission on earth. But do not make the mistake of thinking that I have come to set aside the law and the prophets; I have not come to destroy, but to fulfill, to enlarge and illuminate. I come not to transgress the law but rather to write these new commandments on the tablets of your hearts.

"I demand of you a righteousness that shall exceed the righteousness of those who seek to obtain the Father's favor by almsgiving, prayer, and fasting. If you would enter the kingdom, you must have a righteousness that consists in love, mercy, and truth - the sincere desire to do the will of my Father in heaven."

Then said Simon Peter, "Master, if you have a new commandment, we would hear it. Reveal the new way to us."

Jesus answered Peter, "You have heard it said by those who teach the law: 'You shall not kill; that whosoever kills shall be subject to judgment.' But I look beyond the act to uncover the motive. I declare to you that every one who is angry with his brother is in danger of condemnation. He who nurses hatred in his heart and plans vengeance in his mind stands in danger of judgment. You must judge your fellows by their deeds; the Father in heaven judges by the intent.

"You have heard the teachers of the law say, 'You shall not commit adultery.' But I say to you that every man who looks upon a woman with intent to lust after her has already committed adultery with her in his heart. You can only judge men by their acts, but my Father looks into the hearts of his children and in mercy adjudges them in accordance with their intents and real desires."

Jesus was minded to go on discussing the other commandments when James Zebedee interrupted him, asking, "Master, what shall we teach the people regarding divorcement? Shall we allow a man to divorce his wife as Moses has directed?"

And when Jesus heard this question, he said, "I have not come to legislate but to enlighten. I have come not to reform the kingdoms of this world but rather to establish the kingdom of heaven. It is not the will of the Father that I should yield to the temptation to teach you rules of government, trade, or social behavior, which, while they might be good for today, would be far from suitable for the society of another age. I am on earth solely to comfort the minds, liberate the spirits, and save the souls of men. But I will say, concerning this question of divorcement, that, while Moses looked with favor upon such things, it was not so in the days of Adam and in the Garden of Eden."

After the apostles had talked among themselves for a short time, Jesus went on to say, "Always must you recognize the two viewpoints of all mortal conduct - the human and the divine; the ways of the flesh and the way of the spirit; the estimate of time and the viewpoint of eternity."

And though the twelve could not comprehend all that he taught them, they were truly helped by this instruction.

And then said Jesus, "But you will stumble over my teaching because you are wont to interpret my message literally; you are slow to discern the spirit of my teaching. Again must you remember that you are my messengers; you are beholden to live your lives as I have in spirit lived mine. You are my personal representatives; but do not err in expecting all men to live as you do in every particular. Also must you remember that I have sheep not of this flock, and that I am beholden to them also, to the end that I must provide for them the pattern of doing the will of God while living the life of the mortal nature."

Then asked Nathaniel, "Master, shall we give no place to justice? The law of Moses says, 'An eye for an eye, and a tooth for a tooth.' What shall we say?"

And Jesus answered, "You shall return good for evil. My messengers must not strive with men, but be gentle toward all. Measure for measure shall not be your rule. The rulers of men may have such laws, but not so in the kingdom; mercy always shall determine your judgments and love your conduct. And if these are hard sayings, you can even now turn back. If you find the requirements of apostleship too hard, you may return to the less rigorous pathway of discipleship."

On hearing these startling words, the apostles drew apart by themselves for a while, but they soon returned, and Peter said, "Master, we would go on with you; not one of us would turn back. We are fully prepared to pay the extra price; we will drink the cup. We would be apostles, not merely disciples."

When Jesus heard this, he said, "Be willing, then, to take up your responsibilities and follow me. Do your good deeds in secret; when you give alms, let not the left hand know what the right hand does. And when you pray, go apart by yourselves and use not vain repetitions and meaningless phrases. Always remember that the Father knows what you need even before you ask Him. And be not given to fasting with a sad countenance to be seen by men. As my chosen apostles, now set apart for the service of the kingdom, lay not up for yourselves treasures on earth, but by your unselfish service lay up for yourselves treasures in heaven, for where your treasures are, there will your hearts be also.

"The lamp of the body is the eye; if, therefore, your eye is generous, your whole body will be full of light. But if your eye is selfish, the whole body will be filled with darkness. If the very light which is in you is turned to darkness, how great is that darkness!"

And then Thomas asked Jesus if they should "continue having everything in common."

Said the Master, "Yes, my brethren, I would that we should live together as one understanding family. You are intrusted with a great work, and I crave your undivided service. You know that it has been well said: 'No man can serve two masters.' You cannot sincerely worship God and at the same time wholeheartedly serve mammon. Having now enlisted unreservedly in the work of the kingdom, be not anxious for your lives; much less be concerned with what you shall eat or what you shall drink; nor yet for your bodies, what clothing you shall wear. Already have you learned that willing hands and earnest hearts shall not go hungry. And now, when you prepare to devote all of your energies to the work of the kingdom, be assured that the Father will not be unmindful of your needs. Seek first the kingdom of God, and when you have found entrance thereto, all things needful shall be added to you. Be not, therefore, unduly anxious for the morrow. Sufficient for the day is the trouble thereof."

When Jesus saw they were disposed to stay up all night to ask questions, he said to them, "My brethren, you are earthen vessels; it is best for you to go to your rest so as to be ready for the morrow's work."

But sleep had departed from their eyes. Peter ventured to request of his Master that "I have just a little private talk with you. Not that I would have secrets from my brethren, but I have a troubled spirit, and if, perchance, I should deserve a rebuke from my Master, I could the better endure it alone with you." And Jesus said, "Come with me, Peter" as he led the way into the house.

When Peter returned from the presence of his Master much cheered and greatly encouraged, James decided to go in to talk with Jesus. And so on through the early hours of the morning, the other apostles went in one by one to talk with the Master. When they had all held personal conferences with him save the twins, who had fallen asleep, Andrew went in to Jesus and said, "Master, the twins have fallen asleep in the garden by the fire; shall I arouse them to inquire if they would also talk with you?"

And Jesus smilingly said to Andrew, "They do well; trouble them not." And now the night was passing; the light of another day was dawning.

After a few hours' sleep, when the twelve were assembled for a late breakfast with Jesus, he said, "Now must you begin your work of preaching the glad tidings and instructing believers. Make ready to go to Jerusalem."

After Jesus had spoken, Thomas mustered up courage to say, "I know, Master, that we should now be ready to enter upon the work, but I fear we are not yet able to accomplish this great undertaking. Would you consent for us to stay hereabouts for just a few days more before we begin the work of the kingdom?"

And when Jesus saw that all of his apostles were possessed by this same fear, he said, "It shall be as you have requested; we will remain here over the Sabbath day."

For weeks and weeks small groups of earnest truth seekers, together with curious spectators, had been coming to Bethsaida to see Jesus. Already word about him had spread over the countryside; inquiring groups had come from cities as far away as Tyre, Sidon, Damascus, Caesarea, and Jerusalem. Heretofore, Jesus had greeted these people and taught them concerning the kingdom, but the Master now turned this work over to the twelve. Andrew would select one of the apostles and assign him to a group of visitors, and sometimes all twelve of them were so engaged.

For two days they worked, teaching by day and holding private conferences late into the night. On the third day Jesus visited with Zebedee and Salome while he sent his apostles off to "go fishing, seek carefree change, or perchance visit your families." On Thursday they returned for three more days of teaching.

During this week of rehearsing, Jesus many times repeated to his apostles the two great motives of his post-baptismal mission on earth:

1.    To reveal the Father to man.

2.    To lead men and women to become son-conscious - to faith-realize that they are the children of the Most High.

One week of this varied experience did much for the twelve; some even became over self-confident. At the last conference, the night after the Sabbath, Peter and James came to Jesus, saying, "We are ready; let us now go forth to take the kingdom."

To which Jesus replied, "May your wisdom equal your zeal and your courage atone for your ignorance."

Though the apostles failed to comprehend much of his teaching, they did not fail to grasp the significance of the charmingly beautiful life he lived with them.

Jesus well knew that his apostles were not fully assimilating his teachings. He decided to give some special instruction to Peter, James, and John, hoping they would be able to clarify the ideas of their associates. He saw that, while some features of the idea of a spiritual kingdom were being grasped by the twelve, they steadfastly persisted in attaching these new spiritual teachings directly onto their old and entrenched literal concepts of the kingdom of heaven as a restoration of David's throne and the re-establishment of Israel as a temporal power on earth. Accordingly, on Thursday afternoon Jesus went out from the shore in a boat with Peter, James, and John to talk over the affairs of the kingdom. This was a four hour long teaching conference, embracing scores of questions and answers, and may most profitably be put in this record by reorganizing the summary of this momentous afternoon as it was given by Simon Peter to his brother, Andrew, the following morning:

1. *Doing the Father's will.* Jesus' teaching to trust in the overcare of the heavenly Father was not a blind and passive fatalism. He quoted with approval, on this afternoon, an old Hebrew saying: "He who will not work

shall not eat." He pointed to his own experience as sufficient commentary on his teachings. His precepts about trusting the Father must not be adjudged by the social or economic conditions of modern times or any other age. His instruction embraces the ideal principles of living near God in all ages and on all worlds.

Jesus made clear to the three the difference between the requirements of apostleship and discipleship. And even then he did not forbid the exercise of prudence and foresight by the twelve. What he preached against was not forethought but anxiety, worry. He taught the active and alert submission to God's will. In answer to many of their questions regarding frugality and thriftiness, he simply called attention to his life as carpenter, boatmaker, and fisherman, and to his careful organization of the twelve. He sought to make it clear that the world is not to be regarded as an enemy; that the circumstances of life constitute a divine dispensation working along with the sons and daughters of God.

Jesus had great difficulty in getting them to understand his personal practice of nonresistance. He absolutely refused to defend himself, and it appeared to the apostles that he would be pleased if they would pursue the same policy. He taught them not to resist evil, not to combat injustice or injury, but he did not teach passive tolerance of wrongdoing. And he made it plain on this afternoon that he approved of the social punishment of evildoers and criminals, and that the civil government must sometimes employ force for the maintenance of social order and in the execution of justice.

He never ceased to warn his disciples against the evil practice of *retaliation;* he made no allowance for revenge, the idea of getting even. He deplored the holding of grudges. He disallowed the idea of an eye for an eye and a tooth for a tooth. He discountenanced the whole concept of private and personal revenge, assigning these matters to civil government, on the one hand, and to the judgment of God, on the other. He made it clear to the three that his teachings applied to the *individual,* not the state. He summarized his instructions up to that time regarding these matters, as:

Love your enemies; remember the moral claims of human brotherhood. The futility of evil; A wrong is not righted by vengeance. Do not make the mistake of fighting evil with its own weapons.

Have faith - confidence in the eventual triumph of divine justice and eternal goodness.

*2. Political attitude.* He cautioned his apostles to be discreet in their remarks concerning the strained relations then existing between the Jewish people and the Roman government; he forbade them to become in any way embroiled in these difficulties. He was always careful to avoid the political snares of his enemies, ever making reply, "Render to Caesar the things which are Caesar's and to God the things which are God's." He refused to have his attention diverted from his mission of establishing a new way of salvation; he would not permit himself to be concerned about anything else. In his personal life he was always duly observant of all civil laws and regulations; in all his public teachings he ignored the civic, social, and economic realms. He told the three apostles that he was concerned only with the principles of man's inner and personal spiritual life.

Jesus was not, therefore, a political reformer. He did not come to reorganize the world; even if he had done this, it would have been applicable only to that day and generation. Nevertheless, he did show man the best way of living, and no generation is exempt from the labor of discovering how best to adapt Jesus' life to its own problems. But never make the mistake of identifying Jesus' teachings with any political or economic theory, with any social or industrial system.

*3. Social attitude.* The Jewish rabbis had long debated the question: Who is my neighbor? Jesus came presenting the idea of active and spontaneous kindness, a love of one's fellow men so genuine that it expanded the neighborhood to include the whole world, thereby making all men one's neighbors. But with all this, Jesus was interested only in the individual, not the mass. Jesus was not a sociologist, but he did labor to break down all forms of selfish isolation. He taught pure sympathy, compassion. Michael of Nebadon is a mercy-dominated Son; compassion is his very nature.

The Master did not say that men should never entertain their friends at meat, but he did say that his followers should make feasts for the poor and the unfortunate. Jesus had a firm sense of justice, but it was always tempered with mercy. He did not teach his apostles that they were to be imposed upon by social parasites or professional alms-seekers. The nearest he came to making sociological pronouncements was to say, "Judge not, that you be not judged."

He made it clear that indiscriminate kindness may be blamed for many social evils. The following day Jesus definitely instructed Judas that no apostolic funds were to be given out as alms except upon his request or upon the joint petition of two of the apostles. In all these matters it was the practice of Jesus always to say, "Be as wise as serpents but as harmless as doves." It seemed to be his purpose in all social situations to teach patience, tolerance, and forgiveness.

The family occupied the very center of Jesus' philosophy of life - here and hereafter. He based his teachings about God on the family, while he sought to correct the Jewish tendency to over-honor ancestors. He exalted family life as the highest human duty but made it plain that family relationships must not interfere with religious obligations. He called attention to the fact that the family is a temporal institution; that it does not survive death. Jesus did not hesitate to give up his family when the family ran counter to the Father's will. He taught the new and larger brother/sisterhood of humanity - the children of God. In Jesus' time divorce practices were lax in Palestine and throughout the Roman Empire. He repeatedly refused to lay down laws regarding marriage and divorce, but many of Jesus' early followers had strong opinions on divorce and did not hesitate to attribute them to him. All of the New Testament writers held to these more stringent and advanced ideas about divorce except John Mark.

4. *Economic attitude.* Jesus worked, lived, and traded in the world as he found it. He was not an economic reformer, although he did frequently call attention to the injustice of the unequal distribution of wealth. But he did not offer any suggestions by way of remedy. He made it plain to the three that, while his apostles were not to hold property, he was not preaching against wealth and property, merely its unequal and unfair distribution. He recognized the need for social justice and industrial fairness, but he offered no rules for their attainment. He never taught his followers to avoid earthly possessions, only his twelve apostles. Luke, the physician, was a strong believer in social equality, and he did much to interpret Jesus' sayings in harmony with his personal beliefs. Jesus never personally directed his followers to adopt a communal mode of life; he made no pronouncement of any sort regarding such matters.

Jesus frequently warned his listeners against covetousness, declaring that "a man's happiness consists not in the abundance of his material possessions." He constantly reiterated, "What shall it profit a man if he gain the whole world and lose his own soul?" He made no direct attack on the possession of property, but he did insist that it is eternally essential that spiritual values come first. In his later teachings he sought to correct many erroneous Earth views of life by narrating numerous parables which he presented in the course of his public ministry. Jesus never intended to formulate economic theories; he well knew that each age must evolve its own remedies for existing troubles. And if Jesus were on earth today, living his life in the flesh, he would be a great disappointment to the majority of good men and women for the simple reason that he would not take sides in present-day political, social, or economic disputes. He would remain grandly aloof while teaching you how to perfect your inner spiritual life so as to render you manyfold more competent to attack the solution of your purely human problems.

Jesus would make all his children Godlike and then stand by sympathetically while these children of God solve their own political, social, and economic problems. It was not wealth that he denounced, but what wealth does to the majority of its devotees. On this Thursday afternoon Jesus first told his associates that "it is more blessed to give than to receive."

5. *Personal religion.* You, as did his apostles, should the better understand Jesus' teachings by his life. He lived a perfected life on Earth, and his unique teachings can only be understood when that life is visualized in its immediate background. It is his life, and not his lessons to the twelve or his sermons to the multitudes, that will assist most in revealing the Father's divine character and loving personality.

Jesus did not attack the teachings of the Hebrew prophets or the Greek moralists. The Master recognized the many good things which these great teachers stood for, but he had come down to earth to teach something *additional,* "the voluntary conformity of man's will to God's will." Jesus did not want simply to produce a *religious person,* a mortal wholly occupied with religious feelings and actuated only by spiritual impulses. Could you have had but one look at him, you would have known that Jesus was a real man of great experience in the things of this world. The teachings of Jesus in this respect have been grossly perverted and much misrepresented all down through the centuries of the Christian era; you have also held perverted ideas about the Master's meekness and humility. What he aimed at in his life appears to have been a *superb self-respect.* He only advised men and women to humble themselves that they might become truly exalted; what he really aimed at was true humility toward God. He placed great value upon sincerity - a pure heart. Fidelity was a cardinal virtue in his estimate of character, while *courage* was the very heart of his teachings. "Fear not" was his watchword, and patient endurance his ideal of strength of character. The teachings of Jesus constitute a religion of valor, courage, and heroism. And this is just why he chose as his personal representatives twelve commonplace men, the majority of whom were rugged, virile, and manly fishermen.

Jesus had little to say about the social vices of his day; seldom did he make reference to moral delinquency. He was a positive teacher of true virtue. He studiously avoided the negative method of imparting instruction; he refused to advertise evil. He was not even a moral reformer. He well knew, and so taught his apostles, that the sensual urges of mankind are not suppressed by either religious rebuke or legal prohibitions. His few denunciations were largely directed against pride, cruelty, oppression, and hypocrisy.

Jesus did not vehemently denounce even the Pharisees, as did John. He knew many of the scribes and Pharisees were honest of heart; he understood their enslaving bondage to religious traditions. Jesus laid great emphasis on "first making the tree good." He impressed the three that he valued the whole life, not just a certain few special virtues.

The one thing which John gained from this day's teaching was that the heart of Jesus' religion consisted in the acquirement of a compassionate character coupled with a personality motivated to do the will of the Father in heaven.

Peter grasped the idea that the gospel they were about to proclaim was really a fresh beginning for the whole human race. He conveyed this impression subsequently to Paul, who formulated therefrom his doctrine of Christ as "the second Adam."

James grasped the thrilling truth that Jesus wanted his children on earth to live as though they were already citizens of the completed heavenly kingdom.

Jesus knew each man and woman was different, and he so taught his apostles. He constantly exhorted them to refrain from trying to mold the disciples and believers according to some set pattern. He sought to allow each soul to develop in its own way, a perfecting and separate individual before God. In answer to one of Peter's many questions, the Master said, "I want to set men and women free so that they can start out afresh as little children upon the new and better life." Jesus always insisted that true goodness must be unconscious, in bestowing charity not allowing the left hand to know what the right hand does.

The three apostles were shocked this afternoon when they realized that their Master's religion made no provision for spiritual self-examination. All religions before and after the times of Jesus, even Christianity, carefully provide for conscientious self-examination. But not so with the religion of Jesus of Nazareth. Jesus' philosophy of life is without religious introspection. The carpenter's son never taught character *building;* he taught character *growth,* declaring that the kingdom of heaven is like a mustard seed. But Jesus said nothing that would proscribe self-analysis as a prevention of conceited egotism.

The right to enter the kingdom is conditioned by faith, personal belief. The cost of remaining in the progressive ascent of the kingdom is the pearl of great price, in order to possess which a man sells all that he has.

The teaching of Jesus is a religion for everybody, not alone for weaklings and slaves. His religion never became crystallized (during his day) into creeds and theological laws; he left not a line of writing behind him. His life and teachings were bequeathed the universe as an inspirational and idealistic inheritance suitable for the spiritual guidance and moral instruction of all ages on all worlds. And even today, Jesus' teaching stands apart from all religions, as such, albeit it is the living hope of every one of them.

Jesus did not teach his apostles that religion is man's only earthly pursuit; that was the Jewish idea of serving God. But he did insist that religion was the exclusive business of the twelve. Jesus taught nothing to deter his believers from the pursuit of genuine culture; he only detracted from the tradition-bound religious schools of Jerusalem. He was liberal, bighearted, learned, and tolerant. Self-conscious piety had no place in his philosophy of righteous living.

The Master offered no solutions for the non-religious problems of his own age nor for any subsequent age. Jesus wished to develop spiritual insight into eternal realities and to stimulate initiative in the originality of living; he concerned himself exclusively with the underlying and permanent spiritual needs of the human race. He revealed a goodness equal to God. He exalted love - truth, beauty, and goodness - as the divine ideal and the eternal reality.

The Master came to create in man a new spirit, a new will - to impart a new capacity for knowing the truth, experiencing compassion, and choosing goodness - the will to be in harmony with God's will, coupled with the eternal urge to become perfect, even as the Father in heaven is perfect.

The next Sabbath day Jesus devoted to his apostles, journeying back to the high land where he had ordained them; and there, after a long and beautifully touching personal message of encouragement, he engaged in the solemn act of the consecration of the twelve. This Sabbath afternoon Jesus assembled the apostles around him on the hillside and gave them into the hands of his heavenly Father in preparation for the day when he would be compelled to leave them alone in the world. There was no new teaching on this occasion, just visiting and communion.

Jesus reviewed many features of the ordination sermon, delivered on this same spot, and then, calling them before him one by one, he commissioned them to go forth in the world as his representatives. The Master's consecration charge was: "Go into all the world and preach the glad tidings of the kingdom. Liberate spiritual captives, comfort the oppressed, and minister to the afflicted. Freely you have received, freely give."

Jesus advised them to take neither money nor extra clothing, saying, "The laborer is worthy of his hire." And finally he said: "Behold I send you forth as sheep in the midst of wolves; be you therefore as wise as serpents and as harmless as doves. But take heed, for your enemies will bring you up before their councils, while in their synagogues they will castigate you. Before governors and rulers you will be brought because you believe this gospel, and your very testimony shall be a witness for me to them. And when they lead you to judgment, be not anxious about what you shall say, for the spirit of my Father indwells you and will at such a time speak through you. Some of you will be put to death, and before you establish the kingdom on earth, you will be hated by many peoples because of this gospel; but fear not; I will be with you, and my spirit shall go before you into all the world. And my Father's presence will abide with you while you go first to the Jews, then to the gentiles."

And when they came down from the mountain, they journeyed back to their home in Zebedee's house.

That evening while teaching in the house, for it had begun to rain, Jesus talked at great length, trying to show the twelve what they must *be,* not what they must *do.* They knew only a religion that imposed the *doing* of certain things as the means of attaining righteousness - salvation. But Jesus would reiterate, "In the kingdom you must *be* righteous in order to do the work." Many times did he repeat, "*Be* you therefore perfect, even as your Father in heaven is perfect." All the while was the Master explaining to his bewildered apostles that the salvation which he had come to bring to the world was to be had only by *believing,* by simple and sincere faith. Said Jesus, "John preached a baptism of repentance, sorrow for the old way of living. You are to proclaim the baptism of fellowship with God. Preach repentance to those who stand in need of such teaching, but to those already seeking sincere entrance to the kingdom, open the doors wide and bid them enter into the joyous fellowship of the sons of God." But it was a difficult task to persuade these Galilean fishermen that, in the kingdom, *being* righteous, by faith, must precede *doing* righteousness in the daily life of the mortals of earth.

Another great handicap in this work of teaching the twelve was their tendency to take highly idealistic and spiritual principles of religious truth and remake them into concrete rules of personal conduct. Jesus would present to them the beautiful spirit of the soul's attitude, but they insisted on translating such teachings into rules of personal behavior. Many times, when they did make sure to remember what the Master said, they were almost certain to forget what he did *not* say. But they slowly assimilated his teaching because Jesus *was* all that he taught. What they could not gain from his verbal instruction, they gradually acquired by living with him.

It was not apparent to the apostles that their Master was engaged in living a life of spiritual inspiration for every person of every age on every world of a far-flung universe. Notwithstanding what Jesus told them from time to time, the apostles did not grasp the idea that he was doing a work *on* this world but *for* all other worlds in his vast creation. Jesus lived his earth life on Earth, not to set a personal example of mortal living for the men and women of this world, but rather to create *a high spiritual and inspirational ideal* for all mortal beings on all worlds.

This same evening Thomas asked Jesus: "Master, you say that we must become as little children before we can gain entrance to the Father's kingdom, and yet you have warned us not to be deceived by false prophets nor to become guilty of casting our pearls before swine. Now, I am honestly puzzled. I cannot understand your teaching."

Jesus replied to Thomas, "How long shall I bear with you! Ever you insist on making literal all that I teach. When I asked you to become as little children as the price of entering the kingdom, I referred not to ease of deception, mere willingness to believe, nor to quickness to trust pleasing strangers. What I did desire that you should gather from the illustration was the child-father relationship. You are the child, and it is *your* Father's kingdom you seek to enter. There is present that natural affection between every normal child and its father which insures an understanding and loving relationship, and which forever precludes all disposition to bargain for the Father's love and mercy. And the gospel you are going forth to preach has to do with a salvation growing out of the faith-realization of this very and eternal child-father relationship."

The one characteristic of Jesus' teaching was that the *morality* of his philosophy originated in the personal relation of the individual to God - this very child-father relationship. Jesus placed emphasis on the *individual,* not on the race or nation. While eating supper, Jesus had the talk with Matthew in which he explained that the morality of any act is determined by the individual's motive. Jesus' morality was always positive. The golden rule as restated by Jesus demands active social contact; the older negative rule could be obeyed in isolation. Jesus stripped morality of all rules and ceremonies and elevated it to majestic levels of spiritual thinking and truly righteous living.

This new religion of Jesus was not without its practical implications, but whatever of practical political, social, or economic value there is to be found in his teaching is the natural outworking of this inner experience of the soul as it manifests the fruits of the spirit in the spontaneous daily ministry of genuine personal religious experience.

After Jesus and Matthew had finished talking, Simon Zelotes asked, "But, Master, are *all* men the sons of God?"

And Jesus answered, "Yes, Simon, all men and women are the sons and daughters of God, and that is the good news you are going to proclaim." But the apostles could not grasp such a doctrine; it was a new, strange, and startling announcement. And it was because of his desire to impress this truth upon them that Jesus taught his followers to treat all men and women as their brothers and sisters.

In response to a question asked by Andrew, the Master made it clear that the morality of his teaching was inseparable from the religion of his living. He taught morality, not from the *nature* of man, but from the *relation* of man to God.

John asked Jesus, "Master, what is the kingdom of heaven?"

And Jesus answered, "The kingdom of heaven consists in these three essentials: first, recognition of the fact of the sovereignty of God; second, belief in the truth of sonship with God; and third, faith in the effectiveness of the supreme human desire to do the will of God - to be like God. And this is the good news of the gospel: that by faith every mortal may have all these essentials of salvation."

And now the week of waiting was over, and they prepared to depart on the morrow for Jerusalem.

# BEGINNING THE PUBLIC WORK

O N THE first day of the week, January 19, A.D. 27, Jesus and the twelve apostles made ready to depart from their headquarters in Bethsaida. The twelve knew nothing of their Master's plans except that they were going up to Jerusalem to attend the Passover feast in April, and that it was the intention to journey by way of the Jordan valley. They did not get away from Zebedee's house until near noon because the families of the apostles and others of the disciples had come to say good-bye and wish them well in the new work they were about to begin.

Just before leaving, the apostles missed the Master, and Andrew went out to find him. After a brief search he found Jesus sitting in a boat down the beach, and he was weeping. The twelve had often seen their Master when he seemed to grieve, and they had beheld his brief seasons of serious preoccupation of mind, but none of them had ever seen him weep. Andrew was somewhat startled to see the Master thus affected on the eve of their departure for Jerusalem, and he ventured to approach Jesus and ask: "On this great day, Master, when we are to depart for Jerusalem to proclaim the Father's kingdom, why is it that you weep? Which of us has offended you?"

And Jesus, going back with Andrew to join the twelve, answered him. "No one of you has grieved me. I am saddened only because none of my father Joseph's family have remembered to come over to bid us Godspeed."

At this time Ruth was on a visit to her brother Joseph at Nazareth. Other members of his family were kept away by pride, disappointment, misunderstanding, and petty resentment indulged as a result of hurt feelings.

Capernaum was not far from Tiberias, and the fame of Jesus had begun to spread well over all of Galilee and even to parts beyond. Jesus knew that Herod would soon begin to take notice of his work; so he thought best to journey south and into Judea with his apostles. A company of over one hundred believers desired to go with them, but Jesus spoke to them and besought them not to accompany the apostolic group on their way down the Jordan. Though they consented to remain behind, many of them followed after the Master within a few days.

The first day Jesus and the apostles only journeyed as far as Tarichea, where they rested for the night. The next day they traveled to a point on the Jordan near Pella where John had preached about one year before, and where Jesus had received baptism. Here they tarried for more than two weeks, teaching and preaching. By the end of the first week several hundred people had assembled in a camp near where Jesus and the twelve dwelt, and they had come from Galilee, Phoenicia, Syria, the Decapolis, Perea, and Judea.

Jesus did no public preaching. Andrew divided the multitude and assigned the preachers for the forenoon and afternoon assemblies; after the evening meal Jesus talked with the twelve. He taught them nothing new but reviewed his former teaching and answered their many questions. On one of these evenings he told the twelve something about the forty days which he spent in the hills near this place.

Many of those who came from Perea and Judea had been baptized by John and were interested in finding out more about Jesus' teachings. The apostles made much progress in teaching the disciples of John inasmuch as they did not in any way detract from John's preaching, and since they did not at this time even baptize their new disciples. But it was always a stumbling stone to John's followers that Jesus, if he were all that John had announced, did nothing to get him out of prison. John's disciples never could understand why Jesus did not prevent the cruel death of their beloved leader.

From night to night Andrew carefully instructed his fellow apostles in the delicate and difficult task of getting along smoothly with the followers of John the Baptist. During this first year of Jesus' public ministry more than three fourths of his followers had previously followed John and had received his baptism. This entire year of A.D. 27 was spent in quietly taking over John's work in Perea and Judea.

The night before they left Pella, Jesus gave the apostles some further instruction with regard to the new kingdom. Said the Master: "You have been taught to look for the coming of the kingdom of God, and now I come announcing that this long-looked-for kingdom is near at hand, even that it is already here and in our midst. In every kingdom there must be a king seated upon his throne and decreeing the laws of the realm. And so have you developed a concept of the kingdom of heaven as a glorified rule of the Jewish people over all the peoples of the earth with Messiah sitting on David's throne and from this place of miraculous power promulgating the laws of all the world. But, my children, you see not with the eye of faith, and you hear not with the understanding of the spirit. I declare that the kingdom of heaven is the realization and acknowledgment of God's rule within the hearts of men. True, there is a King in this kingdom, and that King is my Father and your Father. We are indeed his loyal subjects, but far transcending that fact is the transforming truth that we are his children. In my life this truth is to become manifest to all. Our Father also sits upon a throne, but not one made with hands. The throne of the Infinite is the eternal dwelling place of the Father in the heaven of heavens; he fills all things and proclaims his laws to universes upon universes. And the Father also rules within the hearts of his children on earth by the spirit which he has sent to live within the souls of mortal men.

"When you are the subjects of this kingdom, you indeed are made to hear the law of the Universe Ruler; but when, because of the gospel of the kingdom which I have come to declare, you faith-discover yourselves as sons, you henceforth look not upon yourselves as law-subject creatures of an all-powerful king but as privileged sons of a loving and divine Father. Verily, verily, I say to you, when the Father's will is your *law,* you are hardly in the kingdom. But when the Father's will becomes truly your *will,* then are you in very truth in the kingdom because the kingdom has thereby become an established experience in you. When God's will is your law, you are noble slave subjects; but when you believe in this new gospel of divine sonship, my Father's will becomes your will, and you are elevated to the high position of the free children of God, liberated sons of the kingdom."

Some of the apostles grasped something of this teaching, but none of them comprehended the full significance of this tremendous announcement, unless it was James Zebedee. But these words sank into their hearts and came forth to gladden their ministry during later years of service.

The Master and his apostles remained near Amathus for almost three weeks. The apostles continued to preach twice daily to the multitude, and Jesus preached each Sabbath afternoon. It became impossible to continue the Wednesday playtime; so Andrew arranged that two apostles should rest each day of the six days in the week, while all were on duty during the Sabbath services.

Peter, James, and John did most of the public preaching. Philip, Nathaniel, Thomas, and Simon did much of the personal work and conducted classes for special groups of inquirers; the twins continued their general police supervision, while Andrew, Matthew, and Judas developed into a general managerial committee of three, although each of these three also did considerable religious work.

Andrew was much occupied with the task of adjusting the constantly recurring misunderstandings and disagreements between the disciples of John and the newer disciples of Jesus. Serious situations would arise every few days, but Andrew, with the assistance of his apostolic associates, managed to induce the contending parties to come to some sort of agreement, at least temporarily. Jesus refused to participate in any of these conferences; neither would he give any advice about the proper adjustment of these difficulties. He never once offered a suggestion as to how the apostles should solve these perplexing problems.

When Andrew came to Jesus with these questions, he would always say: "It is not wise for the host to participate in the family troubles of his guests; a wise parent never takes sides in the petty quarrels of his own children."

The Master displayed great wisdom and manifested perfect fairness in all of his dealings with his apostles and with all of his disciples. Jesus was truly a master of men; he exercised great influence over his fellow men because of the combined charm and force of his personality. There was a subtle commanding influence in his rugged, nomadic, and homeless life. There was intellectual attractiveness and spiritual drawing power in his authoritative manner of teaching, in his lucid logic, his strength of reasoning, his sagacious insight, his alertness of mind, his matchless poise, and his sublime tolerance. He was simple, manly, honest, and fearless. With all of this physical and intellectual influence manifest in the Master's presence, there were also all those spiritual charms of being which have become associated with his personality; patience, tenderness, meekness, gentleness, and humility.

Jesus of Nazareth was indeed a strong and forceful personality; he was an intellectual power and a spiritual stronghold. His personality not only appealed to the spiritually minded women among his followers, but also to the educated and intellectual Nicodemus and to the hardy Roman soldier, the captain stationed on guard at the cross, who, when he had finished watching the Master die, said, "Truly, this was a Son of God." And red-blooded, rugged Galilean fishermen called him Master.

The pictures of Jesus have been most unfortunate. These paintings of the Christ have exerted a deleterious influence on youth; the temple merchants would hardly have fled before Jesus if he had been such a man as your artists usually have depicted. His was a dignified manhood; he was good, but natural. Jesus did not pose as a mild, sweet, gentle, and kindly mystic. His teaching was thrillingly dynamic. He not only *meant well*, but he went about actually *doing good*.

The Master never said, "Come to me all you who are indolent and all who are dreamers." But he did many times say, "Come to me all you who *labor*, and I will give you rest - spiritual strength." The Master's yoke is, indeed, easy, but even so, he never imposes it; every individual must take this yoke of his own free will.

Jesus portrayed conquest by sacrifice, the sacrifice of pride and selfishness. By showing mercy, he meant to portray spiritual deliverance from all grudges, grievances, anger, and the lust for selfish power and revenge. And when he said, "Resist not evil," he later explained that he did not mean to condone sin or to counsel fraternity with iniquity. He intended the more to teach forgiveness, to "resist not evil treatment of one's personality, evil injury to one's feelings of personal dignity."

While sojourning at Amathus, Jesus spent much time with the apostles instructing them in the new concept of God; again and again did he impress upon them that *God is a Father,* not a great and supreme bookkeeper who is chiefly engaged in making damaging entries against his erring children on earth, recordings of sin and evil to be used against them when he subsequently sits in judgment upon them as the just Judge of all creation. The Jews had long conceived of God as a king over all, even as a Father of the nation, but never before had large numbers of mortal men held the idea of God as a loving Father of the *individual.*

In answer to Thomas's question, "Who is this God of the kingdom?" Jesus replied: "God is *your* Father, and religion - my gospel - is nothing more nor less than the believing recognition of the truth that you are His son. And I am here among you in the flesh to make clear both of these ideas in my life and teachings."

Jesus also sought to free the minds of his apostles from the idea of offering animal sacrifices as a religious duty. But these men, trained in the religion of the daily sacrifice, were slow to comprehend what he meant. Nevertheless, the Master did not grow weary in his teaching. When he failed to reach the minds of all of the apostles by means of one illustration, he would restate his message and employ another type of parable for purposes of illumination.

At this same time Jesus began to teach the twelve more fully concerning their mission "to comfort the afflicted and minister to the sick." The Master taught them much about the whole man - the union of body, mind, and spirit to form the individual man or woman. Jesus told his associates about the three forms of affliction they would meet and went on to explain how they should minister to all who suffer the sorrows of human sickness. He taught them to recognize:

1. Diseases of the flesh — those afflictions commonly regarded as physical sickness.

2. Troubled minds — those nonphysical afflictions that were subsequently looked upon as emotional and mental difficulties and disturbances.

3.The possession of evil spirits.

Jesus explained to his apostles on several occasions the nature, and something concerning the origin, of these evil spirits, in that day often also called unclean spirits. The Master well knew the difference between the possession of evil spirits and insanity, but the apostles did not. Neither was it possible, in view of their limited knowledge of the early history of Earth, for Jesus to undertake to make this matter fully understandable. But he many times said to them, alluding to these evil spirits: "They shall no more molest men when I shall have ascended to my Father in heaven, and after I shall have poured out my spirit upon all flesh in those times when the kingdom will come in great power and spiritual glory."

From week to week and from month to month, throughout this entire year, the apostles paid more and more attention to the healing ministry of the sick.

One of the most eventful of all the evening conferences at Amathus was the session having to do with the discussion of spiritual unity. James Zebedee had asked, "Master, how shall we learn to see alike and thereby enjoy more harmony among ourselves?"

When Jesus heard this question, he was stirred within his spirit, so much so that he replied, "James, James, when did I teach you that you should all see alike? I have come into the world to proclaim spiritual liberty to the end that mortals may be empowered to live individual lives of originality and freedom before God. I do not desire that social harmony and fraternal peace shall be purchased by the sacrifice of free personality and spiritual originality. What I require of you, my apostles, is *spirit unity* - and that you can experience in the joy of your united dedication to the wholehearted doing of the will of my Father in heaven. You do not have to see alike or feel alike or even think alike in order spiritually to *be alike*. Spiritual unity is derived from the consciousness that each of you is indwelt, and increasingly dominated, by the spirit gift of the heavenly Father. Your apostolic harmony must grow out of the fact that the spirit hope of each of you is identical in origin, nature, and destiny.

"In this way you may experience a perfected unity of spirit purpose and spirit understanding growing out of the mutual consciousness of the identity of each of your indwelling Paradise spirits; and you may enjoy all of this profound spiritual unity in the very face of the utmost diversity of your individual attitudes of intellectual thinking, temperamental feeling, and social conduct. Your personalities may be refreshingly diverse and markedly different, while your spiritual natures and spirit fruits of divine worship and brotherly love may be so unified that all who behold your lives will of a surety take cognizance of this spirit identity and soul unity; they will recognize that you have been with me and have thereby learned, and acceptably, how to do the will of the Father in heaven. You can achieve the unity of the service of God even while you render such service in accordance with the technique of your own original endowments of mind, body, and soul.

"Your spirit unity implies two things, which always will be found to harmonize in the lives of individual believers: First, you are possessed with a common motive for life service; you all desire above everything to do the will of the Father in heaven. Second, you all have a common goal of existence; you all purpose to find the Father in heaven, thereby proving to the universe that you have become like him."

Many times during the training of the twelve Jesus reverted to this theme. Repeatedly he told them it was not his desire that those who believed in him should become dogmatized and standardized in accordance with the religious interpretations of even good men. Again and again he warned his apostles against the formulation of creeds and the establishment of traditions as a means of guiding and controlling believers in the gospel of the kingdom.

Near the end of the last week at Amathus, Simon Zelotes brought to Jesus one Teherma, a Persian doing business at Damascus. Teherma had heard of Jesus and had come to Capernaum to see him, and there learning that Jesus had gone with his apostles down the Jordan on the way to Jerusalem, he set out to find him. Andrew had presented Teherma to Simon for instruction. Simon looked upon the Persian as a "fire worshiper," although Teherma took great pains to explain that fire was only the visible symbol of the Pure and Holy One. After talking with Jesus, the Persian signified his intention of remaining for several days to hear the teaching and listen to the preaching.

When Simon Zelotes and Jesus were alone, Simon asked the Master, "Why is it that I could not persuade him? Why did he so resist me and so readily lend an ear to you?"

Jesus answered, "Simon, Simon, how many times have I instructed you to refrain from all efforts to take something *out* of the hearts of those who seek salvation? How often have I told you to labor only to put something *into* these hungry souls? Lead men and women into the kingdom, and the great and living truths of the kingdom will presently drive out all serious error. When you have presented to mortal men and women the good news that God is their Father, you can the easier persuade them that they are in reality children of God. And having done that, you have brought the light of salvation to the those who sit in darkness. Simon, when the Son of Man came first to you, did he come denouncing Moses and the prophets and proclaiming a new and better way of life? I came not to take away that which you had from your forefathers but to show you the perfected vision of that which your fathers saw only in part. Go then, Simon, teaching and preaching the kingdom, and when you have a man safely and securely within the kingdom, then is the time, when such a one shall come to you with inquiries, to impart instruction having to do with the progressive advancement of the soul within the divine kingdom."

Simon was astonished at these words, but he did as Jesus had instructed him, and Teherma, the Persian, was numbered among those who entered the kingdom.

That night Jesus discoursed to the apostles on the new life in the kingdom. He said in part, "When you enter the kingdom, you are reborn. You cannot teach the deep things of the spirit to those who have been born only of the flesh; first see that men are born of the spirit before you seek to instruct them in the advanced ways of the spirit. Do not undertake to show them the beauties of the temple until you have first taken them into the temple. Introduce them to God and *as* the sons and daughters of God before you discourse on the doctrines of the fatherhood of God and the sonship of men and women. Do not strive with them - always be patient. It is not your kingdom; you are only ambassadors. Simply go forth proclaiming: This is the kingdom of heaven - God is your Father and you are His children, and this good news, if you wholeheartedly believe it, *is* your eternal salvation."

The apostles made great progress during the sojourn at Amathus. But they were very much disappointed that Jesus would give them no suggestions about dealing with John's disciples. Even in the important matter of baptism, all that Jesus said was: "John did indeed baptize with water, but when you enter the kingdom of heaven, you shall be baptized with the Spirit."

On February 26, Jesus, his apostles, and a large group of followers journeyed down the Jordan to the ford near Bethany in Perea, the place where John first made proclamation of the coming kingdom. Jesus with his apostles remained here, teaching and preaching, for four weeks before they went on up to Jerusalem.

The second week of the sojourn at Bethany beyond Jordan, Jesus took Peter, James, and John into the hills across the river and south of Jericho for a three days' rest. The Master taught these three many new and advanced truths about the kingdom of heaven. For the purpose of this record we will reorganize and classify these teachings as follows:

Jesus endeavored to make clear that he desired his disciples, having tasted of the good spirit realities of the kingdom, so to live in the world that men, by *seeing* their lives, would become kingdom conscious and hence be led to inquire of believers concerning the ways of the kingdom. All such sincere seekers for the truth are always glad to *hear* the glad tidings of the faith gift which insures admission to the kingdom with its eternal and divine spirit realities.

The Master sought to impress upon all teachers of the gospel of the kingdom that their only business was to reveal God to the individual person as his or her Father - to lead this individual to become son-conscious; then to present this same person to God as His faith-child. Both of these essential revelations are accomplished in Jesus. He became, indeed, "the way, the truth, and the life." The religion of Jesus was wholly based on the living of his bestowal life on earth. When Jesus departed from this world, he left behind no books, laws, or other forms of human organization affecting the religious life of the individual.

Jesus made it plain that he had come to establish personal and eternal relations with man that should forever take precedence over all other human relationships. And he emphasized that this intimate spiritual fellowship was to be extended to all mortals of all ages and of all social conditions among all peoples. The only reward that he held out for his children was: in this world - spiritual joy and divine communion; in the next world - eternal life in the progress of the divine spirit realities of the Paradise Father.

Jesus laid great emphasis upon what he called the two truths of first import in the teachings of the kingdom, and they are: the attainment of salvation by faith, and faith alone, associated with the revolutionary teaching of the attainment of human liberty through the sincere recognition of truth, "You shall know the truth, and the truth shall make you free." Jesus was the truth made manifest in the flesh, and he promised to send his Spirit of Truth into the hearts of all his children after his return to the Father in heaven.

The Master was teaching these apostles the essentials of truth for an entire age on earth. They often listened to his teachings when in reality what he said was intended for the inspiration and edification of other worlds. He exemplified a new and original plan of life. From the human standpoint he was indeed a Jew, but he lived his life for all the worlds as a mortal of the realm.

To insure the recognition of his Father in the unfolding of the plan of the kingdom, Jesus explained that he had purposely ignored the "great men of earth." He began his work with the poor, the very class that had been so neglected by most of the evolutionary religions of preceding times. He despised no man; his plan was worldwide, even universal. He was so bold and emphatic in these announcements that even Peter, James, and John were tempted to think he might possibly be beside himself.

He sought mildly to impart to these apostles the truth that he had come on this bestowal mission, not to set an example for a few earth creatures, but to establish and demonstrate a standard of human life for all peoples upon all worlds throughout his entire universe. And this standard approached the highest perfection, even the final goodness of the Universal Father. But the apostles could not grasp the meaning of his words.

He announced that he had come to function as a teacher, a teacher sent from heaven to present spiritual truth to the material mind. And this is exactly what he did; he was a teacher, not a preacher. From the human viewpoint Peter was a much more effective preacher than Jesus. Jesus' preaching was so effective because of his unique personality, not so much because of compelling oratory or emotional appeal. Jesus spoke directly to men's souls. He was a teacher of mankind's spirit, but through the mind. He lived with men.

It was on this occasion that Jesus intimated to Peter, James, and John that his work on earth was in some respects to be limited by the commission of his "associate on high," referring to the prebestowal instructions of his Paradise brother, Immanuel. He told them that he had come to do his Father's will and only his Father's will. Being thus motivated by a wholehearted singleness of purpose, he was not anxiously bothered by the evil in the world.

The apostles were beginning to recognize the unaffected friendliness of Jesus. Though the Master was easy of approach, he always lived independent of, and above, all human beings. Not for one moment was he ever dominated by any purely mortal influence or subject to frail human judgment. He paid no attention to public opinion, and he was uninfluenced by praise. He seldom paused to correct misunderstandings or to resent misrepresentation. He never asked any man for advice; he never made requests for prayers

James was astonished at how Jesus seemed to see the end from the beginning. The Master rarely appeared to be surprised. He was never excited, vexed, or disconcerted. He never apologized to any man. He was at times saddened, but never discouraged.

More clearly John recognized that, notwithstanding all of his divine endowments, after all, he was human. Jesus lived as a man among men and understood, loved, and knew how to manage men. In his personal life he was so human, and yet so faultless. And he was always unselfish.

Although Peter, James, and John could not understand very much of what Jesus said on this occasion, his gracious words lingered in their hearts, and after the crucifixion and resurrection they came forth greatly to enrich and gladden their subsequent ministry. No wonder these apostles did not fully comprehend the Master's words, for he was projecting to them the plan of a new age.

Throughout the four weeks' sojourn at Bethany beyond Jordan, several times each week Andrew would assign apostolic couples to go up to Jericho for a day or two. John had many believers in Jericho, and the majority of them welcomed the more advanced teachings of Jesus and his apostles. On these Jericho visits the apostles began more specifically to carry out Jesus' instructions to minister to the sick; they visited every house in the city and sought to comfort every afflicted person.

The apostles did some public work in Jericho, but their efforts were chiefly of a more quiet and personal nature. They now made the discovery that the good news of the kingdom was very comforting to the sick; that their message carried healing for the afflicted. And it was in Jericho that Jesus' commission to the twelve to preach the glad tidings of the kingdom and minister to the afflicted was first fully carried into effect.

They stopped in Jericho on the way up to Jerusalem and were overtaken by a delegation from Mesopotamia that had come to confer with Jesus. The apostles had planned to spend but a day here, but when these truth-seekers from the East arrived, Jesus spent three days with them, and they returned to their various homes along the Euphrates happy in the knowledge of the new truths of the kingdom of heaven.

On Monday, the last day of March, Jesus and the apostles began their journey up the hills toward Jerusalem. Lazarus of Bethany had been down to the Jordan twice to see Jesus, and every arrangement had been made for the Master and his apostles to make their headquarters with Lazarus and his sisters at Bethany as long as they might desire to stay in Jerusalem.

The disciples of John remained at Bethany beyond the Jordan, teaching and baptizing the multitudes, so that Jesus was accompanied only by the twelve when he arrived at Lazarus's home. Here Jesus and the apostles tarried for five days, resting and refreshing themselves before going on to Jerusalem for the Passover. It was a great event in the lives of Martha and Mary to have the Master and his apostles in the home of their brother, where they could minister to their needs.

On Sunday morning, April 6, Jesus and the apostles went down to Jerusalem; and this was the first time the Master and all of the twelve had been there together.

# THE PASSOVER AT JERUSALEM

THE MONTH of April Jesus and the apostles worked in Jerusalem, going out of the city each evening to spend the night at Bethany. Jesus himself spent one or two nights each week in Jerusalem at the home of Flavius, a Greek Jew, where many prominent Jews came in secret to interview him.

The first day in Jerusalem Jesus called upon his friend of former years, Annas, the onetime high priest and relative of Salome, Zebedee's wife. Annas had been hearing about Jesus and his teachings, and when Jesus called at the high priest's home, he was received with much reserve. When Jesus perceived Annas's coldness, he took immediate leave, saying as he departed, "Fear is man's chief enslaver and pride his great weakness; will you betray yourself into bondage to both of these destroyers of joy and liberty?" But Annas made no reply. The Master did not again see Annas until the time when he sat with his son-in-law in judgment on the Son of Man.

Throughout this month Jesus or one of the apostles taught daily in the temple. When the Passover crowds were too great to find entrance to the temple teaching, the apostles conducted many teaching groups outside the sacred precincts. The burden of their message was:

1. The kingdom of heaven is at hand.
2. By faith in the fatherhood of God you may enter the kingdom of heaven, thus becoming the sons and daughters of God.
3. Love is the rule of living within the kingdom - supreme devotion to God while loving your neighbor as yourself.
4. Obedience to the will of the Father, yielding the fruits of the spirit in one's personal life, is the law of the kingdom.

The multitudes who came to celebrate the Passover heard this teaching of Jesus, and hundreds of them rejoiced in the good news. The chief priests and rulers of the Jews became much concerned about Jesus and his apostles and debated among themselves as to what should be done with them.

Besides teaching in and about the temple, the apostles and other believers were engaged in doing much personal work among the Passover throngs. These interested men and women carried the news of Jesus' message from this Passover celebration to the uttermost parts of the Roman Empire and also to the East. This was the beginning of the spread of the gospel of the kingdom to the outside world. No longer was the work of Jesus to be confined to Palestine.

There was in Jerusalem in attendance upon the Passover festivities one Jacob, a wealthy Jewish trader from Crete, and he came to Andrew making request to see Jesus privately. Andrew arranged this secret meeting with Jesus at Flavius's home the evening of the next day. This man could not comprehend the Master's teachings, and he came because he desired to inquire more fully about the kingdom of God.

Said Jacob to Jesus, "But, Rabbi, Moses and the olden prophets tell us that Yahweh is a jealous God, a God of great wrath and fierce anger. The prophets say he hates evildoers and takes vengeance on those who obey not His law. You and your disciples teach us that God is a kind and compassionate Father who so loves all men and women that He would welcome them into this new kingdom of heaven, which you proclaim is so near at hand."

When Jacob finished speaking, Jesus replied, "Jacob, you have well stated the teachings of the olden prophets who taught the children of their generation in accordance with the light of their day. Our Father in Paradise is changeless. But the concept of his nature has enlarged and grown from the days of Moses down through the times of Amos and even to the generation of the prophet Isaiah. And now have I come in the flesh to reveal the Father in new glory and to show forth His love and mercy to all men and women on all worlds. As the gospel of this kingdom shall spread over the world with its message of good cheer and good will to all, there will grow up improved and better relations among the families of all nations. As time passes, fathers and their children will love each other more, and thus will be brought about a better understanding of the love of the Father in heaven for His children on earth. Remember, Jacob, that a good and true father not only loves His family as a whole - as a family - but he also truly loves and affectionately cares for each *individual* member."

After considerable discussion of the heavenly Father's character, Jesus paused to say, "You, Jacob, being a father of many, know well the truth of my words."

And Jacob said, "But, Master, who told you I was the father of six children? How did you know this about me?"

And the Master replied, "Suffice it to say that the Father and the Son know all things, for indeed they see all. Loving your children as a father on earth, you must now accept as a reality the love of the heavenly Father for *you* - not just for all the children of Abraham, but for you, your individual soul."

Then Jesus went on to say, "When your children are very young and immature, and when you must chastise them, they may reflect that their father is angry and filled with resentful wrath. Their immaturity cannot penetrate beyond the punishment to discern the father's farseeing and corrective affection. But when these same children become grown-up men and women, would it not be folly for them to cling to these earlier and misconceived notions regarding their father? As men and women they should now discern their father's love in all these early disciplines. And should not mankind, as the centuries pass, come the better to understand the true nature and loving character of the Father in heaven? What profit have you from successive generations of spiritual illumination if you persist in viewing God as Moses and the prophets saw him? I say to you, Jacob, under the bright light of this hour you should see the Father as none of those who have gone before ever beheld Him. And thus seeing Him, you should rejoice to enter the kingdom wherein such a merciful Father rules, and you should seek to have His will of love dominate your life henceforth."

And Jacob answered, "Rabbi, I believe; I desire that you lead me into the Father's kingdom."

The twelve apostles, most of whom had listened to this discussion of the character of God, that night asked Jesus many questions about the Father in heaven. The Master's answers to these questions can best be presented by the following summary in modern phraseology:

Jesus mildly upbraided the twelve, in substance saying: Do you not know the traditions of Israel relating to the growth of the idea of Yahweh, and are you ignorant of the teaching of the Scriptures concerning the doctrine of God? And then did the Master proceed to instruct the apostles about the evolution of the concept of Deity throughout the course of the development of the Jewish people. He called attention to the following phases of the growth of the God idea:

1. *Yahweh* - the god of the Sinai clans. This was the primitive concept of Deity that Moses exalted to the higher level of the Lord God of Israel. The Father in heaven never fails to accept the sincere worship of His children on Earth, no matter how crude their concept of Deity or by what name they symbolize His divine nature.

2. *The Most High.* This concept of the Father in heaven was proclaimed by Melchizedek to Abraham and was carried far from Salem by those who subsequently believed in this enlarged and expanded idea of Deity. Abraham and his brother left Ur because of the establishment of sun

worship, and they became believers in Melchizedek's teaching of El Elyon - the Most High God. Theirs was a composite concept of God, consisting in a blending of their older Mesopotamian ideas and the Most High doctrine.

3. *El Shaddai.* During these early days many of the Hebrews worshiped El Shaddai, the Egyptian concept of the God of heaven, which they learned about during their captivity in the land of the Nile. Long after the times of Melchizedek all three of these concepts of God became joined together to form the doctrine of the creator Deity, the Lord God of Israel.

4. *Elohim.* From the times of Adam the teaching of the Paradise Trinity has persisted. Do you not recall how the Scriptures begin by asserting that "In the beginning the Gods created the heavens and the earth"? This indicates that when that record was made the Trinity concept of three Gods in one had found lodgment in the religion of our forebears.

5. *The Supreme Yahweh.* By the times of Isaiah these beliefs about God had expanded into the concept of a Universal Creator who was simultaneously all-powerful and all-merciful. And this evolving and enlarging concept of God virtually supplanted all previous ideas of Deity in our fathers' religion.

6. *The Father in heaven.* And now do we know God as our Father in heaven. Our teaching provides a religion wherein the believer *is* a child of God. That is the good news of the gospel of the kingdom of heaven. Coexistent with the Father are the Son and the Spirit, and the revelation of the nature and ministry of these Paradise Deities will continue to enlarge and brighten throughout the endless ages of the eternal spiritual progression of the ascending sons and daughters of God. At all times and during all ages the true worship of any human being - as concerns individual spiritual progress - is recognized by the indwelling spirit as homage rendered to the Father in heaven.

Never before had the apostles been so shocked as they were upon hearing this recounting of the growth of the concept of God in the Jewish minds of previous generations; they were too bewildered to ask questions. As they sat before Jesus in silence, the Master continued. "And you would have known these truths had you read the Scriptures. Have you not read in Samuel where it says: 'And the anger of the Lord was kindled against Israel, so much so that He moved David against them, saying, go number Israel and Judah'? And this was not strange because in the days of Samuel the children of Abraham really believed that Yahweh created both good and evil. But when a later writer narrated these events, subsequent to the enlargement of the Jewish concept of the nature of God, he did not dare attribute evil to Yahweh; therefore he said: 'And Satan stood up against Israel and provoked David to number Israel.' Cannot you discern that such records in the Scriptures clearly show how the concept of the nature of God continued to grow from one generation to another?

"Again should you have discerned the growth of the understanding of divine law in perfect keeping with these enlarging concepts of divinity. When the children of Israel came out of Egypt in the days before the enlarged revelation of Yahweh, they had ten commandments which served as their law right up to the times when they were encamped before Sinai. And these ten commandments were:

"1. You shall worship no other god, for the Lord is a jealous God.

"2. You shall not make molten gods.

"3. You shall not neglect to keep the feast of unleavened bread.

"4. Of all the males of men or cattle, the first-born are mine, says the Lord.

"5. Six days you may work, but on the seventh day you shall rest.

"6. You shall not fail to observe the feast of the first fruits and the feast of the ingathering at the end of the year.

"7. You shall not offer the blood of any sacrifice with leavened bread.

"8. The sacrifice of the feast of the Passover shall not be left until morning.

"9. The first of the first fruits of the ground you shall bring to the house of the Lord your God.

"10. You shall not seethe a kid in its mother's milk.

"And then, amidst the thunders and lightnings of Sinai, Moses gave them the new Ten Commandments, which you will all allow are more worthy utterances to accompany the enlarging Yahweh concepts of Deity. And did you never take notice of these commandments as twice recorded in the Scriptures, that in the first case deliverance from Egypt is assigned as the reason for Sabbath keeping, while in a later record the advancing religious beliefs of our forefathers demanded that this be changed to the recognition of the fact of creation as the reason for Sabbath observance?

"And then will you remember that once again - in the greater spiritual enlightenment of Isaiah's day - these ten negative commandments were changed into the great and positive law of love, the injunction to love God supremely and your neighbor as yourself. And it is this supreme law of love for God and for man that I also declare to you as constituting the whole duty of man."

And when he had finished speaking, no man asked him a question. They went, each one to his sleep.

Flavius, the Greek Jew, was a proselyte of the gate, having been neither circumcised nor baptized; and since he was a great lover of the beautiful in art and sculpture, the house which he occupied when sojourning in Jerusalem was a beautiful edifice. This home was exquisitely adorned with priceless treasures that he had gathered up here and there on his world travels. When he first thought of inviting Jesus to his home, he feared that the Master might take offense at the sight of these so-called images. But Flavius was agreeably surprised when Jesus entered the home that, instead of rebuking him for having these supposedly idolatrous objects scattered about the house, he manifested great interest in the entire collection and asked many appreciative questions about each object as Flavius escorted him from room to room, showing him all of his favorite statues.

The Master saw that his host was bewildered at his friendly attitude toward art; therefore, when they had finished the survey of the entire collection, Jesus said, "Because you appreciate the beauty of things created by my Father and fashioned by the artistic hands of man, why should you expect to be rebuked? Because Moses onetime sought to combat idolatry and the worship of false gods, why should all men frown upon the reproduction of grace and beauty? I say to you, Flavius, Moses' children have misunderstood him, and now do they make false gods of even his prohibitions of images and the likeness of things in heaven and on earth. But even if Moses taught such restrictions to the darkened minds of those days, what has that to do with this day when the Father in heaven is revealed as the universal Spirit Ruler over all? And, Flavius, I declare that in the coming kingdom they shall no longer teach, 'Do not worship this and do not worship that'; no longer shall they concern themselves with commands to refrain from this and take care not to do that, but rather shall all be concerned with one supreme duty. And this duty of man and woman is expressed in two great privileges; sincere worship of the infinite Creator, the Paradise Father, and loving service bestowed upon one's fellows. If you love your neighbor as you love yourself, you really know that you are a child of God.

"In an age when my Father was not well understood, Moses was justified in his attempts to withstand idolatry, but in the coming age the Father will have been revealed in the life of the Son; and this new revelation of God will make it forever unnecessary to confuse the Creator Father with idols of stone or images of gold and silver. Henceforth, intelligent men may enjoy the treasures of art without confusing such material appreciation of beauty with the worship and service of the Father in Paradise, the God of all things and all beings."

Flavius believed all that Jesus taught him. The next day he went to Bethany beyond the Jordan and was baptized by the disciples of John. And this he did because the apostles of Jesus did not yet baptize believers. When Flavius returned to Jerusalem, he made a great feast for Jesus and invited sixty of his friends. And many of these guests also became believers in the message of the coming kingdom.

★  ★  ★

One of the great sermons which Jesus preached in the temple this Passover week was in answer to a question asked by one of his hearers, a man from Damascus. This man asked Jesus, "But, Rabbi, how shall we know of a certainty that you are sent by God, and that we may truly enter into this kingdom which you and your disciples declare is near at hand?"

And Jesus answered, "As to my message and the teaching of my disciples, you should judge them by their fruits. If we proclaim to you the truths of the spirit, the spirit will witness in your hearts that our message is genuine. Concerning the kingdom and your assurance of acceptance by the heavenly Father, let me ask what father among you who is a worthy and kindhearted father would keep his son in anxiety or suspense regarding his status in the family or his place of security in the affections of his father's heart? Do you earth fathers take pleasure in torturing your children with uncertainty about their place of abiding love in your human hearts? Neither does your Father in heaven leave His faith children of the spirit in doubtful uncertainty as to their position in the kingdom. If you receive God as your Father, then indeed and in truth are you the children of God. And if you are sons and daughters, then are you secure in the position and standing of all that concerns eternal and divine sonship. If you believe my words, you thereby believe in Him who sent me, and by thus believing in the Father, you have made your status in heavenly citizenship sure. If you do the will of the Father in heaven, you shall never fail in the attainment of the eternal life of progress in the divine kingdom.

"The Supreme Spirit shall bear witness with your spirits that you are truly the children of God. And if you are the sons and daughters of God, then have you been born of the spirit of God; and whosoever has been born of the spirit has in himself the power to overcome all doubt, and this is the victory that overcomes all uncertainty, even your faith.

"Said the Prophet Isaiah, speaking of these times: 'When the spirit is poured upon us from on high, then shall the work of righteousness become peace, quietness, and assurance forever.' And for all who truly believe this gospel, I will become surety for their reception into the eternal mercies and the everlasting life of my Father's kingdom. You, then, who hear this message and believe this gospel of the kingdom are the sons and daughters of God, and you have life everlasting; and the evidence to all the world that you have been born of the spirit is that you sincerely love one another."

The throng of listeners remained many hours with Jesus, asking him questions and listening attentively to his comforting answers. Even the apostles were emboldened by Jesus' teaching to preach the gospel of the kingdom with more power and assurance. This experience at Jerusalem was a great inspiration to the twelve. It was their first contact with such enormous crowds, and they learned many valuable lessons that proved of great assistance in their later work.

★ ★ ★

One evening at the home of Flavius there came to see Jesus one Nicodemus, a wealthy and elderly member of the Jewish Sanhedrin. He had heard much about the teachings of this Galilean, and so he went one afternoon to hear him as he taught in the temple courts. He would have gone often to hear Jesus teach, but he feared to be seen by the people in attendance upon his teaching, for already were the rulers of the Jews so at variance with Jesus that no member of the Sanhedrin would want to be identified in any open manner with him. Accordingly, Nicodemus had arranged with Andrew to see Jesus privately and after nightfall on this particular evening. Peter, James, and John were in Flavius's garden when the interview began, but later they all went into the house where the discourse continued.

In receiving Nicodemus, Jesus showed no particular deference; in talking with him, there was no compromise or undue persuasiveness. The Master made no attempt to repulse his secretive caller, nor did he employ sarcasm. In all his dealings with the distinguished visitor, Jesus was calm, earnest, and dignified. Nicodemus was not an official delegate of the Sanhedrin; he came to see Jesus wholly because of his personal and sincere interest in the Master's teachings.

Upon being presented by Flavius, Nicodemus said, "Rabbi, we know that you are a teacher sent by God, for no mere man could so teach unless God were with him. And I am desirous of knowing more about your teachings regarding the coming kingdom."

Jesus answered Nicodemus, "Verily, verily, I say to you, Nicodemus, except a man be born from above, he cannot see the kingdom of God."

Then replied Nicodemus, "But how can a man be born again when he is old? He cannot enter a second time into his mother's womb to be born."

Jesus said, "Nevertheless, I declare to you, except a man be born of the spirit, he cannot enter into the kingdom of God. That which is born of the flesh is flesh, and that which is born of the spirit is spirit. But you should not marvel that I said you must be born from above. When the wind blows, you hear the rustle of the leaves, but you do not see the wind - whence it comes or whither it goes - and so it is with everyone born of the spirit. With the eyes of the flesh you can behold the manifestations of the spirit, but you cannot actually discern the spirit."

Nicodemus replied, "But I do not understand; how can that be?"

Said Jesus, "Can it be that you are a teacher in Israel and yet ignorant of all this? It becomes, then, the duty of those who know about the realities of the spirit to reveal these things to those who discern only the manifestations of the material world. But will you believe us if we tell you of the heavenly truths? Do you have the courage, Nicodemus, to believe in one who has descended from heaven, even the Son of Man?"

And Nicodemus asked, "But how can I begin to lay hold upon this spirit which is to remake me in preparation for entering into the kingdom?"

Jesus answered, "Already does the spirit of the Father in heaven indwell you. If you would be led by this spirit from above, very soon would you begin to see with the eyes of the spirit, and then by the wholehearted choice of spirit guidance would you be born of the spirit since your only purpose in living would be to do the will of your Father who is in heaven. And so finding yourself born of the spirit and happily in the kingdom of God, you would begin to bear in your daily life the abundant fruits of the spirit."

Nicodemus was thoroughly sincere. He was deeply impressed but went away bewildered. Nicodemus was accomplished in self-development, in self-restraint, and even in high moral qualities. He was refined, egoistic, and altruistic; but he did not know how to *submit* his will to the will of the divine Father as a little child is willing to submit to the guidance and leading of a wise and loving earthly father, thereby becoming in reality a son of God, a progressive heir of the eternal kingdom.

But Nicodemus did summon faith enough to lay hold of the kingdom. He faintly protested when his colleagues of the Sanhedrin sought to condemn Jesus without a hearing; and with Joseph of Arimathea, he later boldly acknowledged his faith and claimed the body of Jesus, even when most of the disciples had fled in fear from the scenes of their Master's final suffering and death.

After the busy period of teaching and personal work of Passover week in Jerusalem, Jesus spent the next Wednesday at Bethany with his apostles, resting. That afternoon, Thomas asked a question that elicited a long and instructive answer. Said Thomas, "Master, on the day we were set apart as ambassadors of the kingdom, you told us many things, instructed us regarding our personal mode of life, but what shall we teach the multitude? How are these people to live after the kingdom more fully comes? Shall your disciples own slaves? Shall your believers court poverty and shun property? Shall mercy alone prevail so that we shall have no more law and justice?"

Jesus and the twelve spent all afternoon and all that evening, after supper, discussing Thomas's questions. For the purposes of this record we present the following summary of the Master's instruction:

Jesus sought first to make plain to his apostles that he himself was on earth living a unique life in the flesh, and that they, the twelve, had been called to participate in this bestowal experience of the Son of Man; and as such coworkers, they, too, must share in many of the special restrictions and obligations of the entire bestowal experience. There was a veiled intimation that the Son of Man was the only person who had ever lived on earth who could simultaneously see into the very heart of God and into the very depths of man's soul.

Very plainly Jesus explained that the kingdom of heaven was an evolutionary experience, beginning here on earth and progressing up through successive life stations to Paradise. In the course of the evening he definitely stated that at some future stage of kingdom development he would revisit this world in spiritual power and divine glory.

He next explained that the "kingdom idea" was not the best way to illustrate man's relation to God; that he employed such figures of speech because the Jewish people were expecting the kingdom, and because John had preached in terms of the coming kingdom. Jesus said, "The people of another age will better understand the gospel of the kingdom when it is presented in terms expressive of the family relationship - when man understands religion as the teaching of the fatherhood of God and the brotherhood of man, sonship with God."

Then the Master discoursed at some length on the earthly family as an illustration of the heavenly family, restating the two fundamental laws of living: the first commandment of love for the father, the head of the family, and the second commandment of mutual love among the children, to love your brother as yourself. And then he explained that such a quality of brotherly affection would invariably manifest itself in unselfish and loving social service.

Following that, came the memorable discussion of the fundamental characteristics of family life and their application to the relationship existing between God and man. Jesus stated that a true family is founded on the following seven facts:

1. *The fact of existence.* The relationships of nature and the phenomena of mortal likenesses are bound up in the family; children inherit certain parental traits. The children take origin in the parents; personality existence depends on the act of the parent. The relationship of father and child is inherent in all nature and pervades all living existences.

2. *Security and pleasure.* True fathers take great pleasure in providing for the needs of their children. Many fathers are not content with supplying the mere wants of their children but enjoy making provision for their pleasures also.

3. *Education and training.* Wise fathers carefully plan for the education and adequate training of their sons and daughters. When young they are prepared for the greater responsibilities of later life.

4. *Discipline and restraint.* Farseeing fathers also make provision for the necessary discipline, guidance, correction, and sometimes restraint of their young and immature offspring.

5. *Companionship and loyalty.* The affectionate father holds intimate and loving intercourse with his children. Always is his ear open to their petitions; he is ever ready to share their hardships and assist them over their difficulties. The father is supremely interested in the progressive welfare of his progeny.

6. *Love and mercy.* A compassionate father is freely forgiving; fathers do not hold vengeful memories against their children. Fathers are not like

judges, enemies, or creditors. Real families are built upon tolerance, patience, and forgiveness.

7. *Provision for the future.* Temporal fathers like to leave an inheritance for their progeny. The family continues from one generation to another. Death only ends one generation to mark the beginning of another. Death terminates an individual life but not necessarily the family.

For hours the Master discussed the application of these features of family life to the relations of man, the earth child, to God, the Paradise Father. And this was his conclusion: "This entire relationship of a son to the Father, I know in perfection, for all that you must attain of sonship in the eternal future I have now already attained. The Son of Man is prepared to ascend to the right hand of the Father, so that in me is the way now open still wider for all of you to see God and, ere you have finished the glorious progression, to become perfect, even as your Father in heaven is perfect."

When the apostles heard these startling words, they recalled the pronouncements which John made at the time of Jesus' baptism, and they also vividly recalled this experience in connection with their preaching and teaching subsequent to the Master's death and resurrection.

Jesus is a divine Son, one in the Universal Father's full confidence. He had been with the Father and comprehended him fully. He had now lived his earth life to the full satisfaction of the Father, and this incarnation in the flesh had enabled him fully to comprehend man. Jesus was the perfection of man; he had attained just such perfection as all true believers are destined to attain in him and through him. Jesus revealed a God of perfection to man and presented in himself the perfected son of the realms to God.

Although Jesus discoursed for several hours, Thomas was not yet satisfied, for he said, "But, Master, we do not find that the Father in heaven always deals kindly and mercifully with us. Many times we grievously suffer on earth, and not always are our prayers answered. Where do we fail to grasp the meaning of your teaching?"

Jesus replied, "Thomas, Thomas, how long before you will acquire the ability to listen with the ear of the spirit? How long will it be before you discern that this kingdom is a spiritual kingdom, and that my Father is also a spiritual being? Do you not understand that I am teaching you as spiritual children in the spirit family of heaven, of which the fatherhead is an infinite and eternal spirit? Will you not allow me to use the earth family as an illustration of divine relationships without so literally applying my teaching to material affairs? In your minds cannot you separate the spiritual realities of the kingdom from the material, social, economic, and political problems of the age? When I speak the language of the spirit, why do you insist on translating my meaning into the language of the flesh just because I presume to employ commonplace and literal relationships for purposes of illustration? My children, I implore that you cease to apply the teaching of the kingdom of the spirit to the sordid affairs of slavery, poverty, houses, and lands, and to the material problems of human equity and justice. These temporal matters are the concern of the men of this world, and while in a way they affect all men, you have been called to represent me in the world, even as I represent my Father. You are spiritual ambassadors of a spiritual kingdom, special representatives of the spirit Father. By this time it should be possible for me to instruct you as full-grown men of the spirit kingdom. Must I ever address you only as children? Will you never grow up in spirit perception? Nevertheless, I love you and will bear with you, even to the very end of our association in the flesh. And even then shall my spirit go before you into all the world."

By the end of April the opposition to Jesus among the Pharisees and Sadducees had become so pronounced that the Master and his apostles decided to leave Jerusalem for a while, going south to work in Bethlehem and Hebron. The entire month of May was spent in doing personal work in these cities and among the people of the surrounding villages. No public preaching was done on this trip, only house-to-house visitation. A part of this time, while the apostles taught the gospel and ministered to the sick, Jesus and Abner spent at Engedi, visiting the Nazarite colony. John the Baptist had gone forth from this place, and Abner had been head of this group. Many of the Nazarite brotherhood became believers in Jesus, but the majority of these ascetic and eccentric men refused to accept him as a teacher sent from heaven because he did not teach fasting and other forms of self-denial.

The people living in this region did not know that Jesus had been born in Bethlehem. They always supposed the Master had been born at Nazareth, as did the vast majority of his disciples, but the twelve knew the facts.

This sojourn in the south of Judea was a restful and fruitful season of labor; many souls were added to the kingdom. By the first days of June the agitation against Jesus had so quieted down in Jerusalem that the Master and the apostles returned to instruct and comfort believers.

Although Jesus and the apostles spent the entire month of June in or near Jerusalem, they did no public teaching during this period. They lived for the most part in tents, which they pitched in a shaded park, or garden, known in that day as Gethsemane. This park was situated on the western slope of the Mount of Olives not far from the brook Kidron. The Sabbath week-ends they usually spent with Lazarus and his sisters at Bethany. Jesus entered within the walls of Jerusalem only a few times, but a large number of interested inquirers came out to Gethsemane to visit with him. One Friday evening Nicodemus and one Joseph of Arimathea ventured out to see Jesus but turned back through fear even after they were standing before the entrance to the Master's tent. And, of course, they did not perceive that Jesus knew all about their doings.

When the rulers of the Jews learned that Jesus had returned to Jerusalem, they prepared to arrest him; but when they observed that he did no public preaching, they concluded that he had become frightened by their previous agitation and decided to allow him to carry on his teaching in this private manner without further molestation. And thus affairs moved along quietly until the last days of June, when one Simon, a member of the Sanhedrin, publicly espoused the teachings of Jesus, after so declaring himself before the rulers of the Jews. Immediately a new agitation for Jesus' apprehension sprang up and grew so strong that the Master decided to retire into the cities of Samaria and the Decapolis.

## GOING THROUGH SAMARIA

A T THE end of June, A.D. 27, because of the increasing opposition of the Jewish religious rulers, Jesus and the twelve departed from Jerusalem, after sending their tents and meager personal effects to be stored at the home of Lazarus at Bethany. Going north into Samaria, they tarried over the Sabbath at Bethel. Here they preached for several days to the people who came from Gophna and Ephraim. A group of citizens from Arimathea and Thamna came over to invite Jesus to visit their villages. The Master and his apostles spent more than two weeks teaching the Jews and Samaritans of this region, many of whom came from as far as Antipatris to hear the good news of the kingdom.

The people of southern Samaria heard Jesus gladly, and the apostles, with the exception of Judas Iscariot, succeeded in overcoming much of their prejudice against the Samaritans. It was very difficult for Judas to love these Samaritans. The last week of July Jesus and his associates made ready to depart for the new Greek cities of Phasaelis and Archelais near the Jordan.

The first half of the month of August the apostolic party made its headquarters at the Greek cities of Archelais and Phasaelis, where they had their first experience preaching to well-nigh exclusive gatherings of gentiles - Greeks, Romans, and Syrians - for few Jews dwelt in these two Greek towns. In contacting with these Roman citizens, the apostles encountered new difficulties in the proclamation of the message of the coming kingdom, and they met with new objections to the teachings of Jesus. At one of the many evening conferences with his apostles, Jesus listened attentively to these objections to the gospel of the kingdom as the twelve repeated their experiences with the subjects of their personal labors.

A question asked by Philip was typical of their difficulties. Said Philip, "Master, these Greeks and Romans make light of our message, saying that such teachings are fit for only weaklings and slaves. They assert that the religion of the heathen is superior to our teaching because it inspires to the acquirement of a strong, robust, and aggressive character. They affirm that we would convert all men into enfeebled specimens of passive nonresisters who would soon perish from the face of the earth. They like you, Master, and freely admit that your teaching is heavenly and ideal, but they will not take us seriously. They assert that your religion is not for this world; that men cannot live as you teach. And now, Master, what shall we say to these gentiles?"

After Jesus had heard similar objections to the gospel of the kingdom presented by Thomas, Nathaniel, Simon Zelotes, and Matthew, he said to the twelve, "I have come into this world to do the will of my Father and to reveal his loving character to all mankind. That, my brethren, is my mission. And this one thing I will do, regardless of the misunderstanding of my teachings by Jews or gentiles of this day or of another generation. But you should not overlook the fact that even divine love has its severe disciplines. A father's love for his son oftentimes impels the father to restrain the unwise acts of his thoughtless offspring. The child does not always comprehend the wise and loving motives of the father's restraining discipline. But I declare to you that my Father in Paradise does rule a universe of universes by the compelling power of his love. Love is the greatest of all spirit realities. Truth is a liberating revelation, but love is the supreme relationship. And no matter what blunders your fellow men make in their world management of today, in an age to come the gospel which I declare to you will rule this very world. The ultimate goal of human progress is the reverent recognition of the fatherhood of God and the loving materialization of the brotherhood of man.

"But who told you that my gospel was intended only for slaves and weaklings? Do you, my chosen apostles, resemble weaklings? Did John look like a weakling? Do you observe that I am enslaved by fear? True, the poor and oppressed of this generation have the gospel preached to them. The religions of this world have neglected the poor, but my Father is no respecter of persons. Besides, the poor of this day are the first to heed the call to repentance and acceptance of sonship. The gospel of the kingdom is to be preached to all mortals - Jew and gentile, Greek and Roman, rich and poor, free and bond - and equally to young and old, male and female.

"Because my Father is a God of love and delights in the practice of mercy, do not imbibe the idea that the service of the kingdom is to be one of monotonous ease. The Paradise ascent is the supreme adventure of all time, the rugged achievement of eternity. The service of the kingdom on earth will call for all the courageous manhood that you and your coworkers can muster. Many of you will be put to death for your loyalty to the gospel of this kingdom. It is easy to die in the line of physical battle when your courage is strengthened by the presence of your fighting comrades, but it requires a higher and more profound form of human courage and devotion calmly and all alone to lay down your life for the love of a truth enshrined in your mortal heart.

"Today, the unbelievers may taunt you with preaching a gospel of nonresistance and with living lives of nonviolence, but you are the first volunteers of a long line of sincere believers in the gospel of this kingdom who will astonish all mankind by their heroic devotion to these teachings. No armies of the world have ever displayed more courage and bravery than will be portrayed by you and your loyal successors who shall go forth to all the world proclaiming the good news - the fatherhood of God and the brotherhood of mankind. The courage of the flesh is the lowest form of bravery. Mind bravery is a higher type of human courage, but the highest and supreme is uncompromising loyalty to the enlightened convictions of profound spiritual realities. And such courage constitutes the heroism of the God-knowing person. And you are all God-knowing men; you are in very truth the personal associates of the Son of Man."

This was not all that Jesus said on that occasion, but it is the introduction of his address, and he went on at great length in amplification and in illustration of this pronouncement. This was one of the most impassioned addresses that Jesus ever delivered to the twelve. Seldom did the Master speak to his apostles with evident strong feeling, but this was one of those few occasions when he spoke with manifest earnestness, accompanied by marked emotion.

The result upon the public preaching and personal ministry of the apostles was immediate; from that very day their message took on a new note of courageous dominance. The twelve continued to acquire the spirit of positive aggression in the new gospel of the kingdom. From this day forward they did not occupy themselves so much with the preaching of the negative virtues and the passive injunctions of their Master's many-sided teaching.

The Master was a perfected specimen of human self-control. When he was reviled, he reviled not; when he suffered, he uttered no threats against his tormentors; when he was denounced by his enemies, he simply committed himself to the righteous judgment of the Father in heaven.

At one of the evening conferences, Andrew asked Jesus, "Master, are we to practice self-denial as John taught us, or are we to strive for the self-control of your teaching? Wherein does your teaching differ from that of John?"

Jesus answered, "John indeed taught you the way of righteousness in accordance with the light and laws of his fathers, and that was the religion of self-examination and self-denial. But I come with a new message of self-forgetfulness and self-control. I show to you the way of life as revealed to me by my Father in heaven.

"Verily, verily, I say to you, he who rules his own self is greater than he who captures a city. Self-mastery is the measure of man's moral nature and the indicator of his spiritual development. In the old order you fasted and prayed; as the new creature of the rebirth of the spirit, you are taught to believe and rejoice. In the

Father's kingdom you are to become new creatures; old things are to pass away; behold I show you how all things are to become new. And by your love for one another you are to convince the world that you have passed from bondage to liberty, from death into life everlasting.

"By the old way you seek to suppress, obey, and conform to the rules of living; by the new way you are first *transformed* by the Spirit of Truth and thereby strengthened in your inner soul by the constant spiritual renewing of your mind, and so are you endowed with the power of the certain and joyous performance of the gracious, acceptable, and perfect will of God. Forget not; it is your personal faith in the exceedingly great and precious promises of God that ensures your becoming partakers of the divine nature. Thus by your faith and the spirit's transformation, you become in reality the temples of God, and His spirit actually dwells within you. If, then, the spirit dwells within you, you are no longer bondslaves of the flesh but free and liberated sons of the spirit. The new law of the spirit endows you with the liberty of self-mastery in place of the old law of the fear of self-bondage and the slavery of self-denial.

"Many times, when you have done evil, you have thought to charge up your acts to the influence of the evil one when in reality you have but been led astray by your own natural tendencies. Did not the Prophet Jeremiah long ago tell you that the human heart is deceitful above all things and sometimes even desperately wicked? How easy for you to become self-deceived and thereby fall into foolish fears, diverse lusts, enslaving pleasures, malice, envy, and even vengeful hatred!

"Salvation is by the regeneration of the spirit and not by the self-righteous deeds of the flesh. You are justified by faith and fellowshipped by grace, not by fear and the self-denial of the flesh, albeit the Father's children who have been born of the spirit are ever and always *masters* of the self and all that pertains to the desires of the flesh. When you know that you are saved by faith, you have real peace with God. And all who follow in the way of this heavenly peace are destined to be sanctified to the eternal service of the ever-advancing sons of the eternal God. Henceforth, it is not a duty but rather your exalted privilege to cleanse yourselves from all evils of mind and body while you seek for perfection in the love of God.

"Your sonship is grounded in faith, and you are to remain unmoved by fear. Your joy is born of trust in the divine word, and you shall not therefore be led to doubt the reality of the Father's love and mercy. It is the very goodness of God that leads men into true and genuine repentance. Your secret of the mastery of self is bound up with your faith in the indwelling spirit, which ever works by love. Even this saving faith you have not of yourselves; it also is the gift of God. And if you are the children of this living faith, you are no longer the bondslaves of self but rather the triumphant masters of yourselves, the liberated sons of God.

"If, then, my children, you are born of the spirit, you are forever delivered from the self-conscious bondage of a life of self-denial and watchcare over the desires of the flesh, and you are translated into the joyous kingdom of the spirit, whence you spontaneously show forth the fruits of the spirit in your daily lives; and the fruits of the spirit are the essence of the highest type of enjoyable and ennobling self-control, even the heights of terrestrial mortal attainment - true self-mastery."

About this time a state of great nervous and emotional tension developed among the apostles and their immediate disciple associates. They had hardly become accustomed to living and working together. They were experiencing increasing difficulties in maintaining harmonious relations with John's disciples. The contact with the gentiles and the Samaritans was a great trial to these Jews. And besides all this, the recent utterances of Jesus had augmented their disturbed state of mind. Andrew was almost beside himself; he did not know what next to do, and so he went to the Master with his problems and perplexities.

When Jesus had listened to the apostolic chief relate his troubles, he said, "Andrew, you cannot talk men out of their perplexities when they reach such a stage of involvement, and when so many persons with strong feelings are concerned. I cannot do what you ask of me - I will not participate in these personal social difficulties - but I will join you in the enjoyment of a three-day period of rest and relaxation. Go to your brethren and announce that all of you are to go with me up on Mount Sartaba, where I desire to rest for a day or two.

"Now you should go to each of your eleven brethren and talk with him privately, saying: 'The Master desires that we go apart with him for a season to rest and relax. Since we all have recently experienced much vexation of spirit and stress of mind, I suggest that no mention be made of our trials and troubles while on this holiday. Can I depend upon you to co-operate with me in this matter?' In this way privately and personally approach each of your brethren." And Andrew did as the Master had instructed him.

This was a marvelous occasion in the experience of each of them; they never forgot the day going up the mountain. Throughout the entire trip hardly a word was said about their troubles. Upon reaching the top of the mountain, Jesus seated them about him while he said, "My brethren, you must all learn the value of rest and the efficacy of relaxation. You must realize that the best method of solving some entangled problems is to forsake them for a time. Then when you go back fresh from your rest or worship, you are able to attack your troubles with a clearer head and a steadier hand, not to mention a more resolute heart. Again, many times your problem is found to have shrunk in size and proportions while you have been resting your mind and body."

The next day Jesus assigned to each of the twelve a topic for discussion. The whole day was devoted to reminiscences and to talking over matters not related to their religious work. They were momentarily shocked when Jesus even neglected to give thanks (verbally) when he broke bread for their noontide lunch. This was the first time they had ever observed him to neglect such formalities.

When they went up the mountain, Andrew's head was full of problems. John was inordinately perplexed in his heart. James was grievously troubled in his soul. Matthew was hard pressed for funds inasmuch as they had been sojourning among the gentiles. Peter was overwrought and had recently been more temperamental than usual. Judas was suffering from a periodic attack of sensitiveness and selfishness. Simon was unusually upset in his efforts to reconcile his patriotism with the love of the brotherhood of man. Philip was more and more nonplused by the way things were going. Nathaniel had been less humorous since they had come in contact with the gentile populations, and Thomas was in the midst of a severe season of depression. Only the twins were normal and unperturbed. All of them were exceedingly perplexed about how to get along peaceably with John's disciples.

The third day when they started down the mountain and back to their camp, a great change had come over them. They had made the important discovery that many human perplexities are in reality nonexistent, that many pressing troubles are the creations of exaggerated fear and the offspring of augmented apprehension. They had learned that all such perplexities are best handled by being forsaken; by going off they had left such problems to solve themselves.

Their return from this holiday marked the beginning of a period of greatly improved relations with the followers of John. Many of the twelve really gave way to mirth when they noted the changed state of everybody's mind and observed the freedom from nervous irritability which had come to them as a result of their three days' vacation from the routine duties of life. There is always danger that monotony of human contact will greatly multiply perplexities and magnify difficulties.

Not many of the gentiles in the two Greek cities of Archelais and Phasaelis believed in the gospel, but the twelve apostles gained a valuable experience in this their first extensive work with exclusively gentile populations. On a Monday morning, about the middle of the month, Jesus said to Andrew, "We go into Samaria." And they set out at once for the city of Sychar, near Jacob's well.

For more than six hundred years the Jews of Judea, and later on those of Galilee also, had been at enmity with the Samaritans. This ill feeling between the Jews and the Samaritans came about in this way: About seven hundred years B.C., Sargon, king of Assyria, in subduing a revolt in central Palestine, carried away and into captivity over twenty-five thousand Jews of the northern kingdom of Israel and installed in their place an almost equal number of the descendants of the Cuthites, Sepharvites, and the Hamathites. Later on, Ashurbanipal sent still other colonies to dwell in Samaria.

The religious enmity between the Jews and the Samaritans dated from the return of the former from the Babylonian captivity, when the Samaritans worked to prevent the rebuilding of Jerusalem. Later they offended the Jews by extending friendly assistance to the armies of Alexander. In return for their friendship Alexander gave the Samaritans permission to build a temple on Mount Gerizim, where they worshiped Yahweh and their tribal gods and offered sacrifices much after the order of the temple services at Jerusalem. At least they continued this worship up to the time of the Maccabees, when John Hyrcanus destroyed their temple on Mount Gerizim. The Apostle Philip, in his labors for the Samaritans after the death of Jesus, held many meetings on the site of this old Samaritan temple.

The antagonisms between the Jews and the Samaritans were time-honored and historic; increasingly since the days of Alexander they had had no dealings with each other. The twelve apostles were not averse to preaching in the Greek and other gentile cities of the Decapolis and Syria, but it was a severe test of their loyalty to the Master when he said, "Let us go into Samaria." But in the year and more they had been with Jesus, they had developed a form of personal loyalty that transcended even their faith in his teachings and their prejudices against the Samaritans.

When the Master and the twelve arrived at Jacob's well, Jesus, being weary from the journey, tarried by the well while Philip took the apostles with him to assist in bringing food and tents from Sychar, for they were disposed to stay in this vicinity for a while. Peter and the Zebedee sons would have remained with Jesus, but he requested that they go with their brethren, saying, "Have no fear for me; these Samaritans will be friendly; only our brethren, the Jews, seek to harm us." And it was almost six o'clock on this summer's evening when Jesus sat down by the well to await the return of the apostles.

The water of Jacob's well was less mineral than that from the wells of Sychar and was therefore much valued for drinking purposes. Jesus was thirsty, but there was no way of getting water from the well. When, therefore, a woman of Sychar came up with her water pitcher and prepared to draw from the well, Jesus said to her, "Give me a drink." This woman of Samaria knew Jesus was a Jew by his appearance and dress, and she surmised that he was a Galilean Jew from his accent. Her name was Nalda and she was a comely creature.

She was much surprised to have a Jewish man thus speak to her at the well and ask for water, for it was not deemed proper in those days for a self-respecting man to speak to a woman in public, much less for a Jew to converse with a Samaritan. Therefore Nalda asked Jesus, "How is it that you, being a Jew, ask for a drink of me, a Samaritan woman?"

Jesus answered, "I have indeed asked you for a drink, but if you could only understand, you would ask me for a draught of the living water."

Then said Nalda, "But, Sir, you have nothing to draw with, and the well is deep; whence, then, have you this living water? Are you greater than our father Jacob who gave us this well, and who drank thereof himself and his sons and his cattle also?"

Jesus replied, "Everyone who drinks of this water will thirst again, but whosoever drinks of the water of the living spirit shall never thirst. And this living water shall become in him a well of refreshment springing up even to eternal life."

Nalda then said, "Give me this water that I thirst not, neither come all the way hither to draw. Besides, anything which a Samaritan woman could receive from such a commendable Jew would be a pleasure."

Nalda did not know how to take Jesus' willingness to talk with her. She beheld in the Master's face the countenance of an upright and holy man, but she mistook friendliness for commonplace familiarity, and she misinterpreted his figure of speech as a form of making advances to her. And being a woman of lax morals, she was minded openly to become flirtatious, when Jesus, looking straight into her eyes, with a commanding voice said, "Woman, go get your husband and bring him hither."

This command brought Nalda to her senses. She saw that she had misjudged the Master's kindness; she perceived that she had misconstrued his manner of speech. She was frightened; she began to realize that she stood in the presence of an unusual person, and groping about in her mind for a suitable reply, in great confusion, she said, "But, Sir, I cannot call my husband, for I have no husband."

Then said Jesus, "You have spoken the truth, for, while you may have once had a husband, he with whom you are now living is not your husband. Better it would be if you would cease to trifle with my words and seek for the living water which I have this day offered you."

By this time Nalda was sobered, and her better self was awakened. She was not an immoral woman wholly by choice. She had been ruthlessly and unjustly cast aside by her husband and in dire straits had consented to live with a certain Greek as his wife, but without marriage. Nalda now felt greatly ashamed that she had so unthinkingly spoken to Jesus, and she most penitently addressed the Master, saying, "My Lord, I repent of my manner of speaking to you, for I perceive that you are a holy man or maybe a prophet." And she was just about to seek direct and personal help from the Master when she did what so many have done before and since; dodged the issue of personal salvation by turning to the discussion of theology and philosophy. She quickly turned the conversation from her own needs to a theological controversy. Pointing over to Mount Gerizim, she continued, "Our fathers worshiped on this mountain, and yet *you* would say that in Jerusalem is the place where men ought to worship; which, then, is the right place to worship God?"

Jesus perceived the attempt of the woman's soul to avoid direct and searching contact with its Maker, but he also saw that there was present in her soul a desire to know the better way of life. After all, there was in Nalda's heart a true thirst for the living water; therefore he dealt patiently with her, saying, "Woman, let me say to you that the day is soon coming when neither on this mountain nor in Jerusalem will you worship the Father. But now you worship that which you know not, a mixture of the religion of many pagan gods and gentile philosophies. The Jews at least know whom they worship; they have removed all confusion by concentrating their worship upon one God, Yahweh. But you should believe me when I say that the hour will soon come - even now is - when all sincere worshipers will worship the Father in spirit and in truth, for it is just such worshipers the Father seeks. God is spirit, and they who worship him must worship him in spirit and in truth. Your salvation comes not from knowing how others should worship or where but by receiving into your own heart this living water which I am offering you even now."

But Nalda would make one more effort to avoid the discussion of the embarrassing question of her personal life on earth and the status of her soul before God. Once more she resorted to questions of general religion, saying, "Yes, I know, Sir, that John has preached about the coming of the Converter, he who will be called the Deliverer, and that, when he shall come, he will declare to us all things..." and Jesus, interrupting Nalda, said with startling assurance, "I who speak to you am he."

This was the first direct, positive, and undisguised pronouncement of his divine nature and sonship which Jesus had made on earth; and it was made to a woman, a Samaritan woman, and a woman of questionable character in the eyes of men up to this moment, but a woman whom the divine eye beheld as having been sinned against more than as sinning of her own desire and as *now* being a human soul who desired salvation, desired it sincerely and wholeheartedly, and that was enough.

As Nalda was about to voice her real and personal longing for better things and a more noble way of living, just as she was ready to speak the real desire of her heart, the twelve apostles returned from Sychar, and coming upon this scene of Jesus' talking so intimately with this woman - this Samaritan woman, and alone - they were more than astonished. They quickly deposited their supplies and drew aside, no man daring to reprove him, while Jesus said to Nalda, "Woman, go your way; God has forgiven you. Henceforth you will live a new life. You have received the living water, and a new joy will spring up within your soul, and you shall become a daughter of the Most High."

And the woman, perceiving the disapproval of the apostles, left her waterpot and fled to the city.

As she entered the city, she proclaimed to everyone she met, "Go out to Jacob's well and go quickly, for there you will see a man who told me all I ever did.

Can this be the Converter?" And ere the sun went down, a great crowd had assembled at Jacob's well to hear Jesus. And the Master talked to them more about
the water of life, the gift of the indwelling spirit.

The apostles never ceased to be shocked by Jesus' willingness to talk with
women, women of questionable character, even immoral women. It was very difficult for Jesus to teach his apostles that women, even so-called immoral women,
have souls which can choose God as their Father, thereby becoming daughters of
God and candidates for life everlasting. Even nineteen centuries later many show
the same unwillingness to grasp the Master's teachings. Even the Christian religion
has been persistently built up around the fact of the death of Christ instead of
around the truth of his life. The world should be more concerned with his happy
and God-revealing life than with his tragic and sorrowful death.

Nalda told this entire story to the Apostle John the next day, but he never revealed it fully to the other apostles, and Jesus did not speak of it in detail to the
twelve.

Nalda told John that Jesus had told her "all I ever did." John many times
wanted to ask Jesus about this visit with Nalda, but he never did. Jesus told her only
one thing about herself, but his look into her eyes and the manner of his dealing
with her had so brought all of her checkered life in panoramic review before her
mind in a moment of time that she associated all of this self-revelation of her past
life with the look and the word of the Master. Jesus never told her she had had five
husbands. She had lived with four different men since her husband cast her aside,
and this, with all her past, came up so vividly in her mind at the moment when she
realized Jesus was a man of God that she subsequently repeated to John that Jesus
had really told her all about herself.

On the evening that Nalda drew the crowd out from Sychar to see Jesus, the
twelve had just returned with food, and they besought Jesus to eat with them
instead of talking to the people, for they had been without food all day and were
hungry. But Jesus knew that darkness would soon be upon them; so he persisted in
his determination to talk to the people before he sent them away. When Andrew
sought to persuade him to eat a bite before speaking to the crowd, Jesus said, "I
have meat to eat that you do not know about."

When the apostles heard this, they said among themselves, "Has any man
brought him aught to eat? Can it be that the woman gave him food as well as
drink?"

When Jesus heard them talking among themselves, before he spoke to the
people, he turned aside and said to the twelve, "My meat is to do the will of Him
who sent me and to accomplish His work. You should no longer say it is such and
such a time until the harvest. Behold these people coming out from a Samaritan

city to hear us; I tell you the fields are already white for the harvest. He who reaps receives wages and gathers this fruit to eternal life; consequently the sowers and the reapers rejoice together. For herein is the saying true: `One sows and another reaps.' I am now sending you to reap that whereon you have not labored; others have labored, and you are about to enter into their labor." This he said in reference to the preaching of John the Baptist.

Jesus and the apostles went into Sychar and preached two days before they established their camp on Mount Gerizim. And many of the dwellers in Sychar believed the gospel and made request for baptism, but the apostles of Jesus did not yet baptize.

The first night of the camp on Mount Gerizim the apostles expected that Jesus would rebuke them for their attitude toward the woman at Jacob's well, but he made no reference to the matter. Instead he gave them that memorable talk on "The realities which are central in the kingdom of God." In any religion it is very easy to allow values to become disproportionate and to permit facts to occupy the place of truth in one's theology. The fact of the cross became the very center of subsequent Christianity; but it is not the central truth of the religion which may be derived from the life and teachings of Jesus of Nazareth.

The theme of Jesus' teaching on Mount Gerizim was: that he wants all men to see God as a Father-friend just as he (Jesus) is a brother-friend. And again and again he impressed upon them that love is the greatest relationship in the world - in the universe - just as truth is the greatest pronouncement of the observation of these divine relationships.

Jesus declared himself so fully to the Samaritans because he could safely do so, and because he knew that he would not again visit the heart of Samaria to preach the gospel of the kingdom.

Jesus and the twelve camped on Mount Gerizim until the end of August. They preached the good news of the kingdom - the fatherhood of God - to the Samaritans in the cities by day and spent the nights at the camp. The work which Jesus and the twelve did in these Samaritan cities yielded many souls for the kingdom and did much to prepare the way for the marvelous work of Philip in these regions after Jesus' death and resurrection, subsequent to the dispersion of the apostles to the ends of the earth by the bitter persecution of believers at Jerusalem.

At the evening conferences on Mount Gerizim, Jesus taught many great truths, and in particular he laid emphasis on the following:

> True religion is the act of an individual soul in its self-conscious relations with the Creator; organized religion is man's attempt to *socialize* the worship of individual religionists.

Worship - contemplation of the spiritual - must alternate with service, contact with material reality. Work should alternate with play; religion should be balanced by humor. Profound philosophy should be relieved by rhythmic poetry. The strain of living - the time-tension of personality - should be relaxed by the restfulness of worship. The feelings of insecurity arising from the fear of personality isolation in the universe should be antidoted by the faith contemplation of the Father and by the attempted realization of the Supreme.

Prayer is designed to make man less thinking but more *realizing;* it is not designed to increase knowledge but rather to expand insight.

Worship is intended to anticipate the better life ahead and then to reflect these new spiritual significances back onto the life which now is. Prayer is spiritually sustaining, but worship is divinely creative.

Worship is the technique of looking to the *One* for the inspiration of service to the *many.* Worship is the yardstick which measures the extent of the soul's detachment from the material universe and its simultaneous and secure attachment to the spiritual realities of all creation.

Prayer is self-reminding - sublime thinking; worship is self-forgetting - superthinking. Worship is effortless attention, true and ideal soul rest, a form of restful spiritual exertion.

Worship is the act of a part identifying itself with the Whole; the finite with the Infinite; the son with the Father; time in the act of striking step with eternity. Worship is the act of the son's or daughter's personal communion with the divine Father, the assumption of refreshing, creative, fraternal, and romantic attitudes by the human soul-spirit.

Although the apostles grasped only a few of his teachings at the camp, other worlds did, and other generations on earth will.

# At Gilboa and in the Decapolis

SEPTEMBER AND October were spent in retirement at a secluded camp upon the slopes of Mount Gilboa. The month of September Jesus spent here alone with his apostles, teaching and instructing them in the truths of the kingdom.

There were a number of reasons why Jesus and his apostles were in retirement at this time on the borders of Samaria and the Decapolis. The Jerusalem religious rulers were very antagonistic; Herod Antipas still held John in prison, fearing either to release or execute him, while he continued to entertain suspicions that John and Jesus were in some way associated. These conditions made it unwise to plan for aggressive work in either Judea or Galilee. There was a third reason: the slowly augmenting tension between the leaders of John's disciples and the apostles of Jesus, which grew worse with the increasing number of believers.

Jesus knew that the days of the preliminary work of teaching and preaching were about over, that the next move involved the beginning of the full and final effort of his life on earth, and he did not wish the launching of this undertaking to be in any manner either trying or embarrassing to John the Baptist. Jesus had therefore decided to spend some time in retirement rehearsing his apostles and then to do some quiet work in the cities of the Decapolis until John should be either executed or released to join them in a united effort.

As time passed, the twelve became more devoted to Jesus and increasingly committed to the work of the kingdom. Their devotion was in large part a matter of personal loyalty. They did not grasp his many-sided teaching; they did not fully comprehend the nature of Jesus or the significance of his bestowal on earth.

Jesus made it plain to his apostles that they were in retirement for three reasons:

1. To confirm their understanding of, and faith in, the gospel of the kingdom.

2. To allow opposition to their work in both Judea and Galilee to quiet down.

3. To await the fate of John the Baptist.

While tarrying on Gilboa, Jesus told the twelve much about his early life and his experiences on Mount Hermon; he also revealed something of what happened in the hills during the forty days immediately after his baptism. And he directly charged them that they should tell no man about these experiences until after he had returned to the Father.

During these September weeks they rested, visited, recounted their experiences since Jesus first called them to service, and engaged in an earnest effort to co-ordinate what the Master had so far taught them. In a measure they all sensed that this would be their last opportunity for prolonged rest. They realized that their next public effort in either Judea or Galilee would mark the beginning of the final proclamation of the coming kingdom, but they had little or no settled idea as to what the kingdom would be when it came. John and Andrew thought the kingdom had already come; Peter and James believed that it was yet to come; Nathaniel and Thomas frankly confessed they were puzzled; Matthew, Philip, and Simon Zelotes were uncertain and confused; the twins were blissfully ignorant of the controversy; and Judas Iscariot was silent, noncommittal.

Much of this time Jesus was alone on the mountain near the camp. Occasionally he took with him Peter, James, or John, but more often he went off to pray or commune alone. Subsequent to the baptism of Jesus and the forty days in the Perean hills, it is hardly proper to speak of these seasons of communion with his Father as prayer, nor is it consistent to speak of Jesus as worshiping, but it is altogether correct to allude to these seasons as personal communion with his Father.

The central theme of the discussions throughout the entire month of September was prayer and worship. After they had discussed worship for some days, Jesus finally delivered his memorable discourse on prayer in answer to Thomas's request: "Master, teach us how to pray."

John had taught his disciples a prayer, a prayer for salvation in the coming kingdom. Although Jesus never forbade his followers to use John's form of prayer, the apostles very early perceived that their Master did not fully approve of the practice of uttering set and formal prayers. Nevertheless, believers constantly requested to be taught how to pray. The twelve longed to know what form of petition Jesus would approve. And it was chiefly because of this need for some simple petition for the common people that Jesus at this time consented, in answer to Thomas's request, to teach them a suggestive form of prayer. Jesus gave this lesson one afternoon in the third week of their sojourn on Mount Gilboa.

"John indeed taught you a simple form of prayer: 'O Father, cleanse us from sin, show us your glory, reveal your love, and let your spirit sanctify our hearts forevermore, Amen!' He taught this prayer that you might have something to teach the multitude. He did not intend that you should use such a set and formal petition as the expression of your own souls in prayer.

"Prayer is entirely a personal and spontaneous expression of the attitude of the soul toward the spirit; prayer should be the communion of sonship and the expression of fellowship. Prayer, when indited by the spirit, leads to co-operative spiritual progress. The ideal prayer is a form of spiritual communion which leads to intelligent worship. True praying is the sincere attitude of reaching heavenward for the attainment of your ideals.

"Prayer is the breath of the soul and should lead you to be persistent in your attempt to ascertain the Father's will. If any one of you has a neighbor, and you go to him at midnight and say: 'Friend, lend me three loaves, for a friend of mine on a journey has come to see me, and I have nothing to set before him'; and if your neighbor answers, 'Trouble me not, for the door is now shut and the children and I are in bed; therefore I cannot rise and give you bread,' you will persist, explaining that your friend hungers, and that you have no food to offer him. I say to you, though your neighbor will not rise and give you bread because he is your friend, yet because of your importunity he will get up and give you as many loaves as you need. If, then, persistence will win favors even from mortal man, how much more will your persistence in the spirit win the bread of life for you from the willing hands of the Father in heaven. Again I say to you: Ask and it shall be given you; seek and you shall find; knock and it shall be opened to you. For every one who asks receives; he who seeks finds; and to him who knocks the door of salvation will be opened.

"Which of you who is a father, if his son asks unwisely, would hesitate to give in accordance with parental wisdom rather than in the terms of the son's faulty petition? If the child needs a loaf, will you give him a stone just because he unwisely asks for it? If your son needs a fish, will you give him a watersnake just because it may chance to come up in the net with the fish and the child foolishly asks for the serpent? If you, then, being mortal and finite, know how to answer prayer and give good and appropriate gifts to your children, how much more shall your heavenly Father give the spirit and many additional blessings to those who ask him? Men ought always to pray and not become discouraged.

"Let me tell you the story of a certain judge who lived in a wicked city. This judge feared not God nor had respect for man. Now there was a needy widow in that city who came repeatedly to this unjust judge, saying, 'Protect me from my adversary.' For some time he would not give ear to her, but presently he said to himself: 'Though I fear not God nor have regard for man, yet because this widow ceases not to trouble me, I will vindicate her lest she wear me out by her continual coming.' These stories I tell you to encourage you to persist in praying and not to intimate that your petitions will change the just and righteous Father above. Your persistence, however, is not to win favor with God but to change your earth attitude and to enlarge your soul's capacity for spirit receptivity.

"But when you pray, you exercise so little faith. Genuine faith will remove mountains of material difficulty which may chance to lie in the path of soul expansion and spiritual progress."

But the apostles were not yet satisfied; they desired Jesus to give them a model prayer which they could teach the new disciples. After listening to this discourse on prayer, James Zebedee said, "Very good, Master, but we do not desire a form of prayer for ourselves so much as for the newer believers who so frequently beseech us, 'Teach us how acceptably to pray to the Father in heaven.'"

When James had finished speaking, Jesus said, "If, then, you still desire such a prayer, I would present the one which I taught my brothers and sisters in Nazareth.

"Our Father who is in heaven, Hallowed be your name.

Your kingdom come; your will be done on earth as it is in heaven.

Give us this day our bread for tomorrow; refresh our souls with the water of life.

And forgive us every one our debts, as we also have forgiven our debtors.

Save us in temptation, deliver us from evil.

And increasingly make us perfect like yourself."

It is not strange that the apostles desired Jesus to teach them a model prayer for believers. John the Baptist had taught his followers several prayers; all great teachers had formulated prayers for their pupils. The religious teachers of the Jews had some twenty-five or thirty set prayers which they recited in the synagogues and even on the street corners. Jesus was particularly averse to praying in public. Up to this time the twelve had heard him pray only a few times. They observed him spending entire nights at prayer or worship, and they were very curious to know the manner or form of his petitions. They were really hard pressed to know what to answer the multitudes when they asked to be taught how to pray as John had taught his disciples.

Jesus taught the twelve always to pray in secret; to go off by themselves amidst the quiet surroundings of nature or to go in their rooms and shut the doors when they engaged in prayer.

After Jesus' death and ascension to the Father it became the practice of many believers to finish this so-called Lord's prayer by the addition of; "In the name of the Lord Jesus Christ." Still later on, two lines were lost in copying, and there was added to this prayer an extra clause, reading; "For yours is the kingdom and the power and the glory, forevermore."

Jesus gave the apostles the prayer in collective form as they had prayed it in the Nazareth home. He never taught a formal personal prayer, only group, family, or social petitions. And he never volunteered to do that.

Jesus taught that effective prayer must be:
1. Unselfish - not alone for oneself.
2. Believing - according to faith.
3. Sincere - honest of heart.
4. Intelligent - according to light.
5. Trustful - in submission to the Father's all-wise will.

When Jesus spent whole nights on the mountain in prayer, it was mainly for his disciples, particularly for the twelve. The Master prayed very little for himself, although he engaged in much worship of the nature of understanding communion with his Paradise Father.

For days after the discourse on prayer the apostles continued to ask the Master questions regarding this all-important and worshipful practice. Jesus' instruction to the apostles during these days, regarding prayer and worship, may be summarized and restated in modern phraseology as follows:

The earnest and longing repetition of any petition, when such a prayer is the sincere expression of a child of God and is uttered in faith, no matter how ill-advised or impossible of direct answer, never fails to expand the soul's capacity for spiritual receptivity.

In all praying, remember that sonship (Ed. Note: sonship is always to be read without connotations of gender) is a *gift*. No child has aught to do with *earning* the status of son or daughter. The earth child comes into being by the will of its parents. Even so, the child of God comes into grace and the new life of the spirit by the will of the Father in heaven. Therefore must the kingdom of heaven - divine sonship - be *received* as by a little child. You earn righteousness - progressive character development - but you receive sonship by grace and through faith.

Prayer led Jesus up to the supercommunion of his soul with the Supreme Rulers of the universe of universes. Prayer will lead the mortals of earth up to the communion of true worship. The soul's spiritual capacity for receptivity determines the quantity of heavenly blessings which can be personally appropriated and consciously realized as an answer to prayer.

Prayer and its associated worship is a technique of detachment from the daily routine of life, from the monotonous grind of material existence. It is an avenue of approach to spiritualized self-realization and individuality of intellectual and religious attainment.

Prayer is an antidote for harmful introspection. At least, prayer as the Master taught it is such a beneficent ministry to the soul. Jesus consistently employed the beneficial influence of praying for one's fellows. The Master usually prayed in the plural, not in the singular. Only in the great crises of his earth life did Jesus ever pray for himself.

Prayer is the breath of the spirit life in the midst of the material civilization of the races of mankind. Worship is salvation for the pleasure-seeking generations of mortals.

As prayer may be likened to recharging the spiritual batteries of the soul, so worship may be compared to the act of tuning in the soul to catch the universe broadcasts of the infinite spirit of the Universal Father.

Prayer is the sincere and longing look of the child to its spirit Father; it is a psychological process of exchanging the human will for the divine will. Prayer is a part of the divine plan for making over that which is into that which ought to be.

One of the reasons why Peter, James, and John, who so often accompanied Jesus on his long night vigils, never heard Jesus pray, was because their Master so rarely uttered his prayers as spoken words. Practically all of Jesus' praying was done in the spirit and in the heart - silently.

Of all the apostles, Peter and James came the nearest to comprehending the Master's teaching about prayer and worship.

From time to time, during the remainder of Jesus' sojourn on earth, he brought to the notice of the apostles several additional forms of prayer, but he did this only in illustration of other matters, and he enjoined that these "parable prayers" should not be taught to the multitudes. Many of them were from other inhabited planets, but this fact Jesus did not reveal to the twelve. Among these prayers were the following:

> Our Father in whom consist the universe realms,
> Uplifted be your name and all-glorious your character.
> Your presence encompasses us, and your glory is manifested
> Imperfectly through us as it is in perfection shown on high.
> Give us this day the vivifying forces of light,
> And let us not stray into the evil bypaths of our imagination,
> For yours is the glorious indwelling, the everlasting power,
> And to us, the eternal gift of the infinite love of your Son.
> Even so, and everlastingly true.

Our creative Parent, who is in the center of the universe,
Bestow upon us your nature and give to us your character.
Make us sons and daughters of yours by grace
And glorify your name through our eternal achievement.
Your adjusting and controlling spirit give to live and dwell within
That we may do your will on this sphere as angels do your bidding in light.
Sustain us this day in our progress along the path of truth.
Deliver us from inertia, evil, and all sinful transgression.
Be patient with us as we show loving-kindness to our fellows.
Shed abroad the spirit of your mercy in our creature hearts.
Lead us by your own hand, step by step, through the uncertain maze of life,
And when our end shall come, receive into your own bosom our faithful spirits.
Even so, not our desires but your will be done.

Our perfect and righteous heavenly Father,
This day guide and direct our journey.
Sanctify our steps and co-ordinate our thoughts.
Ever lead us in the ways of eternal progress.
Fill us with wisdom to the fullness of power
And vitalize us with your infinite energy.
Inspire us with the divine consciousness of
The presence and guidance of the seraphic hosts.
Guide us ever upward in the pathway of light;
Justify us fully in the day of the great judgment.
Make us like yourself in eternal glory
And receive us into your endless service on high.

Our Father who is in the mystery,
Reveal to us your holy character.
Give your children on earth this day
To see the way, the light, and the truth.
Show us the pathway of eternal progress

And give us the will to walk therein.
Establish within us your divine kingship
And thereby bestow upon us the full mastery of self.
Let us not stray into paths of darkness and death;
Lead us everlastingly beside the waters of life.
Hear these our prayers for your own sake;
Be pleased to make us more and more like yourself.
At the end, for the sake of the divine Son,
Receive us into the eternal arms.
Even so, not our will but yours be done.

Glorious Father and Mother, in one parent combined,
Loyal would we be to your divine nature.
Your own self to live again in and through us
By the gift and bestowal of your divine spirit,
Thus reproducing you imperfectly in this sphere
As you are perfectly and majestically shown on high.
Give us day by day your sweet ministry of brotherhood
And lead us moment by moment in the pathway of loving service.
Be you ever and unfailingly patient with us
Even as we show forth your patience to our children.
Give us the divine wisdom that does all things well
And the infinite love that is gracious to every creature.
Bestow upon us your patience and loving-kindness
That our charity may enfold the weak of the realm.
And when our career is finished, make it an honor to your name,
A pleasure to your good spirit, and a satisfaction to our soul helpers.
Not as we wish, our loving Father, but as you desire the eternal good of
your mortal children,
Even so may it be.

Our all-faithful Source and all-powerful Center,
Reverent and holy be the name of your all-gracious Son.
Your bounties and your blessings have descended upon us,
Thus empowering us to perform your will and execute your bidding.
Give us moment by moment the sustenance of the tree of life;
Refresh us day by day with the living waters of the river thereof.

Step by step lead us out of darkness and into the divine light.
Renew our minds by the transformations of the indwelling spirit,
And when the mortal end shall finally come upon us,
Receive us to yourself and send us forth in eternity.
Crown us with celestial diadems of fruitful service,
And we shall glorify the Father, the Son, and the Holy Influence.
Even so, throughout a universe without end.

Our Father who dwells in the secret places of the universe,
Honored be your name, reverenced your mercy, and respected your
judgment.
Let the sun of righteousness shine upon us at noontime,
While we beseech you to guide our wayward steps in the twilight.
Lead us by the hand in the ways of your own choosing
And forsake us not when the path is hard and the hours are dark.
Forget us not as we so often neglect and forget you.
But be you merciful and love us as we desire to love you.
Look down upon us in kindness and forgive us in mercy
As we in justice forgive those who distress and injure us.
May the love, devotion, and bestowal of the majestic Son
Make available life everlasting with your endless mercy and love.
May the God of universes bestow upon us the full measure of his spirit;
Give us grace to yield to the leading of this spirit.
By the loving ministry of devoted seraphic hosts
May the Son guide and lead us to the end of the age.
Make us ever and increasingly like yourself
And at our end receive us into the eternal Paradise embrace.
Even so, in the name of the bestowal Son
And for the honor and glory of the Supreme Father.

Though the apostles were not at liberty to present these prayer lessons in their public teachings, they profited much from all of these revelations in their personal religious experiences. Jesus utilized these and other prayer models as illustrations in connection with the intimate instruction of the twelve, and specific permission has been granted for transcribing these seven specimen prayers into this record.

Around the first of October, Philip and some of his fellow apostles were in a near-by village buying food when they met some of the apostles of John the Baptist. As a result of this chance meeting in the market place there came about a three weeks' conference at the Gilboa camp between the apostles of Jesus and the apostles of John, for John had recently appointed twelve of his leaders to be apostles, following the precedent of Jesus. John had done this in response to the urging of Abner, the chief of his loyal supporters. Jesus was present at the Gilboa camp throughout the first week of this joint conference but absented himself the last two weeks.

By the beginning of the second week of this month, Abner had assembled all of his associates at the Gilboa camp and was prepared to go into council with the apostles of Jesus. For three weeks these twenty-four men were in session three times a day and for six days each week. The first week Jesus mingled with them between their forenoon, afternoon, and evening sessions. They wanted the Master to meet with them and preside over their joint deliberations, but he steadfastly refused to participate in their discussions, though he did consent to speak to them on three occasions. These talks by Jesus to the twenty-four were on sympathy, cooperation, and tolerance.

Andrew and Abner alternated in presiding over these joint meetings of the two apostolic groups. These men had many difficulties to discuss and numerous problems to solve. Again and again would they take their troubles to Jesus, only to hear him say: "I am concerned only with your personal and purely religious problems. I am the representative of the Father to the *individual,* not to the group. If you are in personal difficulty in your relations with God, come to me, and I will hear you and counsel you in the solution of your problem. But when you enter upon the coordination of divergent human interpretations of religious questions and upon the socialization of religion, you are destined to solve all such problems by your own decisions. Albeit, I am ever sympathetic and always interested, and when you arrive at your conclusions touching these matters of nonspiritual import, provided you are all agreed, then I pledge in advance my full approval and hearty co-operation. And now, in order to leave you unhampered in your deliberations, I am leaving you for two weeks. Be not anxious about me, for I will return to you. I will be about my Father's business, for we have other realms besides this one."

After thus speaking, Jesus went down the mountainside, and they saw him no more for two full weeks. And they never knew where he went or what he did during these days. It was some time before the twenty-four could settle down to the serious consideration of their problems, they were so disconcerted by the absence of the Master. However, within a week they were again in the heart of their discussions, and they could not go to Jesus for help.

The first item the group agreed upon was the adoption of the prayer which Jesus had so recently taught them. It was unanimously voted to accept this prayer as the one to be taught believers by both groups of apostles.

They next decided that, as long as John lived, whether in prison or out, both groups of twelve apostles would go on with their work, and that joint meetings for one week would be held every three months at places to be agreed upon from time to time.

But the most serious of all their problems was the question of baptism. Their difficulties were all the more aggravated because Jesus had refused to make any pronouncement upon the subject. They finally agreed: As long as John lived, or until they might jointly modify this decision, only the apostles of John would baptize believers, and only the apostles of Jesus would finally instruct the new disciples. Accordingly, from that time until after the death of John, two of the apostles of John accompanied Jesus and his apostles to baptize believers, for the joint council had unanimously voted that baptism was to become the initial step in the outward alliance with the affairs of the kingdom.

It was next agreed, in case of the death of John, that the apostles of John would present themselves to Jesus and become subject to his direction, and that they would baptize no more unless authorized by Jesus or his apostles.

And then was it voted that, in case of John's death, the apostles of Jesus would begin to baptize with water as the emblem of the baptism of the divine Spirit. As to whether or not *repentance* should be attached to the preaching of baptism was left optional; no decision was made binding upon the group. John's apostles preached, "Repent and be baptized." Jesus' apostles proclaimed, "Believe and be baptized."

And this is the story of the first attempt of Jesus' followers to co-ordinate divergent efforts, compose differences of opinion, organize group undertakings, legislate on outward observances, and socialize personal religious practices.

Many other minor matters were considered and their solutions unanimously agreed upon. These twenty-four men had a truly remarkable experience these two weeks when they were compelled to face problems and compose difficulties without Jesus. They learned to differ, to debate, to contend, to pray, and to compromise, and throughout it all to remain sympathetic with the other person's viewpoint and to maintain at least some degree of tolerance for his honest opinions.

On the afternoon of their final discussion of financial questions, Jesus returned, heard of their deliberations, listened to their decisions, and said, "These, then, are your conclusions, and I shall help you each to carry out the spirit of your united decisions."

Two months and a half from this time John was executed, and throughout this period the apostles of John remained with Jesus and the twelve. They all worked together and baptized believers during this season of labor in the cities of the Decapolis. The Gilboa camp was broken up on November 2, A.D. 27.

Throughout the months of November and December, Jesus and the twenty-four worked quietly in the Greek cities of the Decapolis, chiefly in Scythopolis, Gerasa, Abila, and Gadara. This was really the end of that preliminary period of taking over John's work and organization. Always does the socialized religion of a new revelation pay the price of compromise with the established forms and usages of the preceding religion that it seeks to salvage. Baptism was the price which the followers of Jesus paid in order to carry with them, as a socialized religious group, the followers of John the Baptist. John's followers, in joining Jesus' followers, gave up just about everything except water baptism.

Jesus did little public teaching on this mission to the cities of the Decapolis. He spent considerable time teaching the twenty-four and had many special sessions with John's twelve apostles. In time they became more understanding as to why Jesus did not go to visit John in prison, and why he made no effort to secure his release. But they never could understand why Jesus did no marvelous works, why he refused to produce outward signs of his divine authority. Before coming to the Gilboa camp, they had believed in Jesus mostly because of John's testimony, but soon they were beginning to believe as a result of their own contact with the Master and his teachings.

For these two months the group worked most of the time in pairs, one of Jesus' apostles going out with one of John's. The apostle of John baptized, the apostle of Jesus instructed, while they both preached the gospel of the kingdom as they understood it. And they won many souls among these gentiles and apostate Jews.

Abner, the chief of John's apostles, became a devout believer in Jesus and was later on made the head of a group of seventy teachers whom the Master commissioned to preach the gospel.

The latter part of December they all went over near the Jordan, close by Pella, where they again began to teach and preach. Both Jews and gentiles came to this camp to hear the gospel. It was while Jesus was teaching the multitude one afternoon that some of John's special friends brought the Master the last message that he ever had from the Baptist.

John had now been in prison a year and a half, and most of this time Jesus had labored very quietly; so it was not strange that John should be led to wonder about the kingdom. John's friends interrupted Jesus' teaching to say to him, "John the Baptist has sent us to ask; are you truly the Deliverer, or shall we look for another?"

Jesus paused to say to John's friends, "Go back and tell John that he is not forgotten. Tell him what you have seen and heard, that the poor have good tidings preached to them." And when Jesus had spoken further to the messengers of John, he turned again to the multitude and said, "Do not think that John doubts the gospel of the kingdom. He makes inquiry only to assure his disciples who are also my disciples. John is no weakling. Let me ask you who heard John preach before Herod put him in prison, what did you behold in John; a reed shaken with the wind? A man of changeable moods and clothed in soft raiment? As a rule they who are gorgeously appareled and who live delicately are in kings' courts and in the mansions of the rich. But what did you see when you beheld John? A prophet? Yes, I say to you, and much more than a prophet. Of John it was written: 'Behold, I send my messenger before your face; he shall prepare the way before you.'

"Verily, verily, I say to you, among those born of women there has not arisen a greater than John the Baptist; yet he who is but small in the kingdom of heaven is greater because he has been born of the spirit and knows that he has become a son of God."

Many who heard Jesus that day submitted themselves to John's baptism, thereby publicly professing entrance into the kingdom. And the apostles of John were firmly knit to Jesus from that day forward. This occurrence marked the real union of John's and Jesus' followers.

After the messengers had conversed with Abner, they departed for Machaerus to tell all this to John. He was greatly comforted, and his faith was strengthened by the words of Jesus and the message of Abner.

On this afternoon Jesus continued to teach, saying: "But to what shall I liken this generation? Many of you will receive neither John's message nor my teaching. You are like the children playing in the market place who call to their fellows and say, 'We piped for you and you did not dance; we wailed and you did not mourn.' And so with some of you. John came neither eating nor drinking, and they said he had a devil. The Son of Man comes eating and drinking, and these same people say, 'Behold, a gluttonous man and a partaker of wine, a friend of publicans and sinners!' Truly, wisdom is justified by her children.

"It would appear that the Father in heaven has hidden some of these truths from the wise and haughty, while he has revealed them to babes. But the Father does all things well; the Father reveals himself to the universe by the methods of His own choosing. Come, therefore, all you who labor and are heavy laden, and you shall find rest for your souls. Take upon you the divine yoke, and you will experience the peace of God, which passes all understanding."

John the Baptist was executed by order of Herod Antipas on the evening of January 10, A.D. 28. The next day a few of John's disciples who had gone to Machaerus heard of his execution and, going to Herod, made request for his body, which they put in a tomb, later giving it burial at Sebaste, the home of Abner. The following day, January 12, they started north to the camp of John's and Jesus' apostles near Pella, and they told Jesus about the death of John. When Jesus heard their report, he dismissed the multitude and, calling the twenty-four together, said, "John has left this world. Herod has beheaded him. Tonight go into joint council and arrange your affairs accordingly. There shall be delay no longer. The hour has come to proclaim the kingdom openly and with power. Tomorrow we go into Galilee."

Accordingly, early on the morning of January 13, A.D. 28, Jesus and the apostles, accompanied by some twenty-five disciples, made their way to Capernaum and lodged that night in Zebedee's house.

# FOUR EVENTFUL DAYS AT CAPERNAUM

JESUS AND the apostles arrived in Capernaum the evening of Tuesday, January 13. As usual, they made their headquarters at the home of Zebedee in Bethsaida. Now that John the Baptist had been sent to his death, Jesus prepared to launch out in the first open and public preaching tour of Galilee. The news that Jesus had returned rapidly spread throughout the city, and early the next day, Mary the mother of Jesus hastened away, going over to Nazareth to visit her son Joseph.

Wednesday, Thursday, and Friday Jesus spent at the Zebedee house instructing his apostles preparatory to their first extensive public preaching tour. He also received and taught many earnest inquirers, both singly and in groups. Through Andrew, he arranged to speak in the synagogue on the coming Sabbath day.

Late on Friday evening Jesus' baby sister, Ruth, secretly paid him a visit. They spent almost an hour together in a boat anchored a short distance from the shore. No human being, save John Zebedee, ever knew of this visit, and he was admonished to tell no man. Ruth was the only member of Jesus' family who consistently and unwaveringly believed in the divinity of his earth mission from the times of her earliest spiritual consciousness right on down through his eventful ministry, death, resurrection, and ascension; and she finally passed on to the worlds beyond never having doubted the supernatural character of her father-brother's mission in the flesh. Baby Ruth was the chief comfort of Jesus, as regards his earth family, throughout the trying ordeal of his trial, rejection, and crucifixion.

On Friday morning of this same week, when Jesus was teaching by the seaside, the people crowded him so near the water's edge that he signaled to some fishermen occupying a near-by boat to come to his rescue. Entering the boat, he continued to teach the assembled multitude for more than two hours. This boat was named "Simon"; it was the former fishing vessel of Simon Peter and had been built by Jesus' own hands. On this particular morning the boat was being used by David Zebedee and two associates, who had just come in near shore from a fruitless night of fishing on the lake. They were cleaning and mending their nets when Jesus requested them to come to his assistance.

After Jesus had finished teaching the people, he said to David, "As you were delayed by coming to my help, now let me work with you. Let us go fishing; put out into yonder deep and let down your nets for a draught."

But Simon, one of David's assistants, answered, "Master, it is useless. We toiled all night and took nothing; however, at your bidding we will put out and let down the nets." And Simon consented to follow Jesus' directions because of a gesture made by his master, David. When they had proceeded to the place designated by Jesus, they let down their nets and enclosed such a multitude of fish that they feared the nets would break, so much so that they signaled to their associates on the shore to come to their assistance.

When they had filled all three boats with fish, almost to sinking, this Simon fell down at Jesus' knees, saying, "Depart from me, Master, for I am a sinful man." Simon and all who were concerned in this episode were amazed at the draught of fishes. From that day David Zebedee, this Simon, and their associates forsook their nets and followed Jesus.

But this was in no sense a miraculous draught of fishes. Jesus was a close student of nature; he was an experienced fisherman and knew the habits of the fish in the Sea of Galilee. On this occasion he merely directed these men to the place where the fish were usually to be found at this time of day. But Jesus' followers always regarded this as a miracle.

The next Sabbath, at the afternoon service in the synagogue, Jesus preached his sermon on "The Will of the Father in Heaven." In the morning Simon Peter had preached on "The Kingdom." At the Thursday evening meeting of the synagogue Andrew had taught, his subject being "The New Way." At this particular time more people believed in Jesus in Capernaum than in any other one city on earth.

As Jesus taught in the synagogue this Sabbath afternoon, according to custom he took the first text from the law, reading from the Book of Exodus: "And you shall serve the Lord, your God, and He shall bless your bread and your water, and all sickness shall be taken away from you."

He chose the second text from the Prophets, reading from Isaiah: "Arise and shine, for your light has come, and the glory of the Lord has risen upon you. Darkness may cover the earth and gross darkness the people, but the spirit of the Lord shall arise upon you, and the divine glory shall be seen with you. Even the gentiles shall come to this light, and many great minds shall surrender to the brightness of this light."

shall come to this light, and many great minds shall surrender to the brightness of this light."

This sermon was an effort on Jesus' part to make clear the fact that religion is a *personal experience.* Among other things, the Master said:

"You well know that, while a kindhearted father loves his family as a whole, he so regards them as a group because of his strong affection for each individual member of that family. No longer must you approach the Father in heaven as a child of Israel but as a *child of God.* As a group, you are indeed the children of Israel, but as individuals, each one of you is a child of God. I have come, not to reveal the Father to the children of Israel, but rather to bring this knowledge of God and the revelation of His love and mercy to the individual believer as a genuine personal experience. The prophets have all taught you that Yahweh cares for his people, that God loves Israel. But I have come among you to proclaim a greater truth, one which many of the later prophets also grasped, that God loves *you* - every one of you - as individuals. All these generations have you had a national or racial religion; now have I come to give you a personal religion.

"But even this is not a new idea. Many of the spiritually minded among you have known this truth, inasmuch as some of the prophets have so instructed you. Have you not read in the Scriptures where the Prophet Jeremiah says, 'In those days they shall no more say, the fathers have eaten sour grapes and the children's teeth are set on edge. Every man shall die for his own iniquity; every man who eats sour grapes, his teeth shall be set on edge. Behold, the days shall come when I will make a new covenant with my people, not according to the covenant which I made with their fathers when I brought them out of the land of Egypt, but according to the new way. I will even write my law in their hearts. I will be their God, and they shall be my people. In that day they shall not say, one man to his neighbor, do you know the Lord? Nay! For they shall all know me personally, from the least to the greatest.'

"Have you not read these promises? Do you not believe the Scriptures? Do you not understand that the prophet's words are fulfilled in what you behold this very day? And did not Jeremiah exhort you to make religion an affair of the heart, to relate yourselves to God as individuals? Did not the prophet tell you that the God of heaven would search your individual hearts? And were you not warned that the natural human heart is deceitful above all things and oftentimes desperately wicked?

"Have you not read also where Ezekiel taught even your fathers that religion must become a reality in your individual experiences? No more shall you use the proverb which says, 'The fathers have eaten sour grapes and the children's teeth are set on edge.' 'As I live,' says the Lord God, 'behold all souls are mine; as the soul of the father, so also the soul of the son. Only the soul that sins shall die.' And then Ezekiel foresaw even this day when he spoke in behalf of God, saying, 'A new heart also will I give you, and a new spirit will I put within you.'

"No more should you fear that God will punish a nation for the sin of an individual; neither will the Father in heaven punish one of his believing children for the sins of a nation, albeit the individual member of any family must often suffer the material consequences of family mistakes and group transgressions. Do you not realize that the hope of a better nation - or a better world - is bound up in the progress and enlightenment of the individual?"

Then the Master portrayed that the Father in heaven, after man discerns this spiritual freedom, wills that His children on earth should begin that eternal ascent of the Paradise career which consists in the creature's conscious response to the divine urge of the indwelling spirit to find the Creator, to know God and to seek to become like Him.

The apostles were greatly helped by this sermon. All of them realized more fully that the gospel of the kingdom is a message directed to the individual, not to the nation.

Even though the people of Capernaum were familiar with Jesus' teaching, they were astonished at his sermon on this Sabbath day. He taught, indeed, as one having authority and not as the scribes.

Just as Jesus finished speaking, a young man in the congregation who had been much agitated by his words was seized with a violent epileptic attack and loudly cried out. At the end of the seizure, when recovering consciousness, he spoke in a dreamy state, saying, "What have we to do with you, Jesus of Nazareth? You are the holy one of God; have you come to destroy us?"

Jesus bade the people be quiet and, taking the young man by the hand, said, "Come out of it" - and he was immediately awakened.

This young man was not possessed of an unclean spirit or demon; he was a victim of ordinary epilepsy. But he had been taught that his affliction was due to possession by an evil spirit. He believed this teaching and behaved accordingly in all that he thought or said concerning his ailment. The people all believed that such phenomena were directly caused by the presence of unclean spirits. Accordingly they believed that Jesus had cast a demon out of this man. But Jesus did not at that time cure his epilepsy. Not until later on that day, after sundown, was this man really healed. Long after the day of Pentecost the Apostle John, who was the last to write of Jesus' doings, avoided all reference to these so-called acts of "casting out devils," and this he did in view of the fact that such cases of demon possession never occurred after Pentecost.

As a result of this commonplace incident the report was rapidly spread through Capernaum that Jesus had cast a demon out of a man and miraculously healed him in the synagogue at the conclusion of his afternoon sermon. The Sabbath was just the time for the rapid and effective spreading of such a startling rumor. This report was also carried to all the smaller settlements around Capernaum, and many of the people believed it.

The cooking and the housework at the large Zebedee home, where Jesus and the twelve made their headquarters, was for the most part done by Simon Peter's wife and her mother. Peter's home was near that of Zebedee; and Jesus and his friends stopped there on the way from the synagogue because Peter's wife's mother had for several days been sick with chills and fever. Now it chanced that, at about the time Jesus stood over this sick woman, holding her hand, smoothing her brow, and speaking words of comfort and encouragement, the fever left her. Jesus had not yet had time to explain to his apostles that no miracle had been wrought at the synagogue; and with this incident so fresh and vivid in their minds, and recalling the water and the wine at Cana, they seized upon this coincidence as another miracle, and some of them rushed out to spread the news abroad throughout the city.

Amatha, Peter's mother-in-law, was suffering from malarial fever. She was not miraculously healed by Jesus at this time. Not until several hours later, after sundown, was her cure effected in connection with the extraordinary event that occurred in the front yard of the Zebedee home.

And these cases are typical of the manner in which a wonder-seeking generation and a miracle-minded people unfailingly seized upon all such coincidences as the pretext for proclaiming that another miracle had been wrought by Jesus.

By the time Jesus and his apostles had made ready to partake of their evening meal near the end of this eventful Sabbath day, all Capernaum and its environs were agog over these reputed miracles of healing; and all who were sick or afflicted began preparations to go to Jesus or to have themselves carried there by their friends just as soon as the sun went down. According to Jewish teaching it was not permissible even to go in quest of health during the sacred hours of the Sabbath.

Therefore, as soon as the sun sank beneath the horizon, scores of afflicted men, women, and children began to make their way toward the Zebedee home in Bethsaida. One man started out with his paralyzed daughter just as soon as the sun sank behind his neighbor's house.

The whole day's events had set the stage for this extraordinary sundown scene. Even the text Jesus had used for his afternoon sermon had intimated that sickness should be banished; and he had spoken with such unprecedented power and authority! His message was so compelling! While he made no appeal to human authority, he did speak directly to the consciences and souls of men. Though he did not resort to logic, legal quibbles, or clever sayings, he did make a powerful, direct, clear, and personal appeal to the hearts of his hearers.

That Sabbath was a great day in the earth life of Jesus, yes, in the life of a universe. To all local universe intents and purposes the little Jewish city of Capernaum was the real capital of Nebadon. The handful of Jews in the Capernaum synagogue were not the only beings to hear that momentous closing statement of Jesus' sermon: "Hate is the shadow of fear; revenge the mask of cowardice." Neither could his hearers forget his blessed words, declaring, "Man is the son of God, not a child of the devil."

Soon after the setting of the sun, as Jesus and the apostles still lingered about the supper table, Peter's wife heard voices in the front yard and, on going to the door, saw a large company of sick folks assembling, and that the road from Capernaum was crowded by those who were on their way to seek healing at Jesus' hands. On seeing this sight, she went at once and informed her husband, who told Jesus.

When the Master stepped out of the front entrance of Zebedee's house, his eyes met an array of stricken and afflicted humanity. He gazed upon almost one thousand sick and ailing human beings; at least that was the number of persons gathered together before him. Not all present were afflicted; some had come assisting their loved ones in this effort to secure healing.

The sight of these afflicted mortals, men, women, and children, suffering in large measure as a result of the mistakes and misdeeds of his own trusted Sons of universe administration, peculiarly touched the human heart of Jesus and challenged the divine mercy of this benevolent Creator Son. But Jesus well knew he could never build an enduring spiritual movement upon the foundation of purely material wonders. It had been his consistent policy to refrain from exhibiting his creator prerogatives. Not since Cana had the supernatural or miraculous attended his teaching; still, this afflicted multitude touched his sympathetic heart and mightily appealed to his understanding affection.

A voice from the front yard exclaimed, "Master, speak the word, restore our health, heal our diseases, and save our souls."

No sooner had these words been uttered than a vast retinue of seraphim, physical controllers, Life Carriers, and midwayers, such as always attended this incarnated Creator of a universe, made themselves ready to act with creative power should their Sovereign give the signal. This was one of those moments in the earth career of Jesus in which divine wisdom and human compassion were so interlocked in the judgment of the Son of Man that he sought refuge in appeal to his Father's will.

When Peter implored the Master to heed their cry for help, Jesus, looking down upon the afflicted throng, answered, "I have come into the world to reveal the Father and establish his kingdom. For this purpose have I lived my life to this hour. If, therefore, it should be the will of Him who sent me and not inconsistent with my dedication to the proclamation of the gospel of the kingdom of heaven, I would desire to see my children made whole, and..." but the further words of Jesus were lost in the tumult.

Jesus had passed the responsibility of this healing decision to the ruling of his Father. Evidently the Father's will interposed no objection, for the words of the Master had scarcely been uttered when the assembly of celestial personalities serving under the command of Jesus' Personalized Thought Adjuster was mightily astir. The vast retinue descended into the midst of this motley throng of afflicted mortals, and in a moment of time 683 men, women, and children were made whole, were perfectly healed of all their physical diseases and other material disorders. Such a scene was never witnessed on earth before that day, nor since. And for those of us who were present to behold this creative wave of healing, it was indeed a thrilling spectacle.

But of all the beings who were astonished at this sudden and unexpected outbreak of supernatural healing, Jesus was the most surprised. In a moment when his human interests and sympathies were focused upon the scene of suffering and affliction there spread out before him, he neglected to bear in his human mind the admonitory warnings of his Personalized Adjuster regarding the impossibility of limiting the time element of the creator prerogatives of a Creator Son under certain conditions and in certain circumstances. Jesus desired to see these suffering mortals made whole if his Father's will would not thereby be violated. The Personalized Adjuster of Jesus instantly ruled that such an act of creative energy at that time would not transgress the will of the Paradise Father, and by such a decision - in view of Jesus' preceding expression of healing desire - the creative act *was*. What a *Creator Son* desires and his Father *wills* IS. Not in all of Jesus' subsequent earth life did another such en masse physical healing of mortals take place.

As might have been expected, the fame of this sundown healing at Bethsaida in Capernaum spread throughout all Galilee and Judea and to the regions beyond. Once more were the fears of Herod aroused, and he sent watchers to report on the work and teachings of Jesus and to ascertain if he was the former carpenter of Nazareth or John the Baptist risen from the dead.

Chiefly because of this unintended demonstration of physical healing, henceforth, throughout the remainder of his earth career, Jesus became as much a physician as a preacher. True, he continued his teaching, but his personal work consisted mostly in ministering to the sick and the distressed, while his apostles did the work of public preaching and baptizing believers.

But the majority of those who were recipients of supernatural or creative physical healing at this sundown demonstration of divine energy were not permanently spiritually benefited by this extraordinary manifestation of mercy. A small number were truly edified by this physical ministry, but the spiritual kingdom was not advanced in the hearts of men by this amazing eruption of timeless creative healing.

The healing wonders which every now and then attended Jesus' mission on earth were not a part of his plan of proclaiming the kingdom. They were incidentally inherent in having on earth a divine being of well-nigh unlimited creator prerogatives in association with an unprecedented combination of divine mercy and human sympathy. But such so-called miracles gave Jesus much trouble in that they provided prejudice-raising publicity and afforded much unsought notoriety.

Throughout the evening following this great outburst of healing, the rejoicing and happy throng overran Zebedee's home, and the apostles of Jesus were keyed up to the highest pitch of emotional enthusiasm. From a human standpoint, this was probably the greatest day of all the great days of their association with Jesus. At no time before or after did their hopes surge to such heights of confident expectation. Jesus had told them only a few days before, and when they were yet within the borders of Samaria, that the hour had come when the kingdom was to be proclaimed in *power*, and now their eyes had seen what they supposed was the fulfillment of that promise. They were thrilled by the vision of what was to come if this amazing manifestation of healing power was just the beginning. Their lingering doubts of Jesus' divinity were banished. They were literally intoxicated with the ecstasy of their bewildered enchantment.

But when they sought for Jesus, they could not find him. The Master was much perturbed by what had happened. These men, women, and children who had been healed of diverse diseases lingered late into the evening, hoping for Jesus' return that they might thank him. The apostles could not understand the Master's conduct as the hours passed and he remained in seclusion; their joy would have been full and perfect but for his continued absence. When Jesus did return to their midst, the hour was late, and practically all of the beneficiaries of the healing episode had gone to their homes. Jesus refused the congratulations and adoration of the twelve and the others who had lingered to greet him, only saying, "Rejoice not that my Father is powerful to heal the body, but rather that He is mighty to save the soul. Let us go to our rest, for tomorrow we must be about the Father's business."

And again did twelve disappointed, perplexed, and heart-sorrowing men go to their rest; few of them, except the twins, slept much that night. No sooner would the Master do something to cheer the souls and gladden the hearts of his apostles, than he seemed immediately to dash their hopes in pieces and utterly to demolish the foundations of their courage and enthusiasm. As these bewildered fishermen looked into each other's eyes, there was but one thought: "We cannot understand him. What does all this mean?"

★ ★ ★

Neither did Jesus sleep much that Saturday night. He realized that the world was filled with physical distress and overrun with material difficulties, and he contemplated the great danger of being compelled to devote so much of his time to the care of the sick and afflicted that his mission of establishing the spiritual kingdom in the hearts of men would be interfered with or at least subordinated to the ministry of things physical. Because of these and similar thoughts which occupied the mortal mind of Jesus during the night, he arose that Sunday morning long before daybreak and went all alone to one of his favorite places for communion with the Father. The theme of Jesus' prayer on this early morning was for wisdom and judgment that he might not allow his human sympathy, joined with his divine mercy, to make such an appeal to him in the presence of mortal suffering that all of his time would be occupied with physical ministry to the neglect of the spiritual. Though he did not wish altogether to avoid ministering to the sick, he knew that he must also do the more important work of spiritual teaching and religious training.

Jesus went out in the hills to pray so many times because there were no private rooms suitable for his personal devotions.

Peter could not sleep that night; so, very early, shortly after Jesus had gone out to pray, he aroused James and John, and the three went to find their Master. After more than an hour's search they found Jesus and besought him to tell them the reason for his strange conduct. They desired to know why he appeared to be troubled by the mighty outpouring of the spirit of healing when all the people were overjoyed and his apostles so much rejoiced.

For more than four hours Jesus endeavored to explain to these three apostles what had happened. He taught them about what had transpired and explained the dangers of such manifestations. Jesus confided to them the reason for his coming forth to pray. He sought to make plain to his personal associates the real reasons why the kingdom of the Father could not be built upon wonder-working and physical healing. But they could not comprehend his teaching.

Meanwhile, early Sunday morning, other crowds of afflicted souls and many curiosity seekers began to gather about the house of Zebedee. They clamored to see Jesus. Andrew and the apostles were so perplexed that, while Simon Zelotes talked to the assembly, Andrew, with several of his associates, went to find Jesus. When Andrew had located Jesus in company with the three, he said, "Master, why do you leave us alone with the multitude? Behold, all men seek you; never before have so many sought after your teaching. Even now the house is surrounded by those who have come from near and far because of your mighty works. Will you not return with us to minister to them?"

When Jesus heard this, he answered, "Andrew, have I not taught you and these others that my mission on earth is the revelation of the Father, and my message the proclamation of the kingdom of heaven? How is it, then, that you would have me turn aside from my work for the gratification of the curious and for the satisfaction of those who seek for signs and wonders? Have we not been among these people all these months, and have they flocked in multitudes to hear the good news of the kingdom? Why have they now come to besiege us? Is it not because of the healing of their physical bodies rather than as a result of the reception of spiritual truth for the salvation of their souls? When men are attracted to us because of extraordinary manifestations, many of them come seeking not for truth and salvation but rather in quest of healing for their physical ailments and to secure deliverance from their material difficulties.

"All this time I have been in Capernaum, and both in the synagogue and by the seaside have I proclaimed the good news of the kingdom to all who had ears to hear and hearts to receive the truth. It is not the will of my Father that I should return with you to cater to these curious ones and to become occupied with the ministry of things physical to the exclusion of the spiritual. I have ordained you to preach the gospel and minister to the sick, but I must not become engrossed in healing to the exclusion of my teaching. No, Andrew, I will not return with you. Go and tell the people to believe in that which we have taught them and to rejoice in the liberty of the sons of God, and make ready for our departure for the other cities of Galilee, where the way has already been prepared for the preaching of the good tidings of the kingdom. It was for this purpose that I came forth from the Father. Go, then, and prepare for our immediate departure while I here await your return."

When Jesus had spoken, Andrew and his fellow apostles sorrowfully made their way back to Zebedee's house, dismissed the assembled multitude, and quickly made ready for the journey as Jesus had directed. And so, on the afternoon of Sunday, January 18, A.D. 28, Jesus and the apostles started out upon their first really public and open preaching tour of the cities of Galilee. On this first tour they preached the gospel of the kingdom in many cities, but they did not visit Nazareth.

That Sunday afternoon, shortly after Jesus and his apostles had left for Rimmon, his brothers James and Jude came to see him, calling at Zebedee's house. About noon of that day Jude had sought out his brother James and insisted that they go to Jesus. By the time James consented to go with Jude, Jesus had already departed.

The apostles were loath to leave the great interest which had been aroused at Capernaum. Peter calculated that no less than one thousand believers could have been baptized into the kingdom. Jesus listened to them patiently, but he would not consent to return. Silence prevailed for a season, and then Thomas addressed his fellow apostles, saying, "Let's go! The Master has spoken. No matter if we cannot fully comprehend the mysteries of the kingdom of heaven, of one thing we are certain: We follow a teacher who seeks no glory for himself." And reluctantly they went forth to preach the good tidings in the cities of Galilee.

# FIRST PREACHING TOUR OF GALILEE

HE FIRST public preaching tour of Galilee began on Sunday, January 18, A.D. 28, and continued for about two months, ending with the return to Capernaum on March 17. On this tour Jesus and the twelve apostles, assisted by the former apostles of John, preached the gospel and baptized believers in Rimmon, Jotapata, Ramah, Zebulun, Iron, Gischala, Chorazin, Madon, Cana, Nain, and Endor. In these cities they tarried and taught, while in many other smaller towns they proclaimed the gospel of the kingdom as they passed through.

This was the first time Jesus permitted his associates to preach without restraint. On this tour he cautioned them on only three occasions; he admonished them to remain away from Nazareth and to be discreet when passing through Capernaum and Tiberias. It was a source of great satisfaction to the apostles at last to feel they were at liberty to preach and teach without restriction, and they threw themselves into the work of preaching the gospel, ministering to the sick, and baptizing believers, with great earnestness and joy.

The small city of Rimmon had once been dedicated to the worship of a Babylonian god of the air, Ramman. Many of the earlier Babylonian and later Zoroastrian teachings were still embraced in the beliefs of the Rimmonites; therefore did Jesus and the twenty-four devote much of their time to the task of making plain the difference between these older beliefs and the new gospel of the kingdom. Peter here preached one of the great sermons of his early career on "Aaron and the Golden Calf."

Although many of the citizens of Rimmon became believers in Jesus' teachings, they made great trouble for their brethren in later years. It is difficult to convert nature worshipers to the full fellowship of the adoration of a spiritual ideal during the short space of a single lifetime.

Many of the better of the Babylonian and Persian ideas of light and darkness, good and evil, time and eternity, were later incorporated in the doctrines of so-called Christianity, and their inclusion rendered the Christian teachings more immediately acceptable to the peoples of the Near East. In like manner, the inclusion of many of Plato's theories of the ideal spirit or invisible patterns of all things visible and material, as later adapted by Philo to the Hebrew theology, made Paul's Christian teachings more easy of acceptance by the western Greeks.

It was at Rimmon that Todan first heard the gospel of the kingdom, and he later carried this message into Mesopotamia and far beyond. He was among the first to preach the good news to those who dwelt beyond the Euphrates.

While the common people of Jotapata heard Jesus and his apostles gladly and many accepted the gospel of the kingdom, it was the discourse of Jesus to the twenty-four on the second evening of their sojourn in this small town that distinguishes the Jotapata mission. Nathaniel was confused in his mind about the Master's teachings concerning prayer, thanksgiving, and worship, and in response to his question Jesus spoke at great length in further explanation of his teaching. Summarized in modern phraseology, this discourse may be presented as emphasizing the following points:

1. The conscious and persistent regard for iniquity in the heart of man gradually destroys the prayer connection of the human soul with the spirit circuits of communication between man and his Maker. Naturally God hears the petition of his child, but when the human heart deliberately and persistently harbors the concepts of iniquity, there gradually ensues the loss of personal communion between the earth child and his heavenly Father.

2. That prayer which is inconsistent with the known and established laws of God is an abomination to the Paradise Deities. If man will not listen to the Gods as they speak to their creation in the laws of spirit, mind, and matter, the very act of such deliberate and conscious disdain by the creature turns the ears of spirit personalities away from hearing the personal petitions of such lawless and disobedient mortals. Jesus quoted to his apostles from the Prophet Zechariah: "But they refused to hearken and pulled away the shoulder and stopped their ears that they should not hear. Yes, they made their hearts adamant like a stone, lest they should hear my law and the words which I sent by my spirit through the prophets; therefore did the results of their evil thinking come as a great wrath upon their guilty heads. And so it came to pass that they cried for mercy, but there was no ear open to hear." And then Jesus quoted the proverb of

the wise man who said: "He who turns away his ear from hearing the divine law, even his prayer shall be an abomination."

3. By opening the human end of the channel of the God-man communication, mortals make immediately available the ever-flowing stream of divine ministry to the creatures of the worlds. When man hears God's spirit speak within the human heart, inherent in such an experience is the fact that God simultaneously hears that man's prayer. Even the forgiveness of sin operates in this same unerring fashion. The Father in heaven has forgiven you even before you have thought to ask Him, but such forgiveness is not available in your personal religious experience until such a time as you forgive your fellow men. God's forgiveness in *fact* is not conditioned upon your forgiving your fellows, but in *experience* it is exactly so conditioned. And this fact of the synchrony of divine and human forgiveness was thus recognized and linked together in the prayer that Jesus taught the apostles.

4. There is a basic law of justice in the universe which mercy is powerless to circumvent. The unselfish glories of Paradise are not possible of reception by a thoroughly selfish creature of the realms of time and space. Even the infinite love of God cannot force the salvation of eternal survival upon any mortal creature who does not choose to survive. Mercy has great latitude of bestowal, but, after all, there are mandates of justice which even love combined with mercy cannot effectively abrogate. Again Jesus quoted from the Hebrew scriptures: "I have called and you refused to hear; I stretched out my hand, but no man regarded. You have set at naught all my counsel, and you have rejected my reproof, and because of this rebellious attitude it becomes inevitable that you shall call upon me and fail to receive an answer. Having rejected the way of life, you may seek me diligently in your times of suffering, but you will not find me."

5. They who would receive mercy must show mercy; judge not that you be not judged. With the spirit with which you judge others you also shall be judged. Mercy does not wholly abrogate universe fairness. In the end it will prove true: "Whoso stops his ears to the cry of the poor, he also shall some day cry for help, and no one will hear him." The sincerity of any prayer is the assurance of its being heard; the spiritual wisdom and universe consistency of any petition is the determiner of the time, manner, and degree of the answer. A wise father does not *literally* answer the foolish prayers of his ignorant and inexperienced children, albeit the children may derive much pleasure and real soul satisfaction from the making of such absurd petitions.

6. When you have become wholly dedicated to the doing of the will of the Father in heaven, the answer to all your petitions will be forthcoming be-

cause your prayers will be in full accordance with the Father's will, and the Father's will is ever manifest throughout his vast universe. What the true son or daughter desires and the infinite Father wills IS. Such a prayer cannot remain unanswered, and no other sort of petition can possibly be fully answered.

7. The cry of the righteous is the faith act of the child of God which opens the door of the Father's storehouse of goodness, truth, and mercy, and these good gifts have long been in waiting for the faith-child's approach and personal appropriation. Prayer does not change the divine attitude toward man, but it does change man's attitude toward the changeless Father. The *motive* of the prayer gives it right of way to the divine ear, not the social, economic, or outward religious status of the one who prays.

8. Prayer may not be employed to avoid the delays of time or to transcend the handicaps of space. Prayer is not designed as a technique for aggrandizing self or for gaining unfair advantage over one's fellows. A thoroughly selfish soul cannot pray in the true sense of the word. Said Jesus: "Let your supreme delight be in the character of God, and He shall surely give you the sincere desires of your heart." "Commit your way to the Lord; trust in Him, and He will act." "For the Lord hears the cry of the needy, and He will regard the prayer of the destitute."

9. "I have come forth from the Father; if, therefore, you are ever in doubt as to what you would ask of the Father, ask in my name, and I will present your petition in accordance with your real needs and desires and in accordance with my Father's will." Guard against the great danger of becoming self-centered in your prayers. Avoid praying much for yourself; pray more for the spiritual progress of your brethren. Avoid materialistic praying; pray in the spirit and for the abundance of the gifts of the spirit.

10. When you pray for the sick and afflicted, do not expect that your petitions will take the place of loving and intelligent ministry to the necessities of these afflicted ones. Pray for the welfare of your families, friends, and fellows, but especially pray for those who curse you, and make loving petitions for those who persecute you. "But when to pray, I will not say. Only the spirit that dwells within you may move you to the utterance of those petitions which are expressive of your inner relationship with the Father of spirits."

11. Many resort to prayer only when in trouble. Such a practice is thoughtless and misleading. True, you do well to pray when harassed, but you should also be mindful to speak as a son to your Father even when all goes well with your soul. Let your real petitions always be in secret. Do not let men hear your personal prayers. Prayers of thanksgiving

are appropriate for groups of worshipers, but the prayer of the soul is a personal matter. There is but one form of prayer which is appropriate for all God's children, and that is: "Nevertheless, your will be done."

12. All believers in this gospel should pray sincerely for the extension of the kingdom of heaven. Of all the prayers of the Hebrew scriptures he commented most approvingly on the petition of the Psalmist: "Create in me a clean heart, O God, and renew a right spirit within me. Purge me from secret sins and keep back your servant from presumptuous transgression." Jesus commented at great length on the relation of prayer to careless and offending speech, quoting: "Set a watch, O Lord, before my mouth; keep the door of my lips." "The human tongue," said Jesus, "is a member which few men can tame, but the spirit within can transform this unruly member into a kindly voice of tolerance and an inspiring minister of mercy."

13. Jesus taught that the prayer for divine guidance over the pathway of earthly life was next in importance to the petition for a knowledge of the Father's will. In reality this means a prayer for divine wisdom. Jesus never taught that human knowledge and special skill could be gained by prayer. But he did teach that prayer is a factor in the enlargement of one's capacity to receive the presence of the divine spirit. When Jesus taught his associates to pray in the spirit and in truth, he explained that he referred to praying sincerely and in accordance with one's enlightenment, to praying wholeheartedly and intelligently, earnestly and steadfastly.

14. Jesus warned his followers against thinking that their prayers would be rendered more efficacious by ornate repetitions, eloquent phraseology, fasting, penance, or sacrifices. But he did exhort his believers to employ prayer as a means of leading up through thanksgiving to true worship. Jesus deplored that so little of the spirit of thanksgiving was to be found in the prayers and worship of his followers. He quoted from the Scriptures on this occasion, saying: "It is a good thing to give thanks to the Lord and to sing praises to the name of the Most High, to acknowledge His loving-kindness every morning and His faithfulness every night, for God has made me glad through His work. In everything I will give thanks according to the will of God."

15. And then Jesus said, "Be not constantly overanxious about your common needs. Be not apprehensive concerning the problems of your earthly existence, but in all these things by prayer and supplication, with the spirit of sincere thanksgiving, let your needs be spread out before your Father who is in heaven." Then he quoted from the Scriptures: "I will praise the name of God with a song and will magnify Him with

thanksgiving. And this will please the Lord better than the sacrifice of an ox or bullock with horns and hoofs."

16. Jesus taught his followers that, when they had made their prayers to the Father, they should remain for a time in silent receptivity to afford the indwelling spirit the better opportunity to speak to the listening soul. The spirit of the Father speaks best to man when the human mind is in an attitude of true worship. We worship God by the aid of the Father's indwelling spirit and by the illumination of the human mind through the ministry of truth. Worship, taught Jesus, makes one increasingly like the being who is worshiped. Worship is a transforming experience whereby the finite gradually approaches and ultimately attains the presence of the Infinite.

And many other truths did Jesus tell his apostles about man's communion with God, but not many of them could fully encompass his teaching.

At Ramah Jesus had the memorable discussion with the aged Greek philosopher who taught that science and philosophy were sufficient to satisfy the needs of human experience. Jesus listened with patience and sympathy to this Greek teacher, allowing the truth of many things he said but pointing out that, when he was through, he had failed in his discussion of human existence to explain "whence, why, and whither," and added: "Where you leave off, we begin. Religion is a revelation to man's soul dealing with spiritual realities which the mind alone could never discover or fully fathom. Intellectual strivings may reveal the facts of life, but the gospel of the kingdom unfolds the *truths* of being. You have discussed the material shadows of truth; will you now listen while I tell you about the eternal and spiritual realities which cast these transient time shadows of the material facts of mortal existence?"

For more than an hour Jesus taught this Greek the saving truths of the gospel of the kingdom. The old philosopher was susceptible to the Master's mode of approach, and being sincerely honest of heart, he quickly believed this gospel of salvation.

The apostles were a bit disconcerted by the open manner of Jesus' assent to many of the Greek's propositions, but Jesus afterward privately said to them, "My children, marvel not that I was tolerant of the Greek's philosophy. True and genuine inward certainty does not in the least fear outward analysis, nor does truth resent honest criticism. You should never forget that intolerance is the mask covering up the entertainment of secret doubts as to the trueness of one's belief. No man is at any time disturbed by his neighbor's attitude when he has perfect confidence in the truth of that which he wholeheartedly believes. Courage is the confidence of thoroughgoing honesty about those things which one professes to believe. Sincere men are unafraid of the critical examination of their true convictions and noble ideals."

On the second evening at Ramah, Thomas asked Jesus this question: "Master, how can a new believer in your teaching really know, really be certain, about the truth of this gospel of the kingdom?"

And Jesus said to Thomas: "Your assurance that you have entered into the kingdom family of the Father, and that you will eternally survive with the children of the kingdom, is wholly a matter of personal experience - faith in the word of truth. Spiritual assurance is the equivalent of your personal religious experience in the eternal realities of divine truth and is otherwise equal to your intelligent understanding of truth realities plus your spiritual faith and minus your honest doubts.

"The Son is naturally endowed with the life of the Father. Having been endowed with the living spirit of the Father, you are therefore sons of God. You survive your life in the material world of the flesh because you are identified with the Father's living spirit, the gift of eternal life. Many, indeed, had this life before I came forth from the Father, and many more have received this spirit because they believed my word; but I declare that, when I return to the Father, He will send His spirit into the hearts of all men.

"While you cannot observe the divine spirit at work in your minds, there is a practical method of discovering the degree to which you have yielded the control of your soul powers to the teaching and guidance of this indwelling spirit of the heavenly Father, and that is the degree of your love for your breothers and sisters. This spirit of the Father partakes of the love of the Father, and as it dominates men and women, it unfailingly leads in the directions of divine worship and loving regard for one's fellows. At first you believe that you are sons of God because my teaching has made you more conscious of the inner leadings of our Father's indwelling presence; but presently the Spirit of Truth shall be poured out upon all flesh, and it will live among men and women and teach all mortals, even as I now live among you and speak to you the words of truth. And this Spirit of Truth, speaking for the spiritual endowments of your souls, will help you to know that you are the children of God. It will unfailingly bear witness with the Father's indwelling presence, your spirit, then dwelling in all mortals as it now dwells in some, telling you that you are in reality the children of God.

"Every earth child who follows the leading of this spirit shall eventually know the will of God, and he who surrenders to the will of my Father shall abide forever. The way from the earth life to the eternal estate has not been made plain to you, but there is a way, there always has been, and I have come to make that way new and living. He who enters the kingdom has eternal life already - he shall never perish. But much of this you will the better understand when I shall have returned to the Father and you are able to view your present experiences in retrospect."

And all who heard these blessed words were greatly cheered. The Jewish teachings had been confused and uncertain regarding the survival of the righteous, and it was refreshing and inspiring for Jesus' followers to hear these very definite and positive words of assurance about the eternal survival of all true believers.

The apostles continued to preach and baptize believers, while they kept up the practice of visiting from house to house, comforting the downcast and ministering to the sick and afflicted. The apostolic organization was expanded in that each of Jesus' apostles now had one of John's as an associate; Abner was the associate of Andrew; and this plan prevailed until they went down to Jerusalem for the next Passover.

The special instruction given by Jesus during their stay at Zebulun had chiefly to do with further discussions of the mutual obligations of the kingdom and embraced teaching designed to make clear the differences between personal religious experience and the amities of social religious obligations. This was one of the few times the Master ever discussed the social aspects of religion. Throughout his entire earth life Jesus gave his followers very little instruction regarding the socialization of religion.

In Zebulun the people were of a mixed race, hardly Jew or gentile, and few of them really believed in Jesus, notwithstanding they had heard of the healing of the sick at Capernaum.

At Iron, as in many of even the smaller cities of Galilee and Judea, there was a synagogue, and during the earlier times of Jesus' ministry it was his custom to speak in these synagogues on the Sabbath day. Sometimes he would speak at the morning service, and Peter or one of the other apostles would preach at the afternoon hour. Jesus and the apostles would also often teach and preach at the weekday evening assemblies at the synagogue. Although the religious leaders at Jerusalem became increasingly antagonistic toward Jesus, they exercised no direct control over the synagogues outside of that city. It was not until later in Jesus' public ministry that they were able to create such a widespread sentiment against him as to bring about the almost universal closing of the synagogues to his teaching. At this time all the synagogues of Galilee and Judea were open to him.

Iron was the site of extensive mineral mines for those days, and since Jesus had never shared the life of the miner, he spent most of his time, while sojourning at Iron, in the mines. While the apostles visited the homes and preached in the public places, Jesus worked in the mines with these underground laborers. The fame of Jesus as a healer had spread even to this remote village, and many sick and afflicted sought help at his hands, and many were greatly benefited by his healing ministry. But in none of these cases did the Master perform a so-called miracle of healing save in that of the leper.

Late on the afternoon of the third day at Iron, as Jesus was returning from the mines, he chanced to pass through a narrow side street on his way to his lodging place. As he drew near the squalid hovel of a certain leprous man, the afflicted one, having heard of his fame as a healer, made bold to accost him as he passed his door, saying as he knelt before him, "Lord, if only you would, you could make me clean. I have heard the message of your teachers, and I would enter the kingdom if I could be made clean." And the leper spoke in this way because among the Jews lepers were forbidden even to attend the synagogue or otherwise engage in public worship. This man really believed that he could not be received into the coming kingdom unless he could find a cure for his leprosy.

And when Jesus saw him in his affliction and heard his words of clinging faith, his human heart was touched, and the divine mind was moved with compassion. As Jesus looked upon him, the man fell upon his face and worshiped. Then the Master stretched forth his hand and, touching him, said, "I will - be clean." And immediately he was healed; the leprosy no longer afflicted him.

When Jesus had lifted the man upon his feet, he charged him: "See that you tell no man about your healing but rather go quietly about your business, showing yourself to the priest and offering those sacrifices commanded by Moses in testimony of your cleansing."

But this man did not do as Jesus had instructed him. Instead, he began to publish abroad throughout the town that Jesus had cured his leprosy, and since he was known to all the village, the people could plainly see that he had been cleansed of his disease. He did not go to the priests as Jesus had admonished him. As a result of his spreading abroad the news that Jesus had healed him, the Master was so thronged by the sick that he was forced to rise early the next day and leave the village. Although Jesus did not again enter the town, he remained two days in the outskirts near the mines, continuing to instruct the believing miners further regarding the gospel of the kingdom.

This cleansing of the leper was the first so-called miracle which Jesus had intentionally and deliberately performed up to this time. And this was a case of real leprosy.

From Iron they went to Gischala, spending two days proclaiming the gospel, and then departed for Chorazin, where they spent almost a week preaching the good news; but they were unable to win many believers for the kingdom in Chorazin. In no place where Jesus had taught had he met with such a general rejection of his message. The sojourn at Chorazin was very depressing to most of the apostles, and Andrew and Abner had much difficulty in upholding the courage of their associates. And so, passing quietly through Capernaum, they went on to the village of Madon, where they fared little better. There prevailed in the minds of most of the apostles the idea that their failure to meet with success in these towns so recently visited was due to Jesus' insistence that they refrain, in their teaching and preaching, from referring to him as a healer. How they wished he would cleanse another leper or in some other manner so manifest his power as to attract the attention of the people! But the Master was unmoved by their earnest urging.

The apostolic party was greatly cheered when Jesus announced, "Tomorrow we go to Cana." They knew they would have a sympathetic hearing at Cana, for Jesus was well known there. They were doing well with their work of bringing people into the kingdom when, on the third day, there arrived in Cana a certain prominent citizen of Capernaum, Titus, who was a partial believer, and whose son was critically ill. He heard that Jesus was at Cana; so he hastened over to see him. The believers at Capernaum thought Jesus could heal any sickness.

When this nobleman had located Jesus in Cana, he besought him to hurry over to Capernaum and heal his afflicted son. While the apostles stood by in breathless expectancy, Jesus, looking at the father of the sick boy, said: "How long shall I bear with you? The power of God is in your midst, but except you see signs and behold wonders, you refuse to believe."

But the nobleman pleaded with Jesus, saying, "My Lord, I do believe, but come ere my child perishes, for when I left him he was even then at the point of death."

And when Jesus had bowed his head a moment in silent meditation, he suddenly spoke, "Return to your home; your son will live."

Titus believed the word of Jesus and hastened back to Capernaum. And as he was returning, his servants came out to meet him, saying, "Rejoice, for your son is improved; he lives." Then Titus inquired of them at what hour the boy began to mend, and when the servants answered "yesterday about the seventh hour the fever left him," the father recalled that it was about that hour when Jesus had said, "Your son will live." And Titus henceforth believed with a whole heart, and all his family also believed.

This son became a mighty minister of the kingdom and later yielded up his life with those who suffered in Rome. Though the entire household of Titus, their friends, and even the apostles regarded this episode as a miracle, it was not. At least this was not a miracle of curing physical disease. It was merely a case of preknowledge concerning the course of natural law, just such knowledge as Jesus frequently resorted to subsequent to his baptism.

Again was Jesus compelled to hasten away from Cana because of the undue attention attracted by the second episode of this sort to attend his ministry in this village. The townspeople remembered the water and the wine, and now that he was supposed to have healed the nobleman's son at so great a distance, they came to him, not only bringing the sick and afflicted but also sending messengers requesting that he heal sufferers at a distance. And when Jesus saw that the whole countryside was aroused, he said, "Let us go to Nain."

These people believed in signs; they were a wonder-seeking generation. By this time the people of central and southern Galilee had become miracle minded regarding Jesus and his personal ministry. Scores, hundreds, of honest persons suffering from purely nervous disorders and afflicted with emotional disturbances came into Jesus' presence and then returned home to their friends announcing that Jesus had healed them. And such cases of mental healing these ignorant and simple-minded people regarded as physical healing, miraculous cures.

When Jesus sought to leave Cana and go to Nain, a great multitude of believers and many curious people followed after him. They were bent on beholding miracles and wonders, and they were not to be disappointed. As Jesus and his apostles drew near the gate of the city, they met a funeral procession on its way to the near-by cemetery, carrying the only son of a widowed mother of Nain. This woman was much respected, and half of the village followed the bearers of the bier of this supposedly dead boy. When the funeral procession had come up to Jesus and his followers, the widow and her friends recognized the Master and besought him to bring the son back to life. Their miracle expectancy was aroused to such a high pitch they thought Jesus could cure any human disease, and why could not such a healer even raise the dead? Jesus, while being thus importuned, stepped forward and, raising the covering of the bier, examined the boy. Discovering that the young man was not really dead, he perceived the tragedy which his presence could avert; so, turning to the mother, he said: "Weep not. Your son is not dead; he sleeps. He will be restored to you." And then, taking the young man by the hand, he said, "Awake and arise."

And the youth who was supposed to be dead presently sat up and began to speak, and Jesus sent them back to their homes.

Jesus endeavored to calm the multitude and vainly tried to explain that the lad was not really dead, that he had not brought him back from the grave, but it was useless. The multitude that followed him, and the whole village of Nain, were aroused to the highest pitch of emotional frenzy. Fear seized many, panic others, while still others fell to praying and wailing over their sins. And it was not until long after nightfall that the clamoring multitude could be dispersed. And, of course, notwithstanding Jesus' statement that the boy was not dead, everyone insisted that a miracle had been wrought, even the dead raised. Although Jesus told them the boy was merely in a deep sleep, they explained that that was the manner of his speaking and called attention to the fact that he always in great modesty tried to hide his miracles.

So the word went abroad throughout Galilee and into Judea that Jesus had raised the widow's son from the dead, and many who heard this report believed it. Never was Jesus able to make even all his apostles fully understand that the widow's son was not really dead when he bade him awake and arise. But he did impress them sufficiently to keep it out of all subsequent records except that of

Luke, who recorded it as the episode had been related to him. And again was Jesus so besieged as a physician that he departed early the next day for Endor.

At Endor Jesus escaped for a few days from the clamoring multitudes in quest of physical healing. During their sojourn at this place the Master recounted for the instruction of the apostles the story of King Saul and the witch of Endor. Jesus plainly told his apostles that the stray and rebellious midwayers who had oftentimes impersonated the supposed spirits of the dead would soon be brought under control so that they could no more do these strange things. He told his followers that, after he returned to the Father, and after they had poured out their spirit upon all flesh, no more could such semispirit beings - so-called unclean spirits - possess the feeble- and evil-minded among mortals.

Jesus further explained to his apostles that the spirits of departed human beings do not come back to the world of their origin to communicate with their living fellows. Only after the passing of a dispensational age would it be possible for the advancing spirit of a mortal being to return to earth and then only in exceptional cases and as a part of the spiritual administration of the planet.

When they had rested two days, Jesus said to his apostles: "On the morrow let us return to Capernaum to tarry and teach while the countryside quiets down. At home they will have by this time partly recovered from this sort of excitement."

# THE INTERLUDE VISIT TO JERUSALEM

JESUS AND the apostles arrived in Capernaum on Wednesday, March 17, and spent two weeks at the Bethsaida headquarters before they departed for Jerusalem. These two weeks the apostles taught the people by the seaside while Jesus spent much time alone in the hills about his Father's business. During this period Jesus, accompanied by James and John Zebedee, made two secret trips to Tiberias, where they met with the believers and instructed them in the gospel of the kingdom.

Many of the household of Herod believed in Jesus and attended these meetings. It was the influence of these believers among Herod's official family that had helped to lessen that ruler's enmity toward Jesus. These believers at Tiberias had fully explained to Herod that the "kingdom" which Jesus proclaimed was spiritual in nature and not a political venture. Herod rather believed these members of his own household and therefore did not permit himself to become unduly alarmed by the spreading abroad of the reports concerning Jesus' teaching and healing. He had no objections to Jesus' work as a healer or religious teacher. Notwithstanding the favorable attitude of many of Herod's advisers, and even of Herod himself, there existed a group of his subordinates who were so influenced by the religious leaders at Jerusalem that they remained bitter and threatening enemies of Jesus and the apostles and, later on, did much to hamper their public activities. The greatest danger to Jesus lay in the Jerusalem religious leaders and not in Herod. And it was for this very reason that Jesus and the apostles spent so much time and did most of their public preaching in Galilee rather than at Jerusalem and in Judea.

On the day before they made ready to go to Jerusalem for the feast of the Passover, Mangus, a centurion, or captain, of the Roman guard stationed at Capernaum, came to the rulers of the synagogue and said, "My faithful orderly is sick and at the point of death. Would you, therefore, go to Jesus in my behalf and beseech him to heal my servant?" The Roman captain did this because he thought the Jewish leaders would have more influence with Jesus.

So the elders went to see Jesus and their spokesman said, "Teacher, we earnestly request you to go over to Capernaum and save the favorite servant of the Roman centurion, who is worthy of your notice because he loves our nation and even built us the very synagogue wherein you have so many times spoken."

And when Jesus had heard them, he said, "I will go with you." And as he went with them over to the centurion's house, and before they had entered his yard, the Roman soldier sent his friends out to greet Jesus, instructing them to say: "Lord, trouble not yourself to enter my house, for I am not worthy that you should come under my roof. Neither did I think myself worthy to come to you; wherefore I sent the elders of your own people. But I know that you can speak the word where you stand and my servant will be healed. For I am myself under the orders of others, and I have soldiers under me, and I say to this one go, and he goes; to another come, and he comes, and to my servants do this or do that, and they do it."

And when Jesus heard these words, he turned and said to his apostles and those who were with them, "I marvel at the belief of the gentile. Verily, verily, I say to you, I have not found so great faith, no, not in Israel." Jesus, turning from the house, said, "Let us go hence." And the friends of the centurion went into the house and told Mangus what Jesus had said. And from that hour the servant began to mend and was eventually restored to his normal health and usefulness.

But we never knew just what happened on this occasion. This is simply the record, and as to whether or not invisible beings ministered healing to the centurion's servant, was not revealed to those who accompanied Jesus. We only know of the fact of the servant's complete recovery.

Early on the morning of Tuesday, March 30, Jesus and the apostolic party started on their journey to Jerusalem for the Passover, going by the route of the Jordan valley. They arrived on the afternoon of Friday, April 2, and established their headquarters, as usual, at Bethany. Passing through Jericho, they paused to rest while Judas made a deposit of some of their common funds in the bank of a friend of his family. This was the first time Judas had carried a surplus of money, and this deposit was left undisturbed until they passed through Jericho again when on that last and eventful journey to Jerusalem just before the trial and death of Jesus.

The party had an uneventful trip to Jerusalem, but they had hardly got themselves settled at Bethany when from near and far those seeking healing for their bodies, comfort for troubled minds, and salvation for their souls, began to congregate, so much so that Jesus had little time for rest. Therefore they pitched tents at Gethsemane, and the Master would go back and forth from Bethany to

Gethsemane to avoid the crowds that so constantly thronged him. The apostolic party spent almost three weeks at Jerusalem, but Jesus enjoined them to do no public preaching, only private teaching and personal work.

At Bethany they quietly celebrated the Passover. And this was the first time that Jesus and all of the twelve partook of the bloodless Passover feast. The apostles of John did not eat the Passover with Jesus and his apostles; they celebrated the feast with Abner and many of the early believers in John's preaching. This was the second Passover Jesus had observed with his apostles in Jerusalem.

When Jesus and the twelve departed for Capernaum, the apostles of John did not return with them. Under the direction of Abner they remained in Jerusalem and the surrounding country, quietly laboring for the extension of the kingdom, while Jesus and the twelve returned to work in Galilee. Never again were the twenty-four all together until a short time before the commissioning and sending forth of the seventy evangelists. But the two groups were co-operative, and notwithstanding their differences of opinion, the best of feelings prevailed.

The afternoon of the second Sabbath in Jerusalem, as the Master and the apostles were about to participate in the temple services, John said to Jesus, "Come with me, I would show you something." John conducted Jesus out through one of the Jerusalem gates to a pool of water called Bethesda. Surrounding this pool was a structure of five porches under which a large group of sufferers lingered in quest of healing. This was a hot spring whose reddish-tinged water would bubble up at irregular intervals because of gas accumulations in the rock caverns underneath the pool. This periodic disturbance of the warm waters was believed by many to be due to supernatural influences, and it was a popular belief that the first person who entered the water after such a disturbance would be healed of whatever infirmity he had.

The apostles were somewhat restless under the restrictions imposed by Jesus, and John, the youngest of the twelve, was especially restive under this restraint. He had brought Jesus to the pool thinking that the sight of the assembled sufferers would make such an appeal to the Master's compassion that he would be moved to perform a miracle of healing, and thereby would all Jerusalem be astounded and presently be won to believe in the gospel of the kingdom. John said, "Master, see all of these suffering ones; is there nothing we can do for them?"

And Jesus replied, "John, why would you tempt me to turn aside from the way I have chosen? Why do you go on desiring to substitute the working of wonders and the healing of the sick for the proclamation of the gospel of eternal truth? My son, I may not do that which you desire, but gather together these sick and afflicted that I may speak words of good cheer and eternal comfort to them."

In speaking to those assembled, Jesus said, "Many of you are here, sick and afflicted, because of your many years of wrong living. Some suffer from the accidents of time, others as a result of the mistakes of their forebears, while some of you struggle under the handicaps of the imperfect conditions of your temporal existence. But my Father works, and I would work, to improve your earthly state but more especially to insure your eternal estate. None of us can do much to change the difficulties of life unless we discover the Father in heaven so wills. After all, we are all beholden to do the will of the Eternal. If you could all be healed of your physical afflictions, you would indeed marvel, but it is even greater that you should be cleansed of all spiritual disease and find yourselves healed of all moral infirmities. You are all God's children; you are the sons of the heavenly Father. The bonds of time may seem to afflict you, but the God of eternity loves you. And when the time of judgment shall come, fear not, you shall all find, not only justice, but an abundance of mercy. Verily, verily, I say to you: He who hears the gospel of the kingdom and believes in this teaching of a son and daughter relationship with God, has eternal life; already are such believers passing from judgment and death to light and life. And the hour is coming in which even those who are in the tombs shall hear the voice of the resurrection."

And many of those who heard believed the gospel of the kingdom. Some of the afflicted were so inspired and spiritually revivified that they went about proclaiming that they had also been cured of their physical ailments.

One man who had been many years downcast and grievously afflicted by the infirmities of his troubled mind, rejoiced at Jesus' words and, picking up his bed, went forth to his home, even though it was the Sabbath day. This afflicted man had waited all these years for *somebody* to help him; he was such a victim of the feeling of his own helplessness that he had never once entertained the idea of helping himself which proved to be the one thing he had to do in order to effect recovery - take up his bed and walk.

Then Jesus said to John, "Let us depart ere the chief priests and the scribes come upon us and take offense that we spoke words of life to these afflicted ones." And they returned to the temple to join their companions, and presently all of them departed to spend the night at Bethany. But John never told the other apostles of this visit of himself and Jesus to the pool of Bethesda on this Sabbath afternoon.

On the evening of this same Sabbath day, at Bethany, while Jesus, the twelve, and a group of believers were assembled about the fire in Lazarus's garden, Nathaniel asked Jesus this question: "Master, although you have taught us the positive version of the old rule of life, instructing us that we should do to others as we wish them to do to us, I do not fully discern how we can always abide by such an injunction. Let me illustrate my contention by citing the example of a lustful man who thus wickedly looks upon his intended consort in sin. How can we teach that this evil-intending man should do to others as he would they should do to him?"

When Jesus heard Nathaniel's question, he immediately stood upon his feet and, pointing his finger at the apostle, said, "Nathaniel, Nathaniel! What manner of thinking is going on in your heart? Do you not receive my teachings as one who has been born of the spirit? Do you not hear the truth as men of wisdom and spiritual understanding? When I admonished you to do to others as you would have them do to you, I spoke to men of high ideals, not to those who would be tempted to distort my teaching into a license for the encouragement of evil-doing."

When the Master had spoken, Nathaniel stood up and said, "But, Master, you should not think that I approve of such an interpretation of your teaching. I asked the question because I conjectured that many such men might thus misjudge your admonition, and I hoped you would give us further instruction regarding these matters."

And then when Nathaniel had sat down, Jesus continued speaking. "I well know, Nathaniel, that no such idea of evil is approved in your mind, but I am disappointed in that you all so often fail to put a genuinely spiritual interpretation upon my commonplace teachings, instruction which must be given you in human language and as men must speak. Let me now teach you concerning the differing levels of meaning attached to the interpretation of this rule of living, this admonition to 'do to others that which you desire others to do to you':

"1. *The level of the flesh.* Such a purely selfish and lustful interpretation would be well exemplified by the supposition of your question.

"2. *The level of the feelings.* This plane is one level higher than that of the flesh and implies that sympathy and pity would enhance one's interpretation of this rule of living.

"3. *The level of mind.* Now come into action the reason of mind and the intelligence of experience. Good judgment dictates that such a rule of living should be interpreted in consonance with the highest idealism embodied in the nobility of profound self-respect.

"4. *The level of brotherly love.* Still higher is discovered the level of unselfish devotion to the welfare of one's fellows. On this higher plane of wholehearted social service growing out of the consciousness of the fatherhood of God and the consequent recognition of the brotherhood of man, there is discovered a new and far more beautiful interpretation of this basic rule of life.

"5. *The moral level.* And then when you attain true philosophic levels of interpretation, when you have real insight into the *rightness* and *wrongness* of things, when you perceive the eternal fitness of human relationships, you will begin to view such a problem of interpretation as you would imagine a high-minded, idealistic, wise, and impartial third person would so view and interpret such an injunction as applied to your personal problems of adjustment to your life situations.

"6. *The spiritual level.* And then last, but greatest of all, we attain the level of spirit insight and spiritual interpretation which impels us to recognize in this rule of life the divine command to treat all men as we conceive God would treat them. That is the universe ideal of human relationships. And this is your attitude toward all such problems when your supreme desire is ever to do the Father's will. I would, therefore, that you should do to all men that which you know I would do to them in like circumstances."

Nothing Jesus had said to the apostles up to this time had ever more astonished them. They continued to discuss the Master's words long after he had retired. While Nathaniel was slow to recover from his supposition that Jesus had misunderstood the spirit of his question, the others were more than thankful that their philosophic fellow apostle had had the courage to ask such a thought-provoking question.

One Simon the Pharisee, though not a member of the Jewish Sanhedrin, was influential among the Pharisees of Jerusalem. He was a halfhearted believer, and notwithstanding that he might be severely criticized therefor, he dared to invite Jesus and his personal associates, Peter, James, and John, to his home for a social meal. Simon had long observed the Master and was much impressed with his teachings and even more so with his personality.

The wealthy Pharisees were devoted to almsgiving, and they did not shun publicity regarding their philanthropy. Sometimes they would even blow a trumpet as they were about to bestow charity upon some beggar. It was the custom of these Pharisees, when they provided a banquet for distinguished guests, to leave the doors of the house open so that even the street beggars might come in and, standing around the walls of the room behind the couches of the diners, be in position to receive portions of food which might be tossed to them by the banqueters.

On this particular occasion at Simon's house, among those who came in off the street was a woman of unsavory reputation who had recently become a believer in the good news of the gospel of the kingdom. This woman was well known throughout all Jerusalem as the former keeper of one of the so-called high-class brothels located hard by the temple court of the gentiles. She had, on accepting the teachings of Jesus, closed up her nefarious place of business and had induced the majority of the women associated with her to accept the gospel and change their mode of living; notwithstanding this, she was still held in great disdain by the Pharisees and was compelled to wear her hair down - the badge of harlotry. This unnamed woman had brought with her a large flask of perfumed anointing lotion and, standing behind Jesus as he reclined at meat, began to anoint his feet while she also wet his feet with her tears of gratitude, wiping them with the hair of her head. And when she had finished this anointing, she continued weeping and kissing his feet.

When Simon saw all this, he said to himself, "This man, if he were a prophet, would have perceived who and what manner of woman this is who thus touches him; that she is a notorious sinner."

And Jesus, knowing what was going on in Simon's mind, spoke up, saying, "Simon, I have something which I would like to say to you."

Simon answered, "Teacher, say on."

Then said Jesus, "A certain wealthy moneylender had two debtors. The one owed him five hundred denarii and the other fifty. Now, when neither of them had wherewith to pay, he forgave them both. Which of them do you think, Simon, would love him most?"

Simon answered, "He, I suppose, whom he forgave the most."

And Jesus said, "You have rightly judged," and pointing to the woman, he continued, "Simon, take a good look at this woman. I entered your house as an invited guest, yet you gave me no water for my feet. This grateful woman has washed my feet with tears and wiped them with the hair of her head. You gave me no kiss of friendly greeting, but this woman, ever since she came in, has not ceased to kiss my feet. My head with oil you neglected to anoint, but she has anointed my feet with precious lotions. And what is the meaning of all this? Simply that her many sins have been forgiven, and this has led her to love much. But those who have received but little forgiveness sometimes love but little." And turning around toward the woman, he took her by the hand and, lifting her up, said, "You have indeed repented of your sins, and they are forgiven. Be not discouraged by the thoughtless and unkind attitude of your fellows; go on in the joy and liberty of the kingdom of heaven."

When Simon and his friends who sat at meat with him heard these words, they were the more astonished, and they began to whisper among themselves, "Who is this man that he even dares to forgive sins?"

And when Jesus heard them thus murmuring, he turned to dismiss the woman, saying, "Woman, go in peace; your faith has saved you."

As Jesus arose with his friends to leave, he turned to Simon and said, "I know your heart, Simon, how you are torn betwixt faith and doubts, how you are distraught by fear and troubled by pride; but I pray for you that you may yield to the light and may experience in your station in life just such mighty transformations of mind and spirit as may be comparable to the tremendous changes which the gospel of the kingdom has already wrought in the heart of your unbidden and unwelcome guest. And I declare to all of you that the Father has opened the doors of the heavenly kingdom to all who have the faith to enter, and no man or association of men can close those doors even to the most humble soul or supposedly most flagrant sinner on earth if such sincerely seek an entrance." And Jesus, with Peter,

James, and John, took leave of their host and went to join the rest of the apostles at the camp in the garden of Gethsemane.

That same evening Jesus made the long-to-be-remembered address to the apostles regarding the relative value of status with God and progress in the eternal ascent to Paradise. Said Jesus, "My children, if there exists a true and living connection between the child and the Father, the child is certain to progress continuously toward the Father's ideals. True, the child may at first make slow progress, but the progress is none the less sure. The important thing is not the rapidity of your progress but rather its certainty. Your actual achievement is not so important as the fact that the *direction* of your progress is Godward. What you are becoming day by day is of infinitely more importance than what you are today.

"This transformed woman whom some of you saw at Simon's house today is, at this moment, living on a level which is vastly below that of Simon and his well-meaning associates; but while these Pharisees are occupied with the false progress of the illusion of traversing deceptive circles of meaningless ceremonial services, this woman has, in dead earnest, started out on the long and eventful search for God, and her path toward heaven is not blocked by spiritual pride and moral self-satisfaction. The woman is, humanly speaking, much farther away from God than Simon, but her soul is in progressive motion; she is on the way toward an eternal goal. There are present in this woman tremendous spiritual possibilities for the future. Some of you may not stand high in actual levels of soul and spirit, but you are making daily progress on the living way opened up, through faith, to God. There are tremendous possibilities in each of you for the future. Better by far to have a small but living and growing faith than to be possessed of a great intellect with its dead stores of worldly wisdom and spiritual unbelief."

But Jesus earnestly warned his apostles against the foolishness of the child of God who presumes upon the Father's love. He declared that the heavenly Father is not a lax, loose, or foolishly indulgent parent who is ever ready to condone sin and forgive recklessness. He cautioned his hearers not mistakenly to apply his illustrations of father and child so as to make it appear that God is like some overindulgent and unwise parents who conspire with the foolish of earth to encompass the moral undoing of their thoughtless children, and who are thereby certainly and directly contributing to the delinquency and early demoralization of their own offspring. Said Jesus, "My Father does not indulgently condone those acts and practices of his children which are self-destructive and suicidal to all moral growth and spiritual progress. Such sinful practices are an abomination in the sight of God."

Many other semiprivate meetings and banquets did Jesus attend with the high and the low, the rich and the poor, of Jerusalem before he and his apostles finally departed for Capernaum. And many, indeed, became believers in the gospel of the kingdom and were subsequently baptized by Abner and his associates, who remained behind to foster the interests of the kingdom in Jerusalem and thereabouts.

The last week of April, Jesus and the twelve departed from their Bethany headquarters near Jerusalem and began their journey back to Capernaum by way of Jericho and the Jordan.

The chief priests and the religious leaders of the Jews held many secret meetings for the purpose of deciding what to do with Jesus. They were all agreed that something should be done to put a stop to his teaching, but they could not agree on the method. They had hoped that the civil authorities would dispose of him as Herod had put an end to John, but they discovered that Jesus was so conducting his work that the Roman officials were not much alarmed by his preaching. Accordingly, at a meeting, which was held the day before Jesus' departure for Capernaum, it was decided that he would have to be apprehended on a religious charge and be tried by the Sanhedrin. Therefore a commission of six secret spies was appointed to follow Jesus, to observe his words and acts, and when they had amassed sufficient evidence of lawbreaking and blasphemy, to return to Jerusalem with their report.

These six Jews caught up with the apostolic party, numbering about thirty, at Jericho and, under the pretense of desiring to become disciples, attached themselves to Jesus' family of followers, remaining with the group up to the time of the beginning of the second preaching tour in Galilee; whereupon three of them returned to Jerusalem to submit their report to the chief priests and the Sanhedrin.

Peter preached to the assembled multitude at the crossing of the Jordan, and the following morning they moved up the river toward Amathus. They wanted to proceed straight on to Capernaum, but such a crowd gathered here they remained three days, preaching, teaching, and baptizing. They did not move toward home until early Sabbath morning, the first day of May. The Jerusalem spies were sure they would now secure their first charge against Jesus - that of Sabbath breaking - since he had presumed to start his journey on the Sabbath day. But they were doomed to disappointment because, just before their departure, Jesus called Andrew into his presence and before them all instructed him to proceed for a distance of only one thousand yards, the legal Jewish Sabbath day's journey.

But the spies did not have long to wait for their opportunity to accuse Jesus and his associates of Sabbath breaking. As the company passed along the narrow road, the waving wheat, which was just then ripening, was near at hand on either side, and some of the apostles, being hungry, plucked the ripe grain and ate it. It was customary for travelers to help themselves to grain as they passed along the road, and therefore no thought of wrongdoing was attached to such conduct. But the spies seized upon this as a pretext for assailing Jesus. When they saw Andrew rub the grain in his hand, they went up to him and said, "Do you not know that it is unlawful to pluck and rub the grain on the Sabbath day?"

And Andrew answered, "But we are hungry and rub only sufficient for our needs; and since when did it become sinful to eat grain on the Sabbath day?"

But the Pharisees answered, "You do no wrong in eating, but you do break the law in plucking and rubbing out the grain between your hands; surely your Master would not approve of such acts."

Then said Andrew, "But if it is not wrong to eat the grain, surely the rubbing out between our hands is hardly more work than the chewing of the grain, which you allow; wherefore do you quibble over such trifles?"

When Andrew intimated that they were quibblers, they were indignant, and rushing back to where Jesus walked along, talking to Matthew, they protested, saying, "Behold, Teacher, your apostles do that which is unlawful on the Sabbath day; they pluck, rub, and eat the grain. We are sure you will command them to cease."

And then said Jesus to the accusers, "You are indeed zealous for the law, and you do well to remember the Sabbath day to keep it holy; but did you never read in the Scripture that, one day when David was hungry, he and they who were with him entered the house of God and ate the showbread, which it was not lawful for anyone to eat save the priests? And David also gave this bread to those who were with him. And have you not read in our law that it is lawful to do many needful things on the Sabbath day? And shall I not, before the day is finished, see you eat that which you have brought along for the needs of this day? My good men, you do well to be zealous for the Sabbath, but you would do better to guard the health and well-being of your fellows. I declare that the Sabbath was made for man and not man for the Sabbath. And if you are here present with us to watch my words, then will I openly proclaim that the Son of Man is lord even of the Sabbath."

The Pharisees were astonished and confounded by his words of discernment and wisdom. For the remainder of the day they kept by themselves and dared not ask any more questions.

Jesus' antagonism to the Jewish traditions and slavish ceremonials was always *positive.* It consisted in what he did and in what he affirmed. The Master spent little time in negative denunciations. He taught that those who know God can enjoy the liberty of living without deceiving themselves by the licenses of sinning. Said Jesus to the apostles, "Men, if you are enlightened by the truth and really know what you are doing, you are blessed; but if you know not the divine way, you are unfortunate and already breakers of the law."

It was around noon on Monday, May 3, when Jesus and the twelve came to Bethsaida by boat from Tarichea. They traveled by boat in order to escape those who journeyed with them. But by the next day the others, including the official spies from Jerusalem, had again found Jesus.

On Tuesday evening Jesus was conducting one of his customary classes of questions and answers when the leader of the six spies said to him, "I was today talking with one of John's disciples who is here attending upon your teaching, and we were at a loss to understand why you never command your disciples to fast and pray as we Pharisees fast and as John bade his followers."

And Jesus, referring to a statement by John, answered this questioner, "Do the sons of the bridechamber fast while the bridegroom is with them? As long as the bridegroom remains with them, they can hardly fast. But the time is coming when the bridegroom shall be taken away, and during those times the children of the bridechamber undoubtedly will fast and pray. To pray is natural for the children of light, but fasting is not a part of the gospel of the kingdom of heaven. Be reminded that a wise tailor does not sew a piece of new and unshrunk cloth upon an old garment, lest, when it is wet, it shrink and produce a worse rent. Neither do men put new wine into old wineskins, lest the new wine burst the skins so that both the wine and the skins perish. The wise man puts the new wine into fresh wineskins. Therefore do my disciples show wisdom in that they do not bring too much of the old order over into the new teaching of the gospel of the kingdom. You who have lost your teacher may be justified in fasting for a time. Fasting may be an appropriate part of the law of Moses, but in the coming kingdom the sons of God shall experience freedom from fear and joy in the divine spirit." And when they heard these words, the disciples of John were comforted while the Pharisees themselves were the more confounded.

Then the Master proceeded to warn his hearers against entertaining the notion that all olden teaching should be replaced entirely by new doctrines. Said Jesus, "That which is old and also *true* must abide. Likewise, that which is new but false must be rejected. But that which is new and also true, have the faith and courage to accept. Remember it is written: 'Forsake not an old friend, for the new is not comparable to him. As new wine, so is a new friend; if it becomes old, you shall drink it with gladness.'"

That night, long after the usual listeners had retired, Jesus continued to teach his apostles. He began this special instruction by quoting from the Prophet Isaiah:

"'Why have you fasted? For what reason do you afflict your souls while you continue to find pleasure in oppression and to take delight in injustice? Behold, you fast for the sake of strife and contention and to smite with the fist of wickedness. But you shall not fast in this way to make your voices heard on high.

"'Is it such a fast that I have chosen - a day for a man to afflict his soul? Is it to bow down his head like a bulrush, to grovel in sackcloth and ashes? Will you dare to call this a fast and an acceptable day in the sight of the Lord? Is not this the fast I should choose: to loose the bonds of wickedness, to undo the knots of heavy burdens, to let the oppressed go free, and to break every yoke? Is it not to share my bread with the hungry and to bring those who are homeless and poor to my house? And when I see those who are naked, I will clothe them.

"'Then shall your light break forth as the morning while your health springs forth speedily. Your righteousness shall go before you while the glory of the Lord shall be your rear guard. Then will you call upon the Lord, and He shall answer; you will cry out, and He shall say - Here am I. And all this He will do if you refrain from oppression, condemnation, and vanity. The Father rather desires that you draw out your heart to the hungry, and that you minister to the afflicted souls; then shall your light shine in obscurity, and even your darkness shall be as the noonday. Then shall the Lord guide you continually, satisfying your soul and renewing your strength. You shall become like a watered garden, like a spring whose waters fail not. And they who do these things shall restore the wasted glories; they shall raise up the foundations of many generations; they shall be called the rebuilders of broken walls, the restorers of safe paths in which to dwell.'"

And then long into the night Jesus propounded to his apostles the truth that it was their faith that made them secure in the kingdom of the present and the future, and not their affliction of soul, nor fasting of body. He exhorted the apostles at least to live up to the ideas of the prophet of old and expressed the hope that they would progress far beyond even the ideals of Isaiah and the older prophets. His last words that night were; "Grow in grace by means of that living faith which grasps the fact that you are the children of God while at the same time it recognizes every man and woman as a brother and sister."

It was after two o'clock in the morning when Jesus ceased speaking and every man went to his place for sleep.

# TRAINING EVANGELISTS AT BETHSAIDA

FROM MAY 3 to October 3, A.D. 28, Jesus and the apostolic party were in residence at the Zebedee home at Bethsaida. Throughout this five month period of the dry season an enormous camp was maintained by the seaside near the Zebedee residence, which had been greatly enlarged to accommodate the growing family of Jesus. This seaside camp, occupied by an ever-changing population of truth seekers, healing candidates, and curiosity devotees, numbered from five hundred to fifteen hundred. This tented city was under the general supervision of David Zebedee, assisted by the Alpheus twins. The encampment was a model in order and sanitation as well as in its general administration. The sick of different types were segregated and were under the supervision of a believer physician, a Syrian named Elman.

Throughout this period the apostles would go fishing at least one day a week, selling their catch to David for consumption by the seaside encampment. The funds thus received were turned over to the group treasury. The twelve were permitted to spend one week out of each month with their families or friends.

While Andrew continued in general charge of the apostolic activities, Peter was in full charge of the school of the evangelists. The apostles all did their share in teaching groups of evangelists each forenoon, and both teachers and pupils taught the people during the afternoons. After the evening meal, five nights a week, the apostles conducted question classes for the benefit of the evangelists. Once a week Jesus presided at this question hour, answering the holdover questions from previous sessions.

In five months several thousand came and went at this encampment. Interested persons from every part of the Roman Empire and from the lands east of the Euphrates were in frequent attendance. This was the longest settled and well-organized period of the Master's teaching. Jesus' immediate family spent most of this time at either Nazareth or Cana.

The encampment was not conducted as a community of common interests, as was the apostolic family. David Zebedee managed this large tent city so that it became a self-sustaining enterprise, notwithstanding that no one was ever turned away. This ever-changing camp was an indispensable feature of Peter's evangelistic training school.

Peter, James, and Andrew were the committee designated by Jesus to pass upon applicants for admission to the school of evangelists. All the races and nationalities of the Roman world and the East, as far as India, were represented among the students in this new school of the prophets. This school was conducted on the plan of learning and doing. What the students learned during the forenoon they taught to the assembly by the seaside during the afternoon. After supper they informally discussed both the learning of the forenoon and the teaching of the afternoon.

Each of the apostolic teachers taught his own view of the gospel of the kingdom. They made no effort to teach just alike; there was no standardized or dogmatic formulation of theologic doctrines. Though they all taught the *same truth,* each apostle presented his own personal interpretation of the Master's teaching. And Jesus upheld this presentation of the diversity of personal experience in the things of the kingdom, unfailingly harmonizing and coordinating these many and divergent views of the gospel at his weekly question hours. Notwithstanding this great degree of personal liberty in matters of teaching, Simon Peter tended to dominate the theology of the school of evangelists. Next to Peter, James Zebedee exerted the greatest personal influence.

The one hundred and more evangelists trained during this five months by the seaside represented the material from which (excepting Abner and John's apostles) the later seventy gospel teachers and preachers were drawn. The school of evangelists did not have everything in common to the same degree as did the twelve.

These evangelists, though they taught and preached the gospel, did not baptize believers until after they were later ordained and commissioned by Jesus as the seventy messengers of the kingdom. *Only seven* of the large number healed at the sundown scene at this place were to be found among these evangelistic students. The nobleman's son of Capernaum was one of those trained for gospel service in Peter's school.

In connection with the seaside encampment, Elman, the Syrian physician, with the assistance of a corps of twenty-five young women and twelve men, organized and conducted for four months what should be regarded as the kingdom's first hospital. At this infirmary, located a short distance to the south of the main tented city, they treated the sick in accordance with all known material methods as well as by the spiritual practices of prayer and faith encouragement. Jesus visited the sick of this encampment not less than three times a week and made personal contact with each sufferer. As far as we know, no so-called miracles of supernatural healing occurred among the one thousand afflicted and ailing persons who went away from this infirmary improved or cured. However, the vast majority of these benefited individuals ceased not to proclaim that Jesus had healed them.

Many of the cures effected by Jesus in connection with his ministry in behalf of Elman's patients did, indeed, appear to resemble the working of miracles, but we were instructed that they were only just such transformations of mind and spirit as may occur in the experience of expectant and faith-dominated persons who are under the immediate and inspirational influence of a strong, positive, and beneficent personality whose ministry banishes fear and destroys anxiety.

Elman and his associates endeavored to teach the truth to these sick ones concerning the "possession of evil spirits," but they met with little success. The belief that physical sickness and mental derangement could be caused by the dwelling of a so-called unclean spirit in the mind or body of the afflicted person was well-nigh universal.

In all his contact with the sick and afflicted, when it came to the technique of treatment or the revelation of the unknown causes of disease, Jesus did not disregard the instructions of his Paradise brother, Immanuel, given ere he embarked upon the venture of the incarnation on Earth. Notwithstanding this, those who ministered to the sick learned many helpful lessons by observing the manner in which Jesus inspired the faith and confidence of the sick and suffering.

The camp disbanded a short time before the season for the increase in chills and fever drew on.

Throughout this period Jesus conducted public services at the encampment less than a dozen times and spoke only once in the Capernaum synagogue, the second Sabbath before their departure with the newly trained evangelists upon their second public preaching tour of Galilee.

Not since his baptism had the Master been so much alone as during this period of the evangelists' training encampment at Bethsaida. Whenever any one of the apostles ventured to ask Jesus why he was absent so much from their midst, he would invariably answer that he was "about the Father's business."

During these periods of absence, Jesus was accompanied by only two of the apostles. He had released Peter, James, and John temporarily from their assignment as his personal companions that they might also participate in the work of training the new evangelistic candidates, numbering more than one hundred. When the Master desired to go to the hills about the Father's business, he would summon to accompany him any two of the apostles who might be at liberty. In this way each of the twelve enjoyed an opportunity for close association and intimate contact with Jesus.

It has not been revealed for the purposes of this record, but we have been led to infer that the Master, during many of these solitary seasons in the hills, was in direct and executive association with many of his chief directors of universe affairs. Ever since about the time of his baptism this incarnated Sovereign of our universe had become increasingly and consciously active in the direction of certain phases of universe administration. And we have always held the opinion that, in some way not revealed to his immediate associates, during these weeks of decreased participation in the affairs of earth he was engaged in the direction of those high spirit intelligences who were charged with the running of a vast universe, and that the human Jesus chose to designate such activities on his part as being "about his Father's business."

Many times, when Jesus was alone for hours, but when two of his apostles were near by, they observed his features undergo rapid and multitudinous changes, although they heard him speak no words. Neither did they observe any visible manifestation of celestial beings who might have been in communication with their Master, such as some of them did witness on a subsequent occasion.

It was the habit of Jesus two evenings each week to hold special converse with individuals who desired to talk with him, in a certain secluded and sheltered corner of the Zebedee garden. At one of these evening conversations in private Thomas asked the Master this question: "Why is it necessary for men to be born of the spirit in order to enter the kingdom? Is rebirth necessary to escape the control of the evil one? Master, what is evil?"

When Jesus heard these questions, he said to Thomas:

"Do not make the mistake of confusing *evil* with the *evil one,* more correctly the *iniquitous one.* He whom you call the evil one is the son of self-love, the high administrator who knowingly went into deliberate rebellion against the rule of my Father and His loyal Sons. But I have already vanquished these sinful rebels. Make clear in your mind these different attitudes toward the Father and his universe. Never forget these laws of relation to the Father's will:

"Evil is the unconscious or unintended transgression of the divine law, the Father's will. Evil is likewise the measure of the imperfectness of obedience to the Father's will.

"Sin is the conscious, knowing, and deliberate transgression of the divine law, the Father's will. Sin is the measure of unwillingness to be divinely led and spiritually directed.

"Iniquity is the willful, determined, and persistent transgression of the divine law, the Father's will. Iniquity is the measure of the continued rejection of the Father's loving plan of personality survival and the Sons' merciful ministry of salvation.

"By nature, before the rebirth of the spirit, mortal man is subject to inherent evil tendencies, but such natural imperfections of behavior are neither sin nor iniquity. Mortal man is just beginning his long ascent to the perfection of the Father in Paradise. To be imperfect or partial in natural endowment is not sinful. Man is indeed subject to evil, but he is in no sense the child of the evil one unless he has knowingly and deliberately chosen the paths of sin and the life of iniquity. Evil is inherent in the natural order of this world, but sin is an attitude of conscious rebellion which was brought to this world by those who fell from spiritual light into gross darkness.

"You are confused, Thomas, by the doctrines of the Greeks and the errors of the Persians. You do not understand the relationships of evil and sin because you view mankind as beginning on earth with a perfect Adam and rapidly degenerating, through sin, to man's present deplorable estate. But why do you refuse to comprehend the meaning of the record which discloses how Cain, the son of Adam, went over into the land of Nod and there got himself a wife? And why do you refuse to interpret the meaning of the record which portrays the sons of God finding wives for themselves among the daughters of men?

"Man is, indeed, by nature evil, but not necessarily sinful. The new birth - the baptism of the spirit - is essential to deliverance from evil and necessary for entrance into the kingdom of heaven, but none of this detracts from the fact that man is the child of God. Neither does this inherent presence of potential evil mean that man is in some mysterious way estranged from the Father in heaven so that, as an alien, foreigner, or stepchild, he must in some manner seek for legal adoption by the Father. All such notions are born, first, of your misunderstanding of the Father and, second, of your ignorance of the origin, nature, and destiny of man.

"The Greeks and others have taught you that man is descending from godly perfection steadily down toward oblivion or destruction; I have come to show that man, by entrance into the kingdom, is ascending certainly and surely up to God and divine perfection. Any being who in any manner falls short of the divine and spiritual ideals of the eternal Father's will is potentially evil, but such beings are in no sense sinful, much less iniquitous.

"Thomas, have you not read about this in the Scriptures, where it is written: 'You are the children of the Lord your God.' 'I will be his Father and he shall be my son.' 'I have chosen him to be my son - I will be his Father.' 'Bring my sons from far and my daughters from the ends of the earth; even every one who is called by my name, for I have created them for my glory.' 'You are the sons of the living God.' 'They who have the spirit of God are indeed the sons of God.' While there is a material part of the human father in the natural child, there is a spiritual part of the heavenly Father in every faith-child of the kingdom."

All this and much more Jesus said to Thomas, and much of it the apostle comprehended, although Jesus admonished him to "speak not to the others concerning these matters until after I shall have returned to the Father." And Thomas did not mention this interview until after the Master had departed from this world.

At another of these private interviews in the garden Nathaniel asked Jesus, "Master, though I am beginning to understand why you refuse to practice healing indiscriminately, I am still at a loss to understand why the loving Father in heaven permits so many of his children on earth to suffer so many afflictions."

The Master answered Nathaniel, saying:

"Nathaniel, you and many others are thus perplexed because you do not comprehend how the natural order of this world has been so many times upset by the sinful adventures of certain rebellious traitors to the Father's will. And I have come to make a beginning of setting these things in order. But many ages will be required to restore this part of the universe to former paths and thus release the children of men from the extra burdens of sin and rebellion. The presence of evil alone is sufficient test for the ascension of man; sin is not essential to survival.

"But, my son, you should know that the Father does not purposely afflict his children. Man brings down upon himself unnecessary affliction as a result of his persistent refusal to walk in the better ways of the divine will. Affliction is potential in evil, but much of it has been produced by sin and iniquity. Many unusual events have transpired on this world, and it is not strange that all thinking men should be perplexed by the scenes of suffering and affliction which they witness. But of one thing you may be sure: The Father does not send affliction as an arbitrary punishment for wrongdoing. The imperfections and handicaps of evil are inherent; the penalties of sin are inevitable; the destroying consequences of iniquity are inexorable. Man should not blame God for those afflictions which are the natural result of the life which he chooses to live; neither should man complain of those experiences which are a part of life as it is lived on this world. It is the Father's will that mortal man should work persistently and consistently toward the betterment of his estate on earth. Intelligent application would enable man to overcome much of his earthly misery.

"Nathaniel, it is our mission to help men and women solve their spiritual problems and in this way to quicken their minds so that they may be the better prepared and inspired to go about solving their manifold material problems. I know of your confusion as you have read the Scriptures. All too often there has prevailed a tendency to ascribe to God the responsibility for everything which ignorant man fails to understand. The Father is not personally responsible for all you may fail to comprehend. Do not doubt the love of the Father just because some just and wise law of his ordaining chances to afflict you because you have innocently or deliberately transgressed such a divine ordinance.

"But, Nathaniel, there is much in the Scriptures which would have instructed you if you had only read with discernment. Do you not remember that it is written:

'My son, despise not the chastening of the Lord; neither be weary of his correction, for whom the Lord loves he corrects, even as the father corrects the son in whom he takes delight.' 'The Lord does not afflict willingly.' 'Before I was afflicted, I went astray, but now do I keep the law. Affliction was good for me that I might thereby learn the divine statutes.' 'I know your sorrows. The eternal God is your refuge, while underneath are the everlasting arms.' 'The Lord also is a refuge for the oppressed, a haven of rest in times of trouble.' 'The Lord will strengthen him upon the bed of affliction; the Lord will not forget the sick.' 'As a father shows compassion for his children, so is the Lord compassionate to those who fear Him. He knows your body; he remembers that you are dust.' 'He heals the brokenhearted and binds up their wounds.' 'He is the hope of the poor, the strength of the needy in his distress, a refuge from the storm, and a shadow from the devastating heat.' 'He gives power to the faint, and to them who have no might he increases strength.' 'A bruised reed shall He not break, and the smoking flax He will not quench.' 'When you pass through the waters of affliction, I will be with you, and when the rivers of adversity overflow you, I will not forsake you.' 'He has sent me to bind up the brokenhearted, to proclaim liberty to the captives, and to comfort all who mourn.' 'There is correction in suffering; affliction does not spring forth from the dust.'"

It was this same evening at Bethsaida that John also asked Jesus why so many apparently innocent people suffered from so many diseases and experienced so many afflictions.

In answering John's questions, among many other things, the Master said:

"My son, you do not comprehend the meaning of adversity or the mission of suffering. Have you not read that masterpiece of Semitic literature - the Scripture story of the afflictions of Job? Do you not recall how this wonderful parable begins with the recital of the material prosperity of the Lord's servant? You well remember that Job was blessed with children, wealth, dignity, position, health, and everything else which men value in this temporal life. According to the time-honored teachings of the children of Abraham such material prosperity was all-sufficient evidence of divine favor. But such material possessions and such temporal prosperity do not indicate God's favor. My Father in heaven loves the poor just as much as the rich; he is no respecter of persons.

"Although transgression of divine law is sooner or later followed by the harvest of punishment, while men certainly eventually do reap what they sow, still you should know that human suffering is not always a punishment for antecedent sin. Both Job and his friends failed to find the true answer for their perplexities. And with the light you now enjoy you would hardly assign to either Satan or God the parts they play in this unique parable. While Job did not, through suffering, find the resolution of his intellectual troubles or the solution of his philosophical difficulties, he did achieve great victories; even in the very face of the breakdown of his theological defenses he ascended to those spiritual heights where he could sincerely say, 'I abhor myself'; then was there granted him the salvation of a *vision of God*. So even through misunderstood suffering, Job ascended to the superhuman plane of moral understanding and spiritual insight. When the suffering servant obtains a vision of God, there follows a soul peace which passes all human understanding.

"The first of Job's friends, Eliphaz, exhorted the sufferer to exhibit in his afflictions the same fortitude he had prescribed for others during the days of his prosperity. Said this false comforter: 'Trust in your religion, Job; remember that it is the wicked and not the righteous who suffer. You must deserve this punishment, else you would not be afflicted. You well know that no man can be righteous in God's sight. You know that the wicked never really prosper. Anyway, man seems predestined to trouble, and perhaps the Lord is only chastising you for your own good.' No wonder poor Job failed to get much comfort from such an interpretation of the problem of human suffering.

"But the counsel of his second friend, Bildad, was even more depressing, notwithstanding its soundness from the standpoint of the then accepted theology. Said Bildad: 'God cannot be unjust. Your children must have been sinners since they perished; you must be in error, else you would not be so afflicted. And if you are really righteous, God will certainly deliver you from your afflictions. You should learn from the history of God's dealings with man that the Almighty destroys only the wicked.'

"And then you remember how Job replied to his friends, saying: 'I well know that God does not hear my cry for help. How can God be just and at the same time so utterly disregard my innocence? I am learning that I can get no satisfaction from appealing to the Almighty. Cannot you discern that God tolerates the persecution of the good by the wicked? And since man is so weak, what chance has he for consideration at the hands of an omnipotent God? God has made me as I am, and when He thus turns upon me, I am defenseless. And why did God ever create me just to suffer in this miserable fashion?'

"And who can challenge the attitude of Job in view of the counsel of his friends and the erroneous ideas of God which occupied his own mind? Do you not see that Job longed for a *human* God, that he hungered to commune with a divine Being who knows man's mortal estate and understands that the just must often suffer in innocence as a part of this first life of the long Paradise ascent? Wherefore has the Son of Man come forth from the Father to live such a life in the flesh that he will be able to comfort and succor all those who must henceforth be called upon to endure the afflictions of Job.

"Job's third friend, Zophar, then spoke still less comforting words when he said: 'You are foolish to claim to be righteous, seeing that you are thus afflicted. But I admit that it is impossible to comprehend God's ways. Perhaps there is some hidden purpose in all your miseries.' And when Job had listened to all three of his friends, he appealed directly to God for help, pleading the fact that 'man, born of woman, is few of days and full of trouble.'

"Then began the second session with his friends. Eliphaz grew more stern, accusing, and sarcastic. Bildad became indignant at Job's contempt for his friends. Zophar reiterated his melancholy advice. Job by this time had become disgusted with his friends and appealed again to God, and now he appealed to a just God against the God of injustice embodied in the philosophy of his friends and enshrined even in his own religious attitude. Next Job took refuge in the consolation of a future life in which the inequities of mortal existence may be more justly rectified. Failure to receive help from man drives Job to God. Then ensues the great struggle in his heart between faith and doubt. Finally, the human sufferer begins to see the light of life; his tortured soul ascends to new heights of hope and courage; he may suffer on and even die, but his enlightened soul now utters that cry of triumph, 'My Vindicator lives!'

"Job was altogether right when he challenged the doctrine that God afflicts children in order to punish their parents. Job was ever ready to admit that God is righteous, but he longed for some soul-satisfying revelation of the personal character of the Eternal. And that is our mission on earth. No more shall suffering mortals be denied the comfort of knowing the love of God and understanding the mercy of the Father in heaven. While the speech of God spoken from the whirlwind was a majestic concept for the day of its utterance, you have already learned that the Father does not thus reveal Himself, but rather that He speaks within the human heart as a still, small voice, saying, 'This is the way; walk therein.' Do you not comprehend that God dwells within you, that he has become what you are that He may make you what He is!"

Then Jesus made this final statement: "The Father in heaven does not willingly afflict the children of men. Man suffers, first, from the accidents of time and the imperfections of the evil of an immature physical existence. Next, he suffers the inexorable consequences of sin - the transgression of the laws of life and light. And finally, man reaps the harvest of his own iniquitous persistence in rebellion against the righteous rule of heaven on earth. But man's miseries are not a *personal* visitation of divine judgment. Man can, and will, do much to lessen his temporal sufferings. But once and for all be you delivered from the superstition that God afflicts man at the behest of the evil one. Study the Book of Job just to discover how many wrong ideas of God even good men may honestly entertain; and then note how even the painfully afflicted Job found the God of comfort and salvation in spite of such erroneous teachings. At last his faith pierced the clouds of suffering to discern the light of life pouring forth from the Father as healing mercy and everlasting righteousness."

John pondered these sayings in his heart for many days. His entire afterlife was markedly changed as a result of this conversation with the Master in the garden, and he did much, in later times, to cause the other apostles to change their viewpoints regarding the source, nature, and purpose of commonplace human afflictions. But John never spoke of this conference until after the Master had departed.

The second Sabbath before the departure of the apostles and the new corps of evangelists on the second preaching tour of Galilee, Jesus spoke in the Capernaum synagogue on the "Joys of Righteous Living." When Jesus had finished speaking, a large group of those who were maimed, halt, sick, and afflicted crowded up around him, seeking healing. Also in this group were the apostles, many of the new evangelists, and the Pharisaic spies from Jerusalem. Everywhere that Jesus went (except when in the hills about the Father's business) the six Jerusalem spies were sure to follow.

The leader of the spying Pharisees, as Jesus stood talking to the people, induced a man with a withered hand to approach him and ask if it would be lawful to be healed on the Sabbath day or should he seek help on another day. When Jesus saw the man, heard his words, and perceived that he had been sent by the Pharisees, he said, "Come forward while I ask you a question. If you had a sheep and it should fall into a pit on the Sabbath day, would you reach down, lay hold on it, and lift it out? Is it lawful to do such things on the Sabbath day?"

And the man answered, "Yes, Master, it would be lawful thus to do well on the Sabbath day."

Then said Jesus, speaking to all of them, "I know wherefore you have sent this man into my presence. You would find cause for offense in me if you could tempt me to show mercy on the Sabbath day. In silence you all agreed that it was lawful to lift the unfortunate sheep out of the pit, even on the Sabbath, and I call you to witness that it is lawful to exhibit loving-kindness on the Sabbath day not only to animals but also to men. How much more valuable is a man than a sheep! I proclaim that it is lawful to do good to men on the Sabbath day."

And as they all stood before him in silence, Jesus, addressing the man with the withered hand, said, "Stand up here by my side that all may see you. And now that you may know that it is my Father's will that you do good on the Sabbath day, if you have the faith to be healed, I bid you stretch out your hand."

And as this man stretched forth his withered hand, it was made whole. The people were minded to turn upon the Pharisees, but Jesus bade them be calm, saying, "I have just told you that it is lawful to do good on the Sabbath, to save life, but I did not instruct you to do harm and give way to the desire to kill."

The angered Pharisees went away, and notwithstanding it was the Sabbath day, they hastened forthwith to Tiberias and took counsel with Herod, doing everything in their power to arouse his prejudice in order to secure the Herodians as allies against Jesus. But Herod refused to take action against Jesus, advising that they carry their complaints to Jerusalem.

This is the first case of a miracle to be wrought by Jesus in response to the challenge of his enemies. And the Master performed this so-called miracle, not as a demonstration of his healing power, but as an effective protest against making the Sabbath rest of religion a veritable bondage of meaningless restrictions upon all mankind. This man returned to his work as a stone mason, proving to be one of those whose healing was followed by a life of thanksgiving and righteousness.

The last week of the sojourn at Bethsaida the Jerusalem spies became much divided in their attitude toward Jesus and his teachings. Three of these Pharisees were tremendously impressed by what they had seen and heard. Meanwhile, at Jerusalem, Abraham, a young and influential member of the Sanhedrin, publicly espoused the teachings of Jesus and was baptized in the pool of Siloam by Abner. All Jerusalem was agog over this event, and messengers were immediately dispatched to Bethsaida recalling the six spying Pharisees.

The Greek philosopher who had been won for the kingdom on the previous tour of Galilee returned with certain wealthy Jews of Alexandria, and once more they invited Jesus to come to their city for the purpose of establishing a joint school of philosophy and religion as well as an infirmary for the sick. But Jesus courteously declined the invitation.

About this time there arrived at the Bethsaida encampment a trance prophet from Baghdad, one Kirmeth. This supposed prophet had peculiar visions when in trance and dreamed fantastic dreams when his sleep was disturbed. He created a considerable disturbance at the camp, and Simon Zelotes was in favor of dealing rather roughly with the self-deceived pretender, but Jesus intervened and allowed him entire freedom of action for a few days. All who heard his preaching soon recognized that his teaching was not sound as judged by the gospel of the kingdom. He shortly returned to Baghdad, taking with him only a half dozen unstable and erratic souls. But before Jesus interceded for the Baghdad prophet, David Zebedee, with the assistance of a self-appointed committee, had taken Kirmeth out into the lake and, after repeatedly plunging him into the water, had advised him to depart hence - to organize and build a camp of his own.

On this same day, Beth-Marion, a Phoenician woman, became so fanatical that she went out of her head and, after almost drowning from trying to walk on the water, was sent away by her friends.

The new Jerusalem convert, Abraham the Pharisee, gave all of his worldly goods to the apostolic treasury, and this contribution did much to make possible the immediate sending forth of the one hundred newly trained evangelists. Andrew had already announced the closing of the encampment, and everybody prepared either to go home or else to follow the evangelists into Galilee.

On Friday afternoon, October 1, when Jesus was holding his last meeting with the apostles, evangelists, and other leaders of the disbanding encampment, and with the six Pharisees from Jerusalem seated in the front row of this assembly in the spacious and enlarged front room of the Zebedee home, there occurred one of the strangest and most unique episodes of all Jesus' earth life. The Master was, at this time, speaking as he stood in this large room, which had been built to accommodate these gatherings during the rainy season. The house was entirely surrounded by a vast concourse of people who were straining their ears to catch some part of Jesus' discourse.

While the house was thus thronged with people and entirely surrounded by eager listeners, a man long afflicted with paralysis was carried down from Capernaum on a small couch by his friends. This paralytic had heard that Jesus was about to leave Bethsaida, and having talked with Aaron the stone mason, who had been so recently made whole, he resolved to be carried into Jesus' presence, where he could seek healing. His friends tried to gain entrance to Zebedee's house by both the front and back doors, but too many people were crowded together. But the paralytic refused to accept defeat; he directed his friends to procure ladders by which they ascended to the roof of the room in which Jesus was speaking, and after loosening the tiles, they boldly lowered the sick man on his couch by ropes until the afflicted one rested on the floor immediately in front of the Master. When Jesus saw what they had done, he ceased speaking, while those who were with him in the room marveled at the perseverance of the sick man and his friends.

Said the paralytic, "Master, I would not disturb your teaching, but I am determined to be made whole. I am not like those who received healing and immediately forgot your teaching. I would be made whole that I might serve in the kingdom of heaven."

Now, notwithstanding that this man's affliction had been brought upon him by his own misspent life, Jesus, seeing his faith, said to the paralytic, "Son, fear not; your sins are forgiven. Your faith shall save you."

When the Pharisees from Jerusalem, together with other scribes and lawyers who sat with them, heard this pronouncement by Jesus, they began to say to themselves, "How dare this man thus speak? Does he not understand that such words are blasphemy? Who can forgive sin but God?"

Jesus, perceiving in his spirit that they thus reasoned within their own minds and among themselves, spoke to them, saying, "Why do you so reason in your hearts? Who are you that you sit in judgment over me? What is the difference whether I say to this paralytic, your sins are forgiven, or arise, take up your bed, and walk? But that you who witness all this may finally know that the Son of Man has authority and power on earth to forgive sins, I will say to this afflicted man, Arise, take up your bed, and go to your own house."

And when Jesus had thus spoken, the paralytic arose, and as they made way for him, he walked out before them all. And those who saw these things were amazed. Peter dismissed the assemblage, while many prayed and glorified God, confessing that they had never before seen such strange happenings.

And it was about this time that the messengers of the Sanhedrin arrived to bid the six spies return to Jerusalem. When they heard this message, they fell to earnest debate among themselves; and after they had finished their discussions, the leader and two of his associates returned with the messengers to Jerusalem, while three of the spying Pharisees confessed faith in Jesus and, going immediately to the lake, were baptized by Peter and fellowshipped by the apostles as children of the kingdom.

# THE SECOND PREACHING TOUR

THE SECOND public preaching tour of Galilee began on Sunday, October 3, A.D. 28, and continued for almost three months, ending on December 30. Participating in this effort were Jesus and his twelve apostles, assisted by the newly recruited corps of 117 evangelists and by numerous other interested persons. On this tour they visited Gadara, Ptolemais, Japhia, Dabaritta, Megiddo, Jezreel, Scythopolis, Tarichea, Hippos, Gamala, Bethsaida-Julias, and many other cities and villages.

Before the departure on this Sunday morning Andrew and Peter asked Jesus to give the final charge to the new evangelists, but the Master declined, saying that it was not his province to do those things which others could acceptably perform. After due deliberation it was decided that James Zebedee should administer the charge.

At the conclusion of James's remarks Jesus said to the evangelists, "Go now forth to do the work as you have been charged, and later on, when you have shown yourselves competent and faithful, I will ordain you to preach the gospel of the kingdom."

On this tour only James and John traveled with Jesus. Peter and the other apostles each took with them about one dozen of the evangelists and maintained close contact with them while they carried on their work of preaching and teaching. As fast as believers were ready to enter the kingdom, the apostles would administer baptism. Jesus and his two companions traveled extensively during these three months, often visiting two cities in one day to observe the work of the evangelists and to encourage them in their efforts to establish the kingdom. This entire second preaching tour was principally an effort to afford practical experience for this corps of 117 newly trained evangelists.

Throughout this period and subsequently, up to the time of the final departure of Jesus and the twelve for Jerusalem, David Zebedee maintained a permanent headquarters for the work of the kingdom in his father's house at Bethsaida. This was the clearinghouse for Jesus' work on earth and the relay station for the messenger service that David carried on between the workers in various parts of Palestine and adjacent regions. He did all of this on his own initiative but with the approval of Andrew. David employed forty to fifty messengers in this intelligence division of the rapidly enlarging and extending work of the kingdom. While thus employed, he partially supported himself by spending some of his time at his old work of fishing.

By the time the camp at Bethsaida had been broken up, the fame of Jesus, particularly as a healer, had spread to all parts of Palestine and through all of Syria and the surrounding countries. For weeks after they left Bethsaida, the sick continued to arrive, and when they did not find the Master, on learning from David where he was, they would go in search of him. On this tour Jesus did not deliberately perform any so-called miracles of healing. Nevertheless, scores of afflicted found restoration of health and happiness as a result of the reconstructive power of the intense faith that impelled them to seek for healing.

There began to appear about the time of this mission - and continued throughout the remainder of Jesus' life on earth - a peculiar and unexplained series of healing phenomena. In the course of this three months' tour more than one hundred men, women, and children from Judea, Idumea, Galilee, Syria, Tyre, and Sidon, and from beyond the Jordan were beneficiaries of this unconscious healing by Jesus and, returning to their homes, added to the enlargement of Jesus' fame. And they did this notwithstanding that Jesus would, every time he observed one of these cases of spontaneous healing, directly charge the beneficiary to "tell no man."

It was never revealed to us just what occurred in these cases of spontaneous or unconscious healing. The Master never explained to his apostles how these healings were effected, other than that on several occasions he merely said, "I perceive that power has gone forth from me." On one occasion he remarked when touched by an ailing child, "I perceive that life has gone forth from me."

In the absence of direct word from the Master regarding the nature of these cases of spontaneous healing, it would be presuming on our part to undertake to explain how they were accomplished, but it will be permissible to record our opinion of all such healing phenomena. We believe that many of these apparent miracles of healing, as they occurred in the course of Jesus' earth ministry, were the result of the coexistence of the following three powerful, potent, and associated influences:

1. The presence of strong, dominant, and living faith in the heart of the human being who persistently sought healing, together with the fact that

such healing was desired for its spiritual benefits rather than for purely physical restoration.

2. The existence, concomitant with such human faith, of the great sympathy and compassion of the incarnated and mercy-dominated Creator Son of God, who actually possessed in his person almost unlimited and timeless creative healing powers and prerogatives.

3. Along with the faith of the creature and the life of the Creator it should also be noted that this God-man was the personified expression of the Father's will. If, in the contact of the human need and the divine power to meet it, the Father did not will otherwise, the two became one, and the healing occurred unconsciously to the human Jesus but was immediately recognized by his divine nature. The explanation, then, of many of these cases of healing must be found in a great law which has long been known to us, namely, What the Creator Son desires and the eternal Father wills IS.

It is, then, our opinion that, in the personal presence of Jesus, certain forms of profound human faith were literally and truly *compelling* in the manifestation of healing by certain creative forces and personalities of the universe who were at that time so intimately associated with the Son of Man. It therefore becomes a fact of record that Jesus did frequently suffer men to heal themselves in his presence by their powerful, personal faith.

Many others sought healing for wholly selfish purposes. A rich widow of Tyre, with her retinue, came seeking to be healed of her infirmities, which were many; and as she followed Jesus about through Galilee, she continued to offer more and more money, as if the power of God were something to be purchased by the highest bidder. But never would she become interested in the gospel of the kingdom; it was only the cure of her physical ailments that she sought.

Jesus understood the minds of men. He knew what was in the heart of man, and had his teachings been left as he presented them, the only commentary being the inspired interpretation afforded by his earth life, all nations and all religions of the world would speedily have embraced the gospel of the kingdom. The well-meant efforts of Jesus' early followers to restate his teachings so as to make them the more acceptable to certain nations, races, and religions, only resulted in making such teachings the less acceptable to all other nations, races, and religions.

The Apostle Paul, in his efforts to bring the teachings of Jesus to the favorable notice of certain groups in his day, wrote many letters of instruction and admonition. Other teachers of Jesus' gospel did likewise, but none of them realized that some of these writings would subsequently be brought together by those who would set them forth as the embodiment of the teachings of Jesus. And so, while so-called Christianity does contain more of the Master's gospel than any other religion, it does also contain much that Jesus did not teach. Aside from the incorporation of many teachings from the Persian mysteries and much of the Greek philosophy into early Christianity, two great mistakes were made:

1. The effort to connect the gospel teaching directly onto the Jewish theology, as illustrated by the Christian doctrines of the atonement - the teaching that Jesus was the sacrificed Son who would satisfy the Father's stern justice and appease the divine wrath. These teachings originated in a praiseworthy effort to make the gospel of the kingdom more acceptable to disbelieving Jews. Though these efforts failed as far as winning the Jews was concerned, they did not fail to confuse and alienate many honest souls in all subsequent generations.

2. The second great blunder of the Master's early followers, and one which all subsequent generations have persisted in perpetuating, was to organize the Christian teaching so completely about the *person* of Jesus. This overemphasis of the personality of Jesus in the theology of Christianity has worked to obscure his teachings, and all of this has made it increasingly difficult for Jews, Mohammedans, Hindus, and other Eastern religionists to accept the teachings of Jesus. We would not belittle the place of the person of Jesus in a religion that might bear his name, but we would not permit such consideration to eclipse his inspired life or to supplant his saving message: the fatherhood of God and *the brotherhood of mankind.*

The teachers of the religion of Jesus should approach other religions with the recognition of the truths which are held in common (many of which come directly or indirectly from Jesus' message) while they refrain from placing so much emphasis on the differences.

While, at that particular time, the fame of Jesus rested chiefly upon his reputation as a healer, it does not follow that it continued so to rest. As time passed, more and more he was sought for spiritual help. But it was the physical cures that made the most direct and immediate appeal to the common people. Jesus was increasingly sought by the victims of moral enslavement and mental harassments, and he invariably taught them the way of deliverance. Fathers sought his advice regarding the management of their sons, and mothers came for help in the guidance of their daughters. Those who sat in darkness came to him, and he revealed to them the light of life. His ear was ever open to the sorrows of mankind, and he always helped those who sought his ministry.

When the Creator himself was on earth, incarnated in the likeness of mortal flesh, it was inevitable that some extraordinary things should happen. But you should never approach Jesus through these so-called miraculous occurrences.

Learn to approach the miracle through Jesus, but do not make the mistake of approaching Jesus through the miracle. And this admonition is warranted, notwithstanding that Jesus of Nazareth is the only founder of a religion who performed supermaterial acts on earth.

The most astonishing and the most revolutionary feature of Michael's mission on earth was his attitude toward women. In a day and generation when a man was not supposed to salute even his own wife in a public place, Jesus dared to take women along as teachers of the gospel in connection with his third tour of Galilee. And he had the consummate courage to do this in the face of the rabbinical teaching which declared that it was "better that the words of the law should be burned than delivered to women."

In one generation Jesus lifted women out of the disrespectful oblivion and the slavish drudgery of the ages. And it is the one shameful thing about the religion that presumed to take Jesus' name that it lacked the moral courage to follow this noble example in its subsequent attitude toward women.

As Jesus mingled with the people, they found him entirely free from the superstitions of that day. He was free from religious prejudices; he was never intolerant. He had nothing in his heart resembling social antagonism. While he complied with the good in the religion of his fathers, he did not hesitate to disregard man-made traditions of superstition and bondage. He dared to teach that catastrophes of nature, accidents of time, and other calamitous happenings are not visitations of divine judgments or mysterious dispensations of Providence. He denounced slavish devotion to meaningless ceremonials and exposed the fallacy of materialistic worship. He boldly proclaimed man's spiritual freedom and dared to teach that mortals of the flesh are indeed and in truth children of the living God.

Jesus transcended all the teachings of his forebears when he boldly substituted clean hearts for clean hands as the mark of true religion. He put reality in the place of tradition and swept aside all pretensions of vanity and hypocrisy. And yet this fearless man of God did not give vent to destructive criticism or manifest an utter disregard of the religious, social, economic, and political usages of his day. He was not a militant revolutionist; he was a progressive evolutionist. He engaged in the destruction of that which *was* only when he simultaneously offered his fellows the superior thing that *ought to be*.

Jesus received the obedience of his followers without exacting it. Only three men who received his personal call refused to accept the invitation to discipleship. He exercised a peculiar drawing power over men, but he was not dictatorial. He commanded confidence, and no man ever resented his giving a command. He assumed absolute authority over his disciples, but no one ever objected. He permitted his followers to call him Master.

The Master was admired by all who met him except by those who entertained deep-seated religious prejudices or those who thought they discerned political dangers in his teachings. Men were astonished at the originality and authoritativeness of his teaching. They marveled at his patience in dealing with backward and troublesome inquirers. He inspired hope and confidence in the hearts of all who came under his ministry. Only those who had not met him feared him, and he was hated only by those who regarded him as the champion of that truth which was destined to overthrow the evil and error which they had determined to hold in their hearts at all cost.

On both friends and foes he exercised a strong and peculiarly fascinating influence. Multitudes would follow him for weeks, just to hear his gracious words and behold his simple life. Devoted men and women loved Jesus with a well-nigh superhuman affection. And the better they knew him the more they loved him. And all this is still true; even today and in all future ages, the more men and women come to know this God-man, the more they will love and follow after him.

Notwithstanding the favorable reception of Jesus and his teachings by the common people, the religious leaders at Jerusalem became increasingly alarmed and antagonistic. The Pharisees had formulated a systematic and dogmatic theology. Jesus was a teacher who taught as the occasion served; he was not a systematic teacher. Jesus taught not so much from the law as from life, by parables. (And when he employed a parable for illustrating his message, he designed to utilize just *one* feature of the story for that purpose. Many wrong ideas concerning the teachings of Jesus may be secured by attempting to make allegories out of his parables.)

The religious leaders at Jerusalem were becoming well-nigh frantic as a result of the recent conversion of young Abraham and by the desertion of the three spies who had been baptized by Peter, and who were now out with the evangelists on this second preaching tour of Galilee. The Jewish leaders were increasingly blinded by fear and prejudice, while their hearts were hardened by the continued rejection of the appealing truths of the gospel of the kingdom. When men shut off the appeal to the spirit that dwells within them, there is little that can be done to modify their attitude.

When Jesus first met with the evangelists at the Bethsaida camp, in concluding his address, he said, "You should remember that in body and mind - emotionally - men react individually. The only *uniform* thing about men is the indwelling spirit. Though divine spirits may vary somewhat in the nature and extent of their experience, they react uniformly to all spiritual appeals. Only through, and by appeal to, this spirit can mankind ever attain unity and brotherhood."

But many of the leaders of the Jews had closed the doors of their hearts to the spiritual appeal of the gospel. From this day on they ceased not to plan and plot for the Master's destruction. They were convinced that Jesus must be apprehended, convicted, and executed as a religious offender, a violator of the cardinal teachings of the Jewish sacred law.

★   ★   ★

Jesus did very little public work on this preaching tour, but he conducted many evening classes with the believers in most of the cities and villages where he chanced to sojourn with James and John. At one of these evening sessions one of the younger evangelists asked Jesus a question about anger, and the Master, among other things, said in reply:

"Anger is a material manifestation which represents, in a general way, the measure of the failure of the spiritual nature to gain control of the combined intellectual and physical natures. Anger indicates your lack of tolerant brotherly love plus your lack of self-respect and self-control. Anger depletes the health, debases the mind, and handicaps the spirit teacher of man's soul. Have you not read in the Scriptures that 'wrath kills the foolish man,' and that man 'tears himself in his anger'? That 'he who is slow of wrath is of great understanding,' while 'he who is hasty of temper exalts folly'? You all know that 'a soft answer turns away wrath,' and how `grievous words stir up anger.' 'Discretion defers anger,' while 'he who has no control over his own self is like a defenseless city without walls.' 'Wrath is cruel and anger is outrageous.' 'Angry men stir up strife, while the furious multiply their transgressions.' 'Be not hasty in spirit, for anger rests in the bosom of fools.'"

Before Jesus ceased speaking, he said further, "Let your hearts be so dominated by love that your spirit guide will have little trouble in delivering you from the tendency to give vent to those outbursts of animal anger which are inconsistent with the status of divine sonship."

On this same occasion the Master talked to the group about the desirability of possessing well-balanced characters. He recognized that it was necessary for most men to devote themselves to the mastery of some vocation, but he deplored all tendencies toward overspecialization, toward becoming narrow-minded and circumscribed in life's activities. He called attention to the fact that any virtue, if carried to extremes, may become a vice. Jesus always preached temperance and taught consistency - proportionate adjustment of life problems. He pointed out that overmuch sympathy and pity may degenerate into serious emotional instability; that enthusiasm may drive on into fanaticism. He discussed one of their former associates whose imagination had led him off into visionary and impractical undertakings. At the same time he warned them against the dangers of the dullness of overly conservative mediocrity.

And then Jesus discoursed on the dangers of courage and faith, how they sometimes lead unthinking souls on to recklessness and presumption. He also showed how prudence and discretion, when carried too far, lead to cowardice and failure. He exhorted his hearers to strive for originality while they shunned all tendencies toward eccentricity. He pleaded for sympathy without sentimentality, piety without sanctimoniousness. He taught reverence free from fear and superstition.

It was not so much what Jesus taught about the balanced character that impressed his associates as the fact that his own life was such an eloquent exemplification of his teaching. He lived in the midst of stress and storm, but he never wavered. His enemies continually laid snares for him, but they never entrapped him. The wise and learned endeavored to trip him, but he did not stumble. They sought to embroil him in debate, but his answers were always enlightening, dignified, and final. When he was interrupted in his discourses with multitudinous questions, his answers were always significant and conclusive. Never did he resort to ignoble tactics in meeting the continuous pressure of his enemies, who did not hesitate to employ every sort of false, unfair, and unrighteous mode of attack upon him.

While it is true that many men and women must assiduously apply themselves to some definite pursuit as a livelihood vocation, it is nevertheless wholly desirable that human beings should cultivate a wide range of cultural familiarity with life as it is lived on earth. Truly educated persons are not satisfied with remaining in ignorance of the lives and doings of their fellows.

When Jesus was visiting the group of evangelists working under the supervision of Simon Zelotes, during their evening conference Simon asked the Master, "Why are some persons so much more happy and contented than others? Is contentment a matter of religious experience?"

Among other things, Jesus said in answer to Simon's question:

"Simon, some persons are naturally more happy than others. Much, very much, depends upon the willingness of man to be led and directed by the Father's spirit which lives within him. Have you not read in the Scriptures the words of the wise man, 'The spirit of man is the candle of the Lord, searching all the inward parts'? And also that such spirit-led mortals say: 'The lines are fallen to me in pleasant places; yes, I have a goodly heritage.' 'A little that a righteous man has is better than the riches of many wicked,' for 'a good man shall be satisfied from within himself.' 'A merry heart makes a cheerful countenance and is a continual feast. Better is a little with the reverence of the Lord than great treasure and trouble therewith. Better is a dinner of herbs where love is than a fatted ox and hatred therewith. Better is a little with righteousness than great revenues without rectitude.' 'A merry heart does good like a medicine.' 'Better is a handful with composure than a superabundance with sorrow and vexation of spirit.'

"Much of man's sorrow is born of the disappointment of his ambitions and the wounding of his pride. Although men owe a duty to themselves to make the best of their lives on earth, having thus sincerely exerted themselves, they should cheerfully accept their lot and exercise ingenuity in making the most of that which has fallen to their hands. All too many of man's troubles take origin in the fear soil of his own natural heart. 'The wicked flee when no man pursues.' 'The wicked are like the troubled sea, for it cannot rest, but its waters cast up mire and dirt; there is no peace, says God, for the wicked.'

"Seek not, then, for false peace and transient joy but rather for the assurance of faith and the sureties of divine sonship which yield composure, contentment, and supreme joy in the spirit."

Jesus hardly regarded this world as a "vale of tears." He rather looked upon it as the birth sphere of the eternal and immortal spirits of Paradise ascension, the "vale of soul making."

It was at Gamala, during the evening conference, that Philip said to Jesus: "Master, why is it that the Scriptures instruct us to 'fear the Lord,' while you would have us look to the Father in heaven without fear? How are we to harmonize these teachings?"

And Jesus replied to Philip, saying: "My children, I am not surprised that you ask such questions. In the beginning it was only through fear that man could learn reverence, but I have come to reveal the Father's love so that you will be attracted to the worship of the Eternal by the drawing of a child's affectionate recognition and reciprocation of the Father's profound and perfect love. I would deliver you from the bondage of driving yourselves through slavish fear to the irksome service of a jealous and wrathful King-God. I would instruct you in the Father-child relationship of God and man so that you may be joyfully led into that sublime and supernal free worship of a loving, just, and merciful Father-God.

"The 'fear of the Lord' has had different meanings in the successive ages, coming up from fear, through anguish and dread, to awe and reverence. And now from reverence I would lead you up, through recognition, realization, and appreciation, to *love*. When man recognizes only the works of God, he is led to fear the Supreme; but when man begins to understand and experience the personality and character of the living God, he is led increasingly to love such a good and perfect, universal and eternal Father. And it is just this changing of the relation of man to God that constitutes the mission of the Son of Man on earth.

"Intelligent children do not fear their father in order that they may receive good gifts from his hand; but having already received the abundance of good things bestowed by the dictates of the father's affection for his sons and daughters, these much loved children are led to love their father in responsive recognition and appreciation of such munificent beneficence. The goodness of God leads to repentance; the beneficence of God leads to service; the mercy of God leads to salvation; while the love of God leads to intelligent and freehearted worship.

"Your forebears feared God because he was mighty and mysterious. You shall adore Him because He is magnificent in love, plenteous in mercy, and glorious in truth. The power of God engenders fear in the heart of man, but the nobility and righteousness of His personality beget reverence, love, and willing worship. A dutiful and affectionate son does not fear or dread even a mighty and noble father. I have come into the world to put love in the place of fear, joy in the place of sorrow, confidence in the place of dread, loving service and appreciative worship in the place of slavish bondage and meaningless ceremonies. But it is still true of those who sit in darkness that 'the fear of the Lord is the beginning of wisdom.' But when the light has more fully come, the sons and daughters of God are led to praise the Infinite for what He *is* rather than to fear Him for what He *does*.

"When children are young and unthinking, they must necessarily be admonished to honor their parents; but when they grow older and become somewhat more appreciative of the benefits of the parental ministry and protection, they are led up, through understanding respect and increasing affection, to that level of experience where they actually love their parents for what they are more than for what they have done. The father naturally loves his child, but the child must develop his love for the father from the fear of what the father can do, through awe, dread, dependence, and reverence, to the appreciative and affectionate regard of love.

"You have been taught that you should 'fear God and keep His commandments, for that is the whole duty of man.' But I have come to give you a new and higher commandment. I would teach you to 'love God and learn to do His will, for that is the highest privilege of the liberated sons of God.' Your fathers were taught to 'fear God - the Almighty King.' I teach you, 'Love God - the all-merciful Father.'

"In the kingdom of heaven, which I have come to declare, there is no high and mighty king; this kingdom is a divine family. The universally recognized and unreservedly worshiped center and head of this far-flung brotherhood of intelligent beings is my Father and your Father. I am His Son, and you are also His sons. Therefore it is eternally true that you and I are brethren in the heavenly estate, and all the more so since we have become brethren in the flesh of the earthly life. Cease, then, to fear God as a king or serve Him as a master; learn to reverence Him as the Creator; honor him as the Father of your spirit youth; love him as a merciful defender; and ultimately worship Him as the loving and all-wise Father of your more mature spiritual realization and appreciation.

"Out of your wrong concepts of the Father in heaven grow your false ideas of humility and springs much of your hypocrisy. Man may be a worm of the dust by nature and origin, but when he becomes indwelt by my Father's spirit, that man becomes divine in his destiny. The bestowal spirit of my Father will surely return to the divine source and universe level of origin, and the human soul of mortal man which shall have become the reborn child of this indwelling spirit shall certainly ascend with the divine spirit to the very presence of the eternal Father.

"Humility, indeed, becomes mortal man who receives all these gifts from the Father in heaven, albeit there is a divine dignity attached to all such faith candidates for the eternal ascent of the heavenly kingdom. The meaningless and menial practices of an ostentatious and false humility are incompatible with the appreciation of the source of your salvation and the recognition of the destiny of your spirit-born souls. Humility before God is altogether appropriate in the depths of your hearts; meekness before men is commendable; but the hypocrisy of self-conscious and attention-craving humility is childish and unworthy of the enlightened sons and daughters of the kingdom.

"You do well to be meek before God and self-controlled before men, but let your meekness be of spiritual origin and not the self-deceptive display of a self-conscious sense of self-righteous superiority. The prophet spoke advisedly when he said, 'Walk humbly with God,' for, while the Father in heaven is the Infinite and the Eternal, He also dwells 'with him who is of a contrite mind and a humble spirit.' My Father disdains pride, loathes hypocrisy, and abhors iniquity. And it was to emphasize the value of sincerity and perfect trust in the loving support and faithful guidance of the heavenly Father that I have so often referred to the little child as illustrative of the attitude of mind and the response of spirit which are so essential to the entrance of mortal man into the spirit realities of the kingdom of heaven.

"Well did the Prophet Jeremiah describe many mortals when he said: 'You are near God in the mouth but far from him in the heart.' And have you not also read that direful warning of the prophet who said: 'The priests thereof teach for hire, and the prophets thereof divine for money. At the same time they profess piety and proclaim that the Lord is with them.' Have you not been well warned against those who 'speak peace to their neighbors when mischief is in their hearts,' those who 'flatter with the lips while the heart is given to double-dealing'? Of all the sorrows of a trusting man, none is so terrible as to be 'wounded in the house of a trusted friend.'"

Andrew, in consultation with Simon Peter and with the approval of Jesus, had instructed David at Bethsaida to dispatch messengers to the various preaching groups with instructions to terminate the tour and return to Bethsaida sometime on Thursday, December 30. By supper time on that rainy day all of the apostolic party and the teaching evangelists had arrived at the Zebedee home.

The group remained together over the Sabbath day, being accommodated in the homes of Bethsaida and near-by Capernaum, after which the entire party was granted a two weeks' recess to go home to their families, visit their friends, or go fishing. The two or three days they were together in Bethsaida were, indeed, exhilarating and inspiring; even the older teachers were edified by the young preachers as they narrated their experiences.

Of the 117 evangelists who participated in this second preaching tour of Galilee, only about seventy-five survived the test of actual experience and were on hand to be assigned to service at the end of the two weeks' recess. Jesus, with Andrew, Peter, James, and John, remained at the Zebedee home and spent much time in conference regarding the welfare and extension of the kingdom.

# The Third Preaching Tour

O N SUNDAY evening, January 16, A.D. 29, Abner, with the apostles of John, reached Bethsaida and went into joint conference with Andrew and the apostles of Jesus the next day. Abner and his associates made their headquarters at Hebron and were in the habit of coming up to Bethsaida periodically for these conferences.

Among the many matters considered by this joint conference was the practice of anointing the sick with certain forms of oil in connection with prayers for healing. Again did Jesus decline to participate in their discussions or to express himself regarding their conclusions. The apostles of John had always used the anointing oil in their ministry to the sick and afflicted, and they sought to establish this as a uniform practice for both groups, but the apostles of Jesus refused to bind themselves by such a regulation.

On Tuesday, January 18, the twenty-four were joined by the tested evangelists, about seventy-five in number, at the Zebedee house in Bethsaida preparatory to being sent forth on the third preaching tour of Galilee. This third mission continued for a period of seven weeks.

The evangelists were sent out in groups of five, while Jesus and the twelve traveled together most of the time, the apostles going out two and two to baptize believers as occasion required. For a period of almost three weeks Abner and his associates also worked with the evangelistic groups, advising them and baptizing believers. They visited Magdala, Tiberias, Nazareth, and all the principal cities and villages of central and southern Galilee, all the places previously visited and many others. This was their last message to Galilee, except to the northern portions.

O f all the daring things which Jesus did in connection with his earth career, the most amazing was his sudden announcement on the evening of January 16:

"On the morrow we will set apart ten women for the ministering work of the kingdom."

At the beginning of the two weeks' period during which the apostles and the evangelists were to be absent from Bethsaida on their furlough, Jesus had requested David to summon his parents back to their home and to dispatch messengers calling to Bethsaida ten devout women who had served in the administration of the former encampment and the tented infirmary. These women had all listened to the instruction given the young evangelists, but it had never occurred to either themselves or their teachers that Jesus would dare to commission women to teach the gospel of the kingdom and minister to the sick. These ten women selected and commissioned by Jesus were: Susanna, the daughter of the former chazan of the Nazareth synagogue; Joanna, the wife of Chuza, the steward of Herod Antipas; Elizabeth, the daughter of a wealthy Jew of Tiberias and Sepphoris; Martha, the elder sister of Andrew and Peter; Rachel, the sister-in-law of Jude, the Master's brother in the flesh; Nasanta, the daughter of Elman, the Syrian physician; Milcha, a cousin of the Apostle Thomas; Ruth, the eldest daughter of Matthew Levi; Celta, the daughter of a Roman centurion; and Agaman, a widow of Damascus. Subsequently, Jesus added two other women to this group - Mary Magdalene and Rebecca, the daughter of Joseph of Arimathea.

Jesus authorized these women to effect their own organization and directed Judas to provide funds for their equipment and for pack animals. The ten elected Susanna as their chief and Joanna as their treasurer. From this time on they furnished their own funds; never again did they draw upon Judas for support.

It was most astounding in that day, when women were not even allowed on the main floor of the synagogue (being confined to the women's gallery), to behold them being recognized as authorized teachers of the new gospel of the kingdom. The charge which Jesus gave these ten women as he set them apart for gospel teaching and ministry was the emancipation proclamation which set free all women and for all time; no more was man to look upon woman as his spiritual inferior. This was a decided shock to even the twelve apostles. Notwithstanding they had many times heard the Master say that "in the kingdom of heaven there is neither rich nor poor, free nor bond, male nor female, all are equally the sons and daughters of God," they were literally stunned when he proposed formally to commission these ten women as religious teachers and even to permit their traveling about with them. The whole country was stirred up by this proceeding, the enemies of Jesus making great capital out of this move, but everywhere the women believers in the good news stood staunchly behind their chosen sisters and voiced no uncertain approval of this tardy acknowledgment of woman's place in religious work.

And this liberation of women, giving them due recognition, was practiced by the apostles immediately after the Master's departure, albeit they fell back to the olden customs in subsequent generations. Throughout the early days of the Christian church, women teachers and ministers were called *deaconesses* and were accorded general recognition. But Paul, despite the fact that he conceded all this in theory, never really incorporated it into his own attitude and personally found it difficult to carry out in practice.

As the apostolic party journeyed from Bethsaida, the women traveled in the rear. During the conference time they always sat in a group in front and to the right of the speaker. Increasingly, women had become believers in the gospel of the kingdom, and it had been a source of much difficulty and no end of embarrassment when they had desired to hold personal converse with Jesus or one of the apostles. Now all this was changed. When any of the women believers desired to see the Master or confer with the apostles, they went to Susanna, and in company with one of the twelve women evangelists, they would go at once into the presence of the Master or one of his apostles.

It was at Magdala that the women first demonstrated their usefulness and vindicated the wisdom of their choosing. Andrew had imposed rather strict rules upon his associates about doing personal work with women, especially with those of questionable character. When the party entered Magdala, these ten women evangelists were free to enter the evil resorts and preach the glad tidings directly to all their inmates. And when visiting the sick, these women were able to draw very close in their ministry to their afflicted sisters. As the result of the ministry of these ten women (afterward known as the twelve women) at this place, Mary Magdalene was won for the kingdom. Through a succession of misfortunes and in consequence of the attitude of reputable society toward women who commit such errors of judgment, this woman had found herself in one of the nefarious resorts of Magdala. It was Martha and Rachel who made plain to Mary that the doors of the kingdom were open to even such as she. Mary believed the good news and was baptized by Peter the next day.

Mary Magdalene became the most effective teacher of the gospel among this group of twelve women evangelists. She was set apart for such service, together with Rebecca, at Jotapata about four weeks subsequent to her conversion. Mary and Rebecca, with the others of this group, went on through the remainder of Jesus' life on earth, laboring faithfully and effectively for the enlightenment and uplifting of their downtrodden sisters; and when the last and tragic episode in the drama of Jesus' life was being enacted, notwithstanding the apostles all fled but one, these women were all present, and not one either denied or betrayed him.

The Sabbath services of the apostolic party had been put in the hands of the women by Andrew, upon instructions from Jesus. This meant, of course, that they could not be held in the new synagogue. The women selected Joanna to have charge of this occasion, and the meeting was held in the banquet room of Herod's new palace, Herod being away in residence at Julias in Perea. Joanna read from the Scriptures concerning woman's work in the religious life of Israel, making reference to Miriam, Deborah, Esther, and others.

Late that evening Jesus gave the united group a memorable talk on "Magic and Superstition." In those days the appearance of a bright and supposedly new star was regarded as a token indicating that a great man had been born on earth. Such a star having then recently been observed, Andrew asked Jesus if these beliefs were well founded. In the long answer to Andrew's question the Master entered upon a thoroughgoing discussion of the whole subject of human superstition. The statement which Jesus made at this time may be summarized in modern phraseology as follows:

1. The courses of the stars in the heavens have nothing whatever to do with the events of human life on earth. Astronomy is a proper pursuit of science, but astrology is a mass of superstitious error which has no place in the gospel of the kingdom.

2. The examination of the internal organs of an animal recently killed can reveal nothing about weather, future events, or the outcome of human affairs.

3. The spirits of the dead do not come back to communicate with their families or their onetime friends among the living.

4. Charms and relics are impotent to heal disease, ward off disaster, or influence evil spirits; the belief in all such material means of influencing the spiritual world is nothing but gross superstition.

5. Casting lots, while it may be a convenient way of settling many minor difficulties, is not a method designed to disclose the divine will. Such outcomes are purely matters of material chance. The only means of communion with the spiritual world is embraced in the spirit endowment of mankind, the indwelling spirit of the Father, together with the outpoured spirit of the Son and the omnipresent influence of the Infinite Spirit.

6. Divination, sorcery, and witchcraft are superstitions of ignorant minds, as also are the delusions of magic. The belief in magic numbers, omens of good luck, and harbingers of bad luck, is pure and unfounded superstition.

7. The interpretation of dreams is largely a superstitious and groundless system of ignorant and fantastic speculation. The gospel of the kingdom must have nothing in common with the soothsayer priests of primitive religion.

8. The spirits of good or evil cannot dwell within material symbols of

clay, wood, or metal; idols are nothing more than the material of which they are made.

9. The practices of the enchanters, the wizards, the magicians, and the sorcerers, were derived from the superstitions of the Egyptians, the Assyrians, the Babylonians, and the ancient Canaanites. Amulets and all sorts of incantations are futile either to win the protection of good spirits or to ward off supposed evil spirits.

10. He exposed and denounced their belief in spells, ordeals, bewitching, cursing, signs, mandrakes, knotted cords, and all other forms of ignorant and enslaving superstition.

The next evening, having gathered together the twelve apostles, the apostles of John, and the newly commissioned women's group, Jesus said, "You see for yourselves that the harvest is plenteous, but the laborers are few. Let us all, therefore, pray the Lord of the harvest that He send forth still more laborers into His fields. While I remain to comfort and instruct the younger teachers, I would send out the older ones two and two that they may pass quickly over all Galilee preaching the gospel of the kingdom while it is yet convenient and peaceful." Then he designated the pairs of apostles as he desired them to go forth, and they were: Andrew and Peter, James and John Zebedee, Philip and Nathaniel, Thomas and Matthew, James and Judas Alpheus, Simon Zelotes and Judas Iscariot.

Jesus arranged the date for meeting the twelve at Nazareth, and in parting, he said, "On this mission go not to any city of the gentiles, neither go into Samaria, but go instead to the lost sheep of the house of Israel. Preach the gospel of the kingdom and proclaim the saving truth that mortals are children of God. Remember that the disciple is hardly above his master nor a servant greater than his lord. It is enough for the disciple to be equal with his master and the servant to become like his lord. If some people have dared to call the master of the house an associate of Beelzebub, how much more shall they so regard those of his household! But you should not fear these unbelieving enemies. I declare to you that there is nothing covered up that is not going to be revealed; there is nothing hidden that shall not be known. What I have taught you privately, that preach with wisdom in the open. What I have revealed to you in the inner chamber, that you are to proclaim in due season from the housetops. And I say to you, my friends and disciples, be not afraid of those who can kill the body, but who are not able to destroy the soul; rather put your trust in Him who is able to sustain the body and save the soul.

"Are not two sparrows sold for a penny? And yet I declare that not one of them is forgotten in God's sight. Know you not that the very hairs of your head are all numbered? Fear not, therefore; you are of more value than a great many sparrows. Be not ashamed of my teaching; go forth proclaiming peace and good will, but be not deceived - peace will not always attend your preaching. I came to bring peace on earth, but when men reject my gift, division and turmoil result. When all of a family receive the gospel of the kingdom, truly peace abides in that house; but when some of the family enter the kingdom and others reject the gospel, such division can produce only sorrow and sadness. Labor earnestly to save the whole family lest a man's foes become those of his own household. But, when you have done your utmost for all of every family, I declare to you that he who loves father or mother more than this gospel is not worthy of the kingdom."

When the twelve had heard these words, they made ready to depart. And they did not again come together until the time of their assembling at Nazareth to meet with Jesus and the other disciples as the Master had arranged.

O ne evening at Shunem, after John's apostles had returned to Hebron, and after Jesus' apostles had been sent out two and two, when the Master was engaged in teaching a group of twelve of the younger evangelists who were laboring under the direction of Jacob, together with the twelve women, Rachel asked Jesus this question: "Master, what shall we answer when women ask us, What shall I do to be saved?"

When Jesus heard this question, he answered, "When men and women ask what shall we do to be saved, you shall answer, Believe this gospel of the kingdom; accept divine forgiveness. By faith recognize the indwelling spirit of God, whose acceptance makes you a son of God. Have you not read in the Scriptures where it says, 'In the Lord have I righteousness and strength.' Also where the Father says, 'My righteousness is near; my salvation has gone forth, and my arms shall enfold my people.' 'My soul shall be joyful in the love of my God, for He has clothed me with the garments of salvation and has covered me with the robe of H1is righteousness.' Have you not also read of the Father that His name 'shall be called the Lord our righteousness.' 'Take away the filthy rags of self-righteousness and clothe my son with the robe of divine righteousness and eternal salvation.' It is forever true, 'the just shall live by faith.' Entrance into the Father's kingdom is wholly free, but progress - growth in grace - is essential to continuance therein.

"Salvation is the gift of the Father and is revealed by His Sons. Acceptance by faith on your part makes you a partaker of the divine nature, a son or a daughter of God. By faith you are justified; by faith are you saved; and by this same faith are you eternally advanced in the way of progressive and divine perfection. By faith was Abraham justified and made aware of salvation by the teachings of Melchizedek. All down through the ages has this same faith saved the sons of men, but now has a Son come forth from the Father to make salvation more real and acceptable."

When Jesus had left off speaking, there was great rejoicing among those who had heard these gracious words, and they all went on in the days that followed proclaiming the gospel of the kingdom with new power and with renewed energy and enthusiasm. And the women rejoiced all the more to know they were included in these plans for the establishment of the kingdom on earth.

In summing up his final statement, Jesus said, "You cannot buy salvation; you cannot earn righteousness. Salvation is the gift of God, and righteousness is the natural fruit of the spirit-born life of sonship in the kingdom. You are not to be saved because you live a righteous life; rather is it that you live a righteous life because you have already been saved, have recognized sonship as the gift of God and service in the kingdom as the supreme delight of life on earth. When men and women believe this gospel, which is a revelation of the goodness of God, they will be led to voluntary repentance of all known sin. Realization of sonship is incompatible with the desire to sin. Kingdom believers hunger for righteousness and thirst for divine perfection."

A t the evening discussions Jesus talked upon many subjects. During the remainder of this tour - before they all reunited at Nazareth - he discussed "The Love of God," "Dreams and Visions," "Malice," "Humility and Meekness," "Courage and Loyalty," "Music and Worship," "Service and Obedience," "Pride and Presumption," "Forgiveness in Relation to Repentance," "Peace and Perfection," "Evil Speaking and Envy," "Evil, Sin, and Temptation," "Doubts and Unbelief," "Wisdom and Worship." With the older apostles away, these younger groups of both men and women more freely entered into these discussions with the Master.

After spending two or three days with one group of twelve evangelists, Jesus would move on to join another group, being informed as to the whereabouts and movements of all these workers by David's messengers. This being their first tour, the women remained much of the time with Jesus. Through the messenger service each of these groups was kept fully informed concerning the progress of the tour, and the receipt of news from other groups was always a source of encouragement to these scattered and separated workers.

Before their separation it had been arranged that the twelve apostles, together with the evangelists and the women's corps, should assemble at Nazareth to meet the Master on Friday, March 4. Accordingly, about this time, from all parts of central and southern Galilee these various groups of apostles and evangelists began moving toward Nazareth. By mid-afternoon, Andrew and Peter, the last to arrive, had reached the encampment prepared by the early arrivals and situated on the highlands to the north of the city. And this was the first time Jesus had visited Nazareth since the beginning of his public ministry.

T his Friday afternoon Jesus walked about Nazareth quite unobserved and wholly unrecognized. He passed by the home of his childhood and the carpenter shop and spent a half hour on the hill which he so much enjoyed when a lad. Not since the day of his baptism by John in the Jordan had the Son of Man had such a flood of human emotion stirred up within his soul. While coming down from the mount, he heard the familiar sounds of the trumpet blast announcing the going down of the sun, just as he had so many, many times heard it when a boy growing up in Nazareth. Before returning to the encampment, he walked down by the synagogue where he had gone to school and indulged his mind in many reminiscences of his childhood days. Earlier in the day Jesus had sent Thomas to arrange with the ruler of the synagogue for his preaching at the Sabbath morning service.

The people of Nazareth were never reputed for piety and righteous living. As the years passed, this village became increasingly contaminated by the low moral standards of near-by Sepphoris. Throughout Jesus' youth and young manhood there had been a division of opinion in Nazareth regarding him; there was much resentment when he moved to Capernaum. While the inhabitants of Nazareth had heard much about the doings of their former carpenter, they were offended that he had never included his native village in any of his earlier preaching tours. They had indeed heard of Jesus' fame, but the majority of the citizens were angry because he had done none of his great works in the city of his youth. For months the people of Nazareth had discussed Jesus much, but their opinions were, on the whole, unfavorable toward him.

Thus did the Master find himself in the midst of, not a welcome homecoming, but a decidedly hostile and hypercritical atmosphere. But this was not all. His enemies, knowing that he was to spend this Sabbath day in Nazareth and supposing that he would speak in the synagogue, had hired numerous rough and uncouth men to harass him and in every way possible make trouble.

Most of the older of Jesus' friends, including the doting chazan teacher of his youth, were dead or had left Nazareth, and the younger generation was prone to resent his fame with strong jealousy. They failed to remember his early devotion to his father's family, and they were bitter in their criticism of his neglect to visit his brother and his married sisters living in Nazareth. The attitude of Jesus' family toward him had also tended to increase this unkind feeling of the citizenry. The orthodox among the Jews even presumed to criticize Jesus because he walked too fast on the way to the synagogue this Sabbath morning.


This Sabbath was a beautiful day, and all Nazareth, friends and foes, turned out to hear this former citizen of their town discourse in the synagogue. Many of the apostolic retinue had to remain without the synagogue; there was not room for all who had come to hear him. As a young man Jesus had often spoken in this place of worship, and this morning, when the ruler of the synagogue handed him the roll of sacred writings from which to read the Scripture lesson, none present seemed to recall that this was the very manuscript which he had presented to this synagogue.

The services on this day were conducted just as when Jesus had attended them as a boy. He ascended the speaking platform with the ruler of the synagogue, and the service was begun by the recital of two prayers: "Blessed is the Lord, King of the world, who forms the light and creates the darkness, who makes peace and creates everything; who, in mercy, gives light to the earth and to those who dwell upon it and in goodness, day by day and every day, renews the works of creation. Blessed is the Lord our God for the glory of His handiworks and for the light-giving lights which he has made for His praise. Selah. Blessed is the Lord our God, who has formed the lights."

After a moment's pause they again prayed: "With great love has the Lord our God loved us, and with much overflowing pity has He pitied us, our Father and our King, for the sake of our fathers who trusted in him. You taught them the statutes of life; have mercy upon us and teach us. Enlighten our eyes in the law; cause our hearts to cleave to your commandments; unite our hearts to love and fear your name, and we shall not be put to shame, world without end. For you are a God who prepares salvation, and us have you chosen from among all nations and tongues, and in truth have you brought us near your great name - selah - that we may lovingly praise your unity. Blessed is the Lord, who in love chose his people Israel."

The congregation then recited the Shema, the Jewish creed of faith. This ritual consisted in repeating numerous passages from the law and indicated that the worshipers took upon themselves the yoke of the kingdom of heaven, also the yoke of the commandments as applied to the day and the night.

And then followed the third prayer: "True it is that you are Yahweh, our God and the God of our fathers; our King and the King of our fathers; our Savior and the Savior of our fathers; our Creator and the rock of our salvation; our help and our deliverer. Your name is from everlasting, and there is no God beside you. A new song did they that were delivered sing to your name by the seashore; together did all praise and own you King and say, Yahweh shall reign, world without end. Blessed is the Lord who saves Israel."

The ruler of the synagogue then took his place before the ark, or chest, containing the sacred writings and began the recitation of the nineteen prayer eulogies, or benedictions. But on this occasion it was desirable to shorten the service in order that the distinguished guest might have more time for his discourse; accordingly, only the first and last of the benedictions were recited. The first was: "Blessed is the Lord our God, and the God of our fathers, the God of Abraham, and the God of Isaac, and the God of Jacob; the great, the mighty, and the terrible God, who shows mercy and kindness, who creates all things, who remembers the gracious promises to the fathers and brings a savior to their children's children for his own name's sake, in love. O King, helper, savior, and shield! Blessed are you, O Yahweh, the shield of Abraham."

Then followed the last benediction: "O bestow on your people Israel great peace forever, for you are King and the Lord of all peace. And it is good in your eyes to bless Israel at all times and at every hour with peace. Blessed are you, Yahweh, who blesses his people Israel with peace." The congregation looked not at the ruler as he recited the benedictions. Following the benedictions he offered an informal prayer suitable for the occasion, and when this was concluded, all the congregation joined in saying amen.

Then the chazan went over to the ark and brought out a roll, which he presented to Jesus that he might read the Scripture lesson. It was customary to call upon seven persons to read not less than three verses of the law, but this practice was waived on this occasion that the visitor might read the lesson of his own selection. Jesus, taking the roll, stood up and began to read from Deuteronomy: "For this commandment which I give you this day is not hidden from you, neither is it far off. It is not in heaven, that you should say, who shall go up for us to heaven and bring it down to us that we may hear and do it? Neither is it beyond the sea, that you should say, who will go over the sea for us to bring the commandment to us that we may hear and do it? No, the word of life is very near to you, even in your presence and in your heart, that you may know and obey it."

And when he had ceased reading from the law, he turned to Isaiah and began to read: "The spirit of the Lord is upon me because he has anointed me to preach good tidings to the poor. He has sent me to proclaim release to the captives and the recovering of sight to the blind, to set at liberty those who are bruised and to proclaim the acceptable year of the Lord."

Jesus closed the book and, after handing it back to the ruler of the synagogue, sat down and began to discourse to the people. He began by saying: "Today are these Scriptures fulfilled." And then Jesus spoke for almost fifteen minutes on "The Sons and Daughters of God." Many of the people were pleased with the discourse, and they marveled at his graciousness and wisdom.

It was customary in the synagogue, after the conclusion of the formal service, for the speaker to remain so that those who might be interested could ask him questions. Accordingly, on this Sabbath morning Jesus stepped down into the crowd that pressed forward to ask questions. In this group were many turbulent individuals whose minds were bent on mischief, while about the fringe of this crowd there circulated those debased men who had been hired to make trouble for Jesus. Many of the disciples and evangelists who had remained without now pressed into the synagogue and were not slow to recognize that trouble was brewing. They sought to lead the Master away, but he would not go with them.

Jesus found himself surrounded in the synagogue by a great throng of his enemies and a sprinkling of his own followers, and in reply to their rude questions and sinister banterings he half humorously remarked, "Yes, I am Joseph's son; I am the carpenter, and I am not surprised that you remind me of the proverb, 'Physician heal yourself,' and that you challenge me to do in Nazareth what you have heard I did at Capernaum; but I call you to witness that even the Scriptures declare that 'a prophet is not without honor save in his own country and among his own people.'"

But they jostled him and, pointing accusing fingers at him, said, "You think you are better than the people of Nazareth; you moved away from us, but your brother is a common workman, and your sisters still live among us. We know your mother, Mary. Where are they today? We hear big things about you, but we notice that you do no wonders when you come back."

Jesus answered them, "I love the people who dwell in the city where I grew up, and I would rejoice to see you all enter the kingdom of heaven, but the doing of the works of God is not for me to determine. The transformations of grace are wrought in response to the living faith of those who are the beneficiaries."

Jesus would have good-naturedly managed the crowd and effectively disarmed even his violent enemies had it not been for the tactical blunder of one of his own apostles, Simon Zelotes, who, with the help of Nahor, one of the younger evangelists, had meanwhile gathered together a group of Jesus' friends from among the crowd and, assuming a belligerent attitude, had served notice on the enemies of the Master to go hence. Jesus had long taught the apostles that a soft answer turns away wrath, but his followers were not accustomed to seeing their beloved teacher, whom they so willingly called Master, treated with such discourtesy and disdain. It was too much for them, and they found themselves giving expression to passionate and vehement resentment, all of which only tended to arouse the mob spirit in this ungodly and uncouth assembly. And so, under the leadership of hirelings, these ruffians laid hold upon Jesus and rushed him out of the synagogue to the brow of a near-by precipitous hill, where they were minded to shove him over the edge to his death below. But just as they were about to push him over the edge of the cliff, Jesus turned suddenly upon his captors and, facing them, quietly folded his arms. He said nothing, but his friends were more than astonished when, as he started to walk forward, the mob parted and permitted him to pass on unmolested.

Jesus, followed by his disciples, proceeded to their encampment, where all this was recounted. And they made ready that evening to go back to Capernaum early the next day, as Jesus had directed. This turbulent ending of the third public preaching tour had a sobering effect upon all of Jesus' followers. They were beginning to realize the meaning of some of the Master's teachings; they were awaking to the fact that the kingdom would come only through much sorrow and bitter disappointment.

They left Nazareth this Sunday morning, and traveling by different routes, they all finally assembled at Bethsaida by noon on Thursday, March 10. They came together as a sober and serious group of disillusioned preachers of the gospel of truth and not as an enthusiastic and all-conquering band of triumphant crusaders.

## TARRYING AND TEACHING BY THE SEASIDE

B Y MARCH 10 all of the preaching and teaching groups had forgathered at Bethsaida. Thursday night and Friday many of them went out to fish, while on the Sabbath day they attended the synagogue to hear an aged Jew of Damascus discourse on the glory of father Abraham. Jesus spent most of this Sabbath day alone in the hills. That Saturday night the Master talked for more than an hour to the assembled groups on "The mission of adversity and the spiritual value of disappointment." This was a memorable occasion, and his hearers never forgot the lesson he imparted.

Jesus had not fully recovered from the sorrow of his recent rejection at Nazareth; the apostles were aware of a peculiar sadness mingled with his usual cheerful demeanor. James and John were with him much of the time, Peter being more than occupied with the many responsibilities having to do with the welfare and direction of the new corps of evangelists. This time of waiting before starting for the Passover at Jerusalem, the women spent in visiting from house to house, teaching the gospel, and ministering to the sick in Capernaum and the surrounding cities and villages.

A bout this time Jesus first began to employ the parable method of teaching the multitudes that so frequently gathered about him. Since Jesus had talked with the apostles and others long into the night, on this Sunday morning very few of the group were up for breakfast; so he went out by the seaside and sat alone in the boat, the old fishing boat of Andrew and Peter, which was always kept at his disposal, and meditated on the next move to be made in the work of extending the kingdom. But the Master was not to be alone for long. Very soon the people from Capernaum and near-by villages began to arrive, and by ten o'clock that morning almost one thousand were assembled on shore near Jesus' boat and were clamoring for attention.

Peter was now up and, making his way to the boat, said to Jesus, "Master, shall I talk to them?"

Jesus answered, "No, Peter, I will tell them a story." And then Jesus began the recital of the parable of the sower, one of the first of a long series of such parables which he taught the throngs that followed after him. This boat had an elevated seat on which he sat (for it was the custom to sit when teaching) while he talked to the crowd assembled along the shore.

After Peter had spoken a few words, Jesus said, "A sower went forth to sow, and it came to pass as he sowed that some seed fell by the wayside to be trodden underfoot and devoured by the birds of heaven. Other seed fell upon the rocky places where there was little earth, and immediately it sprang up because there was no depth to the soil, but as soon as the sun shone, it withered because it had no root whereby to secure moisture. Other seed fell among the thorns, and as the thorns grew up, it was choked so that it yielded no grain. Still other seed fell upon good ground and, growing, yielded, some thirtyfold, some sixtyfold, and some a hundredfold." And when he had finished speaking this parable, he said to the multitude, "He who has ears to hear, let him hear."

The apostles and those who were with them, when they heard Jesus teach the people in this manner, were greatly perplexed; and after much talking among themselves, that evening in the Zebedee garden Matthew said to Jesus: "Master, what is the meaning of the dark sayings which you present to the multitude? Why do you speak in parables to those who seek the truth?"

And Jesus answered, "In patience have I instructed you all this time. To you it is given to know the mysteries of the kingdom of heaven, but to the undiscerning multitudes and to those who seek our destruction, from now on, the mysteries of the kingdom shall be presented in parables. And this we will do so that those who really desire to enter the kingdom may discern the meaning of the teaching and thus find salvation, while those who listen only to ensnare us may be the more confounded in that they will see without seeing and will hear without hearing. My children, do you not perceive the law of the spirit which decrees that to him who has shall be given so that he shall have an abundance; but from him who has not shall be taken away even that which he has. Therefore will I henceforth speak to the people much in parables to the end that our friends and those who desire to know the truth may find that which they seek, while our enemies and those who love not the truth may hear without understanding. Many of these people follow not in the way of the truth. The prophet did, indeed, describe all such undiscerning souls when he said: 'For this people's heart has waxed gross, and their ears are dull of hearing, and their eyes they have closed lest they should discern the truth and understand it in their hearts.'" .

The apostles did not fully comprehend the significance of the Master's words. As Andrew and Thomas talked further with Jesus, Peter and the other apostles withdrew to another portion of the garden where they engaged in earnest and prolonged discussion.

Peter and the group about him came to the conclusion that the parable of the sower was an allegory, that each feature had some hidden meaning, and so they decided to go to Jesus and ask for an explanation. Accordingly, Peter approached the Master, saying, "We are not able to penetrate the meaning of this parable, and we desire that you explain it to us since you say it is given us to know the mysteries of the kingdom."

And when Jesus heard this, he said, "My son, I desire to withhold nothing from you, but first suppose you tell me what you have been talking about; what is your interpretation of the parable?"

After a moment of silence, Peter said, "Master, we have talked much concerning the parable, and this is the interpretation I have decided upon: The sower is the gospel preacher; the seed is the word of God. The seed which fell by the wayside represents those who do not understand the gospel teaching. The birds which snatched away the seed that fell upon the hardened ground represent Satan, or the evil one, who steals away that which has been sown in the hearts of these ignorant ones. The seed which fell upon the rocky places, and which sprang up so suddenly, represents those superficial and unthinking persons who, when they hear the glad tidings, receive the message with joy; but because the truth has no real root in their deeper understanding, their devotion is short-lived in the face of tribulation and persecution. When trouble comes, these believers stumble; they fall away when tempted. The seed which fell among thorns represents those who hear the word willingly, but who allow the cares of the world and the deceitfulness of riches to choke the word of truth so that it becomes unfruitful. Now the seed which fell on good ground and sprang up to bear, some thirty, some sixty, and some a hundredfold, represents those who, when they have heard the truth, receive it with varying degrees of appreciation - owing to their differing intellectual endowments - and hence manifest these varying degrees of religious experience."

Jesus, after listening to Peter's interpretation of the parable, asked the other apostles if they did not also have suggestions to offer. To this invitation only Nathaniel responded. Said he, "Master, while I recognize many good things about Simon Peter's interpretation of the parable, I do not fully agree with him. My idea of this parable would be: The seed represents the gospel of the kingdom, while the sower stands for the messengers of the kingdom. The seed which fell by the wayside on hardened ground represents those who have heard but little of the gospel, along with those who are indifferent to the message, and who have hardened their hearts. The birds of the sky that snatched away the seed which fell by the wayside represent one's habits of life, the temptation of evil, and the desires of the flesh. The seed which fell among the rocks stands for those emotional souls who are quick to receive new teaching and equally quick to give up the truth when confronted with the difficulties and realities of living up to this truth; they lack spiritual perception. The seed which fell among the thorns represents those who are attracted to the truths of the gospel; they are minded to follow its teachings, but they are prevented by the pride of life, jealousy, envy, and the anxieties of human existence. The seed which fell on good soil, springing up to bear, some thirty, some sixty, and some a hundredfold, represents the natural and varying degrees of ability to comprehend truth and respond to its spiritual teachings by men and women who possess diverse endowments of spirit illumination."

When Nathaniel had finished speaking, the apostles and their associates fell into serious discussion and engaged in earnest debate, some contending for the correctness of Peter's interpretation, while almost an equal number sought to defend Nathaniel's explanation of the parable. Meanwhile Peter and Nathaniel had withdrawn to the house, where they were involved in a vigorous and determined effort the one to convince and change the mind of the other.

The Master permitted this confusion to pass the point of most intense expression; then he clapped his hands and called them about him. When they had all gathered around him once more, he said, "Before I tell you about this parable, do any of you have aught to say?"

Following a moment of silence, Thomas spoke, "Yes, Master, I wish to say a few words. I remember that you once told us to beware of this very thing. You instructed us that, when using illustrations for our preaching, we should employ true stories, not fables, and that we should select a story best suited to the illustration of the one central and vital truth which we wished to teach the people, and that, having so used the story, we should not attempt to make a spiritual application of all the minor details involved in the telling of the story. I hold that Peter and Nathaniel are both wrong in their attempts to interpret this parable. I admire their ability to do these things, but I am equally sure that all such attempts to make a natural parable yield spiritual analogies in all its features can only result in confusion and serious misconception of the true purpose of such a parable. That I am right is fully proved by the fact that, whereas we were all of one mind an hour ago, now are we divided into two separate groups who hold different opinions concerning this parable and hold such opinions so earnestly as to interfere, in my opinion, with our ability fully to grasp the great truth which you had in mind when you presented this parable to the multitude and subsequently asked us to make comment upon it."

The words which Thomas spoke had a quieting effect on all of them. He caused them to recall what Jesus had taught them on former occasions, and before Jesus resumed speaking, Andrew arose, saying, "I am persuaded that Thomas is right, and I would like to have him tell us what meaning he attaches to the parable of the sower."

After Jesus had beckoned Thomas to speak, he said, "My brethren, I did not wish to prolong this discussion, but if you so desire, I will say that I think this parable was spoken to teach us one great truth. And that is that our teaching of the gospel of the kingdom, no matter how faithfully and efficiently we execute our divine commissions, is going to be attended by varying degrees of success; and that all such differences in results are directly due to conditions inherent in the circumstances of our ministry, conditions over which we have little or no control."

When Thomas had finished speaking, the majority of his fellow preachers were about ready to agree with him, even Peter and Nathaniel were on their way over to speak with him, when Jesus arose and said, "Well done, Thomas; you have discerned the true meaning of parables; but both Peter and Nathaniel have done you all equal good in that they have so fully shown the danger of undertaking to make an allegory out of my parables. In your own hearts you may often profitably engage in such flights of the speculative imagination, but you make a mistake when you seek to offer such conclusions as a part of your public teaching."

Now that the tension was over, Peter and Nathaniel congratulated each other on their interpretations, and with the exception of the Alpheus twins, each of the apostles ventured to make an interpretation of the parable of the sower before they retired for the night. Even Judas Iscariot offered a very plausible interpretation. The twelve would often, among themselves, attempt to figure out the Master's parables as they would an allegory, but never again did they regard such speculations seriously. This was a very profitable session for the apostles and their associates, especially so since from this time on Jesus more and more employed parables in connection with his public teaching.

The apostles were parable-minded, so much so that the whole of the next evening was devoted to the further discussion of parables. Jesus introduced the evening's conference by saying, "My beloved, you must always make a difference in teaching so as to suit your presentation of truth to the minds and hearts before you. When you stand before a multitude of varying intellects and temperaments, you cannot speak different words for each class of hearers, but you can tell a story to convey your teaching; and each group, even each individual, will be able to make his own interpretation of your parable in accordance with his own intellectual and spiritual endowments. You are to let your light shine but do so with wisdom and discretion. No man, when he lights a lamp, covers it up with a vessel or puts it under the bed; he puts his lamp on a stand where all can behold the light. Let me tell you that nothing is hid in the kingdom of heaven which shall not be made manifest; neither are there any secrets which shall not ultimately be made known. Eventually, all these things shall come to light. Think not only of the multitudes and how they hear the truth; take heed also to yourselves how you hear. Remember that I have many times told you: To him who has shall be given more, while from him who has not shall be taken away even that which he thinks he has."

The continued discussion of parables and further instruction as to their interpretation may be summarized and expressed in modern phraseology as follows:

1. Jesus advised against the use of either fables or allegories in teaching the truths of the gospel. He did recommend the free use of parables, especially nature parables. He emphasized the value of utilizing the *analogy* existing between the natural and the spiritual worlds as a means of teaching truth. He frequently alluded to the natural as "the unreal and fleeting shadow of spirit realities."

2. Jesus narrated three or four parables from the Hebrew scriptures, calling attention to the fact that this method of teaching was not wholly new. However, it became almost a new method of teaching as he employed it from this time onward.

3. In teaching the apostles the value of parables, Jesus called attention to the following points:

I. The parable provides for a simultaneous appeal to vastly different levels of mind and spirit. The parable stimulates the imagination, challenges the discrimination, and provokes critical thinking; it promotes sympathy without arousing antagonism.

II. The parable proceeds from the things which are known to the discernment of the unknown. The parable utilizes the material and natural as a means of introducing the spiritual and the supermaterial. Parables favor the making of impartial moral decisions. The parable evades much prejudice and puts new truth gracefully into the mind and does all this with the arousal of a minimum of the self-defense of personal resentment.

III. To reject the truth contained in parabolic analogy requires conscious intellectual action that is directly in contempt of one's honest judgment and fair decision. The parable conduces to the forcing of thought through the sense of hearing.

IV. The use of the parable form of teaching enables the teacher to present new and even startling truths while at the same time he largely avoids all controversy and outward clashing with tradition and established authority.

V. The parable also possesses the advantage of stimulating the memory of the truth taught when the same familiar scenes are subsequently encountered.

In this way Jesus sought to acquaint his followers with many of the reasons underlying his practice of increasingly using parables in his public teaching.

Toward the close of the evening's lesson Jesus made his first comment on the parable of the sower. He said the parable referred to two things: First, it was a review of his own ministry up to that time and a forecast of what lay ahead of him for the remainder of his life on earth. And second, it was also a hint as to what the apostles and other messengers of the kingdom might expect in their ministry from generation to generation as time passed.

Jesus also resorted to the use of parables as the best possible refutation of the studied effort of the religious leaders at Jerusalem to teach that all of his work was done by the assistance of demons and the prince of devils. The appeal to nature was in contravention of such teaching since the people of that day looked upon all natural phenomena as the product of the direct act of spiritual beings and supernatural forces. He also determined upon this method of teaching because it enabled him to proclaim vital truths to those who desired to know the better way while at the same time affording his enemies less opportunity to find cause for offense and for accusations against him.

Before he dismissed the group for the night, Jesus said, "Now will I tell you the last of the parable of the sower. I would test you to know how you will receive this: The kingdom of heaven is also like a man who cast good seed upon the earth; and while he slept by night and went about his business by day, the seed sprang up and grew, and although he knew not how it came about, the plant came to fruit. First there was the blade, then the ear, then the full grain in the ear. And then when the grain was ripe, he put forth the sickle, and the harvest was finished. He who has an ear to hear, let him hear."

Many times did the apostles turn this saying over in their minds, but the Master never made further mention of this addition to the parable of the sower.

The next day Jesus again taught the people from the boat, saying, "The kingdom of heaven is like a man who sowed good seed in his field; but while he slept, his enemy came and sowed weeds among the wheat and hastened away. And so when the young blades sprang up and later were about to bring forth fruit, there appeared also the weeds. Then the servants of this householder came and said to him, 'Sir, did you not sow good seed in your field? Whence then come these weeds?'

And he replied to his servants, 'An enemy has done this.'

The servants then asked their master, 'Would you have us go out and pluck up these weeds?'

But he answered them and said, 'No, lest while you are gathering them up, you uproot the wheat also. Rather let them both grow together until the time of the harvest, when I will say to the reapers, Gather up first the weeds and bind them in bundles to burn and then gather up the wheat to be stored in my barn.'"

After the people had asked a few questions, Jesus spoke another parable. "The kingdom of heaven is like a grain of mustard seed which a man sowed in his field. Now a mustard seed is the least of seeds, but when it is full grown, it becomes the greatest of all herbs and is like a tree so that the birds of heaven are able to come and rest in the branches thereof."

"The kingdom of heaven is also like leaven which a woman took and hid in three measures of meal, and in this way it came about that all of the meal was leavened."

"The kingdom of heaven is also like a treasure hidden in a field, which a man discovered. In his joy he went forth to sell all he had that he might have the money to buy the field."

"The kingdom of heaven is also like a merchant seeking goodly pearls; and having found one pearl of great price, he went out and sold everything he possessed that he might be able to buy the extraordinary pearl."

"Again, the kingdom of heaven is like a sweep net which was cast into the sea, and it gathered up every kind of fish. Now, when the net was filled, the fishermen drew it up on the beach, where they sat down and sorted out the fish, gathering the good into vessels while the bad they threw away."

Many other parables spoke Jesus to the multitudes. In fact, from this time forward he seldom taught the masses except by this means. After speaking to a public audience in parables, he would, during the evening classes, more fully and explicitly expound his teachings to the apostles and the evangelists.

The multitude continued to increase throughout the week. On Sabbath Jesus hastened away to the hills, but when Sunday morning came, the crowds returned. Jesus spoke to them in the early afternoon after the preaching of Peter, and when he had finished, he said to his apostles, "I am weary of the throngs; let us cross over to the other side that we may rest for a day."

On the way across the lake they encountered one of those violent and sudden windstorms which are characteristic of the Sea of Galilee, especially at this season of the year. This body of water is almost seven hundred feet below the level of the sea and is surrounded by high banks, especially on the west. There are steep gorges leading up from the lake into the hills, and as the heated air rises in a pocket over the lake during the day, there is a tendency after sunset for the cooling air of the gorges to rush down upon the lake. These gales come on quickly and sometimes go away just as suddenly.

It was just such an evening gale that caught the boat carrying Jesus over to the other side on this Sunday evening. Three other boats containing some of the younger evangelists were trailing after. This tempest was severe, notwithstanding that it was confined to this region of the lake, there being no evidence of a storm on the western shore. The wind was so strong that the waves began to wash over the boat. The high wind had torn the sail away before the apostles could furl it, and they were now entirely dependent on their oars as they laboriously pulled for the shore, a little more than a mile and a half distant.

Meanwhile Jesus lay asleep in the stern of the boat under a small overhead shelter. The Master was weary when they left Bethsaida, and it was to secure rest that he had directed them to sail him across to the other side. These ex-fishermen were strong and experienced oarsmen, but this was one of the worst gales they had ever encountered. Although the wind and the waves tossed their boat about as though it were a toy ship, Jesus slumbered on undisturbed. Peter was at the right-hand oar near the stern. When the boat began to fill with water, he dropped his oar and, rushing over to Jesus, shook him vigorously in order to awaken him, and when he was aroused, Peter said, "Master, don't you know we are in a violent storm? If you do not save us, we will all perish."

As Jesus came out in the rain, he looked first at Peter, and then peering into the darkness at the struggling oarsmen, he turned his glance back upon Simon Peter, who, in his agitation, had not yet returned to his oar, and said, "Why are all of you so filled with fear? Where is your faith? Peace, be quiet."

Jesus had hardly uttered this rebuke to Peter and the other apostles, he had hardly bidden Peter seek peace wherewith to quiet his troubled soul, when the disturbed atmosphere, having established its equilibrium, settled down into a great calm. The angry waves almost immediately subsided, while the dark clouds, having spent themselves in a short shower, vanished, and the stars of heaven shone overhead. All this was purely coincidental as far as we can judge; but the apostles, particularly Simon Peter, never ceased to regard the episode as a nature miracle. It was especially easy for the men of that day to believe in nature miracles inasmuch as they firmly believed that all nature was a phenomenon directly under the control of spirit forces and supernatural beings.

Jesus plainly explained to the twelve that he had spoken to their troubled spirits and had addressed himself to their fear-tossed minds, that he had not commanded the elements to obey his word, but it was of no avail. The Master's followers always persisted in placing their own interpretation on all such coincidental occurrences. From this day on they insisted on regarding the Master as having absolute power over the natural elements. Peter never grew weary of reciting how "even the winds and the waves obey him."

It was late in the evening when Jesus and his associates reached the shore, and since it was a calm and beautiful night, they all rested in the boats, not going ashore until shortly after sunrise the next morning. When they were gathered together, about forty in all, Jesus said, "Let us go up into yonder hills and tarry for a few days while we ponder over the problems of the Father's kingdom."

☆ ☆ ☆

Although most of the near-by eastern shore of the lake sloped up gently to the highlands beyond, at this particular spot there was a steep hillside, the shore in some places dropping sheer down into the lake.

Pointing up to the side of the near-by hill, Jesus said, "Let us go up on this hillside for our breakfast and under some of the shelters rest and talk."

This entire hillside was covered with caverns that had been hewn out of the rock. Many of these niches were ancient sepulchres. About halfway up the hillside on a small, relatively level spot was the cemetery of the little village of Kheresa. As Jesus and his associates passed near this burial ground, a lunatic who lived in these hillside caverns rushed up to them. This demented man was well known about these parts, having onetime been bound with fetters and chains and confined in one of the grottoes. Long since he had broken his shackles and now roamed at will among the tombs and abandoned sepulchres.

This man, whose name was Amos, was afflicted with a periodic form of insanity. There were considerable spells when he would find some clothing and deport himself fairly well among his fellows. During one of these lucid intervals he had gone over to Bethsaida, where he heard the preaching of Jesus and the apostles, and at that time had become a halfhearted believer in the gospel of the kingdom. But soon a stormy phase of his trouble appeared, and he fled to the tombs, where he moaned, cried out aloud, and so conducted himself as to terrorize all who chanced to meet him.

When Amos recognized Jesus, he fell down at his feet and exclaimed, "I know you, Jesus, but I am possessed of many devils, and I beseech that you will not torment me." This man truly believed that his periodic mental affliction was due to the fact that, at such times, evil or unclean spirits entered into him and dominated his mind and body. His troubles were mostly emotional - his brain was not grossly diseased.

Jesus, looking down upon the man crouching like an animal at his feet, reached down and, taking him by the hand, stood him up and said, "Amos, you are not possessed of a devil; you have already heard the good news that you are a son of God. I command you to come out of this spell."

And when Amos heard Jesus speak these words, there occurred such a transformation in his intellect that he was immediately restored to his right mind and the normal control of his emotions. By this time a considerable crowd had assembled from the near-by village, and these people, augmented by the swine herders from the highland above them, were astonished to see the lunatic sitting with Jesus and his followers, in possession of his right mind and freely conversing with them.

As the swine herders rushed into the village to spread the news of the taming of the lunatic, the dogs charged upon a small and untended herd of about thirty swine and drove most of them over a precipice into the sea. And it was this incidental occurrence, in connection with the presence of Jesus and the supposed miraculous curing of the lunatic, that gave origin to the legend that Jesus had cured Amos by casting a legion of devils out of him, and that these devils had entered into the herd of swine, causing them forthwith to rush headlong to their destruction in the sea below. Before the day was over, this episode was published abroad by the swine tenders, and the whole village believed it. Amos most certainly believed this story; he saw the swine tumbling over the brow of the hill shortly after his troubled mind had quieted down, and he always believed that they carried with them the very evil spirits which had so long tormented and afflicted him. And this had a good deal to do with the permanency of his cure. It is equally true that all of Jesus' apostles (save Thomas) believed that the episode of the swine was directly connected with the cure of Amos.

Jesus did not obtain the rest he was looking for. Most of that day he was thronged by those who came in response to the word that Amos had been cured, and who were attracted by the story that the demons had gone out of the lunatic into the herd of swine. And so, after only one night of rest, early Tuesday morning Jesus and his friends were awakened by a delegation of these swine-raising gentiles who had come to urge that he depart from their midst. Said their spokesman to Peter and Andrew: "Fishermen of Galilee, depart from us and take your prophet with you. We know he is a holy man, but the gods of our country do not know him, and we stand in danger of losing many swine. The fear of you has descended upon us, so that we pray you to go hence."

And when Jesus heard them, he said to Andrew, "Let us return to our place."

As they were about to depart, Amos besought Jesus to permit him to go back with them, but the Master would not consent. Said Jesus to Amos: "Forget not that you are a son of God. Return to your own people and show them what great things God has done for you."

And Amos went about publishing that Jesus had cast a legion of devils out of his troubled soul, and that these evil spirits had entered into a herd of swine, driving them to quick destruction. And he did not stop until he had gone into all the cities of the Decapolis, declaring what great things Jesus had done for him.

## EVENTS LEADING TO THE CAPERNAUM CRISIS

T
HE STORY of the cure of Amos, the Kheresa lunatic, had already reached Bethsaida and Capernaum, so that a great crowd was waiting for Jesus when his boat landed that Tuesday forenoon. Among this throng were the new observers from the Jerusalem Sanhedrin who had come down to Capernaum to find cause for the Master's apprehension and conviction. As Jesus spoke with those who had assembled to greet him, Jairus, one of the rulers of the synagogue, made his way through the crowd and, falling down at his feet, took him by the hand and besought that he would hasten away with him, saying, "Master, my little daughter, an only child, lies in my home at the point of death. I pray that you will come and heal her."

When Jesus heard the request of this father, he said, "I will go with you."

As Jesus went along with Jairus, the large crowd, which had heard the father's request, followed on to see what would happen. Shortly before they reached the ruler's house, as they hastened through a narrow street and as the throng jostled him, Jesus suddenly stopped, exclaiming, "Someone touched me."

And when those who were near him denied that they had touched him, Peter spoke, "Master, you can see that this crowd presses you, threatening to crush us, and yet you say 'someone has touched me.' What do you mean?"

Then Jesus said, "I asked who touched me, for I perceived that living energy had gone forth from me." As Jesus looked about him, his eyes fell upon a near-by woman, who, coming forward, knelt at his feet and said, "For years I have been afflicted with a scourging hemorrhage. I have suffered many things from many physicians; I have spent all my substance, but none could cure me. Then I heard of you, and I thought if I may but touch the hem of his garment, I shall certainly be made whole. And so I pressed forward with the crowd as it moved along until, standing near you, Master, I touched the border of your garment, and I was made whole; I know that I have been healed of my affliction."

When Jesus heard this, he took the woman by the hand and, lifting her up, said, "Daughter, your faith has made you whole; go in peace." It was her *faith* and not her *touch* that made her whole. And this case is a good illustration of many apparently miraculous cures which attended upon Jesus' earth career, but which he in no sense consciously willed. The passing of time demonstrated that this woman was really cured of her malady. Her faith was of the sort that laid direct hold upon the creative power resident in the Master's person. With the faith she had, it was only necessary to approach the Master's person. It was not at all necessary to touch his garment; that was merely the superstitious part of her belief. Jesus called this woman, Veronica of Caesarea Philippi, into his presence to correct two errors which might have lingered in her mind, or which might have persisted in the minds of those who witnessed this healing: He did not want Veronica to go away thinking that her fear in attempting to steal her cure had been honored, or that her superstition in associating the touch of his garment with her healing had been effective. He desired all to know that it was her pure and living *faith* that had wrought the cure.

Jairus was, of course, terribly impatient of this delay in reaching his home; so they now hastened on at quickened pace. Even before they entered the ruler's yard, one of his servants came out, saying, "Trouble not the Master; your daughter is dead."

But Jesus seemed not to heed the servant's words, for, taking with him Peter, James, and John, he turned and said to the grief-stricken father, "Fear not; only believe." When he entered the house, he found the flute-players already there with the mourners, who were making an unseemly tumult; already were the relatives engaged in weeping and wailing. And when he had put all the mourners out of the room, he went in with the father and mother and his three apostles. He had told the mourners that the damsel was not dead, but they laughed him to scorn. Jesus now turned to the mother, saying, "Your daughter is not dead; she is only asleep." And when the house had quieted down, Jesus, going up to where the child lay, took her by the hand and said, "Daughter, I say to you, awake and arise!"

And when the girl heard these words, she immediately rose up and walked across the room. And presently, after she had recovered from her daze, Jesus directed that they should give her something to eat, for she had been a long time without food.

Since there was much agitation in Capernaum against Jesus, he called the family together and explained that the maiden had been in a state of coma following a long fever, and that he had merely aroused her, that he had not raised her from the dead. He likewise explained all this to his apostles, but it was futile; they all believed he had raised the little girl from the dead. What Jesus said in explanation of many of these apparent miracles had little effect on his followers. They were miracle-minded and lost no opportunity to ascribe another wonder to Jesus. Jesus and the apostles returned to Bethsaida after he had specifically charged all of them that they should tell no man.

When he came out of Jairus's house, two blind men led by a dumb boy followed him and cried out for healing. About this time Jesus' reputation as a healer was at its very height. Everywhere he went the sick and the afflicted were waiting for him. The Master now looked much worn, and all of his friends were becoming concerned lest he continue his work of teaching and healing to the point of actual collapse.

Jesus' apostles, let alone the common people, could not understand the nature and attributes of this God-man. Neither has any subsequent generation been able to evaluate what took place on earth in the person of Jesus of Nazareth. And there can never occur an opportunity for either science or religion to check up on these remarkable events for the simple reason that such an extraordinary situation can never again occur, either on this world or on any other world in Michael's creation. Never again, on any world in this entire local universe, will a being appear in the likeness of mortal flesh, at the same time embodying all the attributes of creative energy combined with spiritual endowments which transcend time and most other material limitations.

Never before Jesus was on earth, nor since, has it been possible so directly and graphically to secure the results attendant upon the strong and living faith of mortal men and women. To repeat these phenomena, we would have to go into the immediate presence of Michael, the Creator, and find him as he was in those days - the Son of Man. Likewise, today, while his absence prevents such material manifestations, you should refrain from placing any sort of limitation on the possible exhibition of his *spiritual power.* Though the Master is absent as a material being, he is present as a spiritual influence in the hearts of men. By going away from the world, Jesus made it possible for his spirit to live alongside that of his Father which indwells the minds of all mankind.

Jesus continued to teach the people by day while he instructed the apostles and evangelists at night. On Friday he declared a furlough of one week that all his followers might go home or to their friends for a few days before preparing to go up to Jerusalem for the Passover. But more than one half of his disciples refused to leave him, and the multitude was daily increasing in size, so much so that David Zebedee desired to establish a new encampment, but Jesus refused consent. The Master had so little rest over the Sabbath that on Sunday morning, March 27, he sought to get away from the people. Some of the evangelists were left to talk to the multitude while Jesus and the twelve planned to escape, unnoticed, to the opposite shore of the lake, where they proposed to obtain much needed rest in a beautiful park south of Bethsaida-Julias. This region was a favorite resorting place for Capernaum folks; they were all familiar with these parks on the eastern shore.

But the people would not have it so. They saw the direction taken by Jesus' boat, and hiring every craft available, they started out in pursuit. Those who could not obtain boats fared forth on foot to walk around the upper end of the lake.

By late afternoon more than a thousand persons had located the Master in one of the parks, and he spoke to them briefly, being followed by Peter. Many of these people had brought food with them, and after eating the evening meal, they gathered about in small groups while Jesus' apostles and disciples taught them.

Monday afternoon the multitude had increased to more than three thousand. And still - way into the evening - the people continued to flock in, bringing all manner of sick folks with them. Hundreds of interested persons had made their plans to stop over at Capernaum to see and hear Jesus on their way to the Passover, and they simply refused to be disappointed. By Wednesday noon about five thousand men, women, and children were assembled here in this park to the south of Bethsaida-Julias. The weather was pleasant, it being near the end of the rainy season in this locality.

Philip had provided a three days' supply of food for Jesus and the twelve, which was in the custody of the Mark lad, their boy of all chores. By afternoon of this, the third day for almost half of this multitude, the food the people had brought with them was nearly exhausted. David Zebedee had no tented city here to feed and accommodate the crowds. Neither had Philip made food provision for such a multitude. But the people, even though they were hungry, would not go away. It was being quietly whispered about that Jesus, desiring to avoid trouble with both Herod and the Jerusalem leaders, had chosen this quiet spot outside the jurisdiction of all his enemies as the proper place to be crowned king. The enthusiasm of the people was rising every hour. Not a word was said to Jesus, though, of course, he knew all that was going on. Even the twelve apostles were still tainted with such notions, and especially the younger evangelists. The apostles who favored this attempt to proclaim Jesus king were Peter, John, Simon Zelotes, and Judas Iscariot. Those opposing the plan were Andrew, James, Nathaniel, and Thomas. Matthew, Philip, and the Alpheus twins were noncommittal. The ringleader of this plot to make him king was Joab, one of the young evangelists.

This was the stage setting about five o'clock on Wednesday afternoon, when Jesus asked James Alpheus to summon Andrew and Philip. Said Jesus, "What shall we do with the multitude? They have been with us now three days, and many of them are hungry. They have no food."

Philip and Andrew exchanged glances, and then Philip answered, "Master, you should send these people away so that they may go to the villages around about and buy themselves food."

And Andrew, fearing the materialization of the king plot, quickly joined with Philip, saying, "Yes, Master, I think it best that you dismiss the multitude so that they may go their way and buy food while you secure rest for a season." By this time others of the twelve had joined the conference.

Then said Jesus, "But I do not desire to send them away hungry; can you not feed them?"

This was too much for Philip, and he spoke right up. "Master, in this country place where can we buy bread for this multitude? Two hundred denarii worth would not be enough for lunch."

Before the apostles had an opportunity to express themselves, Jesus turned to Andrew and Philip, saying, "I do not want to send these people away. Here they are, like sheep without a shepherd. I would like to feed them. What food have we with us?"

While Philip was conversing with Matthew and Judas, Andrew sought out the Mark lad to ascertain how much was left of their store of provisions. He returned to Jesus, saying, "The lad has left only five barley loaves and two dried fishes" - and Peter promptly added, "We have yet to eat this evening."

For a moment Jesus stood in silence. There was a faraway look in his eyes. The apostles said nothing. Jesus turned suddenly to Andrew and said, "Bring me the loaves and fishes." And when Andrew had brought the basket to Jesus, the Master said, "Direct the people to sit down on the grass in companies of one hundred and appoint a leader over each group while you bring all of the evangelists here with us."

Jesus took up the loaves in his hands, and after he had given thanks, he broke the bread and gave to his apostles, who passed it on to their associates, who in turn carried it to the multitude. Jesus in like manner broke and distributed the fishes. And this multitude did eat and were filled. And when they had finished eating, Jesus said to the disciples, "Gather up the broken pieces that remain over so that nothing will be lost." And when they had finished gathering up the fragments, they had twelve basketfuls. They who ate of this extraordinary feast numbered about five thousand men, women, and children.

And this is the first and only nature miracle that Jesus performed as a result of his conscious preplanning. It is true that his disciples were disposed to call many things miracles that were not, but this was a genuine supernatural ministration. In this case, so we were taught, Michael multiplied food elements as he always does except for the elimination of the time factor and the visible life channel.

The feeding of the five thousand by supernatural energy was another of those cases where human pity plus creative power equaled that which happened. Now that the multitude had been fed to the full, and since Jesus' fame was then and there augmented by this stupendous wonder, the project to seize the Master and proclaim him king required no further personal direction. The idea seemed to spread through the crowd like a contagion. The reaction of the multitude to this sudden and spectacular supplying of their physical needs was profound and overwhelming. For a long time the Jews had been taught that the Messiah, the son of David, when he should come, would cause the land again to flow with milk and honey, and that the bread of life would be bestowed upon them as manna from heaven was supposed to have fallen upon their forefathers in the wilderness. And was not all of this expectation now fulfilled right before their eyes? When this hungry, undernourished multitude had finished gorging itself with the wonder-food, there was but one unanimous reaction: "Here is our king." The wonder-working deliverer of Israel had come. In the eyes of these simple-minded people the power to feed carried with it the right to rule. No wonder, then, that the multitude, when it had finished feasting, rose as one and shouted, "Make him king!"

This mighty shout enthused Peter and those of the apostles who still retained the hope of seeing Jesus assert his right to rule. But these false hopes were not to live for long. This mighty shout of the multitude had hardly ceased to reverberate from the near-by rocks when Jesus stepped upon a huge stone and, lifting up his right hand to command their attention, said, "My children, you mean well, but you are shortsighted and material-minded."

There was a brief pause; this stalwart Galilean was there majestically posed in the enchanting glow of that eastern twilight. Every inch he looked a king as he continued to speak to this breathless multitude. "You would make me king, not because your souls have been lighted with a great truth, but because your stomachs have been filled with bread. How many times have I told you that my kingdom is not of this world? This kingdom of heaven which we proclaim is a spiritual brotherhood, and no man rules over it seated upon a material throne. My Father in heaven is the all-wise and the all-powerful Ruler over this spiritual family of the sons and daughters of God on earth. Have I so failed in revealing to you the Father of spirits that you would make a king of His Son in the flesh! Now all of you go hence to your own homes. If you must have a king, let the Father of Lights be enthroned in the heart of each of you as the spirit Ruler of all things."

These words of Jesus sent the multitude away stunned and disheartened. Many who had believed in him turned back and followed him no more from that day. The apostles were speechless; they stood in silence gathered about the twelve baskets of the fragments of food; only the chore boy, the Mark lad, spoke, "And he refused to be our king."

Jesus, before going off to be alone in the hills, turned to Andrew and said, "Take your brethren back to Zebedee's house and pray with them, especially for your brother, Simon Peter."

★ ★ ★

The apostles, without their Master - sent off by themselves - entered the boat and in silence began to row toward Bethsaida on the western shore of the lake. None of the twelve was so crushed and downcast as Simon Peter. Hardly a word was spoken; they were all thinking of the Master alone in the hills. Had he forsaken them? He had never before sent them all away and refused to go with them. What could all this mean?

Darkness descended upon them, for there had arisen a strong and contrary wind that made progress almost impossible. As the hours of darkness and hard rowing passed, Peter grew weary and fell into a deep sleep of exhaustion. Andrew and James put him to rest on the cushioned seat in the stern of the boat. While the other apostles toiled against the wind and the waves, Peter dreamed a dream; he saw a vision of Jesus coming to them walking on the sea. When the Master seemed to walk on by the boat, Peter cried out, "Save us, Master, save us." And those who were in the rear of the boat heard him say some of these words. As this apparition of the night season continued in Peter's mind, he dreamed that he heard Jesus say, "Be of good cheer; it is I; be not afraid." This was like the balm of Gilead to Peter's disturbed soul; it soothed his troubled spirit, so that (in his dream) he cried out to the Master, "Lord, if it really is you, bid me come and walk with you on the water." And when Peter started to walk upon the water, the boisterous waves frightened him, and as he was about to sink, he cried out, "Lord, save me!" And many of the twelve heard him utter this cry. Then Peter dreamed that Jesus came to the rescue and, stretching forth his hand, took hold and lifted him up, saying, "O, you of little faith, wherefore did you doubt?"

In connection with the latter part of his dream Peter arose from the seat whereon he slept and actually stepped overboard and into the water. And he awakened from his dream as Andrew, James, and John reached down and pulled him out of the sea.

To Peter this experience was always real. He sincerely believed that Jesus came to them that night. He only partially convinced John Mark, which explains why Mark left a portion of the story out of his narrative. Luke, the physician, who made careful search into these matters, concluded that the episode was a vision of Peter's and therefore refused to give place to this story in the preparation of his narrative.

Thursday morning, before daylight, they anchored their boat offshore near Zebedee's house and sought sleep until about noontime. Andrew was first up and, going for a walk by the sea, found Jesus, in company with their chore boy, sitting on a stone by the water's edge. Notwithstanding that many of the multitude and the young evangelists searched all night and much of the next day about the eastern hills for Jesus, shortly after midnight he and the Mark lad had started to walk around the lake and across the river, back to Bethsaida.

Of the five thousand who were miraculously fed, and who, when their stomachs were full and their hearts empty, would have made him king, only about five hundred persisted in following after him. But before these received word that he was back in Bethsaida, Jesus asked Andrew to assemble the twelve apostles and their associates, including the women, saying, "I desire to speak with them."

And when all were ready, Jesus said, "How long shall I bear with you? Are you all slow of spiritual comprehension and deficient in living faith? All these months have I taught you the truths of the kingdom, and yet are you dominated by material motives instead of spiritual considerations. Have you not even read in the Scriptures where Moses exhorted the unbelieving children of Israel, saying, 'Fear not, stand still and see the salvation of the Lord'? Said the singer: 'Put your trust in the Lord.' 'Be patient, wait upon the Lord and be of good courage. He shall strengthen your heart.' 'Cast your burden on the Lord, and he shall sustain you. Trust Him at all times and pour out your heart to Him, for God is your refuge.' 'He who dwells in the secret place of the Most High shall abide under the shadow of the Almighty.' 'It is better to trust the Lord than to put confidence in human princes.'

"And now do you all see that the working of miracles and the performance of material wonders will not win souls for the spiritual kingdom? We fed the multitude, but it did not lead them to hunger for the bread of life, neither to thirst for the waters of spiritual righteousness. When their hunger was satisfied, they sought not entrance into the kingdom of heaven but rather sought to proclaim the Son of Man king after the manner of the kings of this world, only that they might continue to eat bread without having to toil therefor. And all this, in which many of you did more or less participate, does nothing to reveal the heavenly Father or to advance his kingdom on earth. Have we not sufficient enemies among the religious leaders of the land without doing that which is likely to estrange also the civil rulers? I pray that the Father will anoint your eyes that you may see and open your ears that you may hear, to the end that you may have full faith in the gospel which I have taught you."

Jesus then announced that he wished to withdraw for a few days of rest with his apostles before they made ready to go up to Jerusalem for the Passover, and he forbade any of the disciples or the multitude to follow him. Accordingly they went by boat to the region of Gennesaret for two or three days of rest and sleep. Jesus was preparing for a great crisis of his life on earth, and he therefore spent much time in communion with the Father in heaven.

The news of the feeding of the five thousand and the attempt to make Jesus king aroused widespread curiosity and stirred up the fears of both the religious leaders and the civil rulers throughout all Galilee and Judea. While this great miracle did nothing to further the gospel of the kingdom in the souls of material-minded and halfhearted believers, it did serve the purpose of bringing to a head the miracle-seeking and king-craving proclivities of Jesus' immediate family of apostles and close disciples. This spectacular episode brought an end to the early era of teaching, training, and healing, thereby preparing the way for the inauguration of this last year of proclaiming the higher and more spiritual phases of the new gospel of the kingdom - divine sonship, spiritual liberty, and eternal salvation.

While resting at the home of a wealthy believer in the Gennesaret region, Jesus held informal conferences with the twelve every afternoon. The ambassadors of the kingdom were a serious, sober, and chastened group of disillusioned men. But even after all that had happened, and as subsequent events disclosed, these twelve men were not yet fully delivered from their inbred and long-cherished notions about the coming of the Jewish Messiah. Events of the preceding few weeks had moved too swiftly for these astonished fishermen to grasp their full significance. It requires time for men and women to effect radical and extensive changes in their basic and fundamental concepts of social conduct, philosophic attitudes, and religious convictions.

While Jesus and the twelve were resting at Gennesaret, the multitudes dispersed, some going to their homes, others going on up to Jerusalem for the Passover. In less than one month's time the enthusiastic and open followers of Jesus, who numbered more than fifty thousand in Galilee alone, shrank to less than five hundred. Jesus desired to give his apostles such an experience with the fickleness of popular acclaim that they would not be tempted to rely on such manifestations of transient religious hysteria after he should leave them alone in the work of the kingdom, but he was only partially successful in this effort.

The second night of their sojourn at Gennesaret the Master again told the apostles the parable of the sower and added these words: "You see, my children, the appeal to human feelings is transitory and utterly disappointing; the exclusive appeal to the intellect of man is likewise empty and barren; it is only by making your appeal to the spirit which lives within the human mind that you can hope to achieve lasting success and accomplish those marvelous transformations of human character that are presently shown in the abundant yielding of the genuine fruits of the spirit in the daily lives of all who are thus delivered from the darkness of doubt by the birth of the spirit into the light of faith - the kingdom of heaven."

Jesus taught the appeal to the emotions as the technique of arresting and focusing the intellectual attention. He designated the mind thus aroused and quickened as the gateway to the soul, where there resides that spiritual nature of man which must recognize truth and respond to the spiritual appeal of the gospel in order to afford the permanent results of true character transformations.

Jesus thus endeavored to prepare the apostles for the impending shock - the crisis in the public attitude toward him that was only a few days distant. He explained to the twelve that the religious rulers of Jerusalem would conspire with Herod Antipas to effect their destruction.

The twelve began to realize more fully (though not finally) that Jesus was not going to sit on David's throne. They saw more fully that spiritual truth was not to be advanced by material wonders. They began to realize that the feeding of the five thousand and the popular movement to make Jesus king was the apex of the miracle-seeking, wonder-working expectance of the people and the height of Jesus' acclaim by the populace. They vaguely discerned and dimly foresaw the approaching times of spiritual sifting and cruel adversity. These twelve men were slowly awaking to the realization of the real nature of their task as ambassadors of the kingdom, and they began to gird themselves for the trying and testing ordeals of the last year of the Master's ministry on earth.

Before they left Gennesaret, Jesus instructed them regarding the miraculous feeding of the five thousand, telling them just why he engaged in this extraordinary manifestation of creative power and also assuring them that he did not thus yield to his sympathy for the multitude until he had ascertained that it was "according to the Father's will."

Sunday, April 3, Jesus, accompanied only by the twelve apostles, started from Bethsaida on the journey to Jerusalem. To avoid the multitudes and to attract as little attention as possible, they journeyed by way of Gerasa and Philadelphia. He forbade them to do any public teaching on this trip; neither did he permit them to teach or preach while sojourning in Jerusalem. They arrived at Bethany, near Jerusalem, late on Wednesday evening, April 6. For this one night they stopped at the home of Lazarus, Martha, and Mary, but the next day they separated. Jesus, with John, stayed at the home of a believer named Simon, near the house of Lazarus in Bethany. Judas Iscariot and Simon Zelotes stopped with friends in Jerusalem, while the rest of the apostles sojourned, two and two, in different homes.

Jesus entered Jerusalem only once during this Passover, and that was on the great day of the feast. Many of the Jerusalem believers were brought out by Abner to meet Jesus at Bethany. During this sojourn at Jerusalem the twelve learned how bitter the feeling was becoming toward their Master. They departed from Jerusalem all believing that a crisis was impending.

On Sunday, April 24, Jesus and the apostles left Jerusalem for Bethsaida, going by way of the coast cities of Joppa, Caesarea, and Ptolemais. Thence, overland they went by Ramah and Chorazin to Bethsaida, arriving on Friday, April 29. Immediately on reaching home, Jesus dispatched Andrew to ask of the ruler of the synagogue permission to speak the next day, that being the Sabbath, at the afternoon service. And Jesus well knew that that would be the last time he would ever be permitted to speak in the Capernaum synagogue.

# THE CRISIS AT CAPERNAUM

O N FRIDAY evening, the day of their arrival at Bethsaida, and on Sabbath morning, the apostles noticed that Jesus was seriously occupied with some momentous problem; they were cognizant that the Master was giving unusual thought to some important matter. He ate no breakfast and but little at noontide. All of Sabbath morning and the evening before, the twelve and their associates were gathered together in small groups about the house, in the garden, and along the seashore. There was a tension of uncertainty and a suspense of apprehension resting upon all of them. Jesus had said little to them since they left Jerusalem.

Not in months had they seen the Master so preoccupied and uncommunicative. Even Simon Peter was depressed, if not downcast. Andrew was at a loss to know what to do for his dejected associates. Nathaniel said they were in the midst of the "lull before the storm." Thomas expressed the opinion that "something out of the ordinary is about to happen." Philip advised David Zebedee to "forget about plans for feeding and lodging the multitude until we know what the Master is thinking about." Matthew was putting forth renewed efforts to replenish the treasury. James and John talked over the forthcoming sermon in the synagogue and speculated much as to its probable nature and scope. Simon Zelotes expressed the belief, in reality a hope, that "the Father in heaven may be about to intervene in some unexpected manner for the vindication and support of His Son," while Judas Iscariot dared to indulge the thought that possibly Jesus was oppressed with regrets that "he did not have the courage and daring to permit the five thousand to proclaim him king of the Jews."

It was from among such a group of depressed and disconsolate followers that Jesus went forth on this beautiful Sabbath afternoon to preach his epoch-making sermon in the Capernaum synagogue. The only word of cheerful greeting or well-wishing from any of his immediate followers came from one of the unsuspecting Alpheus twins, who, as Jesus left the house on his way to the synagogue, saluted him cheerily and said, "We pray the Father will help you, and that we may have bigger multitudes than ever."

A distinguished congregation greeted Jesus at three o'clock on this exquisite Sabbath afternoon in the new Capernaum synagogue. Jairus presided and handed Jesus the Scriptures to read. The day before, fifty-three Pharisees and Sadducees had arrived from Jerusalem; more than thirty of the leaders and rulers of the neighboring synagogues were also present. These Jewish religious leaders were acting directly under orders from the Sanhedrin at Jerusalem, and they constituted the orthodox vanguard which had come to inaugurate open warfare on Jesus and his disciples. Sitting by the side of these Jewish leaders, in the synagogue seats of honor, were the official observers of Herod Antipas, who had been directed to ascertain the truth concerning the disturbing reports that an attempt had been made by the populace to proclaim Jesus the king of the Jews, over in the domains of his brother Philip.

Jesus comprehended that he faced the immediate declaration of avowed and open warfare by his increasing enemies, and he elected boldly to assume the offensive. At the feeding of the five thousand he had challenged their ideas of the material Messiah; now he chose again openly to attack their concept of the Jewish deliverer. This crisis, which began with the feeding of the five thousand, and which terminated with this Sabbath afternoon sermon, was the outward turning of the tide of popular fame and acclaim. Henceforth, the work of the kingdom was to be increasingly concerned with the more important task of winning lasting spiritual converts for the truly religious brotherhood of mankind. This sermon marks the crisis in the transition from the period of discussion, controversy, and decision to that of open warfare and final acceptance or final rejection.

The Master well knew that many of his followers were slowly but surely preparing their minds finally to reject him. He likewise knew that many of his disciples were slowly but certainly passing through that training of mind and that discipline of soul which would enable them to triumph over doubt and courageously to assert their full-fledged faith in the gospel of the kingdom. Jesus fully understood how men prepare themselves for the decisions of a crisis and the performance of sudden deeds of courageous choosing by the slow process of the reiterated choosing between the recurring situations of good and evil. He subjected his chosen messengers to repeated rehearsals in disappointment and provided them with frequent and testing opportunities for choosing between the right and the wrong way of meeting spiritual trials. He knew he could depend on his followers, when they met the final test, to make their vital decisions in accordance with prior and habitual mental attitudes and spirit reactions.

This crisis in Jesus' earth life began with the feeding of the five thousand and ended with this sermon in the synagogue; the crisis in the lives of the apostles began with this sermon in the synagogue and continued for a whole year, ending only with the Master's trial and crucifixion.

As they sat there in the synagogue that afternoon before Jesus began to speak, there was just one great mystery, just one supreme question, in the minds of all. Both his friends and his foes pondered just one thought, and that was: "Why did he himself so deliberately and effectively turn back the tide of popular enthusiasm?" And it was immediately before and immediately after this sermon that the doubts and disappointments of his disgruntled adherents grew into unconscious opposition and eventually turned into actual hatred. It was after this sermon in the synagogue that Judas Iscariot entertained his first conscious thought of deserting. But he did, for the time being, effectively master all such inclinations.

Everyone was in a state of perplexity. Jesus had left them dumfounded and confounded. He had recently engaged in the greatest demonstration of supernatural power to characterize his whole career. The feeding of the five thousand was the one event of his earth life which made the greatest appeal to the Jewish concept of the expected Messiah. But this extraordinary advantage was immediately and unexplainedly offset by his prompt and unequivocal refusal to be made king.

On Friday evening, and again on Sabbath morning, the Jerusalem leaders had labored long and earnestly with Jairus to prevent Jesus' speaking in the synagogue, but it was of no avail. Jairus's only reply to all this pleading was: "I have granted this request, and I will not violate my word."

Jesus introduced this sermon by reading from the law as found in Deuteronomy: "But it shall come to pass, if this people will not hearken to the voice of God, that the curses of transgression shall surely overtake them. The Lord shall cause you to be smitten by your enemies; you shall be removed into all the kingdoms of the earth. And the Lord shall bring you and the king you have set up over you into the hands of a strange nation. You shall become an astonishment, a proverb, and a byword among all nations. Your sons and your daughters shall go into captivity. The strangers among you shall rise high in authority while you are brought very low. And these things shall be upon you and your seed forever because you would not hearken to the word of the Lord. Therefore shall you serve your enemies who shall come against you. You shall endure hunger and thirst and wear this alien yoke of iron. The Lord shall bring against you a nation from afar, from the end of the earth, a nation whose tongue you shall not understand, a nation of fierce countenance, a nation which will have little regard for you. And they shall besiege you in all your towns until the high fortified walls wherein you have trusted come down; and all the land shall fall into their hands. And it shall come to pass that you will be driven to eat the fruit of your own bodies, the flesh of your sons and daughters, during this time of siege, because of the straitness wherewith your enemies shall press you."

And when Jesus had finished this reading, he turned to the Prophets and read from Jeremiah: "'If you will not hearken to the words of my servants the prophets whom I have sent you, then will I make this house like Shiloh, and I will make this city a curse to all the nations of the earth.' And the priests and the teachers heard Jeremiah speak these words in the house of the Lord. And it came to pass that, when Jeremiah had made an end of speaking all that the Lord had commanded him to speak to all the people, the priests and teachers laid hold of him, saying, 'You shall surely die.' And all the people crowded around Jeremiah in the house of the Lord. And when the princes of Judah heard these things, they sat in judgment on Jeremiah. Then spoke the priests and the teachers to the princes and to all the people, saying: 'This man is worthy to die, for he has prophesied against our city, and you have heard him with your own ears.' Then spoke Jeremiah to all the princes and to all the people: 'The Lord sent me to prophesy against this house and against this city all the words which you have heard. Now, therefore, amend your ways and reform your doings and obey the voice of the Lord your God that you may escape the evil which has been pronounced against you. As for me, behold I am in your hands. Do with me as seems good and right in your eyes. But know you for certain that, if you put me to death, you shall bring innocent blood upon yourselves and upon this people, for of a truth the Lord has sent me to speak all these words in your ears.'

"The priests and teachers of that day sought to kill Jeremiah, but the judges would not consent, albeit, for his words of warning, they did let him down by cords in a filthy dungeon until he sank in mire up to his armpits. That is what this people did to the Prophet Jeremiah when he obeyed the Lord's command to warn his brethren of their impending political downfall. Today, I desire to ask you: What will the chief priests and religious leaders of this people do with the man who dares to warn them of the day of their spiritual doom? Will you also seek to put to death the teacher who dares to proclaim the word of the Lord, and who fears not to point out wherein you refuse to walk in the way of light which leads to the entrance to the kingdom of heaven?

"What is it you seek as evidence of my mission on earth? We have left you undisturbed in your positions of influence and power while we preached glad tidings to the poor and the outcast. We have made no hostile attack upon that which you hold in reverence but have rather proclaimed new liberty for man's fear-ridden soul. I came into the world to reveal my Father and to establish on earth the spiritual brotherhood of the sons and daughters of God, the kingdom of heaven. And notwithstanding that I have so many times reminded you that my kingdom is not of this world, still has my Father granted you many manifestations of material wonders in addition to more evidential spiritual transformations and regenerations.

"What new sign is it that you seek at my hands? I declare that you already have sufficient evidence to enable you to make your decision. Verily, verily, I say to many who sit before me this day, you are confronted with the necessity of choosing which way you will go; and I say to you, as Joshua said to your forefathers, 'choose you this day whom you will serve.' Today, many of you stand at the parting of the ways.

"Some of you, when you could not find me after the feasting of the multitude on the other side, hired the Tiberias fishing fleet, which a week before had taken shelter near by during a storm, to go in pursuit of me, and what for? Not for truth and righteousness or that you might the better know how to serve and minister to your fellow men! No, but rather that you might have more bread for which you had not labored. It was not to fill your souls with the word of life, but only that you might fill the belly with the bread of ease. And long have you been taught that the Messiah, when he should come, would work those wonders which would make life pleasant and easy for all the chosen people. It is not strange, then, that you who have been thus taught should long for the loaves and the fishes. But I declare to you that such is not the mission of the Son of Man. I have come to proclaim spiritual liberty, teach eternal truth, and foster living faith.

"My brethren, hanker not after the meat which perishes but rather seek for the spiritual food that nourishes even to eternal life; and this is the bread of life which the Son gives to all who will take it and eat, for the Father has given the Son this life without measure. And when you asked me, 'What must we do to perform the works of God?' I plainly told you: 'This is the work of God, that you believe him whom He has sent.'"

And then said Jesus, pointing up to the device of a pot of manna which decorated the lintel of this new synagogue, and which was embellished with grape clusters: "You have thought that your forefathers in the wilderness ate manna - the bread of heaven - but I say to you that this was the bread of earth. While Moses did not give your fathers bread from heaven, my Father now stands ready to give you the true bread of life. The bread of heaven is that which comes down from God and gives eternal life to the men of the world. And when you say to me, Give us this living bread, I will answer: I am this bread of life. He who comes to me shall not hunger, while he who believes me shall never thirst. You have seen me, lived with me, and beheld my works, yet you believe not that I came forth from the Father. But to those who do believe - fear not. All those led of the Father shall come to me, and he who comes to me shall in nowise be cast out.

"And now let me declare to you, once and for all time, that I have come down upon the earth, not to do my own will, but the will of Him who sent me. And this is the final will of Him who sent me, that of all those He has given me I should not lose one. And this is the will of the Father: That every one who beholds the Son and who believes him shall have eternal life. Only yesterday did I feed you with bread for your bodies; today I offer you the bread of life for your hungry souls. Will you now take the bread of the spirit as you then so willingly ate the bread of this world?"

As Jesus paused for a moment to look over the congregation, one of the teachers from Jerusalem (a member of the Sanhedrin) rose up and asked, "Do I understand you to say that you are the bread which comes down from heaven, and that the manna which Moses gave to our fathers in the wilderness did not?"

And Jesus answered the Pharisee, "You understood aright."

Then said the Pharisee: "But are you not Jesus of Nazareth, the son of Joseph, the carpenter? Are not your father and mother, as well as your brothers and sisters, well known to many of us? How then is it that you appear here in God's house and declare that you have come down from heaven?"

By this time there was much murmuring in the synagogue, and such a tumult was threatened that Jesus stood up and said, "Let us be patient; the truth never suffers from honest examination. I am all that you say but more. The Father and I are one; the Son does only that which the Father teaches him, while all those who are given to the Son by the Father, the Son will receive to himself. You have read where it is written in the Prophets, 'You shall all be taught by God,' and that 'Those whom the Father teaches will hear also his Son.' Every one who yields to the teaching of the Father's indwelling spirit will eventually come to me. Not that any man or woman has seen the Father, but the Father's spirit does live within mortals. And the Son who came down from heaven, he has surely seen the Father. And those who truly believe this Son already have eternal life.

"I am this bread of life. Your fathers ate manna in the wilderness and are dead. But this bread which comes down from God, if a man eats thereof, he shall never die in spirit. I repeat, I am this living bread, and every soul who attains the realization of this united nature of God and man shall live forever. And this bread of life which I give to all who will receive is my own living and combined nature. The Father in the Son and the Son one with the Father - that is my life-giving revelation to the world and my saving gift to all nations."

When Jesus had finished speaking, the ruler of the synagogue dismissed the congregation, but they would not depart. They crowded up around Jesus to ask more questions while others murmured and disputed among themselves. And this state of affairs continued for more than three hours. It was well past seven o'clock before the audience finally dispersed.

Many were the questions asked Jesus during this after meeting. Some were asked by his perplexed disciples, but more were asked by caviling unbelievers who sought only to embarrass and entrap him.

One of the visiting Pharisees, mounting a lampstand, shouted out this question: "You tell us that you are the bread of life. How can you give us your flesh to eat or your blood to drink? What avail is your teaching if it cannot be carried out?"

And Jesus answered this question, saying, "I did not teach you that my flesh is the bread of life nor that my blood is the water thereof. But I did say that my life in the flesh is a bestowal of the bread of heaven. The fact of the Word of God bestowed in the flesh and the phenomenon of the Son of Man subject to the will of God, constitute a reality of experience which is equivalent to the divine sustenance. You cannot eat my flesh nor can you drink my blood, but you can become one in spirit with me even as I am one in spirit with the Father. You can be nourished by the eternal word of God, which is indeed the bread of life, and which has been bestowed in the likeness of mortal flesh; and you can be watered in soul by the divine spirit, which is truly the water of life. The Father has sent me into the world to show how He desires to indwell and direct all men; and I have so lived this life in the flesh as to inspire all men likewise ever to seek to know and do the will of the indwelling heavenly Father."

Then one of the Jerusalem spies who had been observing Jesus and his apostles, said, "We notice that neither you nor your apostles wash your hands properly before you eat bread. You must well know that such a practice as eating with defiled and unwashed hands is a transgression of the law of the elders. Neither do you properly wash your drinking cups and eating vessels. Why is it that you show such disrespect for the traditions of the fathers and the laws of our elders?"

And when Jesus heard him speak, he answered, "Why is it that you transgress the commandments of God by the laws of your tradition? The commandment says, 'Honor your father and your mother,' and directs that you share with them your substance if necessary; but you enact a law of tradition which permits undutiful children to say that the money wherewith the parents might have been assisted has been 'given to God.' The law of the elders thus relieves such crafty children of their responsibility, notwithstanding that the children subsequently use all such monies for their own comfort. Why is it that you in this way make void the commandment by your own tradition? Well did Isaiah prophesy of you hypocrites, saying: 'This people honors me with their lips, but their heart is far from me. In vain do they worship me, teaching as their doctrines the precepts of men.'

"You can see how it is that you desert the commandment while you hold fast to the tradition of men. Altogether willing are you to reject the word of God while you maintain your own traditions. And in many other ways do you dare to set up your own teachings above the law and the prophets."

Jesus then directed his remarks to all present. He said, "But hearken to me, all of you. It is not that which enters into the mouth that spiritually defiles the man, but rather that which proceeds out of the mouth and from the heart."

But even the apostles failed fully to grasp the meaning of his words, for Simon Peter also asked him, "Lest some of your hearers be unnecessarily offended, would you explain to us the meaning of these words?"

And then said Jesus to Peter, "Are you also hard of understanding? Know you not that every plant which my heavenly Father has not planted shall be rooted up? Turn now your attention to those who would know the truth. You cannot compel men to love the truth. Many of these teachers are blind guides. And you know that, if the blind lead the blind, both shall fall into the pit. But hearken while I tell you the truth concerning those things which morally defile and spiritually contaminate men. I declare it is not that which enters the body by the mouth or gains access to the mind through the eyes and ears, that defiles the man. Man is only defiled by that evil which may originate within the heart, and which finds expression in the words and deeds of such unholy persons. Do you not know it is from the heart that there come forth evil thoughts, wicked projects of murder, theft, and adulteries, together with jealousy, pride, anger, revenge, railings, and false witness? And it is just such things that defile men, and not that they eat bread with ceremonially unclean hands."

The Pharisaic commissioners of the Jerusalem Sanhedrin were now almost convinced that Jesus must be apprehended on a charge of blasphemy or on one of flouting the sacred law of the Jews; wherefore their efforts to involve him in the discussion of, and possible attack upon, some of the traditions of the elders, or so-called oral laws of the nation. No matter how scarce water might be, these traditionally enslaved Jews would never fail to go through with the required ceremonial washing of the hands before every meal. It was their belief that "it is better to die than to transgress the commandments of the elders." The spies asked this question because it had been reported that Jesus had said, "Salvation is a matter of clean hearts rather than of clean hands." But such beliefs, when they once become a part of one's religion, are hard to get away from. Even many years after this day the Apostle Peter was still held in the bondage of fear to many of these traditions about things clean and unclean, only being finally delivered by experiencing an extraordinary and vivid dream. All of this can the better be understood when it is recalled that these Jews looked upon eating with unwashed hands in the same light as commerce with a harlot, and both were equally punishable by excommunication.

Thus did the Master elect to discuss and expose the folly of the whole rabbinic system of rules and regulations which was represented by the oral law - the traditions of the elders, all of which were regarded as more sacred and more binding upon the Jews than even the teachings of the Scriptures. And Jesus spoke out with less reserve because he knew the hour had come when he could do nothing more to prevent an open rupture of relations with these religious leaders.

☆ ☆ ☆

In the midst of the discussions of this after meeting, one of the Pharisees from Jerusalem brought to Jesus a distraught youth who was possessed of an unruly and rebellious spirit. Leading this demented lad up to Jesus, he said, "What can you do for such affliction as this? Can you cast out devils?"

And when the Master looked upon the youth, he was moved with compassion and, beckoning for the lad to come to him, took him by the hand and said, "You know who I am; come out of him; and I charge one of your loyal fellows to see that you do not return." And immediately the lad was normal and in his right mind.

And this is the first case where Jesus really cast an "evil spirit" out of a human being. All of the previous cases were only supposed possession of the devil; but this was a genuine case of demonic possession, even such as sometimes occurred in those days and right up to the day of Pentecost, when the Master's spirit was poured out upon all flesh, making it forever impossible for these few celestial rebels to take such advantage of certain unstable types of human beings.

When the people marveled, one of the Pharisees stood up and charged that Jesus could do these things because he was in league with devils; that he admitted in the language which he employed in casting out this devil that they were known to each other; and he went on to state that the religious teachers and leaders at Jerusalem had decided that Jesus did all his so-called miracles by the power of Beelzebub, the prince of devils.

Said the Pharisee, "Have nothing to do with this man; he is in partnership with Satan."

Then said Jesus, "How can Satan cast out Satan? A kingdom divided against itself cannot stand; if a house be divided against itself, it is soon brought to desolation. Can a city withstand a siege if it is not united? If Satan casts out Satan, he is divided against himself; how then shall his kingdom stand? But you should know that no one can enter into the house of a strong man and despoil his goods except he first overpower and bind that strong man. And so, if I by the power of Beelzebub cast out devils, by whom do your sons cast them out? Therefore shall they be your judges. But if I, by the spirit of God, cast out devils, then has the kingdom of God truly come upon you. If you were not blinded by prejudice and misled by fear and pride, you would easily perceive that one who is greater than devils stands in your midst. You compel me to declare that he who is not with me is against me, while he who gathers not with me scatters abroad. Let me utter a solemn warning to you who would presume, with your eyes open and with premeditated malice, knowingly to ascribe the works of God to the doings of devils! Verily, verily, I say to you, all your sins shall be forgiven, even all of your blasphemies, but whosoever shall blaspheme against God with deliberation and wicked intention shall never obtain forgiveness. Since such persistent workers of iniquity will never seek nor receive forgiveness, they are guilty of the sin of eternally rejecting divine forgiveness.

"Many of you have this day come to the parting of the ways; you have come to a beginning of the making of the inevitable choice between the will of the Father and the self-chosen ways of darkness. And as you now choose, so shall you eventually be. You must either make the tree good and its fruit good, or else will the tree become corrupt and its fruit corrupt. I declare that in my Father's eternal kingdom the tree is known by its fruits. But some of you who are as vipers, how can you, having already chosen evil, bring forth good fruits? After all, out of the abundance of the evil in your hearts your mouths speak."

Then stood up another Pharisee, who said, "Teacher, we would have you give us a predetermined sign which we will agree upon as establishing your authority and right to teach. Will you agree to such an arrangement?"

And when Jesus heard this, he said, "This faithless and sign-seeking generation seeks a token, but no sign shall be given you other than that which you already have, and that which you shall see when the Son of Man departs from among you."

And when he had finished speaking, his apostles surrounded him and led him from the synagogue. In silence they journeyed home with him to Bethsaida. They were all amazed and somewhat terror-stricken by the sudden change in the Master's teaching tactics. They were wholly unaccustomed to seeing him perform in such a militant manner.

Time and again had Jesus dashed to pieces the hopes of his apostles, repeatedly had he crushed their fondest expectations, but no time of disappointment or season of sorrow had ever equaled that which now overtook them. And, too, there was now admixed with their depression a real fear for their safety. They were all surprisingly startled by the suddenness and completeness of the desertion of the populace. They were also somewhat frightened and disconcerted by the unexpected boldness and assertive determination exhibited by the Pharisees who had come down from Jerusalem. But most of all they were bewildered by Jesus' sudden change of tactics. Under ordinary circumstances they would have welcomed the appearance of this more militant attitude, but coming as it did, along with so much that was unexpected, it startled them.

And now, on top of all of these worries, when they reached home, Jesus refused to eat. For hours he isolated himself in one of the upper rooms. It was almost midnight when Joab, the leader of the evangelists, returned and reported that about one third of his associates had deserted the cause. All through the evening loyal disciples had come and gone, reporting that the revulsion of feeling toward the Master was general in Capernaum. The leaders from Jerusalem were not slow to feed this feeling of disaffection and in every way possible to seek to promote the movement away from Jesus and his teachings. During these trying hours the twelve women were in session over at Peter's house. They were tremendously upset, but none of them deserted.

It was a little after midnight when Jesus came down from the upper chamber and stood among the twelve and their associates, numbering about thirty in all. He said, "I recognize that this sifting of the kingdom distresses you, but it is unavoidable. Still, after all the training you have had, was there any good reason why you should stumble at my words? Why is it that you are filled with fear and consternation when you see the kingdom being divested of these lukewarm multitudes and these halfhearted disciples? Why do you grieve when the new day is dawning for the shining forth in new glory of the spiritual teachings of the kingdom of heaven? If you find it difficult to endure this test, what, then, will you do when the Son of Man must return to the Father? When and how will you prepare yourselves for the time when I ascend to the place whence I came to this world?

"My beloved, you must remember that it is the spirit that quickens; the flesh and all that pertains thereto is of little profit. The words which I have spoken to you are spirit and life. Be of good cheer! I have not deserted you. Many shall be offended by the plain speaking of these days. Already you have heard that many of my disciples have turned back; they walk no more with me. From the beginning I knew that these halfhearted believers would fall out by the way. Did I not choose you twelve men and set you apart as ambassadors of the kingdom? And now at such a time as this would you also desert? Let each of you look to his own faith, for one of you stands in grave danger."

And when Jesus had finished speaking, Simon Peter said, "Yes, Lord, we are sad and perplexed, but we will never forsake you. You have taught us the words of eternal life. We have believed in you and followed with you all this time. We will not turn back, for we know that you are sent by God." And as Peter ceased speaking, they all with one accord nodded their approval of his pledge of loyalty.

Then said Jesus, "Go to your rest, for busy times are upon us; active days are just ahead."

## LAST DAYS AT CAPERNAUM

O N THE eventful Saturday night of April 30, as Jesus was speaking words of comfort and courage to his downcast and bewildered disciples, at Tiberias a council was being held between Herod Antipas and a group of special commissioners representing the Jerusalem Sanhedrin. These scribes and Pharisees urged Herod to arrest Jesus; they did their best to convince him that Jesus was stirring up the populace to dissension and even to rebellion. But Herod refused to take action against him as a political offender. Herod's advisers had correctly reported the episode across the lake when the people sought to proclaim Jesus king and how he rejected the proposal.

One of Herod's official family, Chuza, whose wife belonged to the women's ministering corps, had informed him that Jesus did not propose to meddle with the affairs of earthly rule; that he was only concerned with the establishment of the spiritual brotherhood of his believers, which brotherhood he called the kingdom of heaven. Herod had confidence in Chuza's reports, so much so that he refused to interfere with Jesus' activities. Herod was also influenced at this time, in his attitude toward Jesus, by his superstitious fear of John the Baptist. Herod was one of those apostate Jews who, while he believed nothing, feared everything. He had a bad conscience for having put John to death, and he did not want to become entangled in these intrigues against Jesus. He knew of many cases of sickness which had been apparently healed by Jesus, and he regarded him as either a prophet or a relatively harmless religious fanatic.

When the Jews threatened to report to Caesar that he was shielding a traitorous subject, Herod ordered them out of his council chamber. Thus matters rested for one week, during which time Jesus prepared his followers for the impending dispersion.

F rom May 1 to May 7 Jesus held intimate counsel with his followers at the Zebedee house. Only the tried and trusted disciples were admitted to these conferences. At this time there were only about one hundred disciples who had the moral courage to brave the opposition of the Pharisees and openly declare their adherence to Jesus. With this group he held sessions morning, afternoon, and evening. Small companies of inquirers assembled each afternoon by the seaside, where some of the evangelists or apostles discoursed to them. These groups seldom numbered more than fifty.

On Friday of this week official action was taken by the rulers of the Capernaum synagogue closing the house of God to Jesus and all his followers. This action was taken at the instigation of the Jerusalem Pharisees. Jairus resigned as chief ruler and openly aligned himself with Jesus.

The last of the seaside meetings was held on Sabbath afternoon, May 7. Jesus talked to less than one hundred and fifty who had assembled at that time. This Saturday night marked the time of the lowest ebb in the tide of popular regard for Jesus and his teachings. From then on there was a steady, slow, but more healthful and dependable growth in favorable sentiment; a new following was built up which was better grounded in spiritual faith and true religious experience. The more or less composite and compromising transition stage between the materialistic concepts of the kingdom held by the Master's followers and those more idealistic and spiritual concepts taught by Jesus, had now definitely ended. From now on there was a more open proclamation of the gospel of the kingdom in its larger scope and in its far-flung spiritual implications.

Sunday, May 8, A.D. 29, at Jerusalem, the Sanhedrin passed a decree closing all the synagogues of Palestine to Jesus and his followers. This was a new and unprecedented usurpation of authority by the Jerusalem Sanhedrin. Theretofore each synagogue had existed and functioned as an independent congregation of worshipers and was under the rule and direction of its own board of governors. Only the synagogues of Jerusalem had been subject to the authority of the Sanhedrin. This summary action of the Sanhedrin was followed by the resignation of five of its members. One hundred messengers were immediately dispatched to convey and enforce this decree. Within the short space of two weeks every synagogue in Palestine had bowed to this manifesto of the Sanhedrin except the synagogue at Hebron. The rulers of the Hebron synagogue refused to acknowledge the right of the Sanhedrin to exercise such jurisdiction over their assembly. This refusal to accede to the Jerusalem decree was based on their contention of congregational autonomy rather than on sympathy with Jesus' cause. Shortly thereafter the Hebron synagogue was destroyed by fire.

This same Sunday morning, Jesus declared a week's holiday, urging all of his disciples to return to their homes or friends to rest their troubled souls and speak words of encouragement to their loved ones. He said, "Go to your several places to play or fish while you pray for the extension of the kingdom."

This week of rest enabled Jesus to visit many families and groups about the seaside. He also went fishing with David Zebedee on several occasions, and while he went about alone much of the time, there always lurked nearby two or three of David's most trusted messengers, who had no uncertain orders from their chief respecting the safeguarding of Jesus. There was no public teaching of any sort during this week of rest.

This was the week that Nathaniel and James Zebedee suffered from more than a slight illness. For three days and nights they were acutely afflicted with a painful digestive disturbance. On the third night Jesus sent Salome, James's mother, to her rest, while he ministered to his suffering apostles. Of course Jesus could have instantly healed these two men, but that is not the method of either the Son or the Father in dealing with these commonplace difficulties and afflictions of the children of men on the evolutionary worlds of time and space. Never once, throughout all of his eventful life in the flesh, did Jesus engage in any sort of supernatural ministration to any member of his earth family or in behalf of any one of his immediate followers.

Universe difficulties must be met and planetary obstacles must be encountered as a part of the experience training provided for the growth and development, the progressive perfection, of the evolving souls of mortal creatures. The spiritualization of the human soul requires intimate experience with the educational solving of a wide range of real universe problems. The animal nature and the lower forms of will creatures do not progress favorably in environmental ease. Problematic situations, coupled with exertion stimuli, conspire to produce those activities of mind, soul, and spirit which contribute mightily to the achievement of worthy goals of mortal progression and to the attainment of higher levels of spirit destiny.

On May 16 the second conference at Tiberias between the authorities at Jerusalem and Herod Antipas was convened. Both the religious and the political leaders from Jerusalem were in attendance. The Jewish leaders were able to report to Herod that practically all the synagogues in both Galilee and Judea were closed to Jesus' teachings. A new effort was made to have Herod place Jesus under arrest, but he refused to do their bidding. On May 18, however, Herod did agree to the plan of permitting the Sanhedrin authorities to seize Jesus and carry him to Jerusalem to be tried on religious charges, provided the Roman ruler of Judea concurred in such an arrangement. Meanwhile, Jesus' enemies were industriously spreading the rumor throughout Galilee that Herod had become hostile to Jesus, and that he meant to exterminate all who believed in his teachings.

On Saturday night, May 21, word reached Tiberias that the civil authorities at Jerusalem had no objection to the agreement between Herod and the Pharisees that Jesus be seized and carried to Jerusalem for trial before the Sanhedrin on

450 The Gospel According to Andrew

charges of flouting the sacred laws of the Jewish nation. Accordingly, just before midnight of this day, Herod signed the decree which authorized the officers of the Sanhedrin to seize Jesus within Herod's domains and forcibly to carry him to Jerusalem for trial. Strong pressure from many sides was brought to bear upon Herod before he consented to grant this permission, and he well knew that Jesus could not expect a fair trial before his bitter enemies at Jerusalem.

On this same Saturday night, in Capernaum a group of fifty leading citizens met at the synagogue to discuss the momentous question: "What shall we do with Jesus?" They talked and debated until after midnight, but they could not find any common ground for agreement. Aside from a few persons who inclined to the belief that Jesus might be the Messiah, at least a holy man, or perhaps a prophet, the meeting was divided into four nearly equal groups who held, respectively, the following views of Jesus:

1. That he was a deluded and harmless religious fanatic.
2. That he was a dangerous and designing agitator who might stir up rebellion.
3. That he was in league with devils, that he might even be a prince of devils.
4. That he was beside himself, that he was mad, mentally unbalanced.

There was much talk about Jesus preaching doctrines which were upsetting for the common people; his enemies maintained that his teachings were impractical, that everything would go to pieces if everybody made an honest effort to live in accordance with his ideas. And the men of many subsequent generations have said the same things. Many intelligent and well-meaning men, even in the more enlightened age of these revelations, maintain that modern civilization could not have been built upon the teachings of Jesus; and they are partially right. But all such doubters forget that a much better civilization could have been built upon his teachings, and sometime will be. This world has never seriously tried to carry out the teachings of Jesus on a large scale, notwithstanding that halfhearted attempts have often been made to follow the doctrines of so-called Christianity.

May 22 was an eventful day in the life of Jesus. On this Sunday morning, before daybreak, one of David's messengers arrived in great haste from Tiberias, bringing the word that Herod had authorized, or was about to authorize, the arrest of Jesus by the officers of the Sanhedrin. The receipt of the news of this impending danger caused David Zebedee to arouse his messengers and send them out to all the local groups of disciples, summoning them for an emergency council at seven o'clock that morning. When the sister-in-law of Jude (Jesus' brother) heard this alarming report, she hastened word to all of Jesus' family who dwelt near by, summoning them forthwith to assemble at Zebedee's house. And in response to this hasty call, presently there were assembled Mary, James, Joseph, Jude, and Ruth.

At this early morning meeting Jesus imparted his farewell instructions to the assembled disciples; that is, he bade them farewell for the time being, knowing well that they would soon be dispersed from Capernaum. He directed them all to seek God for guidance and to carry on the work of the kingdom regardless of consequences. The evangelists were to labor as they saw fit until such time as they might be called. He selected twelve of the evangelists to accompany him; the twelve apostles he directed to remain with him no matter what happened. The twelve women he instructed to remain at the Zebedee house and at Peter's house until he should send for them.

Jesus consented to David Zebedee's continuing his countrywide messenger service, and in bidding the Master farewell presently, David said, "Go forth to your work, Master. Don't let the bigots catch you, and never doubt that the messengers will follow after you. My men will never lose contact with you, and through them you shall know of the kingdom in other parts, and by them we will all know about you. Nothing that might happen to me will interfere with this service, for I have appointed first and second leaders, even a third. I am neither a teacher nor a preacher, but it is in my heart to do this, and none can stop me."

About 7:30 this morning Jesus began his parting address to almost one hundred believers who had crowded indoors to hear him. This was a solemn occasion for all present, but Jesus seemed unusually cheerful; he was once more like his normal self. The seriousness of weeks had gone, and he inspired all of them with his words of faith, hope, and courage.

It was about eight o'clock on this Sunday morning when five members of Jesus' earth family arrived on the scene in response to the urgent summons of Jude's sister-in-law. Of all his family in the flesh, only one, Ruth, believed wholeheartedly and continuously in the divinity of his mission on earth. Jude and James, and even Joseph, still retained much of their faith in Jesus, but they had permitted pride to interfere with their better judgment and real spiritual inclinations. Mary was likewise torn between love and fear, between mother love and family pride. Though she was harassed by doubts, she could never quite forget the visit of Gabriel ere Jesus was born. The Pharisees had been laboring to persuade Mary that Jesus was beside himself, demented. They urged her to go with her sons and seek to dissuade him from further efforts at public teaching. They assured Mary that soon Jesus' health would break, and that only dishonor and disgrace could come upon the entire family as a result of allowing him to go on. And so, when the word came from Jude's sister-in-law, all five of them started at once for Zebedee's house, having been together at Mary's home, where they had met with the Pharisees the evening before. They had talked with the Jerusalem leaders long into the night, and all were more or less convinced that Jesus was acting strangely, that he had acted strangely for some time. While Ruth could not explain all of his conduct, she insisted that he had always treated his family fairly and refused to agree to the program of trying to dissuade him from further work.

On the way to Zebedee's house they talked these things over and agreed among themselves to try to persuade Jesus to come home with them, for, said Mary: "I know I could influence my son if he would only come home and listen to me." James and Jude had heard rumors concerning the plans to arrest Jesus and take him to Jerusalem for trial. They also feared for their own safety. As long as Jesus was a popular figure in the public eye, his family allowed matters to drift along, but now that the people of Capernaum and the leaders at Jerusalem had suddenly turned against him, they began keenly to feel the pressure of the supposed disgrace of their embarrassing position.

They had expected to meet Jesus, take him aside, and urge him to go home with them. They had thought to assure him that they would forget his neglect of them - they would forgive and forget - if he would only give up the foolishness of trying to preach a new religion which could bring only trouble to himself and dishonor upon his family. To all of this Ruth would say only: "I will tell my brother that I think he is a man of God, and that I hope he would be willing to die before he would allow these wicked Pharisees to stop his preaching." Joseph promised to keep Ruth quiet while the others labored with Jesus.

When they reached the Zebedee house, Jesus was in the very midst of delivering his parting address to the disciples. They sought to gain entrance to the house, but it was crowded to overflowing. Finally they established themselves on the back porch and had word passed in to Jesus, from person to person, so that it finally was whispered to him by Simon Peter, who interrupted his talking for the purpose and said, "Behold, your mother and your brothers are outside, and they are very anxious to speak with you."

Now it did not occur to his mother how important was the giving of this parting message to his followers, neither did she know that his address was likely to be terminated any moment by the arrival of his apprehenders. She really thought, after so long an apparent estrangement, in view of the fact that she and his brothers had shown the grace actually to come to him, that Jesus would cease speaking and come to them the moment he received word they were waiting.

It was just another of those instances in which his earth family could not comprehend that he must be about his Father's business. And so Mary and the brothers of Jesus were deeply hurt when, notwithstanding that he paused in his speaking to receive the message, instead of his rushing out to greet them, they heard his musical voice speak with increased volume: "Say to my mother and my brothers that they should have no fear for me. The Father who sent me into the world will not forsake me; neither shall any harm come upon my family. Bid them be of good courage and put their trust in the Father of the kingdom. But, after all, who is my mother and who are my brothers?"

And stretching forth his hands toward all of his disciples assembled in the room, he said, "I have no mother; I have no brothers. Behold my mother and behold my brethren! For whosoever does the will of my Father who is in heaven, the same is my mother, my brother, and my sister."

And when Mary heard these words, she collapsed in Jude's arms. They carried her out in the garden to revive her while Jesus spoke the concluding words of his parting message. He would then have gone out to confer with his mother and his brothers, but a messenger arrived in haste from Tiberias bringing word that the officers of the Sanhedrin were on their way with authority to arrest Jesus and carry him to Jerusalem. Andrew received this message and, interrupting Jesus, told it to him.

Andrew did not recall that David had posted some twenty-five sentinels about the Zebedee house, and that no one could take them by surprise; so he asked Jesus what should be done. The Master stood there in silence while his mother, having heard the words, "I have no mother," was recovering from the shock in the garden.

It was at just this time that a woman in the room stood up and exclaimed, "Blessed is the womb that bore you and blessed are the breasts that nursed you."

Jesus turned aside a moment from his conversation with Andrew to answer this woman by saying, "No, rather is the one blessed who hears the word of God and dares to obey it."

Mary and Jesus' brothers thought that Jesus did not understand them, that he had lost interest in them, little realizing that it was they who failed to understand Jesus. Jesus fully understood how difficult it is for men to break with their past. He knew how human beings are swayed by the preacher's eloquence, and how the conscience responds to emotional appeal as the mind does to logic and reason, but he also knew how far more difficult it is to persuade men to *disown the past*.

It is forever true that all who may think they are misunderstood or not appreciated have in Jesus a sympathizing friend and an understanding counselor. He had warned his apostles that a man's foes may be they of his own household, but he had hardly realized how near this prediction would come to apply to his own experience. Jesus did not forsake his earth family to do his Father's work - they forsook him. Later on, after the Master's death and resurrection, when James became connected with the early Christian movement, he suffered immeasurably as a result of his failure to enjoy this earlier association with Jesus and his disciples.

In passing through these events, Jesus chose to be guided by the limited knowledge of his human mind. He desired to undergo the experience with his associates as a mere man. And it was in the human mind of Jesus to see his family before he left. He did not wish to stop in the midst of his discourse and thus render their first meeting after so long a separation such a public affair. He had intended to finish his address and then have a visit with them before leaving, but this plan was thwarted by the conspiracy of events that immediately followed.

The haste of their flight was augmented by the arrival of a party of David's messengers at the rear entrance of the Zebedee home. The commotion produced by these men frightened the apostles into thinking that these new arrivals might be their apprehenders, and in fear of immediate arrest, they hastened through the front entrance to the waiting boat. And all of this explains why Jesus did not see his family waiting on the back porch.

But he did say to David Zebedee as he entered the boat in hasty flight, "Tell my mother and my brothers that I appreciate their coming, and that I intended to see them. Admonish them to find no offense in me but rather to seek for a knowledge of the will of God and for grace and courage to do that will."

And so it was on this Sunday morning, the twenty-second of May, in the year A.D. 29, that Jesus, with his twelve apostles and the twelve evangelists, engaged in this hasty flight from the Sanhedrin officers who were on their way to Bethsaida with authority from Herod Antipas to arrest him and take him to Jerusalem for trial on charges of blasphemy and other violations of the sacred laws of the Jews. It was almost half past eight this beautiful morning when this company of twenty-five manned the oars and pulled for the eastern shore of the Sea of Galilee.

Following the Master's boat was another and smaller craft, containing six of David's messengers, who had instructions to maintain contact with Jesus and his associates and to see that information of their whereabouts and safety was regularly transmitted to the home of Zebedee in Bethsaida, which had served as headquarters for the work of the kingdom for some time. But Jesus was never again to make his home at the house of Zebedee. From now on, throughout the remainder of his earth life, the Master truly "had not where to lay his head." No more did he have even the semblance of a settled abode.

They rowed over to near the village of Kheresa, put their boat in the custody of friends, and began the wanderings of this eventful last year of the Master's life on earth. For a time they remained in the domains of Philip, going from Kheresa up to Caesarea Philippi, thence making their way over to the coast of Phoenicia.

The crowd lingered about the home of Zebedee watching these two boats make their way over the lake toward the eastern shore, and they were well started when the Jerusalem officers hurried up and began their search for Jesus. They refused to believe he had escaped them, and while Jesus and his party were journeying northward through Batanea, the Pharisees and their assistants spent almost a full week vainly searching for him in the neighborhood of Capernaum.

Jesus' family returned to their home in Capernaum and spent almost a week in talking, debating, and praying. They were filled with confusion and consternation. They enjoyed no peace of mind until Thursday afternoon, when Ruth returned from a visit to the Zebedee house, where she learned from David that her father-brother was safe and in good health and making his way toward the Phoenician coast.

# FLEEING THROUGH NORTHERN GALILEE

$S$OON AFTER landing near Kheresa on this eventful Sunday, Jesus and the twenty-four went a little way to the north, where they spent the night in a beautiful park south of Bethsaida-Julias. They were familiar with this camping place, having stopped there in days gone by. Before retiring for the night, the Master called his followers around him and discussed with them the plans for their projected tour through Batanea and northern Galilee to the Phoenician coast.

$S$aid Jesus, "You should all recall how the Psalmist spoke of these times, saying, 'Why do the heathen rage and the peoples plot in vain? The kings of the earth set themselves, and the rulers of the people take counsel together, against the Lord and against his anointed, saying, Let us break the bonds of mercy asunder and let us cast away the cords of love.'

"Today you see this fulfilled before your eyes. But you shall not see the remainder of the Psalmist's prophecy fulfilled, for he entertained erroneous ideas about the Son of Man and his mission on earth. My kingdom is founded on love, proclaimed in mercy, and established by unselfish service. My Father does not sit in heaven laughing in derision at the heathen. He is not wrathful in his great displeasure. True is the promise that the Son shall have these so-called heathen (in reality his ignorant and untaught brethren) for an inheritance. And I will receive these gentiles with open arms of mercy and affection. All this loving-kindness shall be shown the so-called heathen, notwithstanding the unfortunate declaration of the record which intimates that the triumphant Son 'shall break them with a rod of iron and dash them to pieces like a potter's vessel.' The Psalmist exhorted you to 'serve the Lord with fear' - I bid you enter into the exalted privileges of divine sonship by faith; he commands you to rejoice with trembling; I bid you rejoice with assurance. He says, 'Kiss the Son, lest he be angry, and you perish when his wrath is kindled.' But you who have lived with me well know that anger and wrath are not a part of the establishment of the kingdom of heaven in the hearts of men. But the Psalmist did glimpse the true light when, in finishing this exhortation, he said, 'Blessed are they who put their trust in this Son.'"

Jesus continued to teach the twenty-four. "The heathen are not without excuse when they rage at us. Because their outlook is small and narrow, they are able to concentrate their energies enthusiastically. Their goal is near and more or less visible; wherefore do they strive with valiant and effective execution. You who have professed entrance into the kingdom of heaven are altogether too vacillating and indefinite in your teaching conduct. The heathen strike directly for their objectives; you are guilty of too much chronic yearning. If you desire to enter the kingdom, why do you not take it by spiritual assault even as the heathen take a city they lay siege to? You are hardly worthy of the kingdom when your service consists so largely in an attitude of regretting the past, whining over the present, and vainly hoping for the future. Why do the heathen rage? Because they know not the truth. Why do you languish in futile yearning? Because you *obey* not the truth. Cease your useless yearning and go forth bravely doing that which concerns the establishment of the kingdom.

"In all that you do, become not one-sided and overspecialized. The Pharisees who seek our destruction verily think they are doing God's service. They have become so narrowed by tradition that they are blinded by prejudice and hardened by fear. Consider the Greeks, who have a science without religion, while the Jews have a religion without science. And when men become thus misled into accepting a narrow and confused disintegration of truth, their only hope of salvation is to become truth-coordinated - converted.

"Let me emphatically state this eternal truth: If you, by truth coordination, learn to exemplify in your lives this beautiful wholeness of righteousness, your fellow men will then seek after you that they may gain what you have so acquired. The measure wherewith truth seekers are drawn to you represents the measure of your truth endowment, your righteousness. The extent to which you have to go with your message to the people is, in a way, the measure of your failure to live the whole or righteous life, the truth-coordinated life."

And many other things the Master taught his apostles and the evangelists before they bade him good night and sought rest upon their pillows.

On Monday morning, May 23, Jesus directed Peter to go over to Chorazin with the twelve evangelists while he, with the eleven, departed for Caesarea Philippi, going by way of the Jordan to the Damascus-Capernaum road, thence northeast to the junction with the road to Caesarea Philippi, and then on into that city, where they tarried and taught for two weeks. They arrived during the afternoon of Tuesday, May 24.

Peter and the evangelists sojourned in Chorazin for two weeks, preaching the gospel of the kingdom to a small but earnest company of believers. But they were not able to win many new converts. No city of all Galilee yielded so few souls for the kingdom as Chorazin. In accordance with Peter's instructions the twelve evangelists had less to say about healing - things physical - while they preached and taught with increased vigor the spiritual truths of the heavenly kingdom. These two weeks at Chorazin constituted a veritable baptism of adversity for the twelve evangelists in that it was the most difficult and unproductive period in their careers up to this time. Being thus deprived of the satisfaction of winning souls for the kingdom, each of them the more earnestly and honestly took stock of his own soul and its progress in the spiritual paths of the new life.

When it appeared that no more people were minded to seek entrance into the kingdom, Peter, on Tuesday, June 7, called his associates together and departed for Caesarea Philippi to join Jesus and the apostles. They arrived about noontime on Wednesday and spent the entire evening in rehearsing their experiences among the unbelievers of Chorazin. During the discussions of this evening Jesus made further reference to the parable of the sower and taught them much about the meaning of the apparent failure of life undertakings.

Although Jesus did no public work during this two week sojourn near Caesarea Philippi, the apostles held numerous quiet evening meetings in the city, and many of the believers came out to the camp to talk with the Master. Very few were added to the group of believers as a result of this visit. Jesus talked with the apostles each day, and they more clearly discerned that a new phase of the work of preaching the kingdom of heaven was now beginning. They were commencing to comprehend that the "kingdom of heaven is not meat and drink but the realization of the spiritual joy of the acceptance of membership in the divine family og God."

The sojourn at Caesarea Philippi was a real test to the eleven apostles; it was a difficult two weeks for them to live through. They were well-nigh depressed, and they missed the periodic stimulation of Peter's enthusiastic personality. In these times it was truly a great and testing adventure to believe in Jesus and go forth to follow after him. Though they made few converts during these two weeks, they did learn much that was highly profitable from their daily conferences with the Master.

The apostles learned that the Jews were spiritually stagnant and dying because they had crystallized truth into a creed; that when truth becomes formulated as a boundary line of self-righteous exclusiveness instead of serving as signposts of spiritual guidance and progress, such teachings lose their creative and life-giving power and ultimately become merely preservative and fossilizing.

Increasingly they learned from Jesus to look upon human personalities in terms of their possibilities in time and in eternity. They learned that many souls can best be led to love the unseen God by being first taught to love their brethren whom they can see. And it was in this connection that new meaning became attached to the Master's pronouncement concerning unselfish service for one's fellows: "Inasmuch as you did it to one of the least of my brethren, you did it to me."

One of the great lessons of this sojourn at Caesarea had to do with the origin of religious traditions, with the grave danger of allowing a sense of sacredness to become attached to non-sacred things, common ideas, or everyday events. From one conference they emerged with the teaching that true religion was man's heartfelt loyalty to his highest and truest convictions.

Jesus warned his believers that, if their religious longings were only material, increasing knowledge of nature would, by progressive displacement of the supposed supernatural origin of things, ultimately deprive them of their faith in God. But that, if their religion were spiritual, never could the progress of physical science disturb their faith in eternal realities and divine values.

They learned that, when religion is wholly spiritual in motive, it makes all life more worth while, filling it with high purposes, dignifying it with transcendent values, inspiring it with superb motives, all the while comforting the human soul with a sublime and sustaining hope. True religion is designed to lessen the strain of existence; it releases faith and courage for daily living and unselfish serving. Faith promotes spiritual vitality and righteous fruitfulness.

Jesus repeatedly taught his apostles that no civilization could long survive the loss of the best in its religion. And he never grew weary of pointing out to the twelve the great danger of accepting religious symbols and ceremonies in the place of religious experience. His whole earth life was consistently devoted to the mission of thawing out the frozen forms of religion into the liquid liberties of enlightened membership in the family of the divine.

On Thursday morning, June 9, after receiving word regarding the progress of the kingdom brought by the messengers of David from Bethsaida, this group of twenty-five teachers of truth left Caesarea Philippi to begin their journey to the Phoenician coast. They passed around the marsh country, by way of Luz, to the point of junction with the Magdala-Mount Lebanon trail road, thence to the crossing with the road leading to Sidon, arriving there Friday afternoon.

While pausing for lunch under the shadow of an overhanging ledge of rock, near Luz, Jesus delivered one of the most remarkable addresses that his apostles ever listened to throughout all their years of association with him. No sooner had they seated themselves to break bread than Simon Peter asked Jesus, "Master, since the Father in heaven knows all things, and since his spirit is our support in the establishment of the kingdom of heaven on earth, why is it that we flee from the threats of our enemies? Why do we refuse to confront the foes of truth?"

Before Jesus had begun to answer Peter's question, Thomas broke in, asking, "Master, I should really like to know just what is wrong with the religion of our enemies at Jerusalem. What is the real difference between their religion and ours? Why is it we are at such diversity of belief when we all profess to serve the same God?"

And when Thomas had finished, Jesus said, "While I would not ignore Peter's question, knowing full well how easy it would be to misunderstand my reasons for avoiding an open clash with the rulers of the Jews at just this time, still it will prove more helpful to all of you if I choose rather to answer Thomas's question. And that I will proceed to do when you have finished your lunch."

This memorable discourse on religion, summarized and restated in modern phraseology, gave expression to the following truths:

While the religions of the world have a double origin - natural and revelatory - at any one time and among any one people there are to be found three distinct forms of religious devotion. And these three manifestations of the religious urge are:

1. *Primitive religion.* The semi-natural and instinctive urge to fear mysterious energies and worship superior forces, chiefly a religion of the physical nature, the religion of fear.

2. *The religion of civilization.* The advancing religious concepts and practices of the civilizing races - the religion of the mind - the intellectual theology of the authority of established religious tradition.

3. *True religion — the religion of revelation.* The revelation of supernatural values, a partial insight into eternal realities, a glimpse of the goodness and beauty of the infinite character of the Father in heaven - the religion of the spirit as demonstrated in human experience.

The religion of the physical senses and the superstitious fears of natural man, the Master refused to belittle, though he deplored the fact that so much of this primitive form of worship should persist in the religious forms of the more intelligent races of mankind. Jesus made it clear that the great difference between the religion of the mind and the religion of the spirit is that, while the former is upheld by ecclesiastical authority, the latter is wholly based on human experience.

And then the Master, in his hour of teaching, went on to make clear these truths:

Until the races become highly intelligent and more fully civilized, there will persist many of those childlike and superstitious ceremonies which are so characteristic of the evolutionary religious practices of primitive and backward peoples. Until the human race progresses to the level of a higher and more general recognition of the realities of spiritual experience, large numbers of men and women will continue to show a personal preference for those religions of authority which require only intellectual assent, in contrast to the religion of the spirit, which entails active participation of mind and soul in the faith adventure of grappling with the rigorous realities of progressive human experience.

The acceptance of the traditional religions of authority presents the easy way out for man's urge to seek satisfaction for the longings of his spiritual nature. The settled, crystallized, and established religions of authority afford a ready refuge to which the distracted and distraught soul of man may flee when harassed by fear and tormented by uncertainty. Such a religion requires of its devotees, as the price to be paid for its satisfactions and assurances, only a passive and purely intellectual assent.

And for a long time there will live on earth those timid, fearful, and hesitant individuals who will prefer thus to secure their religious consolations, even though, in so casting their lot with the religions of authority, they compromise the sovereignty of personality, debase the dignity of self-respect, and utterly surrender the right to participate in that most thrilling and inspiring of all possible human experiences: the personal quest for truth, the exhilaration of facing the perils of intellectual discovery, the determination to explore the realities of personal religious experience, the supreme satisfaction of experiencing the personal triumph of the actual realization of the victory of spiritual faith over intellectual doubt as it is honestly won in the supreme adventure of all human existence - man seeking God, for himself and as himself, and finding Him.

The religion of the spirit means effort, struggle, conflict, faith, determination, love, loyalty, and progress. The religion of the mind - the theology of authority - requires little or none of these exertions from its formal believers. Tradition is a safe refuge and an easy path for those fearful and halfhearted souls who instinctively shun the spirit struggles and mental uncertainties associated with those faith voyages of daring adventure out upon the high seas of unexplored truth in search for the farther shores of spiritual realities as they may be discovered by the progressive human mind and experienced by the evolving human soul.

And Jesus went on to say, "At Jerusalem the religious leaders have formulated the various doctrines of their traditional teachers and the prophets of other days into an established system of intellectual beliefs, a religion of authority. The appeal of all such religions is largely to the mind. And now are we about to enter upon a deadly conflict with such a religion since we will so shortly begin the bold proclamation of a new religion - a religion which is not a religion in the present-day meaning of that word, a religion that makes its chief appeal to the divine spirit of my Father which resides in the mind of man; a religion which shall derive its authority from the fruits of its acceptance that will so certainly appear in the personal experience of all who really and truly become believers in the truths of this higher spiritual communion."

Pointing out each of the twenty-four and calling them by name, Jesus said, "And now, which one of you would prefer to take this easy path of conformity to an established and fossilized religion, as defended by the Pharisees at Jerusalem, rather than to suffer the difficulties and persecutions attendant upon the mission of proclaiming a better way of salvation to men while you realize the satisfaction of discovering for yourselves the beauties of the realities of a living and personal experience in the eternal truths and supreme grandeurs of the kingdom of heaven? Are you fearful, soft, and ease-seeking? Are you afraid to trust your future in the hands of the God of truth, whose sons you are? Are you distrustful of the Father, whose children you are? Will you go back to the easy path of the certainty and intellectual settledness of the religion of traditional authority, or will you gird yourselves to go forward with me into that uncertain and troublous future of proclaiming the new truths of the religion of the spirit, the kingdom of heaven in the hearts of men?"

All twenty-four of his hearers rose to their feet, intending to signify their united and loyal response to this, one of the few emotional appeals which Jesus ever made to them, but he raised his hand and stopped them, saying, "Go now apart by yourselves, each man alone with the Father, and there find the unemotional answer to my question, and having found such a true and sincere attitude of soul, speak that answer freely and boldly to my Father and your Father, whose infinite life of love is the very spirit of the religion we proclaim."

The evangelists and apostles went apart by themselves for a short time. Their spirits were uplifted, their minds were inspired, and their emotions mightily stirred by what Jesus had said. But when Andrew called them together, the Master said only, "Let us resume our journey. We go into Phoenicia to tarry for a season, and all of you should pray the Father to transform your emotions of mind and body into the higher loyalties of mind and the more satisfying experiences of the spirit."

As they journeyed on down the road, the twenty-four were silent, but presently they began to talk one with another, and by three o'clock that afternoon they could not go farther; they came to a halt, and Peter, going up to Jesus, said, "Master, you have spoken to us the words of life and truth. We would hear more; we beseech you to speak to us further concerning these matters."

And so, while they paused in the shade of the hillside, Jesus continued to teach them regarding the religion of the spirit, in substance saying:

You have come out from among those of your fellows who choose to remain satisfied with a religion of mind, who crave security and prefer conformity. You have elected to exchange your feelings of authoritative certainty for the assurances of the spirit of adventurous and progressive faith. You have dared to protest against the grueling bondage of institutional religion and to reject the authority of the traditions of record which are now regarded as the word of God. Our Father did indeed speak through Moses, Elijah, Isaiah, Amos, and Hosea, but He did not cease to minister words of truth to the world when these prophets of old made an end of their utterances. My Father is no respecter of races or generations in that the word of truth is vouchsafed one age and withheld from another. Commit not the folly of calling that divine which is wholly human, and fail not to discern the words of truth which come not through the traditional oracles of supposed inspiration.

I have called upon you to be born again, to be born of the spirit. I have called you out of the darkness of authority and the lethargy of tradition into the transcendent light of the realization of the possibility of making for yourselves the greatest discovery possible for the human soul to make - the supernal experience of finding God for yourself, in yourself, and of yourself, and of doing all this as a fact in your own personal experience. And so may you pass from death to life, from the authority of tradition to the experience of knowing God; thus will you pass from darkness to light, from a racial faith inherited to a personal faith achieved by actual experience; and thereby will you progress from a theology of mind handed down by your ancestors to a true religion of spirit which shall be built up in your souls as an eternal endowment.

Your religion shall change from the mere intellectual belief in traditional authority to the actual experience of that living faith which is able to grasp the reality of God and all that relates to the divine spirit of the Father. The religion of the mind ties you hopelessly to the past; the religion of the spirit consists in progressive revelation and ever beckons you on toward higher and holier achievements in spiritual ideals and eternal realities.

While the religion of authority may impart a present feeling of settled security, you pay for such a transient satisfaction the price of the loss of your spiritual freedom and religious liberty. My Father does not require of you as the price of entering the kingdom of heaven that you should force yourself to subscribe to a belief in things which are spiritually repugnant, unholy, and untruthful. It is not required of you that your own sense of mercy, justice, and truth should be outraged by submission to an outworn system of religious forms and ceremonies. The religion of the spirit leaves you forever free to follow the truth wherever the leadings of the spirit may take you. And who can judge? Perhaps this spirit may have something to impart to this generation which other generations have refused to hear.

Shame on those false religious teachers who would drag hungry souls back into the dim and distant past and there leave them! And so are these unfortunate persons doomed to become frightened by every new discovery, while they are discomfited by every new revelation of truth. The prophet who said, "He will be kept in perfect peace whose mind is stayed on God," was not a mere intellectual believer in authoritative theology. This truth-knowing human had discovered God; he was not merely talking about God.

I admonish you to give up the practice of always quoting the prophets of old and praising the heroes of Israel, and instead aspire to become living prophets of the Most High and spiritual heroes of the coming kingdom. To honor the God-knowing leaders of the past may indeed be worthwhile, but why, in so doing, should you sacrifice the supreme experience of human existence: finding God for yourselves and knowing him in your own souls?

Every race of mankind has its own mental outlook upon human existence; therefore must the religion of the mind ever run true to these various racial viewpoints. Never can the religions of authority come to unification. Human unity and mortal brotherhood can be achieved only by and through the superendowment of the religion of the spirit. Racial minds may differ, but all mankind is indwelt by the same divine and eternal spirit. The hope of human brotherhood can only be realized when, and as, the divergent mind religions of authority become impregnated with, and overshadowed by, the unifying and ennobling religion of the spirit - the religion of personal spiritual experience.

The religions of authority can only divide men and set them in conscientious array against each other; the religion of the spirit will progressively draw men together and cause them to become understandingly sympathetic with one another. The religions of authority require of men uniformity in belief, but this is impossible of realization in the present state of the world. The religion of the spirit requires only unity of experience - uniformity of destiny - making full allowance for diversity of belief. The religion of the spirit requires only uniformity of insight, not uniformity of viewpoint and outlook. The religion of the spirit does not demand uniformity of intellectual views, only unity of spirit feeling. The religions of authority crystallize into lifeless creeds; the religion of the spirit grows into the increasing joy and liberty of ennobling deeds of loving service and merciful ministration.

But watch, lest any of you look with disdain upon the children of Abraham because they have fallen on these evil days of traditional barrenness. Our forefathers gave themselves up to the persistent and passionate search for God, and they found Him as no other whole race of men have ever known Him since the times of Adam, who knew much of this as he was himself a Son of God. My Father has not failed to mark the long and untiring struggle of Israel, ever since the days of Moses, to find God and to know God. For weary generations the Jews have not ceased to toil, sweat, groan, travail, and endure the sufferings and experience the sorrows of a misunderstood and despised people, all in order that they might come a little nearer the discovery of the truth about God. And, notwithstanding all the failures and falterings of Israel, our fathers progressively, from Moses to the times of Amos and Hosea, did reveal increasingly to the whole world an ever clearer and more truthful picture of the eternal God. And so was the way prepared for the still greater revelation of the Father which you have been called to share.

Never forget there is only one adventure which is more satisfying and thrilling than the attempt to discover the will of the living God, and that is the supreme experience of honestly trying to do that divine will. And fail not to remember that the will of God can be done in any earthly occupation. Some callings are not holy and others secular. All things are sacred in the lives of those who are spirit led; that is, subordinated to truth, ennobled by love, dominated by mercy, and restrained by fairness - justice. The spirit which my Father and I shall send into the world is not only the Spirit of Truth but also the spirit of idealistic beauty.

You must cease to seek for the word of God only on the pages of the olden records of theologic authority. Those who are born of the spirit of God shall henceforth discern the word of God regardless of whence it appears to take origin. Divine truth must not be discounted because the channel of its bestowal is apparently human. Many of your brethren have minds which accept the theory of God while they spiritually fail to realize the presence of God. And that is just the reason why I have so often taught you that the kingdom of heaven can best be realized by acquiring the spiritual attitude of a sincere child. It is not the mental immaturity of the child that I commend to you but rather the *spiritual simplicity* of such an easy-believing and fully-trusting little one. It is not so important that you should know about the fact of God as that you should increasingly grow in the ability to *feel the presence of God*.

When you once begin to find God in your soul, presently you will begin to discover him in other men's souls and eventually in all the creatures and creations of a mighty universe. But what chance does the Father have to appear as a God of supreme loyalties and divine ideals in the souls of men who give little or no time to the thoughtful contemplation of such eternal realities? While the mind is not the seat of the spiritual nature, it is indeed the gateway thereto.

But do not make the mistake of trying to prove to other men that you have found God; you cannot consciously produce such valid proof, albeit there are two positive and powerful demonstrations of the fact that you are God-knowing, and they are:

1. The fruits of the spirit of God showing forth in your daily routine life.
2. The fact that your entire life plan furnishes positive proof that you have unreservedly risked everything you are and have on the adventure of survival after death in the pursuit of the hope of finding the God of eternity, whose presence you have foretasted in time.

Now, mistake not, my Father will ever respond to the faintest flicker of faith. He takes note of the physical and superstitious emotions of the primitive man. And with those honest but fearful souls whose faith is so weak that it amounts to little more than an intellectual conformity to a passive attitude of assent to religions of authority, the Father is ever alert to honor and foster even all such feeble attempts to reach out for him. But you who have been called out of darkness into the light are expected to believe with a whole heart; your faith shall dominate the combined attitudes of body, mind, and spirit.

You are my apostles, and to you religion shall not become a theologic shelter to which you may flee in fear of facing the rugged realities of spiritual progress and idealistic adventure; but rather shall your religion become the fact of real experience which testifies that God has found you, idealized, ennobled, and spiritualized you, and that you have enlisted in the eternal adventure of finding the God who has thus found and sonshipped you.

And when Jesus had finished speaking, he beckoned to Andrew and, pointing to the west toward Phoenicia, said, "Let us be on our way."

# THE SOJOURN AT TYRE AND SIDON

ON FRIDAY afternoon, June 10, Jesus and his associates arrived in the environs of Sidon, where they stopped at the home of a well-to-do woman who had been a patient in the Bethsaida hospital during the times when Jesus was at the height of his popular favor. The evangelists and the apostles were lodged with her friends in the immediate neighborhood, and they rested over the Sabbath day amid these refreshing surroundings. They spent almost two and one-half weeks in Sidon and vicinity before they prepared to visit the coast cities to the north.

This June Sabbath day was one of great quiet. The evangelists and apostles were altogether absorbed in their meditations regarding the discourses of the Master on religion to which they had listened en route to Sidon. They were all able to appreciate something of what he had told them, but none of them fully grasped the import of his teaching.

There lived near the home of Karuska, where the Master lodged, a Syrian woman who had heard much of Jesus as a great healer and teacher, and on this Sabbath afternoon she came over, bringing her little daughter. The child, about twelve years old, was afflicted with a grievous nervous disorder characterized by convulsions and other distressing manifestations.

Jesus had charged his associates to tell no one of his presence at the home of Karuska, explaining that he desired to have a rest. While they had obeyed their Master's instructions, the servant of Karuska had gone over to the house of this Syrian woman, Norana, to inform her that Jesus lodged at the home of her mistress and had urged this anxious mother to bring her afflicted daughter for healing. This mother, of course, believed that her child was possessed by a demon, an unclean spirit.

When Norana arrived with her daughter, the Alpheus twins explained through an interpreter that the Master was resting and could not be disturbed; whereupon Norana replied that she and the child would remain right there until the Master had finished his rest. Peter also endeavored to reason with her and to persuade her to go home. He explained that Jesus was weary with much teaching and healing, and that he had come to Phoenicia for a period of quiet and rest. But it was futile; Norana would not leave. To Peter's entreaties she replied only, "I will not depart until I have seen your Master. I know he can cast the demon out of my child, and I will not go until the healer has looked upon my daughter."

Then Thomas sought to send the woman away but met only with failure. To him she said, "I have faith that your Master can cast out this demon which torments my child. I have heard of his mighty works in Galilee, and I believe in him. What has happened to you, his disciples, that you would send away those who come seeking your Master's help?" And when she had thus spoken, Thomas withdrew.

Then came forward Simon Zelotes to remonstrate with Norana. Said Simon, "Woman, you are a Greek-speaking gentile. It is not right that you should expect the Master to take the bread intended for the children of the favored household and cast it to the dogs."

But Norana refused to take offense at Simon's thrust. She replied only, "Yes, teacher, I understand your words. I am only a dog in the eyes of the Jews, but as concerns your Master, I am a believing dog. I am determined that he shall see my daughter, for I am persuaded that, if he shall but look upon her, he will heal her. And even you, my good man, would not dare to deprive the dogs of the privilege of obtaining the crumbs which chance to fall from the children's table."

At just this time the little girl was seized with a violent convulsion before them all, and the mother cried out, "There, you can see that my child is possessed by an evil spirit. If our need does not impress you, it would appeal to your Master, who I have been told loves all men and dares even to heal the gentiles when they believe. You are not worthy to be his disciples. I will not go until my child has been cured."

Jesus, who had heard all of this conversation through an open window, now came outside, much to their surprise, and said, "O woman, great is your faith, so great that I cannot withhold that which you desire; go your way in peace. Your daughter already has been made whole."

And the little girl was well from that hour. As Norana and the child took leave, Jesus entreated them to tell no one of this occurrence; and while his associates did comply with this request, the mother and the child ceased not to proclaim the fact of the little girl's healing throughout all the countryside and even in Sidon, so much so that Jesus found it advisable to change his lodgings within a few days.

The next day, as Jesus taught his apostles, commenting on the cure of the daughter of the Syrian woman, he said, "And so it has been all the way along; you see for yourselves how the gentiles are able to exercise saving faith in the teachings of the gospel of the kingdom of heaven. Verily, verily, I tell you that the Father's kingdom shall be taken by the gentiles if the children of Abraham are not minded to show faith enough to enter therein."

In entering Sidon, Jesus and his associates passed over a bridge, the first one many of them had ever seen. As they walked over this bridge, Jesus, among other things, said, "This world is only a bridge; you may pass over it, but you should not think to build a dwelling place upon it."

As the twenty-four began their labors in Sidon, Jesus went to stay in a home just north of the city, the house of Justa and her mother, Bernice. Jesus taught the twenty-four each morning at the home of Justa, and they went abroad in Sidon to teach and preach during the afternoons and evenings.

The apostles and the evangelists were greatly cheered by the manner in which the gentiles of Sidon received their message; during their short sojourn many were added to the kingdom. This period of about six weeks in Phoenicia was a very fruitful time in the work of winning souls, but the later Jewish writers of the Gospels were wont lightly to pass over the record of this warm reception of Jesus' teachings by these gentiles at this very time when such a large number of his own people were in hostile array against him.

In many ways these gentile believers appreciated Jesus' teachings more fully than the Jews. Many of these Greek-speaking Syrophoenicians came to know not only that Jesus was like God but also that God was like Jesus. These so-called heathen achieved a good understanding of the Master's teachings about the uniformity of the laws of this world and the entire universe. They grasped the teaching that God is no respecter of persons, races, or nations; that there is no favoritism with the Universal Father; that the universe is wholly and ever law-abiding and unfailingly dependable. These gentiles were not afraid of Jesus; they dared to accept his message. All down through the ages men have not been unable to comprehend Jesus; they have been afraid to.

Jesus made it clear to the twenty-four that he had not fled from Galilee because he lacked courage to confront his enemies. They comprehended that he was not yet ready for an open clash with established religion, and that he did not seek to become a martyr. It was during one of these conferences at the home of Justa that the Master first told his disciples that "even though heaven and earth shall pass away, my words of truth shall not."

The theme of Jesus' instructions during the sojourn at Sidon was spiritual progression. He told them they could not stand still; they must go forward in righteousness or retrogress into evil and sin. He admonished them to "forget those things which are in the past while you push forward to embrace the greater realities of the kingdom." He besought them not to be content with their childhood in the gospel but to strive for the attainment of the full stature of divine sonship in the communion of the spirit and in the fellowship of believers.

Said Jesus, "My disciples must not only cease to do evil but learn to do well; you must not only be cleansed from all conscious sin, but you must refuse to harbor even the feelings of guilt. If you confess your sins, they are forgiven; therefore must you maintain a conscience void of offense."

Jesus greatly enjoyed the keen sense of humor which these gentiles exhibited. It was the sense of humor displayed by Norana, the Syrian woman, as well as her great and persistent faith, that so touched the Master's heart and appealed to his mercy. Jesus greatly regretted that his people - the Jews - were so lacking in humor. He once said to Thomas: "My people take themselves too seriously; they are just about devoid of an appreciation of humor. The burdensome religion of the Pharisees could never have had origin among a people with a sense of humor. They also lack consistency; they strain at gnats and swallow camels."

On Tuesday, June 28, the Master and his associates left Sidon, going up the coast to Porphyreon and Heldua. They were well received by the gentiles, and many were added to the kingdom during this week of teaching and preaching. The apostles preached in Porphyreon and the evangelists taught in Heldua. While the twenty-four were thus engaged in their work, Jesus left them for a period of three or four days, paying a visit to the coast city of Beirut, where he visited with a Syrian named Malach, who was a believer, and who had been at Bethsaida the year before.

On Wednesday, July 6, they all returned to Sidon and tarried at the home of Justa until Sunday morning, when they departed for Tyre, going south along the coast by way of Sarepta, arriving at Tyre on Monday, July 11. By this time the apostles and the evangelists were becoming accustomed to working among these so-called gentiles, who were in reality mainly descended from the earlier Canaanite tribes of still earlier Semitic origin. All of these peoples spoke the Greek language. It was a great surprise to the apostles and evangelists to observe the eagerness of these gentiles to hear the gospel and to note the readiness with which many of them believed.

From July 11 to July 24 they taught in Tyre. Each of the apostles took with him one of the evangelists, and thus two and two they taught and preached in all parts of Tyre and its environs. The polyglot population of this busy seaport heard them gladly, and many were baptized into the outward fellowship of the kingdom.

Jesus maintained his headquarters at the home of a Jew named Joseph, a believer, who lived three or four miles south of Tyre, not far from the tomb of Hiram who had been king of the city-state of Tyre during the times of David and Solomon.

Daily, for this period of two weeks, the apostles and evangelists entered Tyre by way of Alexander's mole to conduct small meetings, and each night most of them would return to the encampment at Joseph's house south of the city. Every day believers came out from the city to talk with Jesus at his resting place. The Master spoke in Tyre only once, on the afternoon of July 20, when he taught the believers concerning the Father's love for all mankind and about the mission of the Son to reveal the Father to all races of men. There was such an interest in the gospel of the kingdom among these gentiles that, on this occasion, the doors of the Melkarth temple were opened to him, and it is interesting to record that in subsequent years a Christian church was built on the very site of this ancient temple.

Many of the leaders in the manufacture of Tyrian purple, the dye that made Tyre and Sidon famous the world over, and which contributed so much to their world-wide commerce and consequent enrichment, believed in the kingdom. When, shortly thereafter, the supply of the sea animals which were the source of this dye began to diminish, these dye makers went forth in search of new habitats of these shellfish. And thus migrating to the ends of the earth, they carried with them the message of the fatherhood of God and the brotherhood of man - the gospel of the kingdom.

On this Wednesday afternoon, in the course of his address, Jesus first told his followers the story of the white lily which rears its pure and snowy head high into the sunshine while its roots are grounded in the slime and muck of the darkened soil beneath. "Likewise," said he, "mortal man, while he has his roots of origin and being in the animal soil of human nature, can by faith raise his spiritual nature up into the sunlight of heavenly truth and actually bear the noble fruits of the spirit."

It was during this same sermon that Jesus made use of his first and only parable having to do with his own trade - carpentry. In the course of his admonition to "Build well the foundations for the growth of a noble character of spiritual endowments," he said, "In order to yield the fruits of the spirit, you must be born of the spirit. You must be taught by the spirit and be led by the spirit if you would live the spirit-filled life among your fellows. But do not make the mistake of the foolish carpenter who wastes valuable time squaring, measuring, and smoothing his worm-eaten and inwardly rotting timber and then, when he has thus bestowed all of his labor upon the unsound beam, must reject it as unfit to enter into the foundations of the building which he would construct to withstand the assaults of time and storm. Let every man make sure that the intellectual and moral foundations of character are such as will adequately support the superstructure of the enlarging and ennobling spiritual nature, which is thus to transform the mortal mind and then, in association with that re-created mind, is to achieve the evolvement of the soul of immortal destiny. Your spirit nature - the jointly created soul - is a living growth, but the mind and morals of the individual are the soil from which these higher manifestations of human development and divine destiny must spring. The soil of the evolving soul is human and material, but the destiny of this combined creature of mind and spirit is spiritual and divine."

On the evening of this same day Nathaniel asked, "Master, why do we pray that God will lead us not into temptation when we well know from your revelation of the Father that he never does such things?"

Jesus answered Nathaniel, "It is not strange that you ask such questions seeing that you are beginning to know the Father as I know him, and not as the early Hebrew prophets so dimly saw him. You well know how our forefathers were disposed to see God in almost everything that happened. They looked for the hand of God in all natural occurrences and in every unusual episode of human experience. They connected God with both good and evil. They thought he softened the heart of Moses and hardened the heart of Pharaoh. When man had a strong urge to do something, good or evil, he was in the habit of accounting for these unusual emotions by remarking: 'The Lord spoke to me saying, do thus and so, or go here and there.' Accordingly, since men so often and so violently ran into temptation, it became the habit of our forefathers to believe that God led them thither for testing, punishing, or strengthening. But you, indeed, now know better. You know that men are all too often led into temptation by the urge of their own selfishness and by the impulses of their animal natures. When you are in this way tempted, I admonish you that, while you recognize temptation honestly and sincerely for just what it is, you intelligently redirect the energies of spirit, mind, and body, which are seeking expression, into higher channels and toward more idealistic goals. In this way may you transform your temptations into the highest types of uplifting mortal ministry while you almost wholly avoid these wasteful and weakening conflicts between the animal and spiritual natures.

"But let me warn you against the folly of undertaking to surmount temptation by the effort of supplanting one desire by another and supposedly superior desire through the mere force of the human will. If you would be truly triumphant over the temptations of the lesser and lower nature, you must come to that place of spiritual advantage where you have really and truly developed an actual interest in, and love for, those higher and more idealistic forms of conduct which your mind is desirous of substituting for these lower and less idealistic habits of behavior that you recognize as temptation. You will in this way be delivered through spiritual transformation rather than be increasingly overburdened with the deceptive suppression of mortal desires. The old and the inferior will be forgotten in the love for the new and the superior. Beauty is always triumphant over ugliness in the hearts of all who are illuminated by the love of truth. There is mighty power in the expulsive energy of a new and sincere spiritual affection. And again I say to you, be not overcome by evil but rather overcome evil with good."

Long into the night the apostles and evangelists continued to ask questions, and from the many answers we would present the following thoughts, restated in modern phraseology:

Forceful ambition, intelligent judgment, and seasoned wisdom are the essentials of material success. Leadership is dependent on natural ability, discretion, will power, and determination. Spiritual destiny is dependent on faith, love, and devotion to truth - hunger and thirst for righteousness - the wholehearted desire to find God and to be like Him.

Do not become discouraged by the discovery that you are human. Human nature may tend toward evil, but it is not inherently sinful. Be not downcast by your failure wholly to forget some of your regrettable experiences. The mistakes which you fail to forget in time will be forgotten in eternity. Lighten your burdens of soul by speedily acquiring a long-distance view of your destiny, a universe expansion of your career.

Make not the mistake of estimating the soul's worth by the imperfections of the mind or by the appetites of the body. Judge not the soul nor evaluate its destiny by the standard of a single unfortunate human episode. Your spiritual destiny is conditioned only by your spiritual longings and purposes.

Religion is the exclusively spiritual experience of the evolving immortal soul of the God-knowing man, but moral power and spiritual energy are mighty forces that may be utilized in dealing with difficult social situations and in solving intricate economic problems. These moral and spiritual endowments make all levels of human living richer and more meaningful.

You are destined to live a narrow and mean life if you learn to love only those who love you. Human love may indeed be reciprocal, but divine love is outgoing in all its satisfaction-seeking. The less of love in any creature's nature, the greater the love need, and the more does divine love seek to satisfy such need. Love is never self-seeking, and it cannot be self-bestowed. Divine love cannot be self-contained; it must be unselfishly bestowed.

Kingdom believers should possess an implicit faith, a wholesouled belief, in the certain triumph of righteousness. Kingdom builders must be undoubting of the truth of the gospel of eternal salvation. Believers must increasingly learn how to step aside from the rush of life - escape the harassments of material existence - while they refresh the soul, inspire the mind, and renew the spirit by worshipful communion.

God-knowing individuals are not discouraged by misfortune or downcast by disappointment. Believers are immune to the depression consequent upon purely material upheavals; spirit livers are not perturbed by the episodes of the material world. Candidates for eternal life are practitioners of an invigorating and constructive technique for meeting all of the vicissitudes and harassments of mortal living. Every day a true believer lives, he finds it *easier* to do the right thing.

Spiritual living mightily increases true self-respect. But self-respect is not self-admiration. Self-respect is always co-ordinate with the love and service of one's fellows. It is not possible to respect yourself more than you love your neighbor; the one is the measure of the capacity for the other.

As the days pass, every true believer becomes more skillful in alluring his fellows into the love of eternal truth. Are you more resourceful in revealing goodness to humanity today than you were yesterday? Are you a better righteousness recommender this year than you were last year? Are you becoming increasingly artistic in your technique of leading hungry souls into the spiritual kingdom?

Are your ideals sufficiently high to insure your eternal salvation while your ideas are so practical as to render you a useful citizen to function on earth in association with your mortal fellows? In the spirit, your citizenship is in heaven; in the flesh, you are still citizens of the earth kingdoms. Render to the Caesars the things which are material and to God those which are spiritual.

The measure of the spiritual capacity of the evolving soul is your faith in truth and your love for man, but the measure of your human strength of character is your ability to resist the holding of grudges and your capacity to withstand brooding in the face of deep sorrow. Defeat is the true mirror in which you may honestly view your real self.

As you grow older in years and more experienced in the affairs of the kingdom, are you becoming more tactful in dealing with troublesome mortals and more tolerant in living with stubborn associates? Tact is the fulcrum of social leverage, and tolerance is the earmark of a great soul. If you possess these rare and charming gifts, as the days pass you will become more alert and expert in your worthy efforts to avoid all unnecessary social misunderstandings. Such wise souls are able to avoid much of the trouble which is certain to be the portion of all who suffer from lack of emotional adjustment, those who refuse to grow up, and those who refuse to grow old gracefully.

Avoid dishonesty and unfairness in all your efforts to preach truth and proclaim the gospel. Seek no unearned recognition and crave no undeserved sympathy. Love, freely receive from both divine and human sources regardless of your deserts, and love freely in return. But in all other things related to honor and adulation seek only that which honestly belongs to you.

The God-conscious mortal is certain of salvation, unafraid of life, honest and consistent., knows how bravely to endure unavoidable suffering, and is uncomplaining when faced by inescapable hardship.

The true believer does not grow weary in well-doing just because he or she is thwarted. Difficulty whets the ardor of the truth lover, while obstacles only challenge the exertions of the undaunted kingdom builder.

And many other things Jesus taught them before they made ready to depart from Tyre.

The day before Jesus left Tyre for the return to the region of the Sea of Galilee, he called his associates together and directed the twelve evangelists to go back by a route different from that which he and the twelve apostles were to take. And after the evangelists here left Jesus, they were never again so intimately associated with him.

About noon on Sunday, July 24, Jesus and the twelve left the home of Joseph, south of Tyre, going down the coast to Ptolemais. Here they tarried for a day, speaking words of comfort to the company of believers resident there. Peter preached to them on the evening of July 25.

On Tuesday they left Ptolemais, going east inland to near Jotapata by way of the Tiberias road. Wednesday they stopped at Jotapata and instructed the believers further in the things of the kingdom. Thursday they left Jotapata, going north on the Nazareth-Mount Lebanon trail to the village of Zebulun, by way of Ramah. They held meetings at Ramah on Friday and remained over the Sabbath. They reached Zebulun on Sunday, the 31st, holding a meeting that evening and departing the next morning.

Leaving Zebulun, they journeyed over to the junction with the Magdala-Sidon road near Gischala, and thence they made their way to Gennesaret on the western shores of the lake of Galilee, south of Capernaum, where they had appointed to meet with David Zebedee, and where they intended to take counsel as to the next move to be made in the work of preaching the gospel of the kingdom.

During a brief conference with David they learned that many leaders were then gathered together on the opposite side of the lake near Kheresa, and accordingly, that very evening a boat took them across. For one day they rested quietly in the hills, going on the next day to the park nearby, where the Master once fed the five thousand. Here they rested for three days and held daily conferences, which were attended by about fifty men and women, the remnants of the once numerous company of believers resident in Capernaum and its environs.

While Jesus was absent from Capernaum and Galilee, the period of the Phoenician sojourn, his enemies reckoned that the whole movement had been broken up and concluded that Jesus' haste in withdrawing indicated he was so thoroughly frightened that he would not likely ever return to bother them. All active opposition to his teachings had about subsided. The believers were beginning to hold public meetings once more, and there was occurring a gradual but effective consolidation of the tried and true survivors of the great sifting through which the gospel believers had just passed.

Philip, the brother of Herod, had become a halfhearted believer in Jesus and sent word that the Master was free to live and work in his domains.

The mandate to close the synagogues of all Jewry to the teachings of Jesus and all his followers had worked adversely upon the scribes and Pharisees. Immediately upon Jesus' removing himself as an object of controversy, there occurred a reaction among the entire Jewish people; there was general resentment against the Pharisees and the Sanhedrin leaders at Jerusalem. Many of the rulers of the synagogues began surreptitiously to open their synagogues to Abner and his associates, claiming that these teachers were followers of John and not disciples of Jesus.

Even Herod Antipas experienced a change of heart and, on learning that Jesus was sojourning across the lake in the territory of his brother Philip, sent word to him that, while he had signed warrants for his arrest in Galilee, he had not so authorized his apprehension in Perea, thus indicating that Jesus would not be molested if he remained outside of Galilee; and he communicated this same ruling to the Jews at Jerusalem.

And that was the situation about the first of August, A.D. 29, when the Master returned from the Phoenician mission and began the reorganization of his scattered, tested, and depleted forces for this last and eventful year of his mission on earth.

The issues of battle are clearly drawn as the Master and his associates prepare to begin the proclamation of a new religion, the religion of the spirit of the living God who dwells in the minds of men and women.

## AT CAESAREA PHILIPPI

**B**EFORE JESUS took the twelve for a short sojourn in the vicinity of Caesarea Philippi, he arranged through the messengers of David to go over to Capernaum on Sunday, August 7, for the purpose of meeting his family. By prearrangement this visit was to occur at the Zebedee boatshop. David Zebedee had arranged with Jude, Jesus' brother, for the presence of the entire Nazareth family - Mary and all of Jesus' brothers and sisters - and Jesus went with Andrew and Peter to keep this appointment. It was certainly the intention of Mary and the children to keep this engagement, but it so happened that a group of the Pharisees, knowing that Jesus was on the opposite side of the lake in Philip's domains, decided to call upon Mary to learn what they could of his whereabouts. The arrival of these Jerusalem emissaries greatly perturbed Mary, and noting the tension and nervousness of the entire family, they concluded that Jesus must have been expected to pay them a visit. Accordingly they installed themselves in Mary's home and, after summoning reinforcements, waited patiently for Jesus' arrival. And this, of course, effectively prevented any of the family from attempting to keep their appointment with Jesus. Several times during the day both Jude and Ruth endeavored to elude the vigilance of the Pharisees in their efforts to send word to Jesus, but it was of no avail.

Early in the afternoon David's messengers brought Jesus word that the Pharisees were encamped on the doorstep of his mother's house, and therefore he made no attempt to visit his family. And so again, through no fault of either, Jesus and his earth family failed to make contact.

**A**s Jesus, with Andrew and Peter, tarried by the lake near the boatshop, a temple-tax collector came upon them and, recognizing Jesus, called Peter to one side and said, "Does not your Master pay the temple tax?"

Peter was inclined to show indignation at the suggestion that Jesus should be expected to contribute to the maintenance of the religious activities of his sworn enemies, but, noting a peculiar expression on the face of the tax collector, he rightly surmised that it was the purpose to entrap them in the act of refusing to pay the customary half shekel for the support of the temple services at Jerusalem. Accordingly, Peter replied, "Why of course the Master pays the temple tax. You wait by the gate, and I will presently return with the tax."

Now Peter had spoken hastily. Judas carried their funds, and he was across the lake. Neither he, his brother, nor Jesus had brought along any money. And knowing that the Pharisees were looking for them, they could not well go to Bethsaida to obtain money.

When Peter told Jesus about the collector and that he had promised him the money, Jesus said, "If you have promised, then should you pay. But wherewith will you redeem your promise? Will you again become a fisherman that you may honor your word? Nevertheless, Peter, it is well in the circumstances that we pay the tax. Let us give these men no occasion for offense at our attitude. We will wait here while you go with the boat and cast for the fish, and when you have sold them at yonder market, pay the collector for all three of us."

All of this had been overheard by the secret messenger of David who stood near by, and who then signaled to an associate, fishing near the shore, to come in quickly. When Peter made ready to go out in the boat for a catch, this messenger and his fisherman friend presented him with several large baskets of fish and assisted him in carrying them to the fish merchant near by, who purchased the catch, paying sufficient, with what was added by the messenger of David, to meet the temple tax for the three. The collector accepted the tax, forgoing the penalty for tardy payment because they had been for some time absent from Galilee.

It is not strange that you have a record of Peter's catching a fish with a shekel in its mouth. In those days there were current many stories about finding treasures in the mouths of fishes; such tales of near miracles were commonplace. So, as Peter left them to go toward the boat, Jesus remarked, half-humorously, "Strange that the sons of the king must pay tribute; usually it is the stranger who is taxed for the upkeep of the court, but it behooves us to afford no stumbling block for the authorities. Go hence! Maybe you will catch the fish with the shekel in its mouth." Jesus having thus spoken, and Peter so soon appearing with the temple tax, it is not surprising that the episode became later expanded into a miracle as recorded by the writer of Matthew's Gospel.

Jesus, with Andrew and Peter, waited by the seashore until nearly sundown. Messengers brought them word that Mary's house was still under surveillance; therefore, when it grew dark, the three waiting men entered their boat and slowly rowed away toward the eastern shore of the Sea of Galilee.

✷ ✷ ✷

On Monday, August 8, while Jesus and the twelve apostles were encamped in Magadan Park, near Bethsaida-Julias, more than one hundred believers, the evangelists, the women's corps, and others interested in the establishment of the kingdom, came over from Capernaum for a conference. And many of the Pharisees, learning that Jesus was here, came also. By this time some of the Sadducees were united with the Pharisees in their effort to entrap Jesus. Before going into the closed conference with the believers, Jesus held a public meeting at which the Pharisees were present, and they heckled the Master and otherwise sought to disturb the assembly.

Said the leader of the disturbers, "Teacher, we would like you to give us a sign of your authority to teach, and then, when the same shall come to pass, all men will know that you have been sent by God."

And Jesus answered them, "When it is evening, you say it will be fair weather, for the heaven is red; in the morning it will be foul weather, for the heaven is red and lowering. When you see a cloud rising in the west, you say showers will come; when the wind blows from the south, you say scorching heat will come. How is it that you so well know how to discern the face of the heavens but are so utterly unable to discern the signs of the times? To those who would know the truth, already has a sign been given; but to an evil-minded and hypocritical generation no sign shall be given."

When Jesus had thus spoken, he withdrew and prepared for the evening conference with his followers. At this conference it was decided to undertake a united mission throughout all the cities and villages of the Decapolis as soon as Jesus and the twelve should return from their proposed visit to Caesarea Philippi. The Master participated in planning for the Decapolis mission and, in dismissing the company, said, "I say to you, beware of the leaven of the Pharisees and the Sadducees. Be not deceived by their show of much learning and by their profound loyalty to the forms of religion. Be only concerned with the spirit of living truth and the power of true religion. It is not the fear of a dead religion that will save you but rather your faith in a living experience in the spiritual realities of the kingdom. Do not allow yourselves to become blinded by prejudice and paralyzed by fear. Neither permit reverence for the traditions so to pervert your understanding that your eyes see not and your ears hear not. It is not the purpose of true religion merely to bring peace but rather to insure progress. And there can be no peace in the heart or progress in the mind unless you fall wholeheartedly in love with truth, the ideals of eternal realities. The issues of life and death are being set before you - the sinful pleasures of time against the righteous realities of eternity. Even now you should begin to find deliverance from the bondage of fear and doubt as you enter upon the living of the new life of faith and hope. And when the feelings of service for your fellow men arise within your soul, do not stifle them; when the emotions of love for your neighbor well up within your heart, give expression to such urges of affection in intelligent ministry to the real needs of your fellows."

★ ★ ★

Early Tuesday morning Jesus and the twelve apostles left Magadan Park for Caesarea Philippi, the capital of the Tetrarch Philip's domain. Caesarea Philippi was situated in a region of wondrous beauty. It nestled in a charming valley between scenic hills where the Jordan poured forth from an underground cave. The heights of Mount Hermon were in full view to the north, while from the hills just to the south a magnificent view was had of the upper Jordan and the Sea of Galilee.

Jesus had gone to Mount Hermon in his early experience with the affairs of the kingdom, and now that he was entering upon the final epoch of his work, he desired to return to this mount of trial and triumph, where he hoped the apostles might gain a new vision of their responsibilities and acquire new strength for the trying times just ahead. As they journeyed along the way, about the time of passing south of the Waters of Merom, the apostles fell to talking among themselves about their recent experiences in Phoenicia and elsewhere and to recounting how their message had been received, and how the different peoples regarded their Master.

As they paused for lunch, Jesus suddenly confronted the twelve with the first question he had ever addressed to them concerning himself. He asked this surprising question, "Who do men say that I am?"

Jesus had spent long months in training these apostles as to the nature and character of the kingdom of heaven, and he well knew the time had come when he must begin to teach them more about his own nature and his personal relationship to the kingdom. And now, as they were seated under the mulberry trees, the Master made ready to hold one of the most momentous sessions of his long association with the chosen apostles.

More than half the apostles participated in answering Jesus' question. They told him that he was regarded as a prophet or as an extraordinary man by all who knew him; that even his enemies greatly feared him, accounting for his powers by the indictment that he was in league with the prince of devils. They told him that some in Judea and Samaria who had not met him personally believed he was John the Baptist risen from the dead. Peter explained that he had been, at sundry times and by various persons, compared with Moses, Elijah, Isaiah, and Jeremiah.

When Jesus had listened to this report, he drew himself upon his feet, and looking down upon the twelve sitting about him in a semicircle, with startling emphasis he pointed to them with a sweeping gesture of his hand and asked, "But who say you that I am?"

There was a moment of tense silence. The twelve never took their eyes off the Master, and then Simon Peter, springing to his feet, exclaimed, "You are the Deliverer, the Son of the living God." And the eleven sitting apostles arose to their feet with one accord, thereby indicating that Peter had spoken for all of them.

When Jesus had beckoned them again to be seated, and while still standing before them, he said, "This has been revealed to you by my Father. The hour has come when you should know the truth about me. But for the time being I charge you that you tell this to no man. Let us go hence."

And so they resumed their journey to Caesarea Philippi, arriving late that evening and stopping at the home of Celsus, who was expecting them. The apostles slept little that night; they seemed to sense that a great event in their lives and in the work of the kingdom had transpired.

Since the occasions of Jesus' baptism by John and the turning of the water into wine at Cana, the apostles had, at various times, virtually accepted him as the Messiah. For short periods some of them had truly believed that he was the expected Deliverer. But hardly would such hopes spring up in their hearts than the Master would dash them to pieces by some crushing word or disappointing deed. They had long been in a state of turmoil due to conflict between the concepts of the expected Messiah which they held in their minds and the experience of their extraordinary association with this extraordinary man which they held in their hearts.

It was late forenoon on this Wednesday when the apostles assembled in Celsus' garden for their noontime meal. During most of the night and since they had arisen that morning, Simon Peter and Simon Zelotes had been earnestly laboring with their brethren to bring them all to the point of the wholehearted acceptance of the Master, not merely as the Messiah, but also as the divine Son of the living God. The two Simons were well-nigh agreed in their estimate of Jesus, and they labored diligently to bring their brethren around to the full acceptance of their views. While Andrew continued as the director-general of the apostolic corps, his brother, Simon Peter, was becoming, increasingly and by common consent, the spokesman for the twelve.

They were all seated in the garden at just about noon when the Master appeared. They wore expressions of dignified solemnity, and all arose to their feet as he approached them. Jesus relieved the tension by that friendly and fraternal smile which was so characteristic of him when his followers took themselves, or some happening related to themselves, too seriously. With a commanding gesture he indicated that they should be seated. Never again did the twelve greet their Master by arising when he came into their presence. They saw that he did not approve of such an outward show of respect.

After they had partaken of their meal and were engaged in discussing plans for the forthcoming tour of the Decapolis, Jesus suddenly looked up into their faces and said, "Now that a full day has passed since you assented to Simon Peter's declaration regarding the identity of the Son of Man, I would ask if you still hold to your decision?"

On hearing this, the twelve stood upon their feet, and Simon Peter, stepping a few paces forward toward Jesus, said, "Yes, Master, we do. We believe that you are the Son of the living God." And Peter sat down with his brethren.

Jesus, still standing, then said to the twelve, "You are my chosen ambassadors, but I know that, in the circumstances, you could not entertain this belief as a result of mere human knowledge. This is a revelation of the spirit of my Father to your inmost souls. And when, therefore, you make this confession by the insight of the spirit of my Father which dwells within you, I am led to declare that upon this foundation will I build the brotherhood of the kingdom of heaven. Upon this rock of spiritual reality will I build the living temple of spiritual fellowship in the eternal realities of my Father's kingdom. All the forces of evil and the hosts of sin shall not prevail against this human fraternity of the divine spirit. And while my Father's spirit shall ever be the divine guide and mentor of all who enter the bonds of this spirit fellowship, to you and your successors I now deliver the keys of the outward kingdom - the authority over things temporal - the social and economic features of this association of men and women as fellows of the kingdom." And again he charged them, for the time being, that they should tell no man that he was the Son of God.

Jesus was beginning to have faith in the loyalty and integrity of his apostles. The Master conceived that a faith which could stand what his chosen representatives had recently passed through would undoubtedly endure the fiery trials which were just ahead and emerge from the apparent wreckage of all their hopes into the new light of a new dispensation and thereby be able to go forth to enlighten a world sitting in darkness. On this day the Master began to believe in the faith of his apostles, save one.

And ever since that day this same Jesus has been building that living temple upon that same eternal foundation of his divine sonship, and those who thereby become self-conscious sons and daughters of God are the human stones which constitute this living temple of sonship erecting to the glory and honor of the wisdom and love of the eternal Father of spirits.

And when Jesus had thus spoken, he directed the twelve to go apart by themselves in the hills to seek wisdom, strength, and spiritual guidance until the time of the evening meal. And they did as the Master admonished them.

The new and vital feature of Peter's confession was the clear-cut recognition that Jesus was the Son of God, of his unquestioned divinity. Ever since his baptism and the wedding at Cana these apostles had variously regarded him as the Messiah, but it was not a part of the Jewish concept of the national deliverer that he should be *divine*. The Jews had not taught that the Messiah would spring from divinity; he was to be the "anointed one," but hardly had they contemplated him as being "the Son of God." In the second confession more emphasis was placed upon the *combined nature,* the supernal fact that he was the Son of Man *and* the Son of God, and it was upon this great truth of the union of the human nature with the divine nature that Jesus declared he would build the kingdom of heaven.

Jesus had sought to live his life on earth and complete his bestowal mission as the Son of Man. His followers were disposed to regard him as the expected Messiah. Knowing that he could never fulfill their Messianic expectations, he endeavored to effect such a modification of their concept of the Messiah as would enable him partially to meet their expectations. But he now recognized that such a plan could hardly be carried through successfully. He therefore elected boldly to disclose the third plan - openly to announce his divinity, acknowledge the truthfulness of Peter's confession, and directly proclaim to the twelve that he was a Son of God.

For three years Jesus had been proclaiming that he was the "Son of Man," while for these same three years the apostles had been increasingly insistent that he was the expected Jewish Messiah. He now disclosed that he was the Son of God, and upon the concept of the *combined nature* of the Son of Man and the Son of God, he determined to build the kingdom of heaven. He had decided to refrain from further efforts to convince them that he was not the Messiah. He now proposed boldly to reveal to them what he *is,* and then to ignore their determination to persist in regarding him as the Messiah.


Jesus and the apostles remained another day at the home of Celsus, waiting for messengers to arrive from David Zebedee with funds. Following the collapse of the popularity of Jesus with the masses there occurred a great falling off in revenue. When they reached Caesarea Philippi, the treasury was empty. Matthew was loath to leave Jesus and his brethren at such a time, and he had no ready funds of his own to hand over to Judas as he had so many times done in the past. However, David Zebedee had foreseen this probable diminution of revenue and had accordingly instructed his messengers that, as they made their way through Judea, Samaria, and Galilee, they should act as collectors of money to be forwarded to the exiled apostles and their Master. And so, by evening of this day, these messengers arrived from Bethsaida bringing funds sufficient to sustain the apostles until their return to embark upon the Decapolis tour. Matthew expected to have money from the sale of his last piece of property in Capernaum by that time, having arranged that these funds should be anonymously turned over to Judas.

Neither Peter nor the other apostles had a very adequate conception of Jesus' divinity. They little realized that this was the beginning of a new epoch in their Master's career on earth, the time when the teacher-healer was becoming the newly conceived Messiah - the Son of God. From this time on a new note appeared in the Master's message. Henceforth his one ideal of living was the revelation of the Father, while his one idea in teaching was to present to his universe the personification of that supreme wisdom which can only be comprehended by living it. He came that we all might have life and have it more abundantly.

Jesus now entered upon the fourth and last stage of his human life in the flesh. The first stage was that of his childhood, the years when he was only dimly conscious of his origin, nature, and destiny as a human being. The second stage was the increasingly self-conscious years of youth and advancing manhood, during which he came more clearly to comprehend his divine nature and human mission. This second stage ended with the experiences and revelations associated with his baptism. The third stage of the Master's earth experience extended from the baptism through the years of his ministry as teacher and healer and up to this momentous hour of Peter's confession at Caesarea Philippi. This third period of his earth life embraced the times when his apostles and his immediate followers knew him as the Son of Man and regarded him as the Messiah. The fourth and last period of his earth career began here at Caesarea Philippi and extended on to the crucifixion. This stage of his ministry was characterized by his acknowledgment of divinity and embraced the labors of his last year in the flesh. During the fourth period, while the majority of his followers still regarded him as the Messiah, he became known to the apostles as the Son of God. Peter's confession marked the beginning of the new period of the more complete realization of the truth of his supreme ministry as a bestowal Son on Earth and for an entire universe, and the recognition of that fact, at least hazily, by his chosen ambassadors.

Thus did Jesus exemplify in his life what he taught in his religion: the growth of the spiritual nature by the technique of living progress. He did not place emphasis, as did his later followers, upon the incessant struggle between the soul and the body. He rather taught that the spirit was easy victor over both and effective in the profitable reconciliation of much of this intellectual and instinctual warfare.

A new significance attaches to all of Jesus' teachings from this point on. Before Caesarea Philippi he presented the gospel of the kingdom as its master teacher. After Caesarea Philippi he appeared not merely as a teacher but as the divine representative of the eternal Father, who is the center and circumference of this spiritual kingdom, and it was required that he do all this as a human being, the Son of Man.

Jesus had sincerely endeavored to lead his followers into the spiritual kingdom as a teacher, then as a teacher-healer, but they would not have it so. He well knew that his earth mission could not possibly fulfill the Messianic expectations of the Jewish people; the olden prophets had portrayed a Messiah which he could never be. He sought to establish the Father's kingdom as the Son of Man, but his followers would not go forward in the adventure. Jesus, seeing this, then elected to meet his believers part way and in so doing prepared openly to assume the role of the bestowal Son of God.

Accordingly, the apostles heard much that was new as Jesus talked to them this day in the garden. And some of these pronouncements sounded strange even to them. Among other startling announcements they listened to such as the following:

"From this time on, if any would have fellowship with us, let them assume the obligations of sonship and follow me. And when I am no more with you, think not that the world will treat you better than it did your Master. If you love me, prepare to prove this affection by your willingness to make the supreme sacrifice."

"And mark well my words: I have not come to call the righteous, but sinners. The Son of Man came not to be ministered to, but to minister and to bestow his life as the gift for all. I declare to you that I have come to seek and to save those who are lost."

"None in this world now see the Father except the Son who came forth from the Father. But if the Son be lifted up, he will draw all men and women to himself, and whosoever believes this truth of the combined nature of the Son shall be endowed with life that is more than age-abiding."

"We may not yet proclaim openly that the Son of Man is the Son of God, but it has been revealed to you; wherefore do I speak boldly to you concerning these mysteries. Though I stand before you in this physical presence, I came forth from God the Father. Before Abraham was, I am. I did come forth from the Father into this world as you have known me, and I declare to you that I must presently leave this world and return to the work of my Father."

"And now can your faith comprehend the truth of these declarations in the face of my warning you that the Son of Man will not meet the expectations of your fathers as they conceived the Messiah? My kingdom is not of this world. Can you believe the truth about me in the face of the fact that, though the foxes have holes and the birds of heaven have nests, I have not where to lay my head?"

"Nevertheless, I tell you that the Father and I are one. He who has seen me has seen the Father. My Father is working with me in all these things, and He will never leave me alone in my mission, even as I will never forsake you when you presently go forth to proclaim this gospel throughout the world."

"And now have I brought you apart with me and by yourselves for a little while that you may comprehend the glory, and grasp the grandeur, of the life to which I have called you: the faith-adventure of the establishment of my Father's kingdom in the hearts of mankind, the building of my fellowship of living association with the souls of all who believe this gospel."

The apostles listened to these bold and startling statements in silence; they were stunned. And they dispersed in small groups to discuss and ponder the Master's words. They had confessed that he was the Son of God, but they could not grasp the full meaning of what they had been led to do.

✳ ✳ ✳

That evening Andrew took it upon himself to hold a personal and searching conference with each of his brethren, and he had profitable and heartening talks
with all of his associates except Judas Iscariot. Andrew had never enjoyed such intimate personal association with Judas as with the other apostles and therefore
had not thought it of serious account that Judas never had freely and confidentially
related himself to the head of the apostolic corps. But Andrew was now so worried
by Judas's attitude that, later on that night, after all the apostles were fast asleep, he
sought out Jesus and presented his cause for anxiety to the Master.

Said Jesus, "It is not amiss, Andrew, that you have come to me with this matter,
but there is nothing more that we can do; only go on placing the utmost confidence
in this apostle. And say nothing to his brethren concerning this talk with me."

And that was all Andrew could elicit from Jesus. Always had there been some
strangeness between this Judean and his Galilean brethren. Judas had been shocked
by the death of John the Baptist, severely hurt by the Master's rebukes on several
occasions, disappointed when Jesus refused to be made king, humiliated when he
fled from the Pharisees, chagrined when he refused to accept the challenge of the
Pharisees for a sign, bewildered by the refusal of his Master to resort to manifestations of power, and now, more recently, depressed and sometimes dejected by an
empty treasury. And Judas missed the stimulus of the multitudes.

Each of the other apostles was, in some and varying measure, likewise affected
by these selfsame trials and tribulations, but they loved Jesus. At least they must have
loved the Master more than did Judas, for they went through with him to the bitter
end.

Being from Judea, Judas took personal offense at Jesus' recent warning to the
apostles to "beware the leaven of the Pharisees"; he was disposed to regard this
statement as a veiled reference to himself. But the great mistake of Judas was: Time
and again, when Jesus would send his apostles off by themselves to pray, Judas, instead of engaging in sincere communion with the spiritual forces of the universe,
indulged in thoughts of human fear while he persisted in the entertainment of subtle
doubts about the mission of Jesus as well as giving in to his unfortunate tendency to
harbor feelings of revenge.

And now Jesus would take his apostles along with him to Mount Hermon, where
he had appointed to inaugurate his fourth phase of earth ministry as the Son of God.
Some of them were present at his baptism in the Jordan and had witnessed the beginning of his career as the Son of Man, and he desired that some of them should also
be present to hear his authority for the assumption of the new and public role of a
Son of God. Accordingly, on the morning of Friday, August 12, Jesus said to the twelve,
"Lay in provisions and prepare yourselves for a journey to yonder mountain, where
the spirit bids me go to be endowed for the finish of my work on earth. And I would
take my brethren along that they may also be strengthened for the trying times of going
with me through this experience."

# THE MOUNT OF TRANSFIGURATION

I T WAS near sundown on Friday afternoon, August 12, A.D. 29, when Jesus and his associates reached the foot of Mount Hermon, near the very place where the lad Tiglath once waited while the Master ascended the mountain alone to settle the spiritual destinies of Earth and technically to terminate the Lucifer rebellion. And here they sojourned for two days in spiritual preparation for the events so soon to follow.

In a general way, Jesus knew beforehand what was to transpire on the mountain, and he much desired that all his apostles might share this experience. It was to fit them for this revelation of himself that he tarried with them at the foot of the mountain. But they could not attain those spiritual levels which would justify their exposure to the full experience of the visitation of the celestial beings so soon to appear on earth. And since he could not take all of his associates with him, he decided to take only the three who were in the habit of accompanying him on such special vigils. Accordingly, only Peter, James, and John shared even a part of this unique experience with the Master.

Early on the morning of Monday, August 15, Jesus and the three apostles began the ascent of Mount Hermon, and this was six days after the memorable noontide confession of Peter by the roadside under the mulberry trees.

Jesus had been summoned to go up on the mountain, apart by himself, for the transaction of important matters having to do with the progress of his bestowal in the flesh as this experience was related to the universe of his own creation. It is significant that this extraordinary event was timed to occur while Jesus and the apostles were in the lands of the gentiles, and that it actually transpired on a mountain of the gentiles.

They reached their destination, about halfway up the mountain, shortly before noon, and while eating lunch, Jesus told the three apostles something of his experience in the hills to the east of Jordan shortly after his baptism and also some more of his experience on Mount Hermon in connection with his former visit to this lonely retreat.

When a boy, Jesus used to ascend the hill near his home and dream of the battles which had been fought by the armies of empires on the plain of Esdraelon; now he ascended Mount Hermon to receive the endowment which was to prepare him to descend upon the plains of the Jordan to enact the closing scenes of the drama of his bestowal on Earth. The Master could have relinquished the struggle this day on Mount Hermon and returned to his rule of the universe domains, but he not only chose to meet the requirements of his order of divine sonship embraced in the mandate of the Eternal Son on Paradise, but he also elected to meet the last and full measure of the present will of his Paradise Father. On this day in August three of his apostles saw him decline to be invested with full universe authority. They looked on in amazement as the celestial messengers departed, leaving him alone to finish out his earth life as the Son of Man and the Son of God.

The faith of the apostles was at a high point at the time of the feeding of the five thousand, and then it rapidly fell almost to zero. Now, as a result of the Master's admission of his divinity, the lagging faith of the twelve arose in the next few weeks to its highest pitch, only to undergo a progressive decline. The third revival of their faith did not occur until after the Master's resurrection.

It was about three o'clock on this beautiful afternoon that Jesus took leave of the three apostles, saying, "I go apart by myself for a season to commune with the Father and his messengers; I bid you tarry here and, while awaiting my return, pray that the Father's will may be done in all your experience in connection with the further bestowal mission of the Son of Man." And after saying this to them, Jesus withdrew for a long conference with Gabriel and the Father Melchizedek, not returning until about six o'clock.

When Jesus saw their anxiety over his prolonged absence, he said, "Why were you afraid? You well know I must be about my Father's business; wherefore do you doubt when I am not with you? I now declare that the Son of Man has chosen to go through his full life in your midst and as one of you. Be of good cheer; I will not leave you until my work is finished."

As they partook of their meager evening meal, Peter asked the Master, "How long do we remain on this mountain away from our brethren?"

And Jesus answered, "Until you shall see the glory of the Son of Man and know that whatsoever I have declared to you is true." And they talked over the affairs of the Lucifer rebellion while seated about the glowing embers of their fire until darkness drew on and the apostles' eyes grew heavy, for they had begun their journey very early that morning.

When the three had been fast asleep for about half an hour, they were suddenly awakened by a near-by crackling sound, and much to their amazement and consternation, on looking about them, they beheld Jesus in intimate converse with two brilliant beings clothed in the habiliments of the light of the celestial world. And Jesus' face and form shone with the luminosity of a heavenly light. These three conversed in a strange language, but from certain things said, Peter erroneously conjectured that the beings with Jesus were Moses and Elijah; in reality, they were Gabriel and the Father Melchizedek. The physical controllers had arranged for the apostles to witness this scene because of Jesus' request.

The three apostles were so badly frightened that they were slow in collecting their wits, but Peter, who was first to recover himself, said, as the dazzling vision faded from before them and they observed Jesus standing alone, "Jesus, Master, it is good to have been here. We rejoice to see this glory. We are loath to go back down to the inglorious world. If you are willing, let us abide here, and we will erect three tents, one for you, one for Moses, and one for Elijah." And Peter said this because of his confusion, and because nothing else came into his mind at just that moment.

While Peter was yet speaking, a silvery cloud drew near and overshadowed the four of them. The apostles now became greatly frightened, and as they fell down on their faces to worship, they heard a voice, the same that had spoken on the occasion of Jesus' baptism, say: "This is my beloved Son; give heed to him."

And when the cloud vanished, again was Jesus alone with the three, and he reached down and touched them, saying, "Arise and be not afraid; you shall see greater things than this." But the apostles were truly afraid; they were a silent and thoughtful trio as they made ready to descend the mountain shortly before midnight.

For about half the distance down the mountain not a word was spoken. Jesus then began the conversation by remarking, "Make certain that you tell no man, not even your brethren, what you have seen and heard on this mountain until the Son of Man has risen from the dead."

The three apostles were shocked and bewildered by the Master's words, "until the Son of Man has risen from the dead." They had so recently reaffirmed their faith in him as the Deliverer, the Son of God, and they had just beheld him transfigured in glory before their very eyes, and now he began to talk about "rising from the dead"!

Peter shuddered at the thought of the Master's dying - it was too disagreeable an idea to entertain - and fearing that James or John might ask some question relative to this statement, he thought best to start up a diverting conversation and, not knowing what else to talk about, gave expression to the first thought coming into his mind, which was: "Master, why is it that the scribes say that Elijah must first come before the Messiah shall appear?"

And Jesus, knowing that Peter sought to avoid reference to his death and resurrection, answered, "Elijah indeed comes first to prepare the way for the Son of Man, who must suffer many things and finally be rejected. But I tell you that Elijah has already come, and they received him not but did to him whatsoever they willed." And then did the three apostles perceive that he referred to John the Baptist as Elijah. Jesus knew that, if they insisted on regarding him as the Messiah, then must John be the Elijah of the prophecy.

Jesus enjoined silence about their observation of the foretaste of his postresurrection glory because he did not want to foster the notion that, being now received as the Messiah, he would in any degree fulfill their erroneous concepts of a wonder-working deliverer. Although Peter, James, and John pondered all this in their minds, they spoke not of it to any man until after the Master's resurrection.

As they continued to descend the mountain, Jesus said, "You would not receive me as the Son of Man; therefore have I consented to be received in accordance with your settled determination, but, mistake not, the will of my Father must prevail. If you thus choose to follow the inclination of your own wills, you must prepare to suffer many disappointments and experience many trials, but the training which I have given you should suffice to bring you triumphantly through even these sorrows of your own choosing."

Jesus did not take Peter, James, and John with him up to the mount of the transfiguration because they were in any sense better prepared than the other apostles to witness what happened, or because they were spiritually more fit to enjoy such a rare privilege. Not at all. He well knew that none of the twelve were spiritually qualified for this experience; therefore did he take with him only the three apostles who were assigned to accompany him at those times when he desired to be alone to enjoy solitary communion.

That which Peter, James, and John witnessed on the mount of transfiguration was a fleeting glimpse of a celestial pageant which transpired that eventful day on Mount Hermon. The transfiguration was the occasion of:

1. The acceptance of the fullness of the bestowal of the incarnated life of Michael on Earth by the Eternal Mother-Son of Paradise (Ed. Note: the second person of the Trinity). As far as concerned the requirements of the Eternal Son, Jesus had now received assurance of their fulfillment. And Gabriel brought Jesus that assurance.

2. The testimony of the satisfaction of the Infinite Spirit as to the fullness of the Earth bestowal in the likeness of mortal flesh. The universe representative of the Infinite Spirit, the immediate associate of Michael on Salvington and his ever-present coworker, on this occasion spoke through the Father Melchizedek.

Jesus welcomed this testimony regarding the success of his earth mission presented by the messengers of the Eternal Son and the Infinite Spirit, but he noted that his Father did not indicate that the Earth bestowal was finished; only did the unseen presence of the Father bear witness through Jesus' Personalized Adjuster, saying, "This is my beloved Son; give heed to him." And this was spoken in words to be heard also by the three apostles.

After this celestial visitation Jesus sought to know his Father's will and decided to pursue the mortal bestowal to its natural end. This was the significance of the transfiguration to Jesus. To the three apostles it was an event marking the entrance of the Master upon the final phase of his earth career as the Son of God and the Son of Man.

After the formal visitation of Gabriel and the Father Melchizedek, Jesus held informal converse with these, his Sons of ministry, and communed with them concerning the affairs of the universe.

It was shortly before breakfast time on this Tuesday morning when Jesus and his companions arrived at the apostolic camp. As they drew near, they discerned a considerable crowd gathered around the apostles and soon began to hear the loud words of argument and disputation of this group of about fifty persons, embracing the nine apostles and a gathering equally divided between Jerusalem scribes and believing disciples who had tracked Jesus and his associates in their journey from Magadan.

Although the crowd engaged in numerous arguments, the chief controversy was about a certain citizen of Tiberias who had arrived the preceding day in quest of Jesus. This man, James of Safed, had a son about fourteen years old, an only child, who was severely afflicted with epilepsy. In addition to this nervous malady this lad had become possessed by one of those wandering, mischievous, and rebellious midwayers who were then present on earth and uncontrolled, so that the youth was both epileptic and demon-possessed.

For almost two weeks this anxious father, a minor official of Herod Antipas, had wandered about through the western borders of Philip's domains, seeking Jesus that he might entreat him to cure this afflicted son. And he did not catch up with the apostolic party until about noon of this day when Jesus was up on the mountain with the three apostles.

The nine apostles were much surprised and considerably perturbed when this man, accompanied by almost forty other persons who were looking for Jesus, suddenly came upon them. At the time of the arrival of this group the nine apostles, at least the majority of them, had succumbed to their old temptation - that of discussing who should be greatest in the coming kingdom; they were busily arguing about the probable positions which would be assigned the individual apostles.

They simply could not free themselves entirely from the long-cherished idea of the material mission of the Messiah. And now that Jesus himself had accepted their confession that he was indeed the Deliverer - at least he had admitted the fact of his divinity - what was more natural than that, during this period of separation from the Master, they should fall to talking about those hopes and ambitions which were uppermost in their hearts. And they were engaged in these discussions when James of Safed and his fellow seekers after Jesus came upon them.

Andrew stepped up to greet this father and his son, saying, "Whom do you seek?"

Said James, "My good man, I search for your Master. I seek healing for my afflicted son. I would have Jesus cast out this devil that possesses my child." And then the father proceeded to relate to the apostles how his son was so afflicted that he had many times almost lost his life as a result of these malignant seizures.

As the apostles listened, Simon Zelotes and Judas Iscariot stepped into the presence of the father, saying, "We can heal him; you need not wait for the Master's return. We are ambassadors of the kingdom; no longer do we hold these things in secret. Jesus is the Deliverer, and the keys of the kingdom have been delivered to us."

By this time Andrew and Thomas were in consultation at one side. Nathaniel and the others looked on in amazement; they were all aghast at the sudden boldness, if not presumption, of Simon and Judas. Then said the father, "If it has been given you to do these works, I pray that you will speak those words which will deliver my child from this bondage."

Then Simon stepped forward and, placing his hand on the head of the child, looked directly into his eyes and commanded: "Come out of him, you unclean spirit; in the name of Jesus obey me." But the lad had only a more violent fit, while the scribes mocked the apostles in derision, and the disappointed believers suffered the taunts of these unfriendly critics.

Andrew was deeply chagrined at this ill-advised effort and its dismal failure. He called the apostles aside for conference and prayer. After this season of meditation, feeling keenly the sting of their defeat and sensing the humiliation resting upon all of them, Andrew sought, in a second attempt, to cast out the demon, but only failure crowned his efforts. Andrew frankly confessed defeat and requested the father to remain with them overnight or until Jesus' return, saying, "Perhaps this sort goes not out except by the Master's personal command."

And so, while Jesus was descending the mountain with the exuberant and ecstatic Peter, James, and John, their nine brethren likewise were sleepless in their confusion and downcast humiliation. They were a dejected and chastened group. But James of Safed would not give up. Although they could give him no idea as to when Jesus might return, he decided to stay on until the Master came back.

★ ★ ★

As Jesus drew near, the nine apostles were more than relieved to welcome him, and they were greatly encouraged to behold the good cheer and unusual enthusiasm which marked the countenances of Peter, James, and John. They all rushed forward to greet Jesus and their three brethren. As they exchanged greetings, the crowd came up, and Jesus asked, "What were you disputing about as we drew near?"

But before the disconcerted and humiliated apostles could reply to the Master's question, the anxious father of the afflicted lad stepped forward and, kneeling at Jesus' feet, said, "Master, I have a son, an only child, who is possessed by an evil spirit. Not only does he cry out in terror, foam at the mouth, and fall like a dead person at the time of seizure, but oftentimes this evil spirit which possesses him rends him in convulsions and sometimes has cast him into the water and even into the fire. With much grinding of teeth and as a result of many bruises, my child wastes away. His life is worse than death; his mother and I are of a sad heart and a broken spirit. About noon yesterday, seeking for you, I caught up with your disciples, and while we were waiting, your apostles sought to cast out this demon, but they could not do it. And now, Master, will you do this for us, will you heal my son?"

When Jesus had listened to this recital, he touched the kneeling father and bade him rise while he gave the near-by apostles a searching survey. Then said Jesus to all those who stood before him, "O faithless and perverse generation, how long shall I bear with you? How long shall I be with you? How long ere you learn that the works of faith come not forth at the bidding of doubting unbelief?" And then, pointing to the bewildered father, Jesus said, "Bring hither your son."

And when James had brought the lad before Jesus, he asked, "How long has the boy been afflicted in this way?"

The father answered, "Since he was a very young child." And as they talked, the youth was seized with a violent attack and fell in their midst, gnashing his teeth and foaming at the mouth. After a succession of violent convulsions he lay there before them as one dead.

Now did the father again kneel at Jesus' feet while he implored the Master, saying, "If you can cure him, I beseech you to have compassion on us and deliver us from this affliction."

And when Jesus heard these words, he looked down into the father's anxious face, saying, "Question not my Father's power of love, only the sincerity and reach of your faith. All things are possible to him who really believes."

And then James of Safed spoke those long-to-be-remembered words of commingled faith and doubt, "Lord, I believe. I pray you help my unbelief."

When Jesus heard these words, he stepped forward and, taking the lad by the hand, said, "I will do this in accordance with my Father's will and in honor of living faith. My son, arise! Come out of him, disobedient spirit, and go not back into him."

And placing the hand of the lad in the hand of the father, Jesus said, "Go your way. The Father has granted the desire of your soul."

And all who were present, even the enemies of Jesus, were astonished at what they saw.

It was indeed a disillusionment for the three apostles who had so recently enjoyed the spiritual ecstasy of the scenes and experiences of the transfiguration, so soon to return to this scene of the defeat and discomfiture of their fellow apostles. But it was ever so with these twelve ambassadors of the kingdom. They never failed to alternate between exaltation and humiliation in their life experiences.

This was a true healing of a double affliction, a physical ailment and a spirit malady. And the lad was permanently cured from that hour.

When James had departed with his restored son, Jesus said, "We go now to Caesarea Philippi; make ready at once." And they were a quiet group as they journeyed southward while the crowd followed on behind.

They remained overnight with Celsus, and that evening in the garden, after they had eaten and rested, the twelve gathered about Jesus, and Thomas said, "Master, while we who tarried behind still remain ignorant of what transpired up on the mountain, and which so greatly cheered our brethren who were with you, we crave to have you talk with us concerning our defeat and instruct us in these matters, seeing that those things which happened on the mountain cannot be disclosed at this time."

And Jesus answered Thomas, saying, "Everything which your brethren heard on the mountain shall be revealed to you in due season. But I will now show you the cause of your defeat in that which you so unwisely attempted. While your Master and his companions, your brethren, ascended yonder mountain yesterday to seek for a larger knowledge of the Father's will and to ask for a richer endowment of wisdom effectively to do that divine will, you who remained on watch here with instructions to strive to acquire the mind of spiritual insight and to pray with us for a fuller revelation of the Father's will, failed to exercise the faith at your command but, instead, yielded to the temptation and fell into your old evil tendencies to seek for yourselves preferred places in the kingdom of heaven - the material and temporal kingdom which you persist in contemplating. And you cling to these erroneous concepts in spite of the reiterated declaration that my kingdom is not of this world.

"No sooner does your faith grasp the identity of the Son of Man than your selfish desire for worldly preferment creeps back upon you, and you fall to discussing among yourselves as to who should be greatest in the kingdom of heaven, a kingdom which, as you persist in conceiving it, does not exist, nor ever shall. Have not

I told you that he who would be greatest in the kingdom of my Father's spiritual brotherhood must become little in his own eyes and thus become the server of his brethren? Spiritual greatness consists in an understanding love that is Godlike and not in an enjoyment of the exercise of material power for the exaltation of self. In what you attempted, in which you so completely failed, your purpose was not pure. Your motive was not divine. Your ideal was not spiritual. Your ambition was not altruistic. Your procedure was not based on love, and your goal of attainment was not the will of the Father in heaven.

"How long will it take you to learn that you cannot time-shorten the course of established natural phenomena except when such things are in accordance with the Father's will? Nor can you do spiritual work in the absence of spiritual power. And you can do neither of these, even when their potential is present, without the existence of that third and essential human factor, the personal experience of the possession of living faith. Must you always have material manifestations as an attraction for the spiritual realities of the kingdom? Can you not grasp the spirit significance of my mission without the visible exhibition of unusual works? When can you be depended upon to adhere to the higher and spiritual realities of the kingdom regardless of the outward appearance of all material manifestations?"

When Jesus had thus spoken to the twelve, he added, "And now go to your rest, for on the morrow we return to Magadan and there take counsel concerning our mission to the cities and villages of the Decapolis. And in the conclusion of this day's experience, let me declare to each of you that which I spoke to your brethren on the mountain, and let these words find a deep lodgment in your hearts: The Son of Man now enters upon the last phase of the bestowal. We are about to begin those labors which shall presently lead to the great and final testing of your faith and devotion when I shall be delivered into the hands of the men who seek my destruction. And remember what I am saying to you: The Son of Man will be put to death, but he shall rise again."

They retired for the night, sorrowful. They were bewildered; they could not comprehend these words. And while they were afraid to ask aught concerning what he had said, they did recall all of it subsequent to his resurrection.

Early this Wednesday morning Jesus and the twelve departed from Caesarea Philippi for Magadan Park near Bethsaida-Julias. The apostles had slept very little that night, so they were up early and ready to go. Even the stolid Alpheus twins had been shocked by this talk about the death of Jesus. As they journeyed south, just beyond the Waters of Merom they came to the Damascus road, and desiring to avoid the scribes and others whom Jesus knew would presently be coming along after them, he directed that they go on to Capernaum by the Damascus road which passes through Galilee. And he did this because he knew that those who followed after him would go on down over the east Jordan road since they reckoned that Jesus and the apostles would fear to pass through the territory of Herod Antipas. Jesus sought to elude his critics and the crowd that followed him that he might be alone with his apostles this day.

They traveled on through Galilee until well past the time for their lunch, when they stopped in the shade to refresh themselves. And after they had partaken of food, Andrew, speaking to Jesus, said, "Master, my brethren do not comprehend your deep sayings. We have come fully to believe that you are the Son of God, and now we hear these strange words about leaving us, about dying. We do not understand your teaching. Are you speaking to us in parables? We pray you to speak to us directly and in undisguised form."

In answer to Andrew, Jesus said, "My brethren, it is because you have confessed that I am the Son of God that I am constrained to begin to unfold to you the truth about the end of the bestowal of the Son of Man on earth. You insist on clinging to the belief that I am the Messiah, and you will not abandon the idea that the Messiah must sit upon a throne in Jerusalem; wherefore do I persist in telling you that the Son of Man must presently go to Jerusalem, suffer many things, be rejected by the scribes, the elders, and the chief priests, and after all this be killed and raised from the dead. And I speak not a parable to you; I speak the truth to you that you may be prepared for these events when they suddenly come upon us."

And while he was yet speaking, Simon Peter, rushing impetuously toward him, laid his hand upon the Master's shoulder and said, "Master, be it far from us to contend with you, but I declare that these things shall never happen to you."

Peter spoke thus because he loved Jesus; but the Master's human nature recognized in these words of well-meant affection the subtle suggestion of temptation that he change his policy of pursuing to the end his earth bestowal in accordance with the will of his Paradise Father. And it was because he detected the danger of permitting the suggestions of even his affectionate and loyal friends to dissuade him, that he turned upon Peter and the other apostles, saying, "Get you behind me. You savor of the spirit of the adversary, the tempter. When you talk in this manner, you are not on my side but rather on the side of our enemy. In this way do you make your love for me a stumbling block to my doing the Father's will. Mind not the ways of men but rather the will of God."

After they had recovered from the first shock of Jesus' stinging rebuke, and before they resumed their journey, the Master spoke further. "If any man would come after me, let him disregard himself, take up his responsibilities daily, and follow me. For whosoever would save his life selfishly, shall lose it, but whosoever loses his life for my sake and the gospel's, shall save it. What does it profit a man to gain the whole world and lose his own soul? What would a man give in exchange for eternal life? Be not ashamed of me and my words in this sinful and hypocritical generation, even as I will not be ashamed to acknowledge you when in glory I appear before my Father in the presence of all the celestial hosts. Nevertheless, many of you now standing before me shall not taste death till you see this kingdom of God come with power."

And thus did Jesus make plain to the twelve the painful and conflicting path which they must tread if they would follow him. What a shock these words were to these Galilean fishermen who persisted in dreaming of an earthly kingdom with positions of honor for themselves! But their loyal hearts were stirred by this courageous appeal, and not one of them was minded to forsake him. Jesus was not sending them alone into the conflict; he was leading them. He asked only that they bravely follow.

Slowly the twelve were grasping the idea that Jesus was telling them something about the possibility of his dying. They only vaguely comprehended what he said about his death, while his statement about rising from the dead utterly failed to register in their minds. As the days passed, Peter, James, and John, recalling their experience upon the mount of the transfiguration, arrived at a fuller understanding of certain of these matters.

In all the association of the twelve with their Master, only a few times did they see that flashing eye and hear such swift words of rebuke as were administered to Peter and the rest of them on this occasion. Jesus had always been patient with their human shortcomings, but not so when faced by an impending threat against the program of implicitly carrying out his Father's will regarding the remainder of his earth career. The apostles were literally stunned; they were amazed and horrified. They could not find words to express their sorrow. Slowly they began to realize what the Master must endure, and that they must go through these experiences with him, but they did not awaken to the reality of these coming events until long after these early hints of the impending tragedy of his latter days.

In silence Jesus and the twelve started for their camp at Magadan Park, going by way of Capernaum. As the afternoon wore on, though they did not converse with Jesus, they talked much among themselves while Andrew talked with the Master.

Entering Capernaum at twilight, they went by unfrequented thoroughfares directly to the home of Simon Peter for their evening meal. While David Zebedee made ready to take them across the lake, they lingered at Simon's house, and Jesus, looking up at Peter and the other apostles, asked, "As you walked along together this afternoon, what was it that you talked about so earnestly among yourselves?"

The apostles held their peace because many of them had continued the discussion begun at Mount Hermon as to what positions they were to have in the coming kingdom; who should be the greatest, and so on.

Jesus, knowing what it was that occupied their thoughts that day, beckoned to one of Peter's little ones and, setting the child down among them, said, "Verily, verily, I say to you, except you turn about and become more like this child, you will make little progress in the kingdom of heaven. Whosoever shall humble himself and become as this little one, the same shall become greatest in the kingdom of heaven. And whoso receives such a little one receives me. And they who receive me receive also Him who sent me. If you would be first in the kingdom, seek to minister these good truths to your brethren in the flesh. But whosoever causes one of these little ones to stumble, it would be better for him if a millstone were hanged about his neck and he were cast into the sea. If the things you do with your hands, or the things you see with your eyes give offense in the progress of the kingdom, sacrifice these cherished idols, for it is better to enter the kingdom minus many of the beloved things of life rather than to cling to these idols and find yourself shut out of the kingdom. But most of all, see that you despise not one of these little ones, for their angels do always behold the faces of the heavenly hosts."
When Jesus had finished speaking, they entered the boat and sailed across to Magadan.

## THE DECAPOLIS TOUR

WHEN JESUS and the twelve arrived at Magadan Park, they found awaiting them a group of almost one hundred evangelists and disciples, including the women's corps, and they were ready immediately to begin the teaching and preaching tour of the cities of the Decapolis.

On this Thursday morning, August 18, the Master called his followers together and directed that each of the apostles should associate himself with one of the twelve evangelists, and that with others of the evangelists they should go out in twelve groups to labor in the cities and villages of the Decapolis. The women's corps and others of the disciples he directed to remain with him. Jesus allotted four weeks to this tour, instructing his followers to return to Magadan not later than Friday, September 16. He promised to visit them often during this time. In the course of this month these twelve groups labored in Gerasa, Gamala, Hippos, Zaphon, Gadara, Abila, Edrei, Philadelphia, Heshbon, Dium, Scythopolis, and many other cities. Throughout this tour no miracles of healing or other extraordinary events occurred.

One evening at Hippos, in answer to a disciple's question, Jesus taught the lesson on forgiveness.

Said the Master, "If a kindhearted man has a hundred sheep and one of them goes astray, does he not immediately leave the ninety and nine and go out in search of the one that has gone astray? And if he is a good shepherd, will he not keep up his quest for the lost sheep until he finds it? And then, when the shepherd has found his lost sheep, he lays it over his shoulder and, going home rejoicing, calls to his friends and neighbors, 'Rejoice with me, for I have found my sheep that was lost.' I declare that there is more joy in heaven over one sinner who repents than over ninety and nine righteous persons who need no repentance. Even so, it is not the will of my Father in heaven that one of these little ones should go astray, much less that they should perish. In your religion God may receive repentant sinners; in the gospel of the kingdom the Father goes forth to find them even before they have seriously thought of repentance.

"The Father in heaven loves his children, and therefore should you learn to love one another; the Father in heaven forgives you your sins; therefore should you learn to forgive one another. If your brother sins against you, go to him and with tact and patience show him his fault. And do all this between you and him alone. If he will listen to you, then have you won your brother. But if your brother will not hear you, if he persists in the error of his way, go again to him, taking with you one or two mutual friends that you may thus have two or even three witnesses to confirm your testimony and establish the fact that you have dealt justly and mercifully with your offending brother. Now if he refuses to hear your brethren, you may tell the whole story to the congregation, and then, if he refuses to hear the brotherhood, let them take such action as they deem wise; let such an unruly member become an outcast from the kingdom. While you cannot pretend to sit in judgment on the souls of your fellows, and while you may not forgive sins or otherwise presume to usurp the prerogatives of the supervisors of the heavenly hosts, at the same time, it has been committed to your hands that you should maintain temporal order in the kingdom on earth.

"While you may not meddle with the divine decrees concerning eternal life, you shall determine the issues of conduct as they concern the temporal welfare of the brotherhood on earth. And so, in all these matters connected with the discipline of the brotherhood, whatsoever you shall decree on earth shall be recognized in heaven. Although you cannot determine the eternal fate of the individual, you may legislate regarding the conduct of the group, for, where two or three of you agree concerning any of these things and ask of me, it shall be done for you if your petition is not inconsistent with the will of my Father in heaven. And all this is ever true, for, where two or three believers are gathered together, there am I in the midst of them."

Simon Peter was the apostle in charge of the workers at Hippos, and when he heard Jesus thus speak, he asked, "Lord, how often shall my brother sin against me, and I forgive him? Until seven times?"

And Jesus answered Peter, "Not only seven times but even to seventy times and seven. Therefore may the kingdom of heaven be likened to a certain king who ordered a financial reckoning with his stewards. And when they had begun to conduct this examination of accounts, one of his chief retainers was brought before him confessing that he owed his king ten thousand talents. Now this officer of the king's court pleaded that hard times had come upon him, and that he did not have wherewith to pay this obligation. And so the king commanded that his property be confiscated, and that his children be sold to pay his debt. When this chief steward heard this stern decree, he fell down on his face before the king and implored him to have mercy and grant him more time, saying, 'Lord, have a little more patience with me, and I will pay you all.' And when the king looked upon this negligent servant and his family, he was moved with compassion. He ordered that he should be released, and that the loan should be wholly forgiven.

"And this chief steward, having thus received mercy and forgiveness at the hands of the king, went about his business, and finding one of his subordinate stewards who owed him a mere hundred denarii, he laid hold upon him and, taking him by the throat, said, 'Pay me all you owe.' And then did this fellow steward fall down before the chief steward and, beseeching him, said, 'Only have patience with me, and I will presently be able to pay you.' But the chief steward would not show mercy to his fellow steward but rather had him cast in prison until he should pay his debt. When his fellow servants saw what had happened, they were so distressed that they went and told their lord and master, the king. When the king heard of the doings of his chief steward, he called this ungrateful and unforgiving man before him and said, 'You are a wicked and unworthy steward. When you sought for compassion, I freely forgave you your entire debt. Why did you not also show mercy to your fellow steward, even as I showed mercy to you?' And the king was so very angry that he delivered his ungrateful chief steward to the jailers that they might hold him until he had paid all that was due. And even so shall my heavenly Father show the more abundant mercy to those who freely show mercy to their fellows. How can you come to God asking consideration for your shortcomings when you are wont to chastise your brethren for being guilty of these same human frailties? I say to all of you: Freely you have received the good things of the kingdom; therefore freely give to your fellows on earth."

Thus did Jesus teach the dangers and illustrate the unfairness of sitting in personal judgment upon one's fellows. Discipline must be maintained, justice must be administered, but in all these matters the wisdom of the brotherhood should prevail. Jesus invested legislative and judicial authority in the *group*, not in the *individual*. Even this investment of authority in the group must not be exercised as personal authority. There is always danger that the verdict of an individual may be warped by prejudice or distorted by passion. Group judgment is more likely to remove the dangers and eliminate the unfairness of personal bias. Jesus sought always to minimize the elements of unfairness, retaliation, and vengeance.

[The use of the term seventy-seven as an illustration of mercy and forbearance was derived from the Scriptures referring to Lamech's exultation because of the metal weapons of his son Tubal-Cain, who, comparing these superior instruments with those of his enemies, exclaimed: "If Cain, with no weapon in his hand, was avenged seven times, I shall now be avenged seventy-seven."]

★ ★ ★

Jesus went over to Gamala to visit John and those who worked with him at that place. That evening, after the session of questions and answers, John said to Jesus, "Master, yesterday I went over to Ashtaroth to see a man who was teaching in your name and even claiming to be able to cast out devils. Now this fellow had never been with us, neither does he follow after us; therefore I forbade him to do such things."

Then said Jesus, "Forbid him not. Do you not perceive that this gospel of the kingdom shall presently be proclaimed in all the world? How can you expect that all who will believe the gospel shall be subject to your direction? Rejoice that already our teaching has begun to manifest itself beyond the bounds of our personal influence. Do you not see, John, that those who profess to do great works in my name must eventually support our cause? They certainly will not be quick to speak evil of me. My son, in matters of this sort it would be better for you to reckon that he who is not against us is for us. In the generations to come many who are not wholly worthy will do many strange things in my name, but I will not forbid them. I tell you that, even when a cup of cold water is given to a thirsty soul, the Father's messengers shall ever make record of such a service of love."

This instruction greatly perplexed John. Had he not heard the Master say, "He who is not with me is against me"? And he did not perceive that in this case Jesus was referring to man's personal relation to the spiritual teachings of the kingdom, while in the other case reference was made to the outward and far-flung social relations of believers regarding the questions of administrative control and the jurisdiction of one group of believers over the work of other groups which would eventually compose the forthcoming world-wide brotherhood.

But John oftentimes recounted this experience in connection with his subsequent labors in behalf of the kingdom. Nevertheless, many times did the apostles take offense at those who made bold to teach in the Master's name. To them it always seemed inappropriate that those who had never sat at Jesus' feet should dare to teach in his name.

This man whom John forbade to teach and work in Jesus' name did not heed the apostle's injunction. He went right on with his efforts and raised up a considerable company of believers at Kanata before going on into Mesopotamia. This man, Aden, had been led to believe in Jesus through the testimony of the demented man whom Jesus had healed near Kheresa, and who so confidently believed that the supposed evil spirits which the Master cast out of him entered the herd of swine and rushed them headlong over the cliff to their destruction.

At Edrei, where Thomas and his associates labored, Jesus spent a day and a night and, in the course of the evening's discussion, gave expression to the principles which should guide those who preach truth, and which should activate all who teach the gospel of the kingdom. Summarized and restated in modern phraseology, Jesus taught:

Always respect the personality of man. Never should a righteous cause be promoted by force; spiritual victories can be won only by spiritual power. This injunction against the employment of material influences refers to psychic force as well as to physical force. Overpowering arguments and mental superiority are not to be employed to coerce men and women into the kingdom. Man's mind is not to be crushed by the mere weight of logic or overawed by shrewd eloquence. While emotion as a factor in human decisions cannot be wholly eliminated, it should not be directly appealed to in the teachings of those who would advance the cause of the kingdom. Make your appeals directly to the divine spirit that dwells within the minds of men. Do not appeal to fear, pity, or mere sentiment. In appealing to men, be fair; exercise self-control and exhibit due restraint; show proper respect for the personalities of your pupils. Remember that I have said: "Behold, I stand at the door and knock, and if any man will open, I will come in."

In bringing men and women into the kingdom, do not lessen or destroy their self-respect. While overmuch self-respect may destroy proper humility and end in pride, conceit, and arrogance, the loss of self-respect often ends in paralysis of the will. It is the purpose of this gospel to restore self-respect to those who have lost it and to restrain it in those who have it. Make not the mistake of only condemning the wrongs in the lives of your pupils; remember also to accord generous recognition for the most praiseworthy things in their lives. Forget not that I will stop at nothing to restore self-respect to those who have lost it, and who really desire to regain it.

Take care that you do not wound the self-respect of timid and fearful souls. Do not indulge in sarcasm at the expense of my simple-minded brethren. Be not cynical with my fear-ridden children. Idleness is destructive of self-respect; therefore, admonish your brethren ever to keep busy at their chosen tasks, and put forth every effort to secure work for those who find themselves without employment.

Never be guilty of such unworthy tactics as endeavoring to frighten men and women into the kingdom. A loving father does not frighten his children into yielding obedience to his just requirements.

Sometime the children of the kingdom will realize that strong feelings of emotion are not equivalent to the leadings of the divine spirit. To be strongly and strangely impressed to do something or to go to a certain place, does not necessarily mean that such impulses are the leadings of the indwelling spirit.

Forewarn all believers regarding the fringe of conflict which must be traversed by all who pass from the life as it is lived in the flesh to the higher life as it is lived in the spirit. To those who live quite wholly within either realm, there is little conflict or confusion, but all are doomed to experience more or less uncertainty during the times of transition between the two levels of living. In entering the kingdom, you cannot escape its responsibilities or avoid its obligations, but remember: The gospel yoke is easy and the burden of truth is light.

The world is filled with hungry souls who famish in the very presence of the bread of life; men die searching for the very God who lives within them. Men seek for the treasures of the kingdom with yearning hearts and weary feet when they are all within the immediate grasp of living faith. Faith is to religion what sails are to a ship; it is an addition of power, not an added burden of life. There is but one struggle for those who enter the kingdom, and that is to fight the good fight of faith. The believer has only one battle, and that is against doubt - unbelief.

In preaching the gospel of the kingdom, you are simply teaching friendship with God. And this fellowship will appeal alike to men and women in that both will find that which most truly satisfies their characteristic longings and ideals. Tell my children that I am not only tender of their feelings and patient with their frailties, but that I am also ruthless with sin and intolerant of iniquity. I am indeed meek and humble in the presence of my Father, but I am equally and relentlessly inexorable where there is deliberate evil-doing and sinful rebellion against the will of my Father in heaven.

You shall not portray your teacher as a man of sorrows. Future generations shall know also the radiance of our joy, the buoyancy of our good will, and the inspiration of our good humor. We proclaim a message of good news which is infectious in its transforming power. Our religion is throbbing with new life and new meanings. Those who accept this teaching are filled with joy and in their hearts are constrained to rejoice evermore. Increasing happiness is always the experience of all who are certain about God.

Teach all believers to avoid leaning upon the insecure props of false sympathy. You cannot develop strong characters out of the indulgence of self-pity; honestly endeavor to avoid the deceptive influence of mere fellowship in misery. Extend sympathy to the brave and courageous while you withhold overmuch pity from those cowardly souls who only halfheartedly stand up before the trials of living. Offer not consolation to those who lie down before their troubles without a struggle. Sympathize not with your fellows merely that they may sympathize with you in return.

When my children once become self-conscious of the assurance of the divine presence, such a faith will expand the mind, ennoble the soul, reinforce the personality, augment the happiness, deepen the spirit perception, and enhance the power to love and be loved.

Teach all believers that those who enter the kingdom are not thereby rendered immune to the accidents of time or to the ordinary catastrophes of nature. Believing the gospel will not prevent getting into trouble, but it will insure that you shall be *unafraid* when trouble does overtake you. If you dare to believe in me and wholeheartedly proceed to follow after me, you shall most certainly by so doing enter upon the sure pathway to trouble. I do not promise to deliver you from the waters of adversity, but I do promise to go with you through all of them.

And much more did Jesus teach this group of believers before they made ready for the night's sleep. And they who heard these sayings treasured them in their hearts and did often recite them for the edification of the apostles and disciples who were not present when they were spoken.

And then went Jesus over to Abila, where Nathaniel and his associates labored. Nathaniel was much bothered by some of Jesus' pronouncements that seemed to detract from the authority of the recognized Hebrew scriptures. Accordingly, on this night, after the usual period of questions and answers, Nathaniel took Jesus away from the others and asked, "Master, could you trust me to know the truth about the Scriptures? I observe that you teach us only a portion of the sacred writings - the best as I view it - and I infer that you reject the teachings of the rabbis to the effect that the words of the law are the very words of God, having been with God in heaven even before the times of Abraham and Moses. What is the truth about the Scriptures?"

When Jesus heard the question of his bewildered apostle, he answered, "Nathaniel, you have rightly judged; I do not regard the Scriptures as do the rabbis. I will talk with you about this matter on condition that you do not relate these things to your brethren, who are not all prepared to receive this teaching. The words of the law of Moses and the teachings of the Scriptures were not in existence before Abraham. Only in recent times have the Scriptures been gathered together as we now have them. While they contain the best of the higher thoughts and longings of the Jewish people, they also contain much that is far from being representative of the character and teachings of the Father in heaven; wherefore must I choose from among the better teachings those truths which are to be gleaned for the gospel of the kingdom.

"These writings are the work of men, some of them holy men, others not so holy. The teachings of these books represent the views and extent of enlightenment of the times in which they had their origin. As a revelation of truth, the last are more dependable than the first. The Scriptures are faulty and altogether human in origin, but mistake not, they do constitute the best collection of religious wisdom and spiritual truth to be found in all the world at this time.

"Many of these books were not written by the persons whose names they bear, but that in no way detracts from the value of the truths which they contain. If the story of Jonah should not be a fact, even if Jonah had never lived, still would the profound truth of this narrative, the love of God for Nineveh and the so-called heathen, be nonetheless precious in the eyes of all those who love their fellow men. The Scriptures are sacred because they present the thoughts and acts of men who were searching for God, and who in these writings left on record their highest concepts of righteousness, truth, and holiness. The Scriptures contain much that is true, very much, but in the light of your present teaching, you know that these writings also contain much that is misrepresentative of the Father in heaven, the loving God I have come to reveal to all the worlds.

"Nathaniel, never permit yourself for one moment to believe the Scripture records which tell you that the God of love directed your forefathers to go forth in battle to slay all their enemies - men, women, and children. Such records are the words of men, not very holy men, and they are not the word of God. The Scriptures always have, and always will, reflect the intellectual, moral, and spiritual status of those who create them. Have you not noted that the concepts of Yahweh grow in beauty and glory as the prophets make their records from Samuel to Isaiah? And you should remember that the Scriptures are intended for religious instruction and spiritual guidance. They are not the works of either historians or philosophers.

"The thing most deplorable is not merely this erroneous idea of the absolute perfection of the Scripture record and the infallibility of its teachings, but rather the confusing misinterpretation of these sacred writings by the tradition-enslaved scribes and Pharisees at Jerusalem. And now will they employ both the doctrine of the inspiration of the Scriptures and their misinterpretations thereof in their determined effort to withstand these newer teachings of the gospel of the kingdom. Nathaniel, never forget, the Father does not limit the revelation of truth to any one generation or to any one people. Many earnest seekers after the truth have been, and will continue to be, confused and disheartened by these doctrines of the perfection of the Scriptures.

"The authority of truth is the very spirit that indwells its living manifestations, and not the dead words of the less illuminated and supposedly inspired men of another generation. And even if these holy men of old lived inspired and spirit-filled lives, that does not mean that their *words* were similarly spiritually inspired. Today we make no record of the teachings of this gospel of the kingdom lest, when I have gone, you speedily become divided up into sundry groups of truth contenders as a result of the diversity of your interpretation of my teachings. For this generation it is best that we *live* these truths while we shun the making of records.

"Mark you well my words, Nathaniel, nothing which human nature has touched can be regarded as infallible. Through the mind of man divine truth may indeed shine forth, but always of relative purity and partial divinity. The creature may crave infallibility, but only the Creators possess it.

"But the greatest error of the teaching about the Scriptures is the doctrine of their being sealed books of mystery and wisdom which only the wise minds of the nation dare to interpret. The revelations of divine truth are not sealed except by human ignorance, bigotry, and narrow-minded intolerance. The light of the Scriptures is only dimmed by prejudice and darkened by superstition. A false fear of sacredness has prevented religion from being safeguarded by common sense. The fear of the authority of the sacred writings of the past effectively prevents the honest souls of today from accepting the new light of the gospel, the light which these very God-knowing men of another generation so intensely longed to see.

"But the saddest feature of all is the fact that some of the teachers of the sanctity of this traditionalism know this very truth. They more or less fully understand these limitations of Scripture, but they are moral cowards, intellectually dishonest. They know the truth regarding the sacred writings, but they prefer to withhold such disturbing facts from the people. And thus do they pervert and distort the Scriptures, making them the guide to slavish details of the daily life and an authority in things nonspiritual instead of appealing to the sacred writings as the repository of the moral wisdom, religious inspiration, and the spiritual teaching of the God-knowing men of other generations."

Nathaniel was enlightened, and shocked, by the Master's pronouncement. He long pondered this talk in the depths of his soul, but he told no man concerning this conference until after Jesus' ascension; and even then he feared to impart the full story of the Master's instruction.

At Philadelphia, where James was working, Jesus taught the disciples about the positive nature of the gospel of the kingdom. When, in the course of his remarks, he intimated that some parts of the Scripture were more truth-containing than others and admonished his hearers to feed their souls upon the best of the spiritual food, James interrupted the Master, asking, "Would you be good enough, Master, to suggest to us how we may choose the better passages from the Scriptures for our personal edification?"

And Jesus replied, "Yes, James, when you read the Scriptures look for those eternally true and divinely beautiful teachings, such as:

"Create in me a clean heart, O Lord.

"The Lord is my shepherd; I shall not want.

"You should love your neighbor as yourself.

"For I, the Lord your God, will hold your right hand, saying, fear not; I will help you.

"Neither shall the nations learn war any more."

And this is illustrative of the way Jesus, day by day, appropriated the cream of the Hebrew scriptures for the instruction of his followers and for inclusion in the teachings of the new gospel of the kingdom. Other religions had suggested the thought of the nearness of God to man, but Jesus made the care of God for man like the solicitude of a loving father for the welfare of his dependent children and then made this teaching the cornerstone of his religion. And thus did the doctrine of the fatherhood of God make imperative the practice of the brotherhood of man. The worship of God and the service of man became the sum and substance of his religion. Jesus took the best of the Jewish religion and translated it to a worthy setting in the new teachings of the gospel of the kingdom.

Jesus put the spirit of positive action into the passive doctrines of the Jewish religion. In the place of negative compliance with ceremonial requirements, Jesus enjoined the positive doing of that which his new religion required of those who accepted it. Jesus' religion consisted not merely in *believing,* but in actually *doing,* those things which the gospel required. He did not teach that the essence of his religion consisted in social service, but rather that social service was one of the certain effects of the possession of the spirit of true religion.

Jesus did not hesitate to appropriate the better half of a Scripture while he repudiated the lesser portion. His great exhortation, "Love your neighbor as yourself," he took from the Scripture which reads: "You shall not take vengeance against the children of your people, but you shall love your neighbor as yourself." Jesus appropriated the positive portion of this Scripture while rejecting the negative part. He even opposed negative or purely passive nonresistance. Said he: "When an enemy smites you on one cheek, do not stand there dumb and passive but in positive attitude turn the other; that is, do the best thing possible actively to lead your brother in error away from the evil paths into the better ways of righteous living." Jesus required his followers to react positively and aggressively to every life situation. The turning of the other cheek, or whatever act that may typify, demands initiative, necessitates vigorous, active, and courageous expression of the believer's personality.

Jesus did not advocate the practice of negative submission to the indignities of those who might purposely seek to impose upon the practitioners of nonresistance to evil, but rather that his followers should be wise and alert in the quick and positive reaction of good to evil to the end that they might effectively overcome evil with good. Forget not, the truly good is invariably more powerful than the most malignant evil. The Master taught a positive standard of righteousness: "Whosoever wishes to be my disciple, let him disregard himself and take up the full measure of his responsibilities daily to follow me." And he so lived himself in that "he went about doing good." And this aspect of the gospel was well illustrated by many parables which he later spoke to his followers. He never exhorted his followers patiently to bear their obligations but rather with energy and enthusiasm to live up to the full measure of their human responsibilities and divine privileges in the kingdom of God.

When Jesus instructed his apostles that they should, when one unjustly took away the coat, offer the other garment, he referred not so much to a literal second coat as to the idea of doing something *positive* to save the wrongdoer in the place of the olden advice to retaliate - "an eye for an eye" and so on. Jesus abhorred the idea either of retaliation or of becoming just a passive sufferer or victim of injustice. On this occasion he taught them the three ways of contending with, and resisting, evil:

1. To return evil for evil — the positive but unrighteous method.
2. To suffer evil without complaint and without resistance - the purely negative method.
3. To return good for evil, to assert the will so as to become master of the situation, to overcome evil with good - the positive and righteous method.

One of the apostles once asked, "Master, what should I do if a stranger forced me to carry his pack for a mile?"

Jesus answered, "Do not sit down and sigh for relief while you berate the stranger under your breath. Righteousness comes not from such passive attitudes. If you can think of nothing more effectively positive to do, you can at least carry the pack a second mile. That will of a certainty challenge the unrighteous and ungodly stranger."

The Jews had heard of a God who would forgive repentant sinners and try to forget their misdeeds, but not until Jesus came, did men hear about a God who went in search of lost sheep, who took the initiative in looking for sinners, and who rejoiced when he found them willing to return to the Father's house. This positive note in religion Jesus extended even to his prayers. And he converted the negative golden rule into a positive admonition of human fairness.

In all his teaching Jesus unfailingly avoided distracting details. He shunned flowery language and avoided the mere poetic imagery of a play upon words. He habitually put large meanings into small expressions. For purposes of illustration Jesus reversed the current meanings of many terms, such as salt, leaven, fishing, and little children. He most effectively employed the antithesis, comparing the minute to the infinite and so on. His pictures were striking, such as, "The blind leading the blind." But the greatest strength to be found in his illustrative teaching was its naturalness. Jesus brought the philosophy of religion from heaven down to earth. He portrayed the elemental needs of the soul with a new insight and a new bestowal of affection.

The mission of four weeks in the Decapolis was moderately successful. Hundreds of souls were received into the kingdom, and the apostles and evangelists had a valuable experience in carrying on their work without the inspiration of the immediate personal presence of Jesus.

On Friday, September 16, the entire corps of workers assembled by prearrangement at Magadan Park. On the Sabbath day a council of more than one hundred believers was held at which the future plans for extending the work of the kingdom were fully considered. The messengers of David were present and made reports concerning the welfare of the believers throughout Judea, Samaria, Galilee, and adjoining districts.

Few of Jesus' followers at this time fully appreciated the great value of the services of the messenger corps. Not only did the messengers keep the believers throughout Palestine in touch with each other and with Jesus and the apostles, but during these dark days they also served as collectors of funds, not only for the sustenance of Jesus and his associates, but also for the support of the families of the twelve apostles and the twelve evangelists.

About this time Abner moved his base of operations from Hebron to Bethlehem, and this latter place was also the headquarters in Judea for David's messengers. David maintained an overnight relay messenger service between Jerusalem and Bethsaida. These runners left Jerusalem each evening, relaying at Sychar and Scythopolis, arriving in Bethsaida by breakfast time the next morning.

Jesus and his associates now prepared to take a week's rest before they made ready to start upon the last epoch of their labors in behalf of the kingdom. This was their last rest, for the Perean mission developed into a campaign of preaching and teaching which extended right on down to the time of their arrival at Jerusalem and of the enactment of the closing episodes of Jesus' earth career.

# RODAN OF ALEXANDRIA

O N SUNDAY morning, September 18, Andrew announced that no work would be planned for the coming week. All of the apostles, except Nathaniel and Thomas, went home to visit their families or to sojourn with friends. This week Jesus enjoyed a period of almost complete rest, but Nathaniel and Thomas were very busy with their discussions with a certain Greek philosopher from Alexandria named Rodan. This Greek had recently become a disciple of Jesus through the teaching of one of Abner's associates who had conducted a mission at Alexandria. Rodan was now earnestly engaged in the task of harmonizing his philosophy of life with Jesus' new religious teachings, and he had come to Magadan hoping that the Master would talk these problems over with him. He also desired to secure a firsthand and authoritative version of the gospel from either Jesus or one of his apostles. Though the Master declined to enter into such a conference with Rodan, he did receive him graciously and immediately directed that Nathaniel and Thomas should listen to all he had to say and tell him about the gospel in return.

E arly Monday morning, Rodan began a series of ten addresses to Nathaniel, Thomas, and a group of some two dozen believers who chanced to be at Magadan. These talks, condensed, combined, and restated in modern phraseology, present the following thoughts for consideration:

Human life consists in three great drives - urges, desires, and lures. Strong character, commanding personality, is only acquired by converting the natural urge of life into the social art of living, by transforming present desires into those higher longings which are capable of lasting attainment, while the commonplace lure of existence must be transferred from one's conventional and established ideas to the higher realms of unexplored ideas and undiscovered ideals.

The more complex civilization becomes, the more difficult will become the art of living. The more rapid the changes in social usage, the more complicated will become the task of character development. Every ten generations mankind must learn anew the art of living if progress is to continue. And if man becomes so ingenious that he more rapidly adds to the complexities of society, the art of living will need to be remastered in less time, perhaps every single generation. If the evolution of the art of living fails to keep pace with the technique of existence, humanity will quickly revert to the simple urge of living - the attainment of the satisfaction of present desires. Thus will humanity remain immature; society will fail in growing up to full maturity.

Social maturity is equivalent to the degree to which man is willing to surrender the gratification of mere transient and present desires for the entertainment of those superior longings, the striving for whose attainment affords the more abundant satisfactions of progressive advancement toward permanent goals. But the true badge of social maturity is the willingness of a people to surrender the right to live peaceably and contentedly under the ease-promoting standards of the lure of established beliefs and conventional ideas for the disquieting and energy-requiring lure of the pursuit of the unexplored possibilities of the attainment of undiscovered goals of idealistic spiritual realities.

Animals respond nobly to the urge of life, but only man can attain the art of living, albeit the majority of mankind only experience the animal urge to live. Animals know only this blind and instinctive urge; man is capable of transcending this urge to natural function. Man may elect to live upon the high plane of intelligent art, even that of celestial joy and spiritual ecstasy. Animals make no inquiry into the purposes of life; therefore they never worry, neither do they commit suicide. Suicide among men testifies that such beings have emerged from the purely animal stage of existence, and to the further fact that the exploratory efforts of such human beings have failed to attain the artistic levels of mortal experience. Animals know not the meaning of life; man not only possesses capacity for the recognition of values and the comprehension of meanings, but he also is conscious of the meaning of meanings - he is self-conscious of insight.

When men dare to forsake a life of natural craving for one of adventurous art and uncertain logic, they must expect to suffer the consequent hazards of emotional casualties - conflicts, unhappiness, and uncertainties - at least until the time of their attainment of some degree of intellectual and emotional maturity. Discouragement, worry, and indolence are positive evidence of moral immaturity. Human society is confronted with two problems: attainment of the maturity of the individual and attainment of the maturity of the race. The mature human being soon begins to look upon all other mortals with feelings of tenderness and with emotions of tolerance. Mature men view immature folks with the love and consideration that parents bear their children.

Successful living is nothing more or less than the art of the mastery of dependable techniques for solving common problems. The first step in the solution of any problem is to locate the difficulty, to isolate the problem, and frankly to recognize its nature and gravity. The great mistake is that, when life problems excite our profound fears, we refuse to recognize them. Likewise, when the acknowledgment of our difficulties entails the reduction of our long-cherished conceit, the admission of envy, or the abandonment of deep-seated prejudices, the average person prefers to cling to the old illusions of safety and to the long-cherished false feelings of security. Only a brave person is willing honestly to admit, and fearlessly to face, what a sincere and logical mind discovers.

The wise and effective solution of any problem demands that the mind shall be free from bias, passion, and all other purely personal prejudices which might interfere with the disinterested survey of the actual factors that go to make up the problem presenting itself for solution. The solution of life problems requires courage and sincerity. Only honest and brave individuals are able to follow valiantly through the perplexing and confusing maze of living to where the logic of a fearless mind may lead. And this emancipation of the mind and soul can never be effected without the driving power of an intelligent enthusiasm which borders on religious zeal. It requires the lure of a great ideal to drive man on in the pursuit of a goal that is beset with difficult material problems and manifold intellectual hazards.

Even though you are effectively armed to meet the difficult situations of life, you can hardly expect success unless you are equipped with that wisdom of mind and charm of personality which enable you to win the hearty support and co-operation of your fellows. You cannot hope for a large measure of success in either secular or religious work unless you can learn how to persuade your fellows, to prevail with men. You simply must have tact and tolerance.

But the greatest of all methods of problem solving I have learned from Jesus, your Master. I refer to that which he so consistently practices, and which he has so faithfully taught you, the isolation of worshipful meditation. In this habit of Jesus' going off so frequently by himself to commune with the Father in heaven is to be found the technique, not only of gathering strength and wisdom for the ordinary conflicts of living, but also of appropriating the energy for the solution of the higher problems of a moral and spiritual nature. But even correct methods of solving problems will not compensate for inherent defects of personality or atone for the absence of the hunger and thirst for true righteousness.

I am deeply impressed with the custom of Jesus in going apart by himself to engage in these seasons of solitary survey of the problems of living; to seek for new stores of wisdom and energy for meeting the manifold demands of social service; to quicken and deepen the supreme purpose of living by actually subjecting the total personality to the consciousness of contacting with divinity; to grasp for possession of new and better methods of adjusting oneself to the ever-changing situations of living existence; to effect those vital reconstructions and readjustments of one's personal attitudes which are so essential to enhanced insight into everything worthwhile and real; and to do all of this with an eye single to the glory of God - to breathe in sincerity your Master's favorite prayer, "Not my will, but yours, be done."

This worshipful practice of your Master brings that relaxation which renews the mind; that illumination which inspires the soul; that courage which enables one bravely to face one's problems; that self-understanding which obliterates debilitating fear; and that consciousness of union with divinity which equips man with the assurance that enables him to dare to be Godlike. The relaxation of worship, or spiritual communion as practiced by the Master, relieves tension, removes conflicts, and mightily augments the total resources of the personality. And all this philosophy, plus the gospel of the kingdom, constitutes the new religion as I understand it.

Prejudice blinds the soul to the recognition of truth, and prejudice can be removed only by the sincere devotion of the soul to the adoration of a cause that is all-embracing and all-inclusive of one's fellow men. Prejudice is inseparably linked to selfishness. Prejudice can be eliminated only by the abandonment of self-seeking and by substituting therefor the quest of the satisfaction of the service of a cause that is not only greater than self, but one that is even greater than all humanity - the search for God, the attainment of divinity. The evidence of maturity of personality consists in the transformation of human desire so that it constantly seeks for the realization of those values which are highest and most divinely real.

In a continually changing world, in the midst of an evolving social order, it is impossible to maintain settled and established goals of destiny. Only those who have discovered and embraced the living God as the eternal goal of infinite attainment can experience stability of personality. And thus to transfer one's goal from time to eternity, from earth to Paradise, from the human to the divine, requires that man shall become regenerated, converted, be born again; that he shall become the re-created child of the divine spirit; that he shall gain entrance into the brotherhood of the kingdom of heaven. All philosophies and religions which fall short of these ideals are immature. The philosophy that I teach, linked with the gospel that you preach, represents the new religion of maturity, the ideal of all future generations. And this is true because our ideal is final, infallible, eternal, universal, absolute, and infinite.

My philosophy gave me the urge to search for the realities of true attainment, the goal of maturity. But my urge was impotent; my search lacked driving power; my quest suffered from the absence of certainty of directionization. And these deficiencies have been abundantly supplied by this new gospel of Jesus, with its enhancement of insights, elevation of ideals, and settledness of goals. Without doubts and misgivings I can now wholeheartedly enter upon the eternal venture.

There are just two ways in which mortals may live together: the material or animal way and the spiritual or human way. By the use of signals and sounds animals are able to communicate with each other in a limited way. But such forms of communication do not convey meanings, values, or ideas. The one distinction between man and the animal is that man can communicate with his fellows by means of *symbols* which most certainly designate and identify meanings, values, ideas, and even ideals.

Since animals cannot communicate ideas to each other, they cannot develop personality. Man develops personality because he can thus communicate with his fellows concerning both ideas and ideals.

It is this ability to communicate and share meanings that constitutes human culture and enables man, through social associations, to build civilizations. Knowledge and wisdom become cumulative because of man's ability to communicate these possessions to succeeding generations. And thereby arise the cultural activities of the race: art, science, religion, and philosophy.

Symbolic communication between human beings predetermines the bringing into existence of social groups. The most effective of all social groups is the family, more particularly the *two parents*. Personal affection is the spiritual bond which holds together these material associations. Such an effective relationship is also possible between two persons of the same sex, as is so abundantly illustrated in the devotions of genuine friendships.

These associations of friendship and mutual affection are socializing and ennobling because they encourage and facilitate the following essential factors of the higher levels of the art of living:

1. *Mutual self-expression and self-understanding.* Many noble human impulses die because there is no one to hear their expression. Truly, it is not good for man to be alone. Some degree of recognition and a certain amount of appreciation are essential to the development of human character. Without the genuine love of a home, no child can achieve the full development of normal character. Character is something more than mere mind and morals. Of all social relations calculated to develop character, the most effective and ideal is the affectionate and understanding friendship of man and woman in the mutual embrace of intelligent wedlock. Marriage, with its manifold relations, is best designed to draw forth those precious impulses and those higher motives that are indispensable to the development of a strong character. I do not hesitate thus to glorify family life, for your Master has wisely chosen the father-child relationship as the very cornerstone of this new gospel of the king-

dom. And such a matchless community of relationship, man and woman in the fond embrace of the highest ideals of time, is so valuable and satisfying an experience that it is worth any price, any sacrifice, requisite for its possession.

2. *Union of souls — the mobilization of wisdom.* Every human being sooner or later acquires a certain concept of this world and a certain vision of the next. Now it is possible, through personality association, to unite these views of temporal existence and eternal prospects. Thus does the mind of one augment its spiritual values by gaining much of the insight of the other. In this way men enrich the soul by pooling their respective spiritual possessions. Likewise, in this same way, man is enabled to avoid that ever-present tendency to fall victim to distortion of vision, prejudice of viewpoint, and narrowness of judgment. Fear, envy, and conceit can be prevented only by intimate contact with other minds. I call your attention to the fact that the Master never sends you out alone to labor for the extension of the kingdom; he always sends you out two and two. And since wisdom is superknowledge, it follows that, in the union of wisdom, the social group, small or large, mutually shares all knowledge.

3. *The enthusiasm for living.* Isolation tends to exhaust the energy charge of the soul. Association with one's fellows is essential to the renewal of the zest for life and is indispensable to the maintenance of the courage to fight those battles consequent upon the ascent to the higher levels of human living. Friendship enhances the joys and glorifies the triumphs of life. Loving and intimate human associations tend to rob suffering of its sorrow and hardship of much of its bitterness. The presence of a friend enhances all beauty and exalts every goodness. By intelligent symbols man is able to quicken and enlarge the appreciative capacities of his friends. One of the crowning glories of human friendship is this power and possibility of the mutual stimulation of the imagination. Great spiritual power is inherent in the consciousness of wholehearted devotion to a common cause, mutual loyalty to a cosmic Deity.

4. *The enhanced defense against all evil.* Personality association and mutual affection is an efficient insurance against evil. Difficulties, sorrow, disappointment, and defeat are more painful and disheartening when borne alone. Association does not transmute evil into righteousness, but it does aid in greatly lessening the sting. Said your Master, "Happy are they who mourn" - if a friend is at hand to comfort. There ispositive strength in the knowledge that you live for the welfare of others, and that these others likewise live for your welfare and advancement. Man languishes in isolation. Human beings unfailingly become discouraged when they view only the transitory transactions of time. The

present, when divorced from the past and the future, becomes exasperatingly trivial. Only a glimpse of the circle of eternity can inspire man to do his best and can challenge the best in him to do its utmost. And when man is thus at his best, he lives most unselfishly for the good of others, his fellow sojourners in time and eternity.

I repeat, such inspiring and ennobling association finds its ideal possibilities in the human marriage relation. True, much is attained out of marriage, and many, many marriages utterly fail to produce these moral and spiritual fruits. Too many times marriage is entered by those who seek other values which are lower than these superior accompaniments of human maturity. Ideal marriage must be founded on something more stable than the fluctuations of sentiment and the fickleness of mere sex attraction; it must be based on genuine and mutual personal devotion. And thus, if you can build up such trustworthy and effective small units of human association, when these are assembled in the aggregate, the world will behold a great and glorified social structure, the civilization of mortal maturity. Such a race might begin to realize something of your Master's ideal of "peace on earth and good will among men." While such a society would not be perfect or entirely free from evil, it would at least approach the stabilization of maturity.

The effort toward maturity necessitates work, and work requires energy. Whence the power to accomplish all this? The physical things can be taken for granted, but the Master has well said, "Man cannot live by bread alone." Granted the possession of a normal body and reasonably good health, we must next look for those lures that will act as a stimulus to call forth man's slumbering spiritual forces. Jesus has taught us that God lives in man; then how can we induce man to release these soul-bound powers of divinity and infinity? How shall we induce men to let go of God that he may spring forth to the refreshment of our own souls while in transit outward and then to serve the purpose of enlightening, uplifting, and blessing countless other souls? How best can I awaken these latent powers for good which lie dormant in your souls? One thing I am sure of: Emotional excitement is not the ideal spiritual stimulus. Excitement does not augment energy; it rather exhausts the powers of both mind and body. Whence then comes the energy to do these great things? Look to your Master. Even now he is out in the hills taking in power while we are here giving out energy. The secret of this entire problem is wrapped up in spiritual communion, in worship. From the human standpoint it is a question of combined meditation and relaxation. Meditation makes the contact of mind with spirit; relaxation determines the capacity for spiritual receptivity. And this interchange of strength for weakness, courage for fear, the will of God for the mind of self, constitutes worship. At least, that is the way the philosopher views it.

When these experiences are frequently repeated, they crystallize into habits, strength-giving and worshipful habits, and such habits eventually formulate themselves into a spiritual character, and such a character is finally recognized by one's fellows as a *mature personality*. These practices are difficult and time-consuming at first, but when they become habitual, they are at once restful and timesaving. The more complex society becomes, and the more the lures of civilization multiply, the more urgent will become the necessity for God-knowing individuals to form such protective habitual practices designed to conserve and augment their spiritual energies.

Another requirement for the attainment of maturity is the cooperative adjustment of social groups to an ever-changing environment. The immature individual arouses the antagonisms of his fellows; the mature man wins the hearty cooperation of his associates, thereby many times multiplying the fruits of his life efforts.

My philosophy tells me that there are times when I must fight, if need be, for the defense of my concept of righteousness, but I doubt not that the Master, with a more mature type of personality, would easily and gracefully gain an equal victory by his superior and winsome technique of tact and tolerance. All too often, when we battle for the right, it turns out that both the victor and the vanquished have sustained defeat. I heard the Master say only yesterday that the "wise man, when seeking entrance through the locked door, would not destroy the door but rather would seek for the key wherewith to unlock it." Too often we engage in a fight merely to convince ourselves that we are not afraid.

This new gospel of the kingdom renders a great service to the art of living in that it supplies a new and richer incentive for higher living. It presents a new and exalted goal of destiny, a supreme life purpose. And these new concepts of the eternal and divine goal of existence are in themselves transcendent stimuli, calling forth the reaction of the very best that is resident in man's higher nature. On every mountaintop of intellectual thought are to be found relaxation for the mind, strength for the soul, and communion for the spirit. From such vantagepoints of high living, man is able to transcend the material irritations of the lower levels of thinking; worry, jealousy, envy, revenge, and the pride of immature personality. These high-climbing souls deliver themselves from a multitude of the crosscurrent conflicts of the trifles of living, thus becoming free to attain consciousness of the higher currents of spirit concept and celestial communication. But the life purpose must be jealously guarded from the temptation to seek for easy and transient attainment; likewise must it be so fostered as to become immune to the disastrous threats of fanaticism.

While you have an eye single to the attainment of eternal realities, you must also make provision for the necessities of temporal living. While the spirit is our goal, the flesh is a fact. Occasionally the necessities of living may fall into our hands by accident, but in general, we must intelligently work for them. The two major problems of life are making a temporal living and the achievement of eternal survival. And even the problem of making a living requires religion for its ideal solution. These are both highly personal problems. True religion, in fact, does not function apart from the individual.

The essentials of the temporal life, as I see them, are:

1. Good physical health.
2. Clear and clean thinking.
3. Ability and skill.
4. Wealth - the goods of life.
5. Ability to withstand defeat.
6. Culture - education and wisdom.

Even the physical problems of bodily health and efficiency are best solved when they are viewed from the religious standpoint of our Master's teaching: That the body and mind of man are the dwelling place of the gift of the Gods, the spirit of God becoming the spirit of man. The mind of man thus becomes the mediator between material things and spiritual realities.

It requires intelligence to secure one's share of the desirable things of life. It is wholly erroneous to suppose that faithfulness in doing one's daily work will insure the rewards of wealth. Barring the occasional and accidental acquirement of wealth, the material rewards of the temporal life are found to flow in certain well-organized channels, and only those who have access to these channels may expect to be well rewarded for their temporal efforts. Poverty must ever be the lot of all men who seek for wealth in isolated and individual channels. Wise planning, therefore, becomes the one thing essential to worldly prosperity. Success requires not only devotion to one's work but also that one should function as a part of some one of the channels of material wealth. If you are unwise, you can bestow a devoted life upon your generation without material reward; if you are an accidental beneficiary of the flow of wealth, you may roll in luxury even though you have done nothing worthwhile for your fellow men.

Ability is that which you inherit, while skill is what you acquire. Life is not real to one who cannot do some one thing well, expertly. Skill is one of the real sources of the satisfaction of living. Ability implies the gift of foresight, farseeing vision. Be not deceived by the tempting rewards of dishonest achievement; be willing to toil for the later returns inherent in honest endeavor. The wise man is able to distinguish between means and ends; otherwise, sometimes overplanning for the future defeats its own high purpose. As a pleasure seeker you should aim always to be a producer as well as a consumer.

Train your memory to hold in sacred trust the strength-giving and worthwhile episodes of life, which you can recall at will for your pleasure and edification.

When men react to religion in the tribal, national, or racial sense, it is because they look upon those without their group as not being truly human. We always look upon the object of our religious loyalty as being worthy of the reverence of all men. Religion can never be a matter of mere intellectual belief or philosophic reasoning; religion is always and forever a mode of reacting to the situations of life; it is a species of conduct. Religion embraces thinking, feeling, and acting reverently toward some reality that we deem worthy of universal adoration.

If something has become a religion in your experience, it is self-evident that you already have become an active evangelist of that religion since you deem the supreme concept of your religion as being worthy of the worship of all mankind, all universe intelligences. If you are not a positive and missionary evangelist of your religion, you are self-deceived in that what you call a religion is only a traditional belief or a mere system of intellectual philosophy. If your religion is a spiritual experience, your object of worship must be the universal spirit reality and ideal of all your spiritualized concepts. All religions based on fear, emotion, tradition, and philosophy I term the intellectual religions, while those based on true spirit experience I would term the true religions. The object of religious devotion may be material or spiritual, true or false, real or unreal, human or divine. Religions can therefore be either good or evil.

Morality and religion are not necessarily the same. A system of morals, by grasping an object of worship, may become a religion. A religion, by losing its universal appeal to loyalty and supreme devotion, may devolve into a system of philosophy or a code of morals. This thing, being, state, or order of existence, or possibility of attainment which constitutes the supreme ideal of religious loyalty, and which is the recipient of the religious devotion of those who worship, is God. Regardless of the name applied to this ideal of spirit reality, it is God.

The social characteristics of a true religion consist in the fact that it invariably seeks to convert the individual and to transform the world. Religion implies the existence of undiscovered ideals that far transcend the known standards of ethics and morality embodied in even the highest social usages of the most mature institutions of civilization. Religion reaches out for undiscovered ideals, unexplored realities, superhuman values, divine wisdom, and true spirit attainment. True religion does all of this; all other beliefs are not worthy of the name. You cannot have a genuine spiritual religion without the supreme and supernal ideal of an eternal God. A religion without this God is an invention of man, a human institution of lifeless intellectual beliefs and meaningless emotional ceremonies. A religion might claim as the object of its devotion a great ideal. But such ideals of unreality are not attainable; such a concept is illusionary. The only ideals susceptible of human attainment are the divine realities of the infinite values resident in the spiritual fact of the eternal God.

The word God, the *idea* of God as contrasted with the *ideal* of God, can become a part of any religion, no matter how puerile or false that religion may chance to be. And this idea of God can become anything that those who entertain it may choose to make it. The lower religions shape their ideas of God to meet the natural state of the human heart; the higher religions demand that the human heart shall be changed to meet the demands of the ideals of true religion.

The religion of Jesus transcends all our former concepts of the idea of worship in that he not only portrays his Father as the ideal of infinite reality but positively declares that this divine source of values and the eternal center of the universe is truly and personally attainable by every mortal creature who chooses to enter the kingdom of heaven on earth, thereby acknowledging the acceptance of sonship with God and brotherhood with man. That, I submit, is the highest concept of religion the world has ever known, and I pronounce that there can never be a higher since this gospel embraces the infinity of realities, the divinity of values, and the eternity of universal attainments. Such a concept constitutes the achievement of the experience of the idealism of the supreme and the ultimate.

I am not only intrigued by the consummate ideals of this religion of your Master, but I am mightily moved to profess my belief in his announcement that these ideals of spirit realities are attainable; that you and I can enter upon this long and eternal adventure with his assurance of the certainty of our ultimate arrival at the portals of Paradise. My brethren, I am a believer, I have embarked; I am on my way with you in this eternal venture. The Master says he came from the Father, and that he will show us the way. I am fully persuaded he speaks the truth. I am finally convinced that there are no attainable ideals of reality or values of perfection apart from the eternal and universal Father.

I come, then, to worship, not merely the God of existences, but the God of the possibility of all future existences. Therefore must your devotion to a supreme ideal, if that ideal is real, be devotion to this God of past, present, and future universes of things and beings. And there is no other God, for there cannot possibly be any other God. All other gods are figments of the imagination, illusions of mortal mind, distortions of false logic, and the self-deceptive idols of those who create them. Yes, you can have a religion without this God, but it does not mean anything. And if you seek to substitute the word God for the reality of this ideal of the living God, you have only deluded yourself by putting an idea in the place of an ideal, a divine reality. Such beliefs are merely religions of wishful fancy.

I see in the teachings of Jesus, religion at its best. This gospel enables us to seek for the true God and to find him. But are we willing to pay the price of this entrance into the kingdom of heaven? Are we willing to be born again? To be remade? Are we willing to be subject to this terrible and testing process of self-destruction and soul reconstruction? Has not the Master said: "Whoso would save his life must lose it. Think not that I have come to bring peace but rather a soul struggle"? True, after we pay the price of dedication to the Father's will, we do experience great peace provided we continue to walk in these spiritual paths of consecrated living.

Now are we truly forsaking the lures of the known order of existence while we unreservedly dedicate our quest to the lures of the unknown and unexplored order of the existence of a future life of adventure in the spirit worlds of the higher idealism of divine reality. And we seek for those symbols of meaning wherewith to convey to our fellow men these concepts of the reality of the idealism of the religion of Jesus, and we will not cease to pray for that day when all mankind shall be thrilled by the communal vision of this supreme truth. Just now, our focalized concept of the Father, as held in our hearts, is that God is spirit; as conveyed to our fellows, that God is love.

The religion of Jesus demands living and spiritual experience. Other religions may consist in traditional beliefs, emotional feelings, philosophic consciousness, and all of that, but the teaching of the Master requires the attainment of actual levels of real spirit progression.

The consciousness of the impulse to be like God is not true religion. The feelings of the emotion to worship God are not true religion. The knowledge of the conviction to forsake self and serve God is not true religion. The wisdom of the reasoning that this religion is the best of all is not religion as a personal and spiritual experience. True religion has reference to destiny and reality of attainment as well as to the reality and idealism of that which is wholeheartedly faith-accepted. And all of this must be made personal to us by the revelation of the Spirit of Truth.

And thus ended the dissertations of the Greek philosopher, one of the greatest of his race, who had become a believer in the gospel of Jesus.

O N SUNDAY, September 25, A.D. 29, the apostles and the evangelists assembled at Magadan. After a long conference that evening with his associates, Jesus surprised all by announcing that early the next day he and the twelve apostles would start for Jerusalem to attend the feast of tabernacles. He directed that the evangelists visit the believers in Galilee, and that the women's corps return for a while to Bethsaida.

When the hour came to leave for Jerusalem, Nathaniel and Thomas were still in the midst of their discussions with Rodan of Alexandria, and they secured the Master's permission to remain at Magadan for a few days. And so, while Jesus and the ten were on their way to Jerusalem, Nathaniel and Thomas were engaged in earnest debate with Rodan. The week prior, in which Rodan had expounded his philosophy, Thomas and Nathaniel had alternated in presenting the gospel of the kingdom to the Greek philosopher. Rodan discovered that he had been well instructed in Jesus' teachings by one of the former apostles of John the Baptist who had been his teacher at Alexandria.

There was one matter on which Rodan and the two apostles did not see alike, and that was the personality of God. Rodan readily accepted all that was presented to him regarding the attributes of God, but he contended that the Father in heaven is not, cannot be, a person as man conceives personality. While the apostles found themselves in difficulty trying to prove that God is a person, Rodan found it still more difficult to prove He is not a person.

Rodan contended that the fact of personality consists in the coexistent fact of full and mutual communication between beings of equality, beings who are capable of sympathetic understanding. Said Rodan, "In order to be a person, God must have symbols of spirit communication which would enable Him to become fully understood by those who make contact with Him. But since God is infinite and eternal, the Creator of all other beings, it follows that, as regards beings of equality, God is alone in the universe. There are none equal to Him; there are none with whom He can communicate as an equal. God indeed may be the source of all personality, but as such He is transcendent to personality, even as the Creator is above and beyond the creature."

This contention greatly troubled Thomas and Nathaniel, and they had asked Jesus to come to their rescue, but the Master refused to enter into their discussions. He did say to Thomas, "It matters little what *idea* of the Father you may entertain as long as you are spiritually acquainted with the *ideal* of His infinite and eternal nature."

Thomas contended that God does communicate with man, and therefore that the Father is a person, even within the definition of Rodan. This the Greek rejected on the ground that God does not reveal himself personally; that He is still a mystery. Then Nathaniel appealed to his own personal experience with God, and that Rodan allowed, affirming that he had recently had similar experiences, but these experiences, he contended, proved only the *reality* of God, not His *personality*.

By Monday night Thomas gave up. But by Tuesday night Nathaniel had won Rodan to believe in the personality of the Father, and he effected this change in the Greek's views by the following steps of reasoning:

1. The Father in Paradise does enjoy equality of communication with at least two other beings who are fully equal to Himself and wholly like Himself - the Eternal Mother-Son and the Infinite Spirit. In view of the doctrine of the Trinity, the Greek was compelled to concede the personality possibility of the Universal Father. (It was the later consideration of these discussions that led to the enlarged conception of the Trinity in the minds of the twelve apostles. Of course, it was the general belief that Jesus was the Eternal Son.)

2. Since Jesus was equal with the Father, and since this Son had achieved the manifestation of personality to his earth children, such a phenomenon constituted proof of the fact, and demonstration of the possibility, of the possession of personality by all three of the Godheads and forever settled the question regarding the ability of God to communicate with man and the possibility of man's communicating with God.

3. That Jesus was on terms of mutual association and perfect communication with man; that Jesus was the Son of God. That the relation of Son and Father presupposes equality of communication and mutuality of sympathetic understanding; that Jesus and the Father were one. That Jesus maintained at one and the same time understanding communication with both God and man, and that, since both God and man comprehended the meaning of the symbols of Jesus' communication, both God

and man possessed the attributes of personality in so far as the requirements of the ability of intercommunication were concerned. That the personality of Jesus demonstrated the personality of God, while it proved conclusively the presence of God in man. That two things which are related to the same thing are related to each other.

4. That personality represents man's highest concept of human reality and divine values; that God also represents man's highest concept of divine reality and infinite values; therefore, that God must be a divine and infinite personality, a personality in reality although infinitely and eternally transcending man's concept and definition of personality, but nevertheless always and universally a personality.

5. That God must be a personality since he is the Creator of all personality and the destiny of all personality. Rodan had been tremendously influenced by the teaching of Jesus, "Be you therefore perfect, even as your Father in heaven is perfect."

When Rodan heard these arguments, he said, "I am convinced. I will confess God as a person if you will permit me to qualify my confession of such a belief by attaching to the meaning of personality a group of extended values, such as superhuman, transcendent, supreme, infinite, eternal, final, and universal. I am now convinced that, while God must be infinitely more than a personality, he cannot be anything less. I am satisfied to end the argument and to accept Jesus as the personal revelation of the Father and the satisfaction of all unsatisfied factors in logic, reason, and philosophy."

Since Nathaniel and Thomas had so fully approved Rodan's views of the gospel of the kingdom, there remained only one more point to consider, the teaching dealing with the divine nature of Jesus, a doctrine only so recently publicly announced. Nathaniel and Thomas jointly presented their views of the divine nature of the Master, and the following narrative is a condensed, rearranged, and restated presentation of their teaching:

1. Jesus has admitted his divinity, and we believe him. Many remarkable things have happened in connection with his ministry which we can understand only by believing that he is the Son of God as well as the Son of Man.

2. His life association with us exemplifies the ideal of human friendship; only a divine being could possibly be such a human friend. He is the most truly unselfish person we have ever known. He is the friend even of sinners; he dares to love his enemies. He is very loyal to us. While he does not hesitate to reprove us, it is plain to all that he truly loves us. The

better you know him, the more you will love him. You will be charmed by his unswerving devotion. Through all these years of our failure to comprehend his mission, he has been a faithful friend. While he makes no use of flattery, he does treat us all with equal kindness; he is invariably tender and compassionate. He has shared his life and everything else with us. We are a happy community; we share all things in common. We do not believe that a mere human could live such a blameless life under such trying circumstances.

3. We think Jesus is divine because he never does wrong; he makes no mistakes. His wisdom is extraordinary; his piety superb. He lives day by day in perfect accord with the Father's will. He never repents of misdeeds because he transgresses none of the Father's laws. He prays for us and with us, but he never asks us to pray for him. We believe that he is consistently sinless. We do not think that one who is only human ever professed to live such a life. He claims to live a perfect life, and we acknowledge that he does. Our piety springs from repentance, but his piety springs from righteousness. He even professes to forgive sins and does heal diseases. No mere man would sanely profess to forgive sin; that is a divine prerogative. And he has seemed to be thus perfect in his righteousness from the times of our first contact with him. We grow in grace and in the knowledge of the truth, but our Master exhibits maturity of righteousness to start with. All men, good and evil, recognize these elements of goodness in Jesus. And yet never is his piety obtrusive or ostentatious. He is both meek and fearless. He seems to approve of our belief in his divinity. He is either what he professes to be, or else he is the greatest hypocrite and fraud the world has ever known. We are persuaded that he is just what he claims to be.

4. The uniqueness of his character and the perfection of his emotional control convince us that he is a combination of humanity and divinity. He unfailingly responds to the spectacle of human need; suffering never fails to appeal to him. His compassion is moved alike by physical suffering, mental anguish, or spiritual sorrow. He is quick to recognize and generous to acknowledge the presence of faith or any other grace in his fellow men. He is so just and fair and at the same time so merciful and considerate. He grieves over the spiritual obstinacy of the people and rejoices when they consent to see the light of truth.

5. He seems to know the thoughts of men's minds and to understand the longings of their hearts. And he is always sympathetic with our troubled spirits. He seems to possess all our human emotions, but they are magnificently glorified. He strongly loves goodness and equally hates sin. He possesses a superhuman consciousness of the presence of Deity. He

prays like a man but performs like a God. He seems to foreknow things; he even now dares to speak about his death, some mystic reference to his future glorification. While he is kind, he is also brave and courageous. He never falters in doing his duty.

6. We are constantly impressed by the phenomenon of his superhuman knowledge. Hardly does a day pass but something transpires to disclose that the Master knows what is going on away from his immediate presence. He also seems to know about the thoughts of his associates. He undoubtedly has communion with celestial personalities; he unquestionably lives on a spiritual plane far above the rest of us. Everything seems to be open to his unique understanding. He asks us questions to draw us out, not to gain information.

7. Recently the Master does not hesitate to assert his superhumanity. From the day of our ordination as apostles right on down to recent times, he has never denied that he came from the Father above. He speaks with the authority of a divine teacher. The Master does not hesitate to refute the religious teachings of today and to declare the new gospel with positive authority. He is assertive, positive, and authoritative. Even John the Baptist, when he heard Jesus speak, declared that he was the Son of God. He seems to be so sufficient within himself. He craves not the support of the multitude; he is indifferent to the opinions of men. He is brave and yet so free from pride.

8. He constantly talks about God as an ever-present associate in all that he does. He goes about doing good, for God seems to be in him. He makes the most astounding assertions about himself and his mission on earth, statements which would be absurd if he were not divine. He once declared, "Before Abraham was, I am." He has definitely claimed divinity; he professes to be in partnership with God. He well-nigh exhausts the possibilities of language in the reiteration of his claims of intimate association with the heavenly Father. He even dares to assert that he and the Father are one. He says that anyone who has seen him has seen the Father. And he says and does all these tremendous things with such childlike naturalness. He alludes to his association with the Father in the same manner that he refers to his association with us. He seems to be so sure about God and speaks of these relations in such a matter-of-fact way.

9. In his prayer life he appears to communicate directly with his Father. We have heard few of his prayers, but these few would indicate that he talks with God, as it were, face to face. He seems to know the future as well as the past. He simply could not be all of this and do all of these extraordinary things unless he were something more than human. We

know he is human, we are sure of that, but we are almost equally sure that he is also divine. We believe that he is divine. We are convinced that he is the Son of Man and the Son of God.

When Nathaniel and Thomas had concluded their conferences with Rodan, they hurried on toward Jerusalem to join their fellow apostles, arriving on Friday of that week. This had been a great experience in the lives of all three of these believers, and the other apostles learned much from the recounting of these experiences by Nathaniel and Thomas.

Rodan made his way back to Alexandria, where he long taught his philosophy in the school of Meganta. He became a mighty man in the later affairs of the kingdom of heaven; he was a faithful believer to the end of his earth days, yielding up his life in Greece with others when the persecutions were at their height.

Consciousness of divinity was a gradual growth in the mind of Jesus up to the occasion of his baptism. After he became fully self-conscious of his divine nature, prehuman existence, and universe prerogatives, he seems to have possessed the power of variously limiting his human consciousness of his divinity. It appears to us that from his baptism until the crucifixion it was entirely optional with Jesus whether to depend only on the human mind or to utilize the knowledge of both the human and the divine minds. At times he appeared to avail himself of only that information which was resident in the human intellect. On other occasions he appeared to act with such fullness of knowledge and wisdom as could be afforded only by the utilization of the superhuman content of his divine consciousness.

We can understand his unique performances only by accepting the theory that he could, at will, self-limit his divinity consciousness. We are fully cognizant that he frequently withheld from his associates his foreknowledge of events, and that he was aware of the nature of their thinking and planning. We understand that he did not wish his followers to know too fully that he was able to discern their thoughts and to penetrate their plans. He did not desire too far to transcend the concept of the human as it was held in the minds of his apostles and disciples.

We are utterly at a loss to differentiate between his practice of self-limiting his divine consciousness and his technique of concealing his preknowledge and thought discernment from his human associates. We are convinced that he used both of these techniques, but we are not always able, in a given instance, to specify which method he may have employed. We frequently observed him acting with only the human content of consciousness; then would we behold him in conference with the directors of the celestial hosts of the universe and discern the undoubted functioning of the divine mind. And then on almost numberless occasions did we witness the working of this combined personality of man and God as it was activated by the apparent perfect union of the human and the divine minds. This is the limit of our knowledge of such phenomena; we really do not actually know the full truth about this mystery.

# AT THE FEAST OF TABERNACLES

W HEN JESUS started up to Jerusalem with the ten apostles, he planned to go through Samaria, that being the shorter route. Accordingly, they passed down the eastern shore of the lake and, by way of Scythopolis, entered the borders of Samaria. Near nightfall Jesus sent Philip and Matthew over to a village on the eastern slopes of Mount Gilboa to secure lodging for the company. It so happened that these villagers were greatly prejudiced against the Jews, even more so than the average Samaritans, and these feelings were heightened at this particular time as so many were on their way to the feast of tabernacles. These people knew very little about Jesus, and they refused him lodging because he and his associates were Jews. When Matthew and Philip manifested indignation and informed these Samaritans that they were declining to entertain the Holy One of Israel, the infuriated villagers chased them out of the little town with sticks and stones.

After Philip and Matthew had returned to their fellows and reported how they had been driven out of the village, James and John stepped up to Jesus and said, "Master, we pray you to give us permission to bid fire come down from heaven to devour these insolent and impenitent Samaritans."

But when Jesus heard these words of vengeance, he turned upon the sons of Zebedee and severely rebuked them, "You know not what manner of attitude you manifest. Vengeance savors not of the outlook of the kingdom of heaven. Rather than dispute, let us journey over to the little village by the Jordan ford." Thus because of sectarian prejudice these Samaritans denied themselves the honor of showing hospitality to the Creator Son of a universe.

Jesus and the ten stopped for the night at the village near the Jordan ford. Early the next day they crossed the river and continued on to Jerusalem by way of the east Jordan highway, arriving at Bethany late Wednesday evening. Thomas and Nathaniel arrived on Friday, having been delayed by their conferences with Rodan.

Jesus and the twelve remained in the vicinity of Jerusalem until the end of the following month (October), about four and one-half weeks. Jesus himself went into the city only a few times, and these brief visits were made during the days of the feast of tabernacles. He spent a considerable portion of October with Abner and his associates at Bethlehem.

Long before they fled from Galilee, the followers of Jesus had implored him to go to Jerusalem to proclaim the gospel of the kingdom in order that his message might have the prestige of having been preached at the center of Jewish culture and learning; but now that he had actually come to Jerusalem to teach, they were afraid for his life. Knowing that the Sanhedrin had sought to bring Jesus to Jerusalem for trial and recalling the Master's recently reiterated declarations that he must be subject to death, the apostles had been literally stunned by his sudden decision to attend the feast of tabernacles. To all their previous entreaties that he go to Jerusalem he had replied, "The hour has not yet come." Now, to their protests of fear he answered only, "But the hour has come."

During the feast of tabernacles Jesus went boldly into Jerusalem on several occasions and publicly taught in the temple. This he did in spite of the efforts of his apostles to dissuade him. Though they had long urged him to proclaim his message in Jerusalem, they now feared to see him enter the city at this time, knowing full well that the scribes and Pharisees were bent on bringing about his death.

Jesus' bold appearance in Jerusalem more than ever confused his followers. Many of his disciples, and even Judas Iscariot, the apostle, had dared to think that Jesus had fled in haste into Phoenicia because he feared the Jewish leaders and Herod Antipas. They failed to comprehend the significance of the Master's movements. His presence in Jerusalem at the feast of tabernacles, even in opposition to the advice of his followers, sufficed forever to put an end to all whisperings about fear and cowardice.

During the feast of tabernacles, thousands of believers from all parts of the Roman Empire saw Jesus, heard him teach, and many even journeyed out to Bethany to confer with him regarding the progress of the kingdom in their home districts.

There were many reasons why Jesus was able publicly to preach in the temple courts throughout the days of the feast, and chief of these was the fear that had come over the officers of the Sanhedrin as a result of the secret division of sentiment in their own ranks. It was a fact that many of the members of the Sanhedrin either secretly believed in Jesus or else were decidedly averse to arresting him during the feast, when such large numbers of people were present in Jerusalem, many of whom either believed in him or were at least friendly to the spiritual movement which he sponsored.

The efforts of Abner and his associates throughout Judea had also done much to consolidate sentiment favorable to the kingdom, so much so that the enemies of Jesus dared not be too outspoken in their opposition. This was one of the reasons why Jesus could publicly visit Jerusalem and live to go away. One or two months before this he would certainly have been put to death.

But the audacious boldness of Jesus in publicly appearing in Jerusalem over-awed his enemies; they were not prepared for such a daring challenge. Several times during this month the Sanhedrin made feeble attempts to place the Master under arrest, but nothing came of these efforts. His enemies were so taken aback by Jesus' unexpected public appearance in Jerusalem that they conjectured he must have been promised protection by the Roman authorities. Knowing that Philip (Herod Antipas's brother) was almost a follower of Jesus, the members of the Sanhedrin speculated that Philip had secured for Jesus promises of protection against his enemies. Jesus had departed from their jurisdiction before they awakened to the realization that they had been mistaken in the belief that his sudden and bold appearance in Jerusalem had been due to a secret understanding with the Roman officials.

Only the twelve apostles had known that Jesus intended to attend the feast of tabernacles when they had departed from Magadan. The other followers of the Master were greatly astonished when he appeared in the temple courts and began publicly to teach, and the Jewish authorities were surprised beyond expression when it was reported that he was teaching in the temple.

Although his disciples had not expected Jesus to attend the feast, the vast majority of the pilgrims from afar who had heard of him entertained the hope that they might see him at Jerusalem. And they were not disappointed, for on several occasions he taught in Solomon's Porch and elsewhere in the temple courts. These teachings were really the official or formal announcement of the divinity of Jesus to the Jewish people and to the whole world.

The multitudes who listened to the Master's teachings were divided in their opinions. Some said he was a good man; some a prophet; some that he was truly the Messiah; others said he was a mischievous meddler, that he was leading the people astray with his strange doctrines. His enemies hesitated to denounce him openly for fear of his friendly believers, while his friends feared to acknowledge him openly for fear of the Jewish leaders, knowing that the Sanhedrin was determined to put him to death. But even his enemies marveled at his teaching, knowing that he had not been instructed in the schools of the rabbis.

Every time Jesus went to Jerusalem, his apostles were filled with terror. They were the more afraid as, from day to day, they listened to his increasingly bold pronouncements regarding the nature of his mission on earth. They were unaccustomed to hearing Jesus make such positive claims and such amazing assertions even when preaching among his friends.

★ ★ ★

The first afternoon that Jesus taught in the temple, a considerable company sat listening to his words depicting the liberty of the new gospel and the joy of those who believe the good news, when a curious listener interrupted him to ask, "Teacher, how is it you can quote the Scriptures and teach the people so fluently when I am told that you are untaught in the learning of the rabbis?"

Jesus replied, "No man has taught me the truths which I declare to you. And this teaching is not mine but His who sent me. If any man really desires to do my Father's will, he shall certainly know about my teaching, whether it be God's or whether I speak for myself. He who speaks for himself seeks his own glory, but when I declare the words of the Father, I thereby seek the glory of Him who sent me. But before you try to enter into the new light, should you not rather follow the light you already have? Moses gave you the law, yet how many of you honestly seek to fulfill its demands? Moses in this law enjoins you, saying, 'You shall not kill'; notwithstanding this command some of you seek to kill the Son of Man."

When the crowd heard these words, they fell to wrangling among themselves. Some said he was mad; some that he had a devil. Others said this was indeed the prophet of Galilee whom the scribes and Pharisees had long sought to kill. Some said the religious authorities were afraid to molest him; others thought that they laid not hands upon him because they had become believers in him. After considerable debate one of the crowd stepped forward and asked Jesus, "Why do the rulers seek to kill you?"

And he replied, "The rulers seek to kill me because they resent my teaching about the good news of the kingdom, a gospel that sets men free from the burdensome traditions of a formal religion of ceremonies which these teachers are determined to uphold at any cost. They circumcise in accordance with the law on the Sabbath day, but they would kill me because I once on the Sabbath day set free a man held in the bondage of affliction. They follow after me on the Sabbath to spy on me but would kill me because on another occasion I chose to make a grievously stricken man completely whole on the Sabbath day. They seek to kill me because they well know that, if you honestly believe and dare to accept my teaching, their system of traditional religion will be overthrown, forever destroyed. Thus will they be deprived of authority over that to which they have devoted their lives since they steadfastly refuse to accept this new and more glorious gospel of the kingdom of God. And now do I appeal to every one of you: Judge not according to outward appearances but rather judge by the true spirit of these teachings; judge righteously."

Then said another inquirer, "Yes, Teacher, we do look for the Messiah, but when he comes, we know that his appearance will be in mystery. We know whence you are. You have been among your brethren from the beginning. The deliverer will come in power to restore the throne of David's kingdom. Do you really claim to be the Messiah?"

And Jesus replied, "You claim to know me and to know whence I am. I wish your claims were true, for indeed then would you find abundant life in that knowledge. But I declare that I have not come to you for myself; I have been sent by the Father, and He who sent me is true and faithful. By refusing to hear me, you are refusing to receive Him who sends me. You, if you will receive this gospel, shall come to know Him who sent me. I know the Father, for I have come from the Father to declare and reveal Him to you."

The agents of the scribes wanted to lay hands upon him, but they feared the multitude, for many believed in him. Jesus' work since his baptism had become well known to all Jewry, and as many of these people recounted these things, they said among themselves: "Even though this teacher is from Galilee, and even though he does not meet all of our expectations of the Messiah, we wonder if the deliverer, when he does come, will really do anything more wonderful than this Jesus of Nazareth has already done?"

When the Pharisees and their agents heard the people talking this way, they took counsel with their leaders and decided that something should be done forthwith to put a stop to these public appearances of Jesus in the temple courts. The leaders of the Jews, in general, were disposed to avoid a clash with Jesus, believing that the Roman authorities had promised him immunity. They could not otherwise account for his boldness in coming at this time to Jerusalem; but the officers of the Sanhedrin did not wholly believe this rumor. They reasoned that the Roman rulers would not do such a thing secretly and without the knowledge of the highest governing body of the Jewish nation. Accordingly, Eber, the proper officer of the Sanhedrin, with two assistants was dispatched to arrest Jesus.

As Eber made his way toward Jesus, the Master said, "Fear not to approach me. Draw near while you listen to my teaching. I know you have been sent to apprehend me, but you should understand that nothing will befall the Son of Man until his hour comes. You are not arrayed against me; you come only to do the bidding of your masters, and even these rulers of the Jews verily think they are doing God's service when they secretly seek my destruction.

"I bear none of you ill will. The Father loves you, and therefore do I long for your deliverance from the bondage of prejudice and the darkness of tradition. I offer you the liberty of life and the joy of salvation. I proclaim the new and living way, the deliverance from evil and the breaking of the bondage of sin. I have come that you might have life, and have it eternally. You seek to be rid of me and my disquieting teachings. If you could only realize that I am to be with you only a little while! In just a short time I go to Him who sent me into this world. And then will many of you diligently seek me, but you shall not discover my presence, for where

I am about to go you cannot come. But all who truly seek to find me shall some-time attain the life that leads to my Father's presence."

Some of the scoffers said among themselves, "Where will this man go that we cannot find him? Will he go to live among the Greeks? Will he destroy himself? What can he mean when he declares that soon he will depart from us, and that we cannot go where he goes?"

Eber and his assistants refused to arrest Jesus; they returned to their meeting place without him. When, therefore, the chief priests and the Pharisees upbraided Eber and his assistants because they had not brought Jesus with them, Eber only replied, "We feared to arrest him in the midst of the multitude because many believe in him. Besides, we never heard a man speak like this man. There is something out of the ordinary about this teacher. You would all do well to go over to hear him."

And when the chief rulers heard these words, they were astonished and spoke tauntingly to Eber, "Are you also led astray? Are you about to believe in this deceiver? Have you heard that any of our learned men or any of the rulers have believed in him? Have any of the scribes or the Pharisees been deceived by his clever teachings? How does it come that you are influenced by the behavior of this ignorant multitude who know not the law or the prophets? Do you not know that such untaught people are accursed?"

And then answered Eber, "Even so, my masters, but this man speaks to the multitude words of mercy and hope. He cheers the downhearted, and his words were comforting even to our souls. What can there be wrong in these teachings even though he may not be the Messiah of the Scriptures? And even then does not our law require fairness? Do we condemn a man before we hear him?"

And the chief of the Sanhedrin was wroth with Eber and, turning upon him, said, "Have you gone mad? Are you by any chance also from Galilee? Search the Scriptures, and you will discover that out of Galilee arises no prophet, much less the Messiah."

The Sanhedrin disbanded in confusion, and Jesus withdrew to Bethany for the night.

It was during this visit to Jerusalem that Jesus dealt with a certain woman of evil repute who was brought into his presence by her accusers and his enemies. The distorted record you have of this episode would suggest that this woman had been brought before Jesus by the scribes and Pharisees, and that Jesus so dealt with them as to indicate that these religious leaders of the Jews might themselves have been guilty of immorality. Jesus well knew that, while these scribes and Pharisees were spiritually blind and intellectually prejudiced by their loyalty to tradition, they were to be numbered among the most thoroughly moral men of that day and generation.

What really happened was this: Early the third morning of the feast, as Jesus approached the temple, he was met by a group of the hired agents of the Sanhedrin who were dragging a woman along with them. As they came near, the spokesman said, "Master, this woman was taken in adultery - in the very act. Now, the law of Moses commands that we should stone such a woman. What do you say should be done with her?"

It was the plan of Jesus' enemies, if he upheld the law of Moses requiring that the self-confessed transgressor be stoned, to involve him in difficulty with the Roman rulers, who had denied the Jews the right to inflict the death penalty without the approval of a Roman tribunal. If he forbade stoning the woman, they would accuse him before the Sanhedrin of setting himself up above Moses and the Jewish law. If he remained silent, they would accuse him of cowardice. But the Master so managed the situation that the whole plot fell to pieces of its own sordid weight.

This woman, once comely, was the wife of an inferior citizen of Nazareth, a man who had been a troublemaker for Jesus throughout his youthful days. The man, having married this woman, did most shamefully force her to earn their living by making commerce of her body. He had come up to the feast at Jerusalem that his wife might thus prostitute her physical charms for financial gain. He had entered into a bargain with the hirelings of the Jewish rulers thus to betray his own wife in her commercialized vice. And so they came with the woman and her companion in transgression for the purpose of ensnaring Jesus into making some statement that could be used against him in case of his arrest.

Jesus, looking over the crowd, saw her husband standing behind the others. He knew what sort of man he was and perceived that he was a party to the despicable transaction. Jesus first walked around to near where this degenerate husband stood and wrote upon the sand a few words which caused him to depart in haste. Then he came back before the woman and wrote again upon the ground for the benefit of her would-be accusers; and when they read his words, they, too, went away, one by one. And when the Master had written in the sand the third time, the woman's companion in evil took his departure, so that, when the Master raised himself up from this writing, he beheld the woman standing alone before him. Jesus said, "Woman, where are your accusers? Did no man remain to stone you?"

And the woman, lifting up her eyes, answered, "No man, Lord."

And then said Jesus, "I know about you; neither do I condemn you. Go your way in peace." And this woman, Hildana, forsook her wicked husband and joined herself to the disciples of the kingdom.

The presence of people from all of the known world, from Spain to India, made the feast of tabernacles an ideal occasion for Jesus for the first time publicly to proclaim his full gospel in Jerusalem. At this feast the people lived much in the open air, in leafy booths. It was the feast of the harvest ingathering, and coming, as it did, in the cool of the autumn months, it was more generally attended by the Jews of the world than was the Passover at the end of the winter or Pentecost at the beginning of summer. The apostles at last beheld their Master making the bold announcement of his mission on earth before the entire world, as it were.

This was the feast of feasts, since any sacrifice not made at the other festivals could be made at this time. This was the occasion of the reception of the temple offerings; it was a combination of vacation pleasures with the solemn rites of religious worship. Here was a time of racial rejoicing, mingled with sacrifices, Levitical chants, and the solemn blasts of the silvery trumpets of the priests. At night the impressive spectacle of the temple and its pilgrim throngs was brilliantly illuminated by the great candelabras which burned brightly in the court of the women as well as by the glare of scores of torches standing about the temple courts. The entire city was gaily decorated except the Roman castle of Antonia, which looked down in grim contrast upon this festive and worshipful scene. And how the Jews did hate this ever-present reminder of the Roman yoke!

Seventy bullocks were sacrificed during the feast, the symbol of the seventy nations of heathendom. The ceremony of the outpouring of the water symbolized the outpouring of the divine spirit. This ceremony of the water followed the sunrise procession of the priests and Levites. The worshipers passed down the steps leading from the court of Israel to the court of the women while successive blasts were blown upon the silvery trumpets. And then the faithful marched on toward the beautiful gate, which opened upon the court of the gentiles. Here they turned about to face westward, to repeat their chants, and to continue their march for the symbolic water.

On the last day of the feast almost four hundred and fifty priests with a corresponding number of Levites officiated. At daybreak the pilgrims assembled from all parts of the city, each carrying in the right hand a sheaf of myrtle, willow, and palm branches, while in the left hand each one carried a branch of the paradise apple - the citron, or the "forbidden fruit." These pilgrims divided into three groups for this early morning ceremony. One band remained at the temple to attend the morning sacrifices; another group marched down below Jerusalem to near Maza to cut the willow branches for the adornment of the sacrificial altar, while the third group formed a procession to march from the temple behind the water priest, who, to the sound of the silvery trumpets, bore the golden pitcher which was to contain the symbolic water, out through Ophel to near Siloam, where was located the fountain gate. After the golden pitcher had been filled at the pool of Siloam, the procession marched back to the temple, entering by way of the water gate and going directly to the court of the priests, where the priest bearing the water pitcher was joined by the priest bearing the wine for the drink offering. These two priests then repaired to the silver funnels leading to the base of the altar and poured the contents of the pitchers therein. The execution of this rite of pouring the wine and the water was the signal for the assembled pilgrims to begin the chanting of the Psalms from 113 to 118 inclusive, in alternation with the Levites. And as they repeated these lines, they would wave their sheaves at the altar. Then followed the sacrifices for the day, associated with the repeating of the Psalm for the day, the Psalm for the last day of the feast being the eighty-second, beginning with the fifth verse.

On the evening of the next to the last day of the feast, when the scene was brilliantly illuminated by the lights of the candelabras and the torches, Jesus stood up in the midst of the assembled throng and said, "I am the light of the world. He who follows me shall not walk in darkness but shall have the light of life. Presuming to place me on trial and assuming to sit as my judges, you declare that, if I bear witness of myself, my witness cannot be true. But never can the creature sit in judgment on the Creator. Even if I do bear witness about myself, my witness is everlastingly true, for I know whence I came, who I am, and whither I go. You who would kill the Son of Man know not whence I came, who I am, or whither I go. You only judge by the appearances of the flesh; you do not perceive the realities of the spirit. I judge no man, not even my archenemy. But if I should choose to judge, my judgment would be true and righteous, for I would judge not alone but in association with my Father, who sent me into the world, and who is the source of all true judgment. You even allow that the witness of two reliable persons may be accepted - well, then, I bear witness of these truths; so also does my Father in heaven. And when I told you this yesterday, in your darkness you asked me, 'Where is your Father?' Truly, you know neither me nor my Father, for if you had known me, you would also have known the Father.

"I have already told you that I am going away, and that you will seek me and not find me, for where I am going you cannot come. You who would reject this light are from beneath; I am from above. You who prefer to sit in darkness are of this world; I am not of this world, and I live in the eternal light of the Father of lights. You all have had abundant opportunity to learn who I am, but you shall have still other evidence confirming the identity of the Son of Man. I am the light of life, and every one who deliberately and with understanding rejects this saving light shall die in his sins. Much I have to tell you, but you are unable to receive my words. However, He who sent me is true and faithful; my Father loves even His erring children. And all that my Father has spoken I also proclaim to the world.

"When the Son of Man is lifted up, then shall you all know that I am he, and that I have done nothing of myself but only as the Father has taught me. I speak these words to you and to your children. And He who sent me is even now with me; He has not left me alone, for I do always that which is pleasing in His sight."

As Jesus thus taught the pilgrims in the temple courts, many believed. And no man dared to lay hands upon him.

✫ ✫ ✫

On the last day, the great day of the feast, as the procession from the pool of Siloam passed through the temple courts, and just after the water and the wine had been poured down upon the altar by the priests, Jesus, standing among the pilgrims, said, "If any man thirst, let him come to me and drink. From the Father above I bring to this world the water of life. He who believes me shall be filled with the spirit which this water represents, for even the Scriptures have said, 'Out of him shall flow rivers of living waters.' When the Son of Man has finished his work on earth, there shall be poured out upon all flesh the living Spirit of Truth. Those who receive this spirit shall never know spiritual thirst."

Jesus did not interrupt the service to speak these words. He addressed the worshipers immediately after the chanting of the Hallel, the responsive reading of the Psalms accompanied by waving of the branches before the altar. Just here was a pause while the sacrifices were being prepared, and it was at this time that the pilgrims heard the fascinating voice of the Master declare that he was the giver of living water to every spirit-thirsting soul.

At the conclusion of this early morning service Jesus continued to teach the multitude. "Have you not read in the Scripture: 'Behold, as the waters are poured out upon the dry ground and spread over the parched soil, so will I give the spirit of holiness to be poured out upon your children for a blessing even to your children's children'? Why will you thirst for the ministry of the spirit while you seek to water your souls with the traditions of men, poured from the broken pitchers of ceremonial service? That which you see going on about this temple is the way in which your fathers sought to symbolize the bestowal of the divine spirit upon the children of faith, and you have done well to perpetuate these symbols, even down to this day. But now has come to this generation the revelation of the Father of spirits through the bestowal of His Son, and all of this will certainly be followed by the bestowal of the spirit of the Father and the Son upon the children of men. To every one who has faith shall this bestowal of the spirit become the true teacher of the way which leads to life everlasting, to the true waters of life in the kingdom of heaven on earth and in the Father's Paradise over there."

And Jesus continued to answer the questions of both the multitude and the Pharisees. Some thought he was a prophet; some believed him to be the Messiah; others said he could not be the Christ, seeing that he came from Galilee, and that the Messiah must restore David's throne. Still they dared not arrest him.

On the afternoon of the last day of the feast and after the apostles had failed in their efforts to persuade him to flee from Jerusalem, Jesus again went into the temple to teach. Finding a large company of believers assembled in Solomon's Porch, he spoke to them, saying, "If my words abide in you and you are minded to do the will of my Father, then are you truly my disciples. You shall know the truth, and the truth shall make you free. I know how you will answer me: We are the children of Abraham, and we are in bondage to none; how then shall we be made free? Even so, I do not speak of outward subjection to another's rule; I refer to the liberties of the soul. Verily, verily, I say to you, everyone who commits sin is the bondservant of sin. And you know that the bondservant is not likely to abide forever in the master's house. You also know that the son does remain in his father's house. If, therefore, the Son shall make you free, shall make you sons, you shall be free indeed.

"I know that you are Abraham's seed, yet your leaders seek to kill me because my word has not been allowed to have its transforming influence in their hearts. Their souls are sealed by prejudice and blinded by the pride of revenge. I declare to you the truth which the eternal Father shows me, while these deluded teachers seek to do the things which they have learned only from their temporal fathers. And when you reply that Abraham is your father, then do I tell you that, if you were the children of Abraham, you would do the works of Abraham. Some of you believe my teaching, but others seek to destroy me because I have told you the truth which I received from God. But Abraham did not so treat the truth of God. I perceive that some among you are determined to do the works of the evil one. If God were your Father, you would know me and love the truth which I reveal. Will you not see that I come forth from the Father, that I am sent by God, that I am not doing this work of myself? Why do you not understand my words? Is it because you have chosen to become the children of evil? If you are the children of darkness, you will hardly walk in the light of the truth which I reveal. The children of evil follow only in the ways of their father, who was a deceiver and stood not for the truth because there came to be no truth in him. But now comes the Son of Man speaking and living the truth, and many of you refuse to believe.

"Which of you convicts me of sin? If I, then, proclaim and live the truth shown me by the Father, why do you not believe? He who is of God hears gladly the words of God; for this cause many of you hear not my words, because you are not of God. Your teachers have even presumed to say that I do my works by the power of the prince of devils. One nearby has just said that I have a devil, that I am a child of the devil. But all of you who deal honestly with your own souls know full well that I am not a devil. You know that I honor the Father even while you would dishonor me. I seek not my own glory, only the glory of my Paradise Father. And I do not judge you, for there is one who judges for me.

"Verily, verily, I say to you who believe the gospel that, if a man will keep this word of truth alive in his heart, he shall never taste death. And now just at my side a scribe says this statement proves that I have a devil, seeing that Abraham is dead, also the prophets. And he asks, 'Are you so much greater than Abraham and the prophets that you dare to stand here and say that whoso keeps your word shall not taste death? Who do you claim to be that you dare to utter such blasphemies?' And I say to all such that, if I glorify myself, my glory is as nothing. But it is the Father who shall glorify me, even the same Father whom you call God. But you have failed to know this your God and my Father, and I have come to bring you together; to show you how to become truly the sons and daughters of God. Though you know not the Father, I truly know Him. Even Abraham rejoiced to see my day, and by faith he saw it and was glad."

When the unbelieving Jews and the agents of the Sanhedrin who had gathered about by this time heard these words, they raised a tumult, shouting, "You are not fifty years of age, and yet you talk about seeing Abraham; you are a child of the devil!"

Jesus was unable to continue the discourse. He only said as he departed, "Verily, verily, I say to you, before Abraham was, I am."

Many of the unbelievers rushed forth for stones to cast at him, and the agents of the Sanhedrin sought to place him under arrest, but the Master quickly made his way through the temple corridors and escaped to a secret meeting place near Bethany where Martha, Mary, and Lazarus awaited him.

It had been arranged that Jesus should lodge with Lazarus and his sisters at a friend's house, while the apostles were scattered here and there in small groups, these precautions being taken because the Jewish authorities were again becoming bold with their plans to arrest him.

For years it had been the custom for these three to drop everything and listen to Jesus' teaching whenever he chanced to visit them. With the loss of their parents, Martha had assumed the responsibilities of the home life, and so on this occasion, while Lazarus and Mary sat at Jesus' feet drinking in his refreshing teaching, Martha made ready to serve the evening meal. It should be explained that Martha was unnecessarily distracted by numerous needless tasks, and that she was cumbered by many trivial cares; that was her disposition.

As Martha busied herself with all these supposed duties, she was perturbed because Mary did nothing to help. Therefore she went to Jesus and said, "Master, do you not care that my sister has left me alone to do all of the serving? Will you not bid her to come and help me?"

Jesus answered, "Martha, Martha, why are you always anxious about so many things and troubled by so many trifles? Only one thing is really worthwhile, and since Mary has chosen this good and needful part, I shall not take it away from her. But when will both of you learn to live as I have taught you: both serving in cooperation and both refreshing your souls in unison? Can you not learn that there is a time for everything - that the lesser matters of life should give way before the greater things of the heavenly kingdom?"

Throughout the week that followed the feast of tabernacles, scores of believers forgathered at Bethany and received instruction from the twelve apostles. The Sanhedrin made no effort to molest these gatherings since Jesus was not present; he was throughout this time working with Abner and his associates in Bethlehem. The day following the close of the feast, Jesus had departed for Bethany, and he did not again teach in the temple during this visit to Jerusalem.

At this time, Abner was making his headquarters at Bethlehem, and from that center many workers had been sent to the cities of Judea and southern Samaria and even to Alexandria. Within a few days of his arrival, Jesus and Abner completed the arrangements for the consolidation of the work of the two groups of apostles.

Throughout his visit to the feast of tabernacles, Jesus had divided his time about equally between Bethany and Bethlehem. At Bethany he spent considerable time with his apostles; at Bethlehem he gave much instruction to Abner and the other former apostles of John. And it was this intimate contact that finally led them to believe in him. These former apostles of John the Baptist were influenced by the courage he displayed in his public teaching in Jerusalem as well as by the sympathetic understanding they experienced in his private teaching at Bethlehem. These influences finally and fully won over each of Abner's associates to a wholehearted acceptance of the kingdom and all that such a step implied.

Before leaving Bethlehem for the last time, the Master made arrangements for them all to join him in the united effort which was to precede the ending of his earth career in the flesh. It was agreed that Abner and his associates were to join Jesus and the twelve in the near future at Magadan Park.

In accordance with this understanding, early in November Abner and his eleven fellows cast their lot with Jesus and the twelve and labored with them as one organization right on down to the crucifixion.

In the latter part of October Jesus and the twelve withdrew from the immediate vicinity of Jerusalem. On Sunday, October 30, Jesus and his associates left the city of Ephraim, where he had been resting in seclusion for a few days, and, going by the west Jordan highway directly to Magadan Park, arrived late on the afternoon of Wednesday, November 2.

The apostles were greatly relieved to have the Master back on friendly soil; no more did they urge him to go up to Jerusalem to proclaim the gospel of the kingdom.

# ORDINATION OF THE SEVENTY AT MAGADAN

A FEW days after the return of Jesus and the twelve to Magadan from Jerusalem, Abner and a group of some fifty disciples arrived from Bethlehem. At this time there were also assembled at Magadan Camp the evangelistic corps, the women's corps, and about one hundred and fifty other true and tried disciples from all parts of Palestine. After devoting a few days to visiting and the reorganization of the camp, Jesus and the twelve began a course of intensive training for this special group of believers, and from this well-trained and experienced aggregation of disciples the Master subsequently chose the seventy teachers and sent them forth to proclaim the gospel of the kingdom. This regular instruction began on Friday, November 4, and continued until Sabbath, November 19.

Jesus gave a talk to this company each morning. Peter taught methods of public preaching; Nathaniel instructed them in the art of teaching; Thomas explained how to answer questions; while Matthew directed the organization of their group finances. The other apostles also participated in this training in accordance with their special experience and natural talents.

The seventy were ordained by Jesus on Sabbath afternoon, November 19, at the Magadan Camp, and Abner was placed at the head of these gospel preachers and teachers. This corps of seventy consisted of Abner and ten of the former apostles of John, fifty-one of the earlier evangelists, and eight other disciples who had distinguished themselves in the service of the kingdom.

About two o'clock on this Sabbath afternoon, between showers of rain, a company of believers, augmented by the arrival of David and the majority of his messenger corps and numbering over four hundred, assembled on the shore of the lake of Galilee to witness the ordination of the seventy.

Before Jesus laid his hands upon the heads of the seventy to set them apart as gospel messengers, addressing them, he said, "The harvest is indeed plenteous, but the laborers are few; therefore I exhort all of you to pray that the Lord of the harvest will send still other laborers into his harvest. I am about to set you apart as messengers of the kingdom; I am about to send you to Jew and gentile as lambs among wolves. As you go your ways, two and two, I instruct you to carry neither purse nor extra clothing, for you go forth on this first mission for only a short season. Salute no man by the way, attend only to your work. Whenever you go to stay at a home, first say: Peace be to this household. If those who love peace live therein, you shall abide there; if not, then shall you depart. And having selected this home, remain there for your stay in that city, eating and drinking whatever is set before you. And you do this because the laborer is worthy of his sustenance. Move not from house to house because a better lodging may be offered. Remember, as you go forth proclaiming peace on earth and good will among men, you must contend with bitter and self-deceived enemies; therefore be as wise as serpents while you are also as harmless as doves.

"And everywhere you go, preach, saying, 'The kingdom of heaven is at hand,' and minister to all who may be sick in either mind or body. Freely you have received of the good things of the kingdom; freely give. If the people of any city receive you, they shall find an abundant entrance into the Father's kingdom; but if the people of any city refuse to receive this gospel, still shall you proclaim your message as you depart from that unbelieving community, saying, even as you leave, to those who reject your teaching: 'Notwithstanding you reject the truth, it remains that the kingdom of God has come near you.' He who hears you hears me. And he who hears me hears Him who sent me. He who rejects your gospel message rejects me. And he who rejects me rejects Him who sent me."

When Jesus had thus spoken to the seventy, he began with Abner and, as they knelt in a circle about him, laid his hands upon the head of every one of the seventy.

Early the next morning Abner sent the seventy messengers into all the cities of Galilee, Samaria, and Judea. And these thirty-five couples went forth preaching and teaching for about six weeks, all of them returning to the new camp near Pella, in Perea, on Friday, December 30.

Over fifty disciples who sought ordination and appointment to membership in the seventy were rejected by the committee appointed by Jesus to select these candidates. This committee consisted of Andrew, Abner, and the acting head of the evangelistic corps. In all cases where this committee of three were not unanimous in agreement, they brought the candidate to Jesus, and while the Master never rejected a single person who craved ordination as a gospel messenger, there were more than a dozen who, when they had talked with Jesus, no more desired to become gospel messengers.

One earnest disciple came to Jesus, saying, "Master, I would be one of your new apostles, but my father is very old and near death; could I be permitted to return home to bury him?"

To this man Jesus said, "My son, the foxes have holes, and the birds of heaven have nests, but the Son of Man has nowhere to lay his head. You are a faithful disciple, and you can remain such while you return home to minister to your loved ones, but not so with my gospel messengers. They have forsaken all to follow me and proclaim the kingdom. If you would be an ordained teacher, you must let others bury the dead while you go forth to publish the good news." And this man went away in great disappointment.

Another disciple came to the Master and said, "I would become an ordained messenger, but I would like to go to my home for a short while to comfort my family."

And Jesus replied, "If you would be ordained, you must be willing to forsake all. The gospel messengers cannot have divided affections. No man, having put his hand to the plough, if he turns back, is worthy to become a messenger of the kingdom."

Then Andrew brought to Jesus a certain rich young man who was a devout believer, and who desired to receive ordination. This young man, Matadormus, was a member of the Jerusalem Sanhedrin; he had heard Jesus teach and had been subsequently instructed in the gospel of the kingdom by Peter and the other apostles. Jesus talked with Matadormus concerning the requirements of ordination and requested that he defer decision until after he had thought more fully about the matter. Early the next morning, as Jesus was going for a walk, this young man accosted him and said, "Master, I would know from you the assurances of eternal life. Seeing that I have observed all the commandments from my youth, I would like to know what more I must do to gain eternal life?"

In answer to this question Jesus said, "If you keep all the commandments - do not commit adultery, do not kill, do not steal, do not bear false witness, do not defraud, honor your parents - you do well, but salvation is the reward of faith, not merely of works. Do you believe this gospel of the kingdom?"

And Matadormus answered, "Yes, Master, I do believe everything you and your apostles have taught me."

And Jesus said, "Then are you indeed my disciple and a child of the kingdom."

Then said the young man, "But, Master, I am not content to be your disciple; I would be one of your new messengers."

When Jesus heard this, he looked down upon him with a great love and said, "I will have you to be one of my messengers if you are willing to pay the price, if you will supply the one thing which you lack."

Matadormus replied, "Master, I will do anything if I may be allowed to follow you."

Jesus, kissing the kneeling young man on the forehead, said, "If you would be my messenger, go and sell all that you have and, when you have bestowed the proceeds upon the poor or upon your brethren, come and follow me, and you shall have treasure in the kingdom of heaven."

When Matadormus heard this, his countenance fell. He arose and went away sorrowful, for he had great possessions. This wealthy young Pharisee had been raised to believe that wealth was the token of God's favor. Jesus knew that he was not free from the love of himself and his riches. The Master wanted to deliver him from the *love* of wealth, not necessarily from the wealth. While the disciples of Jesus did not part with all their worldly goods, the apostles and the seventy did. Matadormus desired to be one of the seventy new messengers, and that was the reason for Jesus' requiring him to part with all of his temporal possessions.

Almost every human being has some one thing which is held on to as a pet evil, and which the entrance into the kingdom of heaven requires as a part of the price of admission. If Matadormus had parted with his wealth, it probably would have been put right back into his hands for administration as treasurer of the seventy. For later on, after the establishment of the church at Jerusalem, he did obey the Master's injunction, although it was then too late to enjoy membership in the seventy, and he became the treasurer of the Jerusalem church, of which James the Lord's brother in the flesh was the head.

Thus always it was and forever will be: Earth-children must arrive at their own decisions. There is a certain range of the freedom of choice which mortals may exercise. The forces of the spiritual world will not coerce men and women; they allow them to go the way of their own choosing.

Jesus foresaw that Matadormus, with his riches, could not possibly become an ordained associate of men who had forsaken all for the gospel; at the same time, he saw that, without his riches, he would become the ultimate leader of all of them. But, like Jesus' own brethren, he never became great in the kingdom because he deprived himself of that intimate and personal association with the Master which might have been his experience had he been willing to do at this time the very thing which Jesus asked, and which, several years subsequently, he actually did.

Riches have nothing directly to do with entrance into the kingdom of heaven, but the *love of wealth does.* The spiritual loyalties of the kingdom are incompatible with servility to materialistic mammon. Men and women may not share their supreme loyalty to a spiritual ideal with a material devotion.

Jesus never taught that it was wrong to have wealth. He required only the twelve and the seventy to dedicate all of their worldly possessions to the common cause. Even then, he provided for the profitable liquidation of their property, as in the case of the Apostle Matthew. Jesus many times advised his well-to-do disciples as he had taught the rich man when in Rome. The Master regarded the wise investment of excess earnings as a legitimate form of insurance against future and unavoidable adversity. When the apostolic treasury was overflowing, Judas put funds on deposit to be used subsequently when they might suffer greatly from a diminution of income. This Judas did after consultation with Andrew. Jesus never personally had anything to do with the apostolic finances except in the disbursement of alms. But there was one economic abuse that he many times condemned, and that was the unfair exploitation of the weak, unlearned, and less fortunate of men by their strong, keen, and more intelligent fellows. Jesus declared that such inhuman treatment of men, women, and children was incompatible with the ideals of the brotherhood of the kingdom of heaven.

By the time Jesus had finished talking with Matadormus, Peter and a number of the apostles had gathered about him, and as the rich young man was departing, Jesus turned around to face the apostles and said, "You see how difficult it is for those who have riches to enter fully into the kingdom of God! Spiritual worship cannot be shared with material devotions; no man can serve two masters. You have a saying that it is 'easier for a camel to go through the eye of a needle than for the heathen to inherit eternal life.' And I declare that it is as easy for this camel to go through the needle's eye as for these self-satisfied rich ones to enter the kingdom of heaven."

When Peter and the apostles heard these words, they were astonished exceedingly, so much so that Peter said, "Who then, Lord, can be saved? Shall all who have riches be kept out of the kingdom?"

And Jesus replied, "No, Peter, but all who put their trust in riches shall hardly enter into the spiritual life that leads to eternal progress. But even then, much which is impossible to man is not beyond the reach of the Father in heaven; rather should we recognize that with God all things are possible."

As they went off by themselves, Jesus was grieved that Matadormus did not remain with them, for he greatly loved him. And when they had walked down by the lake, they sat there beside the water, and Peter, speaking for the twelve (who were all present by this time), said, "We are troubled by your words to the rich young man. Shall we require those who would follow you to give up all their worldly goods?"

And Jesus said, "No, Peter, only those who would become apostles, and who desire to live with me as you do and as one family. But the Father requires that the affections of His children be pure and undivided. Whatever thing or person comes between you and the love of the truths of the kingdom, must be surrendered. If one's wealth does not invade the precincts of the soul, it is of no consequence in the spiritual life of those who would enter the kingdom."

And then said Peter, "But, Master, we have left everything to follow you, what then shall we have?"

And Jesus spoke to all of the twelve, "Verily, verily, I say to you, there is no man who has left wealth, home, wife, brethren, parents, or children for my sake and for the sake of the kingdom of heaven who shall not receive manifold more in this world, perhaps with some persecutions, and in the world to come eternal life. But many who are first shall be last, while the last shall often be first. The Father deals with His creatures in accordance with their needs and in obedience to His just laws of merciful and loving consideration for the welfare of a universe.

"The kingdom of heaven is like a householder who was a large employer of men, and who went out early in the morning to hire laborers to work in his vineyard. When he had agreed with the laborers to pay them a denarius a day, he sent them into the vineyard. Then he went out about nine o'clock, and seeing others standing in the market place idle, he said to them, 'Go you also to work in my vineyard, and whatsoever is right I will pay you.' And they went at once to work. Again he went out about twelve and about three and did likewise. And going to the market place about five in the afternoon, he found still others standing idle, and he inquired of them, 'Why do you stand here idle all the day?' And the men answered, 'Because nobody has hired us.' Then said the householder, 'Go you also to work in my vineyard, and whatever is right I will pay you.'

"When evening came, this owner of the vineyard said to his steward, 'Call the laborers and pay them their wages, beginning with the last hired and ending with the first.' When those who were hired about five o'clock came, they received a denarius each, and so it was with each of the other laborers. When the men who were hired at the beginning of the day saw how the later comers were paid, they expected to receive more than the amount agreed upon. But like the others every man received only a denarius. And when each had received his pay, they complained to the householder, saying, 'These men who were hired last worked only one hour, and yet you have paid them the same as us who have borne the burden of the day in the scorching sun.'

"Then answered the householder, 'My friends, I do you no wrong. Did not each of you agree to work for a denarius a day? Take now that which is yours and go your way, for it is my desire to give to those who came last as much as I have given to you. Is it not lawful for me to do what I will with my own? Or do you begrudge my generosity because I desire to be good and to show mercy?'"

★ ★ ★

It was a stirring time about the Magadan Camp the day the seventy went forth on their first mission. Early that morning, in his last talk with the seventy, Jesus placed emphasis on the following:

1. The gospel of the kingdom must be proclaimed to all the world, to gentile as well as to Jew.

2. While ministering to the sick, refrain from teaching the expectation of miracles.

3. Proclaim a spiritual brotherhood of the sons and daughters of God, not an outward kingdom of worldly power and material glory.

4. Avoid loss of time through overmuch social visiting and other trivialities which might detract from wholehearted devotion to preaching the gospel.

5. If the first house to be selected for a headquarters proves to be a worthy home, abide there throughout the sojourn in that city.

6. Make clear to all faithful believers that the time for an open break with the religious leaders of the Jews at Jerusalem has now come.

7. Teach that man's whole duty is summed up in this one commandment: Love the Lord your God with all your mind and soul and your neighbor as yourself. (This they were to teach as man's whole duty in place of the 613 rules of living expounded by the Pharisees.)

When Jesus had talked thus to the seventy in the presence of all the apostles and disciples, Simon Peter took them off by themselves and preached to them their ordination sermon, which was an elaboration of the Master's charge given at the time he laid his hands upon them and set them apart as messengers of the kingdom. Peter exhorted the seventy to cherish in their experience the following virtues:

1. *Consecrated devotion.* To pray always for more laborers to be sent forth into the gospel harvest. He explained that, when one so prays, he will the more likely say, "Here am I; send me." He admonished them to neglect not their daily worship.

2. *True courage.* He warned them that they would encounter hostility and be certain to meet with persecution. Peter told them their mission was no undertaking for cowards and advised those who were afraid to step out before they started. But none withdrew.

3. *Faith and trust.* They must go forth on this short mission wholly unprovided for; they must trust the Father for food and shelter and all other things needful.

4. *Zeal and initiative.* They must be possessed with zeal and intelligent enthusiasm; they must attend strictly to their Master's business. Oriental salutation was a lengthy and elaborate ceremony; therefore had they

been instructed to "salute no man by the way," which was a common method of exhorting one to go about his business without the waste of time. It had nothing to do with the matter of friendly greeting.

5. *Kindness and courtesy.* The Master had instructed them to avoid unnecessary waste of time in social ceremonies, but he enjoined courtesy toward all with whom they should come in contact. They were to show every kindness to those who might entertain them in their homes. They were strictly warned against leaving a modest home to be entertained in a more comfortable or influential one.

6. *Ministry to the sick.* The seventy were charged by Peter to search out the sick in mind and body and to do everything in their power to bring about the alleviation or cure of their maladies.

And when they had been thus charged and instructed, they started out, two and two, on their mission in Galilee, Samaria, and Judea.

Although the Jews had a peculiar regard for the number seventy, sometimes considering the nations of heathendom as being seventy in number, and although these seventy messengers were to go with the gospel to all peoples, still as far as we can discern, it was only coincidental that this group happened to number just seventy. Certain it was that Jesus would have accepted no less than half a dozen others, but they were unwilling to pay the price of forsaking wealth and families.

Jesus and the twelve now prepared to establish their last headquarters in Perea, near Pella, where the Master was baptized in the Jordan. The last ten days of November were spent in council at Magadan, and on Tuesday, December 6, the entire company of almost three hundred started out at daybreak with all their effects to lodge that night near Pella by the river. This was the same site, by the spring, that John the Baptist had occupied with his camp several years before.

After the breaking up of the Magadan Camp, David Zebedee returned to Bethsaida and began immediately to curtail the messenger service. The kingdom was taking on a new phase. Daily, pilgrims arrived from all parts of Palestine and even from remote regions of the Roman Empire. Believers occasionally came from Mesopotamia and from the lands east of the Tigris. Accordingly, on Sunday, December 18, David, with the help of his messenger corps, loaded on to the pack animals the camp equipage, then stored in his father's house, with which he had formerly conducted the camp of Bethsaida by the lake. Bidding farewell to Bethsaida for the time being, he proceeded down the lake shore and along the Jordan to a point about one-half mile north of the apostolic camp; and in less than a week he was prepared to offer hospitality to almost fifteen hundred pilgrim visitors. The apostolic camp could accommodate about five hundred. This was the rainy season in Palestine, and these accommodations were required to take care of the ever-increasing number of inquirers, mostly earnest, who came into Perea to see Jesus and to hear his teaching.

David did all this on his own initiative, though he had taken counsel with Philip and Matthew at Magadan. He employed the larger part of his former messenger corps as his helpers in conducting this camp; he now used less than twenty men on regular messenger duty. Near the end of December and before the return of the seventy, almost eight hundred visitors were gathered about the Master, and they found lodging in David's camp.

On Friday, December 30, while Jesus was away in the nearby hills with Peter, James, and John, the seventy messengers were arriving by couples, accompanied by numerous believers, at the Pella headquarters. All seventy were assembled at the teaching site about five o'clock when Jesus returned to the camp. The evening meal was delayed for more than an hour while these enthusiasts for the gospel of the kingdom related their experiences. David's messengers had brought much of this news to the apostles during previous weeks, but it was truly inspiring to hear these newly ordained teachers of the gospel personally tell how their message had been received by hungry Jews and gentiles. At last Jesus was able to see men going out to spread the good news without his personal presence. The Master now knew that he could leave this world without seriously hindering the progress of the kingdom.

When the seventy related how "even the devils were subject" to them, they referred to the wonderful cures they had wrought in the cases of victims of nervous disorders. Nevertheless, there had been a few cases of real spirit possession relieved by these ministers, and referring to these, Jesus said, "It is not strange that these disobedient minor spirits should be subject to you, seeing that I beheld Satan falling as lightning from heaven. But rejoice not so much over this, for I declare to you that, as soon as I return to my Father, we will send forth our spirits into the very minds of men so that no more can these few lost spirits enter the minds of unfortunate mortals. I rejoice with you that you have power with men, but be not lifted up because of this experience but the rather rejoice that your names are written on the rolls of heaven, and that you are thus to go forward in an endless career of spiritual conquest."

And it was at this time, just before partaking of the evening meal, that Jesus experienced one of those rare moments of emotional ecstasy which his followers had occasionally witnessed. He said, "I thank you, my Father, Lord of heaven and earth, that, while this wonderful gospel was hidden from the wise and self-righteous, the spirit has revealed these spiritual glories to these children of the kingdom. Yes, my Father, it must have been pleasing in your sight to do this, and I rejoice to know that the good news will spread to all the world even after I shall have returned to you and the work which you have given me to perform. I am mightily moved as I realize you are about to deliver all authority into my hands, that only you really know who I am, and that only I really know you, and those to whom I have revealed you. And when I have finished this revelation to my brethren in the flesh, I will continue the revelation to your creatures on high."

When Jesus had thus spoken to the Father, he turned aside to speak to his apostles and ministers. "Blessed are the eyes which see and the ears which hear these things. Let me say to you that many prophets and many of the great men of the past ages have desired to behold what you now see, but it was not granted them. And many generations of the children of light yet to come will, when they hear of these things, envy you who have heard and seen them."

Then, speaking to all the disciples, he said, "You have heard how many cities and villages have received the good news of the kingdom, and how my ministers and teachers have been received by both the Jew and the gentile. And blessed indeed are these communities which have elected to believe the gospel of the kingdom. But woe upon the light-rejecting inhabitants of Chorazin, Bethsaida-Julias, and Capernaum, the cities which did not well receive these messengers. I declare that, if the mighty works done in these places had been done in Tyre and Sidon, the people of these so-called heathen cities would have long since repented in sackcloth and ashes. It shall indeed be more tolerable for Tyre and Sidon in the day of judgment."

The next day being the Sabbath, Jesus went apart with the seventy and said, "I did indeed rejoice with you when you came back bearing the good tidings of the reception of the gospel of the kingdom by so many people scattered throughout Galilee, Samaria, and Judea. But why were you so surprisingly elated? Did you not expect that your message would manifest power in its delivery? Did you go forth with so little faith in this gospel that you come back in surprise at its effectiveness? And now, while I would not quench your spirit of rejoicing, I would sternly warn you against the subtleties of pride, spiritual pride. If you could understand the downfall of Lucifer, the iniquitous one, you would solemnly shun all forms of spiritual pride.

"You have entered upon this great work of teaching mortals that they are children of God. I have shown you the way; go forth to do your duty and be not weary in well doing. To you and to all who shall follow in your steps down through the ages, let me say, I always stand near, and my invitation-call is, and ever shall be; Come to me all you who labor and are heavy laden, and I will give you rest. Take my yoke upon you and learn of me, for I am true and loyal, and you shall find spiritual rest for your souls."

And they found the Master's words to be true when they put his promises to the test. And since that day countless thousands also have tested and proved the surety of these same promises.

✡ ✡ ✡

The next few days were busy times in the Pella camp; preparations for the Perean mission were being completed. Jesus and his associates were about to enter upon their last mission, the three month tour of all Perea, which terminated only upon the Master's entering Jerusalem for his final labors on earth. Throughout this period the headquarters of Jesus and the twelve apostles was maintained here at the Pella camp.

It was no longer necessary for Jesus to go abroad to teach the people. They now came to him in increasing numbers each week and from all parts, not only from Palestine but from the whole Roman world and from the Near East. Although the Master participated with the seventy in the tour of Perea, he spent much of his time at the Pella camp, teaching the multitude and instructing the twelve. Throughout this three months' period at least ten of the apostles remained with Jesus.

The women's corps also prepared to go out, two and two, with the seventy to labor in the larger cities of Perea. This original group of twelve women had recently trained a larger corps of fifty women in the work of home visitation and in the art of ministering to the sick and the afflicted. Perpetua, Simon Peter's wife, became a member of this new division of the women's corps and was intrusted with the leadership of the enlarged women's work under Abner. After Pentecost she remained with her illustrious husband, accompanying him on all of his missionary tours; and on the day Peter was crucified in Rome, she was fed to the wild beasts in the arena. This new women's corps also had as members the wives of Philip and Matthew and the mother of James and John.

The work of the kingdom now prepared to enter upon its terminal phase under the personal leadership of Jesus. And this present phase was one of spiritual depth in contrast with the miracle-minded and wonder-seeking multitudes who followed after the Master during the former days of popularity in Galilee. However, there were still any number of his followers who were material-minded, and who failed to grasp the truth that the kingdom of heaven is the spiritual brotherhood of man founded on the eternal fact of the universal fatherhood of God.

## At the Feast of Dedication

A
S THE camp at Pella was being established, Jesus, taking with him Nathaniel and Thomas, secretly went up to Jerusalem to attend the feast of the dedication. Not until they passed over the Jordan at the Bethany ford, did the two apostles become aware that their Master was going on to Jerusalem. When they perceived that he really intended to be present at the feast of dedication, they remonstrated with him most earnestly, and using every sort of argument, they sought to dissuade him. But their efforts were of no avail; Jesus was determined to visit Jerusalem. To all their entreaties and to all their warnings emphasizing the folly and danger of placing himself in the hands of the Sanhedrin, he would reply only, "I would give these teachers in Israel another opportunity to see the light, before my hour comes."

On they went toward Jerusalem, the two apostles continuing to express their feelings of fear and to voice their doubts about the wisdom of such an apparently presumptuous undertaking. They reached Jericho about half past four and prepared to lodge there for the night.

That evening a considerable company gathered about Jesus and the two apostles to ask questions, many of which the apostles answered, while others the Master discussed. In the course of the evening a certain lawyer, seeking to entangle Jesus in a compromising disputation, said, "Teacher, I would like to ask you just what I should do to inherit eternal life?"

Jesus answered, "What is written in the law and the prophets; how do you read the Scriptures?"

The lawyer, knowing the teachings of both Jesus and the Pharisees, answered, "To love the Lord God with all your heart, soul, mind, and strength, and your neighbor as yourself."

Then said Jesus, "You have answered right; this, if you really do, will lead to life everlasting."

But the lawyer was not wholly sincere in asking this question, and desiring to justify himself while also hoping to embarrass Jesus, he ventured to ask still another question. Drawing a little closer to the Master, he said, "But, Teacher, I should like you to tell me just who is my neighbor?" The lawyer asked this question hoping to entrap Jesus into making some statement that would contravene the Jewish law which defined one's neighbor as "the children of one's people." The Jews looked upon all others as "gentile dogs." This lawyer was somewhat familiar with Jesus' teachings and therefore well knew that the Master thought differently; thus he hoped to lead him into saying something which could be construed as an attack upon the sacred law.

But Jesus discerned the lawyer's motive, and instead of falling into the trap, he proceeded to tell his hearers a story, a story which would be fully appreciated by any Jericho audience. Said Jesus, "A certain man was going down from Jerusalem to Jericho, and he fell into the hands of cruel brigands, who robbed him, stripped him and beat him, and departing, left him half dead. Very soon, by chance, a certain priest was going down that way, and when he came upon the wounded man, seeing his sorry plight, he passed by on the other side of the road. And in like manner a Levite also, when he came along and saw the man, passed by on the other side. Now, about this time, a certain Samaritan, as he journeyed down to Jericho, came across this wounded man; and when he saw how he had been robbed and beaten, he was moved with compassion, and going over to him, he bound up his wounds, pouring on oil and wine, and setting the man upon his own beast, brought him here to the inn and took care of him. And on the morrow he took out some money and, giving it to the host, said, 'Take good care of my friend, and if the expense is more, when I come back again, I will repay you.' Now let me ask you: Which of these three turned out to be the neighbor of him who fell among the robbers?"

And when the lawyer perceived that he had fallen into his own snare, he answered, "He who showed mercy on him."

And Jesus said, "Go and do likewise."

The lawyer answered, "He who showed mercy," that he might refrain from even speaking that odious word, Samaritan. The lawyer was forced to give the very answer to the question, "Who is my neighbor?" which Jesus wished given, and which, if Jesus had so stated, would have directly involved him in the charge of heresy. Jesus not only confounded the dishonest lawyer, but he told his hearers a story which was at the same time a beautiful admonition to all his followers and a stunning rebuke to all Jews regarding their attitude toward the Samaritans. And this story has continued to promote brotherly love among all who have subsequently believed the gospel of Jesus.

★ ★ ★

Jesus had attended the feast of tabernacles that he might proclaim the gospel to the pilgrims from all parts of the empire; he now went up to the feast of the dedication for just one purpose: to give the Sanhedrin and the Jewish leaders another chance to see the light. The principal event of these few days in Jerusalem occurred on Friday night at the home of Nicodemus. Here were gathered together some twenty-five Jewish leaders who believed Jesus' teaching. Among this group were fourteen men who were then, or had recently been, members of the Sanhedrin. This meeting was attended by Eber, Matadormus, and Joseph of Arimathea.

On this occasion Jesus' hearers were all learned men, and both they and his two apostles were amazed at the breadth and depth of the remarks which the Master made to this distinguished group. Not since the times when he had taught in Alexandria, Rome, and in the islands of the Mediterranean, had he exhibited such learning and shown such a grasp of the affairs of men, both secular and religious.

When this little meeting broke up, all went away mystified by the Master's personality, charmed by his gracious manner, and in love with the man. They had sought to advise Jesus concerning his desire to win the remaining members of the Sanhedrin. The Master listened attentively, but silently, to all their proposals. He well knew none of their plans would work. He surmised that the majority of the Jewish leaders never would accept the gospel of the kingdom; nevertheless, he gave them all this one more chance to choose. But when he went forth that night, with Nathaniel and Thomas, to lodge on the Mount of Olives, he had not yet decided upon the method he would pursue in bringing his work once more to the notice of the Sanhedrin.

That night Nathaniel and Thomas slept little; they were too much amazed by what they had heard at Nicodemus's house. They thought much over the final remark of Jesus regarding the offer of the former and present members of the Sanhedrin to go with him before the seventy. The Master said, "No, my brethren, it would be to no purpose. You would multiply the wrath to be visited upon your own heads, but you would not in the least mitigate the hatred which they bear me. Go, each of you, about the Father's business as the spirit leads you while I once more bring the kingdom to their notice in the manner which my Father may direct."

The next morning the three went over to Martha's home at Bethany for breakfast and then went immediately into Jerusalem. This Sabbath morning, as Jesus and his two apostles drew near the temple, they encountered a well-known beggar, a man who had been born blind, sitting at his usual place. Although these mendicants did not solicit or receive alms on the Sabbath day, they were permitted thus to sit in their usual places. Jesus paused and looked upon the beggar. As he gazed upon this man who had been born blind, the idea came into his mind as to how he would once more bring his mission on earth to the notice of the Sanhedrin and the other Jewish leaders and religious teachers.

As the Master stood there before the blind man, engrossed in deep thought, Nathaniel, pondering the possible cause of this man's blindness, asked, "Master, who did sin, this man or his parents, that he should be born blind?"

The rabbis taught that all such cases of blindness from birth were caused by sin. Not only were children conceived and born in sin, but a child could be born blind as a punishment for some specific sin committed by its father. They even taught that a child itself might sin before it was born into the world. They also taught that such defects could be caused by some sin or other indulgence of the mother while carrying the child.

There was, throughout all these regions, a lingering belief in reincarnation. The older Jewish teachers, together with Plato, Philo, and many of the Essenes, tolerated the theory that men may reap in one incarnation what they have sown in a previous existence; thus in one life they were believed to be expiating the sins committed in preceding lives. The Master found it difficult to make men believe that their souls had not had previous existences.

However, inconsistent as it seems, while such blindness was supposed to be the result of sin, the Jews held that it was meritorious in a high degree to give alms to these blind beggars. It was the custom of these blind men constantly to chant to the passers-by, "O tenderhearted, gain merit by assisting the blind."

Jesus entered into the discussion of this case with Nathaniel and Thomas, not only because he had already decided to use this blind man as the means of that day bringing his mission once more prominently to the notice of the Jewish leaders, but also because he always encouraged his apostles to seek for the true causes of all phenomena, natural or spiritual. He had often warned them to avoid the common tendency to assign spiritual causes to commonplace physical events.

Jesus decided to use this beggar in his plans for that day's work, but before doing anything for the blind man, Josiah by name, he proceeded to answer Nathaniel's question. Said the Master, "Neither did this man sin nor his parents that the works of God might be manifest in him. This blindness has come upon him in the natural course of events, but we must now do the works of Him who sent me, while it is still day, for the night will certainly come when it will be impossible to do the work we are about to perform. When I am in the world, I am the light of the world, but in only a little while I will not be with you."

When Jesus had spoken, he said to Nathaniel and Thomas, "Let us create the sight of this blind man on this Sabbath day that the scribes and Pharisees may have the full occasion which they seek for accusing the Son of Man." Then, stooping over, he spat on the ground and mixed the clay with the spittle, and speaking of all this so that the blind man could hear, he went up to Josiah and put the clay over his sightless eyes, saying, "Go, my son, wash away this clay in the pool of Siloam, and immediately you shall receive your sight." And when Josiah had so washed in the pool of Siloam, he returned to his friends and family, seeing.

Having always been a beggar, he knew nothing else; so, when the first excitement of the creation of his sight had passed, he returned to his usual place of alms-seeking. His friends, neighbors, and all who had known him aforetime, when they observed that he could see, all said, "Is this not Josiah the blind beggar?" Some said it was he, while others said, "No, it is one like him, but this man can see." But when they asked the man himself, he answered, "I am he."

When they began to inquire of him how he was able to see, he answered them, "A man called Jesus came by this way, and when talking about me with his friends, he made clay with spittle, anointed my eyes, and directed that I should go and wash in the pool of Siloam. I did what this man told me, and immediately I received my sight. And that is only a few hours ago. I do not yet know the meaning of much that I see."

And when the people who began to gather about him asked where they could find the strange man who had healed him, Josiah could answer only that he did not know.

This is one of the strangest of all the Master's miracles. This man did not ask for healing. He did not know that the Jesus who had directed him to wash at Siloam, and who had promised him vision, was the prophet of Galilee who had preached in Jerusalem during the feast of tabernacles. This man had little faith that he would receive his sight, but the people of that day had great faith in the efficacy of the spittle of a great or holy man; and from Jesus' conversation with Nathaniel and Thomas, Josiah had concluded that his would-be benefactor was a great man, a learned teacher or a holy prophet; accordingly he did as Jesus directed him.

Jesus made use of the clay and the spittle and directed him to wash in the symbolic pool of Siloam for three reasons:

1. This was not a miracle response to the individual's faith. This was a wonder that Jesus chose to perform for a purpose of his own, but which he so arranged that this man might derive lasting benefit therefrom.

2. As the blind man had not asked for healing, and since the faith he had was slight, these material acts were suggested for the purpose of encouraging him. He did believe in the superstition of the efficacy of spittle, and he knew the pool of Siloam was a semisacred place. But he would hardly have gone there had it not been necessary to wash away the clay of his anointing. There was just enough ceremony about the transaction to induce him to act.

3. But Jesus had a third reason for resorting to these material means in connection with this unique transaction: This was a miracle wrought purely in obedience to his own choosing, and thereby he desired to teach his followers of that day and all subsequent ages to refrain from

despising or neglecting material means in the healing of the sick. He wanted to teach them that they must cease to regard miracles as the only method of curing human diseases.

Jesus gave this man his sight by miraculous working, on this Sabbath morning and in Jerusalem near the temple, for the prime purpose of making this act an open challenge to the Sanhedrin and all the Jewish teachers and religious leaders. This was his way of proclaiming an open break with the Pharisees. He was always positive in everything he did. And it was for the purpose of bringing these matters before the Sanhedrin that Jesus brought his two apostles to this man early in the afternoon of this Sabbath day and deliberately provoked those discussions which compelled the Pharisees to take notice of the miracle.

By midafternoon the healing of Josiah had raised such a discussion around the temple that the leaders of the Sanhedrin decided to convene the council in its usual temple meeting place. And they did this in violation of a standing rule which forbade the meeting of the Sanhedrin on the Sabbath day. Jesus knew that Sabbath breaking would be one of the chief charges to be brought against him when the final test came, and he desired to be brought before the Sanhedrin for adjudication of the charge of having healed a blind man on the Sabbath day, when the very session of the high Jewish court sitting in judgment on him for this act of mercy would be deliberating on these matters on the Sabbath day and in direct violation of their own self-imposed laws.

But they did not call Jesus before them; they feared to. Instead, they sent forthwith for Josiah. After some preliminary questioning, the spokesman for the Sanhedrin (about fifty members being present) directed Josiah to tell them what had happened to him. Since his healing that morning Josiah had learned from Thomas, Nathaniel, and others that the Pharisees were angry about his healing on the Sabbath, and that they were likely to make trouble for all concerned; but Josiah did not yet perceive that Jesus was he who was called the Deliverer. So, when the Pharisees questioned him, he said, "This man came along, put clay upon my eyes, told me to go wash in Siloam, and I do now see."

One of the older Pharisees, after making a lengthy speech, said, "This man cannot be from God because you can see that he does not observe the Sabbath. He violates the law, first, in making the clay, then, in sending this beggar to wash in Siloam on the Sabbath day. Such a man cannot be a teacher sent from God."

Then one of the younger men who secretly believed in Jesus, said, "If this man is not sent by God, how can he do these things? We know that one who is a common sinner cannot perform such miracles. We all know this beggar and that he was born blind; now he sees. Will you still say that this prophet does all these wonders by the power of the prince of devils?"

And for every Pharisee who dared to accuse and denounce Jesus one would arise to ask entangling and embarrassing questions, so that a serious division arose among them. The presiding officer saw whither they were drifting, and in order to allay the discussion, he prepared further to question the man himself. Turning to Josiah, he said, "What do you have to say about this man, this Jesus, whom you claim opened your eyes?"

And Josiah answered, "I think he is a prophet."

The leaders were greatly troubled and, knowing not what else to do, decided to send for Josiah's parents to learn whether he had actually been born blind. They were loath to believe that the beggar had been healed.

It was well known about Jerusalem, not only that Jesus was denied entrance into all synagogues, but that all who believed in his teaching were likewise cast out of the synagogue, excommunicated from the congregation of Israel; and this meant denial of all rights and privileges of every sort throughout all Jewry except the right to buy the necessaties of life.

When, therefore, Josiah's parents, poor and fear-burdened souls, appeared before the august Sanhedrin, they were afraid to speak freely. Said the spokesman of the court, "Is this your son? And do we understand aright that he was born blind? If this is true, how is it that he can now see?"

And then Josiah's father, seconded by his mother, answered, "We know that this is our son, and that he was born blind, but how it is that he has come to see, or who it was that opened his eyes, we know not. Ask him; he is of age; let him speak for himself."

They now called Josiah up before them a second time. They were not getting along well with their scheme of holding a formal trial, and some were beginning to feel strange about doing this on the Sabbath; accordingly, when they recalled Josiah, they attempted to ensnare him by a different mode of attack. The officer of the court spoke to the former blind man, saying, "Why do you not give God the glory for this? Why do you not tell us the whole truth about what happened? We all know that this man is a sinner. Why do you refuse to discern the truth? You know that both you and this man stand convicted of Sabbath breaking. Will you not atone for your sin by acknowledging God as your healer, if you still claim that your eyes have this day been opened?"

But Josiah was neither dumb nor lacking in humor; so he replied to the officer of the court, "Whether this man is a sinner, I know not; but one thing I do know; that, whereas I was blind, now I see."

And since they could not entrap Josiah, they sought further to question him, asking, "Just how did he open your eyes? What did he actually do to you? What did he say to you? Did he ask you to believe in him?"

Josiah replied, somewhat impatiently, "I have told you exactly how it all happened, and if you did not believe my testimony, why would you hear it again? Would you by any chance also become his disciples?"

When Josiah had thus spoken, the Sanhedrin broke up in confusion, almost violence, for the leaders rushed upon Josiah, angrily exclaiming, "You may talk about being this man's disciple, but we are disciples of Moses, and we are the teachers of the laws of God. We know that God spoke through Moses, but as for this man Jesus, we know not whence he is."

Then Josiah, standing upon a stool, shouted abroad to all who could hear, saying, "Hearken, you who claim to be the teachers of all Israel, while I declare to you that herein is a great marvel since you confess that you know not whence this man is, and yet you know of a certainty, from the testimony which you have heard, that he opened my eyes. We all know that God does not perform such works for the ungodly; that God would do such a thing only at the request of a true worshiper - for one who is holy and righteous. You know that not since the beginning of the world have you ever heard of the opening of the eyes of one who was born blind. Look, then, all of you, upon me and realize what has been done this day in Jerusalem! I tell you, if this man were not from God, he could not do this."

And as the Sanhedrists departed in anger and confusion, they shouted to him, "You were altogether born in sin, and do you now presume to teach us? Maybe you were not really born blind, and even if your eyes were opened on the Sabbath day, this was done by the power of the prince of devils." And they went at once to the synagogue to cast out Josiah.

Josiah entered this trial with meager ideas about Jesus and the nature of his healing. Most of the daring testimony which he so cleverly and courageously bore before this supreme tribunal of all Israel developed in his mind as the trial proceeded along such unfair and unjust lines.

All of the time this Sabbath-breaking session of the Sanhedrin was in progress in one of the temple chambers, Jesus was walking about near at hand, teaching the people in Solomon's Porch, hoping that he would be summoned before the Sanhedrin where he could tell them the good news of the liberty and joy of divine sonship in the kingdom of God. But they were afraid to send for him. They were always disconcerted by these sudden and public appearances of Jesus in Jerusalem. The very occasion they had so ardently sought, Jesus now gave them, but they feared to bring him before the Sanhedrin even as a witness, and even more they feared to arrest him.

This was midwinter in Jerusalem, and the people sought the partial shelter of Solomon's Porch; and as Jesus lingered, the crowds asked him many questions, and he taught them for more than two hours. Some of the Jewish teachers sought to entrap him by publicly asking him, "How long will you hold us in suspense? If you are the Messiah, why do you not plainly tell us?"

Said Jesus, "I have told you about myself and my Father many times, but you will not believe me. Can you not see that the works I do in my Father's name bear witness for me? But many of you believe not because you belong not to my fold. The teacher of truth attracts only those who hunger for the truth and who thirst for righteousness. My sheep hear my voice and I know them and they follow me. And to all who follow my teaching I give eternal life; they shall never perish, and no one shall snatch them out of my hand. My Father, who has given me these children, is greater than all, so that no one is able to pluck them out of my Father's hand. The Father and I are one."

Some of the unbelieving Jews rushed over to where they were still building the temple to pick up stones to cast at Jesus, but the believers restrained them.

Jesus continued his teaching. "Many loving works have I shown you from the Father, so that now would I inquire for which one of these good works do you think to stone me?"

And then answered one of the Pharisees, "For no good work would we stone you but for blasphemy, inasmuch as you, being a man, dare to make yourself equal with God."

And Jesus answered, "You charge the Son of Man with blasphemy because you refused to believe me when I declared to you that I was sent by God. If I do not the works of God, believe me not, but if I do the works of God, even though you believe not in me, I should think you would believe the works. But that you may be certain of what I proclaim, let me again assert that the Father is in me and I in the Father, and that, as the Father dwells in me, so will I dwell in every one who believes this gospel."

And when the people heard these words, many of them rushed out to lay hands upon the stones to cast at him, but he passed out through the temple precincts; and meeting Nathaniel and Thomas, who had been in attendance upon the session of the Sanhedrin, he waited with them near the temple until Josiah came from the council chamber.

Jesus and the two apostles did not go in search of Josiah at his home until they heard he had been cast out of the synagogue. When they came to his house, Thomas called him out in the yard, and Jesus, speaking to him, said, "Josiah, do you believe in the Son of God?"

And Josiah answered, "Tell me who he is that I may believe in him."

And Jesus said, "You have both seen and heard him, and it is he who now speaks to you."

And Josiah said, "Lord, I believe," and falling down, he worshiped.

When Josiah learned that he had been cast out of the synagogue, he was at first greatly downcast, but he was much encouraged when Jesus directed that he should immediately prepare to go with them to the camp at Pella. This simple-minded man of Jerusalem had indeed been cast out of a Jewish synagogue, but behold the Creator of a universe leading him forth to become associated with the spiritual nobility of that day and generation.

And now Jesus left Jerusalem, not again to return until near the time when he prepared to leave this world. With the two apostles and Josiah the Master went back to Pella. And Josiah proved to be one of the recipients of the Master's miraculous ministry who turned out fruitfully, for he became a lifelong preacher of the gospel of the kingdom.

# THE PEREAN MISSION BEGINS

O
N TUESDAY, January 3, A.D. 30, Abner, the former chief of the twelve apostles of John the Baptist, a Nazarite and onetime head of the Nazarite school at Engedi, now chief of the seventy messengers of the kingdom, called his associates together and gave them final instructions before sending them on a mission to all of the cities and villages of Perea. This Perean mission continued for almost three months and was the last ministry of the Master. From these labors Jesus went directly to Jerusalem to pass through his final experiences in the flesh. The seventy, supplemented by the periodic labors of Jesus and the twelve apostles, worked in the following cities and towns and some fifty additional villages: Zaphon, Gadara, Macad, Arbela, Ramath, Edrei, Bosora, Caspin, Mispeh, Gerasa, Ragaba, Succoth, Amathus, Adam, Penuel, Capitolias, Dion, Hatita, Gadda, Philadelphia, Jogbehah, Gilead, Beth-Nimrah, Tyrus, Elealah, Livias, Heshbon, Callirrhoe, Beth-Peor, Shittim, Sibmah, Medeba, Beth-Meon, Areopolis, and Aroer.

Throughout this tour of Perea the women's corps, now numbering sixty-two, took over most of the work of ministration to the sick. This was the final period of the development of the higher spiritual aspects of the gospel of the kingdom, and there was, accordingly, an absence of miracle working. No other part of Palestine was so thoroughly worked by the apostles and disciples of Jesus, and in no other region did the better classes of citizens so generally accept the Master's teaching. Perea at this time was about equally gentile and Jewish, the Jews having been generally removed from these regions during the times of Judas Maccabee. Perea was the most beautiful and picturesque province of all Palestine. It was generally referred to by the Jews as "the land beyond the Jordan."

Throughout this period Jesus divided his time between the camp at Pella and trips with the twelve to assist the seventy in the various cities where they taught and preached. Under Abner's instructions the seventy baptized all believers, although Jesus had not so charged them.

By the middle of January more than twelve hundred persons were gathered together at Pella, and Jesus taught this multitude at least once each day when he was in residence at the camp, usually speaking at nine o'clock in the morning if not prevented by rain. Peter and the other apostles taught each afternoon. The evenings Jesus reserved for the usual sessions of questions and answers with the twelve and other advanced disciples. The evening groups averaged about fifty.

By the middle of March, the time when Jesus began his journey toward Jerusalem, over four thousand persons composed the large audience that heard Jesus or Peter preach each morning. The Master chose to terminate his work on earth when the interest in his message had reached a high point, the highest point attained under this second or non-miraculous phase of the progress of the kingdom. While three-quarters of the multitude were truth seekers, there were also present a large number of Pharisees from Jerusalem and elsewhere, together with many doubters and cavilers.

Jesus and the twelve apostles devoted much of their time to the multitude assembled at the Pella camp. The twelve paid little or no attention to the fieldwork, only going out with Jesus to visit Abner's associates from time to time. Abner was very familiar with the Perean district since this was the region in which his former master, John the Baptist, had done most of his work. After beginning the Perean mission, Abner and the seventy never returned to the Pella camp.

A company of over three hundred Jerusalemites, Pharisees and others, followed Jesus north to Pella when he hastened away from the jurisdiction of the Jewish rulers at the ending of the feast of the dedication; and it was in the presence of these Jewish teachers and leaders, as well as in the hearing of the twelve apostles, that Jesus preached the sermon on the "Good Shepherd."

After half an hour of informal discussion, speaking to a group of about one hundred, Jesus said, "On this night I have much to tell you, and since many of you are my disciples and some of you my bitter enemies, I will present my teaching in a parable, so that you may each take for yourself that which finds a reception in your heart.

"Tonight, here before me are men who would be willing to die for me and for this gospel of the kingdom, and some of them will so offer themselves in the years to come; and here also are some of you, slaves of tradition, who have followed me down from Jerusalem, and who, with your darkened and deluded leaders, seek to kill the Son of Man. The life which I now live in the flesh shall judge both of you, the true shepherds and the false shepherds. If the false shepherd were blind, he would have no sin, but you claim that you see; you profess to be teachers in Israel; therefore does your sin remain upon you.

"The true shepherd gathers his flock into the fold for the night in times of danger. And when the morning has come, he enters into the fold by the door, and when he calls, the sheep know his voice. Every shepherd who gains entrance to the sheepfold by any other means than by the door is a thief and a robber. The true shepherd enters the fold after the porter has opened the door for him, and his sheep, knowing his voice, come out at his word; and when they that are his are thus brought forth, the true shepherd goes before them; he leads the way and the sheep follow him. His sheep follow him because they know his voice; they will not follow a stranger. They will flee from the stranger because they know not his voice. This multitude which is gathered about us here are like sheep without a shepherd, but when we speak to them, they know the shepherd's voice, and they follow after us; at least, those who hunger for truth and thirst for righteousness do. Some of you are not of my fold; you know not my voice, and you do not follow me. And because you are false shepherds, the sheep know not your voice and will not follow you."

And when Jesus had spoken this parable, no one asked him a question. After a time he began again to speak and went on to discuss the parable. "You who would be the undershepherds of my Father's flocks must not only be worthy leaders, but you must also *feed* the flock with good food; you are not true shepherds unless you lead your flocks into green pastures and beside still waters.

"And now, lest some of you too easily comprehend this parable, I will declare that I am both the door to the Father's sheepfold and at the same time the true shepherd of my Father's flocks. Every shepherd who seeks to enter the fold without me shall fail, and the sheep will not hear his voice. I, with those who minister with me, am the door. Every soul who enters upon the eternal way by the means I have created and ordained shall be saved and will be able to go on to the attainment of the eternal pastures of Paradise.

"But I also am the true shepherd who is willing even to lay down his life for the sheep. The thief breaks into the fold only to steal, and to kill, and to destroy; but I have come that you all may have life and have it more abundantly. He who is a hireling, when danger arises, will flee and allow the sheep to be scattered and destroyed; but the true shepherd will not flee when the wolf comes; he will protect his flock and, if necessary, lay down his life for his sheep. Verily, verily, I say to you, friends and enemies, I am the true shepherd; I know my own and my own know me. I will not flee in the face of danger. I will finish this service of the completion of my Father's will, and I will not forsake the flock that the Father has intrusted to my keeping.

"But I have many other sheep not of this fold, and these words are true not only of this world. These other sheep also hear and know my voice, and I have promised the Father that they shall all be brought into one fold, one family of the sons and daughters of God. And then shall you all know the voice of one shepherd, the true shepherd, and shall all acknowledge the fatherhood of God.

"And so shall you know why the Father loves me and has put all of His flocks in this domain in my hands for keeping; it is because the Father knows that I will not falter in the safeguarding of the sheepfold, that I will not desert my sheep, and that, if it shall be required, I will not hesitate to lay down my life in the service of his manifold flocks. But, mind you, if I lay down my life, I will take it up again. No man nor any other creature can take away my life. I have the right and the power to lay down my life, and I have the same power and right to take it up again. You cannot understand this, but I received such authority from my Father even before this world was."

When they heard these words, his apostles were confused, his disciples were amazed, while the Pharisees from Jerusalem and around about went out into the night, saying, "He is either mad or has a devil."

But even some of the Jerusalem teachers said, "He speaks like one having authority; besides, who ever saw one having a devil open the eyes of a man born blind and do all of the wonderful things which this man has done?"

On the morrow about half of these Jewish teachers professed belief in Jesus, and the other half in dismay returned to Jerusalem and their homes.

By the end of January the Sabbath-afternoon multitudes numbered almost three thousand. On Saturday, January 28, Jesus preached the memorable sermon on "Trust and Spiritual Preparedness."

After preliminary remarks by Simon Peter, the Master said,

"What I have many times said to my apostles and to my disciples, I now declare to this multitude: Beware of the leaven of the Pharisees which is hypocrisy, born of prejudice and nurtured in traditional bondage, albeit many of these Pharisees are honest of heart and some of them abide here as my disciples. Presently all of you shall understand my teaching, for there is nothing now covered that shall not be revealed. That which is now hid from you shall all be made known when the Son of Man has completed his mission on earth and in the flesh.

"Soon, very soon, will the things which our enemies now plan in secrecy and in darkness be brought out into the light and be proclaimed from the housetops. But I say to you, my friends, when they seek to destroy the Son of Man, be not afraid of them. Fear not those who, although they may be able to kill the body, after that have no more power over you. I admonish you to fear none, in heaven or on earth, but to rejoice in the knowledge of him who has power to deliver you from all unrighteousness and to present you blameless before the judgment seat of a universe.

"Are not five sparrows sold for two pennies? And yet, when these birds flit about in quest of their sustenance, not one of them exists without the knowledge of the Father, the source of all life. To the seraphic guardians the very hairs of your head are numbered. And if all of this is true, why should you live in fear of the many trifles which come up in your daily lives? I say to you: Fear not; you are of much more value than many sparrows.

"All of you who have had the courage to confess faith in my gospel before men I will presently acknowledge before the angels of heaven; but he who shall knowingly deny the truth of my teachings before men shall be denied by his guardian of destiny even before the angels of heaven.

"Say what you will about the Son of Man, and it shall be forgiven you; but he who presumes to blaspheme against God shall hardly find forgiveness. When men go so far as knowingly to ascribe the doings of God to the forces of evil, such deliberate rebels will hardly seek forgiveness for their sins.

"And when our enemies bring you before the rulers of the synagogues and before other high authorities, be not concerned about what you should say and be not anxious as to how you should answer their questions, for the spirit that dwells within you shall certainly teach you in that very hour what you should say in honor of the gospel of the kingdom.

"How long will you tarry in the valley of decision? Why do you halt between two opinions? Why should the Jews or the gentiles hesitate to accept the good news that they are sons and daughters of the eternal God? How long will it take us to persuade you to enter joyfully into your spiritual inheritance? I came into this world to reveal the Father to you and to lead you to the Father. The first I have done, but the last I may not do without your consent; the Father never compels any man to enter the kingdom. The invitation ever has been and always will be: Whosoever will, let him come and freely partake of the water of life."

When Jesus had finished speaking, many went forth to be baptized by the apostles in the Jordan while he listened to the questions of those who remained.

As the apostles baptized believers, the Master talked with those who tarried. And a certain young man said to him, "Master, my father died leaving much property to me and my brother, but my brother refuses to give me that which is my own. Will you, then, bid my brother divide this inheritance with me?"

Jesus was mildly indignant that this material-minded youth should bring up for discussion such a question of business; but he proceeded to use the occasion for the impartation of further instruction. Said Jesus, "Man, who made me a divider over you? Where did you get the idea that I give attention to the material affairs of this world?" And then, turning to all who were about him, he said, "Take heed and keep yourselves free from covetousness; a man's life consists not in the abundance of the things which he may possess. Happiness comes not from the power of wealth, and joy springs not from riches. Wealth, in itself, is not a curse, but the love of riches many times leads to such devotion to the things of this world that the soul becomes blinded to the beautiful attractions of the spiritual realities of the kingdom of God on earth and to the joys of eternal life in heaven.

"Let me tell you a story of a certain rich man whose ground brought forth plentifully; and when he had become very rich, he began to reason with himself, saying, 'What shall I do with all my riches? I now have so much that I have no place to store my wealth.' And when he had meditated on his problem, he said, 'This I will do; I will pull down my barns and build greater ones, and thus will I have abundant room in which to store my fruits and my goods. Then can I say to my soul, soul, you have much wealth laid up for many years; take now your ease; eat, drink, and be merry, for you are rich and increased in goods.'

"But this rich man was also foolish. In providing for the material requirements of his mind and body, he had failed to lay up treasures in heaven for the satisfaction of the spirit and for the salvation of the soul. And even then he was not to enjoy the pleasure of consuming his hoarded wealth, for that very night was his soul required of him. That night there came the brigands who broke into his house to kill him, and after they had plundered his barns, they burned that which remained. And for the property which escaped the robbers his heirs fell to fighting among themselves. This man laid up treasures for himself on earth, but he was not rich toward God."

Jesus thus dealt with the young man and his inheritance because he knew that his trouble was covetousness. Even if this had not been the case, the Master would not have interfered, for he never meddled with the temporal affairs of even his apostles, much less his disciples.

When Jesus had finished his story, another man rose up and asked him, "Master, I know that your apostles have sold all their earthly possessions to follow you, and that they have all things in common as do the Essenes, but would you have all of us who are your disciples do likewise? Is it a sin to possess honest wealth?"

And Jesus replied, "My friend, it is not a sin to have honorable wealth; but it is a sin if you convert the wealth of material possessions into *treasures* which may absorb your interests and divert your affections from devotion to the spiritual pursuits of the kingdom. There is no sin in having honest possessions on earth provided your *treasure* is in heaven, for where your treasure is, there will your heart be also. There is a great difference between wealth which leads to covetousness and selfishness and that which is held and dispensed in the spirit of stewardship by those who have an abundance of this world's goods, and who so bountifully contribute to the support of those who devote all their energies to the work of the kingdom. Many of you who are here and without money are fed and lodged in yonder tented city because liberal men and women of means have given funds to your host, David Zebedee, for such purposes.

"But never forget that, after all, wealth is unenduring. The love of riches all too often obscures and even destroys the spiritual vision. Fail not to recognize the danger of wealth's becoming, not your servant, but your master."

Jesus did not teach nor countenance improvidence, idleness, indifference to providing the physical necessities for one's family, or dependence upon alms. But he did teach that the material and temporal must be subordinated to the welfare of the soul and the progress of the spiritual nature in the kingdom of heaven.

Then, as the people went down by the river to witness the baptizing, the first man came privately to Jesus about his inheritance inasmuch as he thought Jesus had dealt harshly with him; and when the Master had again heard him, he replied, "My son, why do you miss the opportunity to feed upon the bread of life on a day like this in order to indulge your covetous disposition? Do you not know that the Jewish laws of inheritance will be justly administered if you will go with your complaint to the court of the synagogue? Can you not see that my work has to do with making sure that you know about your heavenly inheritance? Have you not read the Scripture: 'There is he who waxes rich by his wariness and much pinching, and this is the portion of his reward: Whereas he says, I have found rest and now shall be able to eat continually of my goods, yet he knows not what time shall bring upon him, and also that he must leave all these things to others when he dies.' Have you not read the commandment: 'You shall not covet.' And again, 'They have eaten and filled themselves and waxed fat, and then did they turn to other gods.' Have you read in the Psalms that 'the Lord abhors the covetous,' and that 'the little a righteous man has is better than the riches of many wicked.' 'If riches increase, set not your heart upon them.' Have you read where Jeremiah said, 'Let not the rich man glory in his riches'; and Ezekiel spoke truth when he said, 'With their mouths they make a show of love, but their hearts are set upon their own selfish gain.'"

Jesus sent the young man away, saying to him, "My son, what shall it profit you if you gain the whole world and lose your own soul?"

To another standing near by who asked Jesus how the wealthy would stand in the day of judgment, he replied, "I have come to judge neither the rich nor the poor, but the lives men live will sit in judgment on all. Whatever else may concern the wealthy in the judgment, at least three questions must be answered by all who acquire great wealth, and these questions are:

"1. How much wealth did you accumulate?
"2. How did you get this wealth?
"3. How did you use your wealth?"

Then Jesus went into his tent to rest for a while before the evening meal. When the apostles had finished with the baptizing, they came also and would have talked with him about wealth on earth and treasure in heaven, but he was asleep.

That evening after supper, when Jesus and the twelve gathered together for their daily conference, Andrew asked, "Master, while we were baptizing the believers, you spoke many words to the lingering multitude which we did not hear. Would you be willing to repeat these words for our benefit?"

And in response to Andrew's request, Jesus said, "Yes, Andrew, I will speak to you about these matters of wealth and self-support, but my words to you, the apostles, must be somewhat different from those spoken to the disciples and the multitude since you have forsaken everything, not only to follow me, but to be ordained as ambassadors of the kingdom. Already have you had several years' experience, and you know that the Father whose kingdom you proclaim will not forsake you. You have dedicated your lives to the ministry of the kingdom; therefore be not anxious or worried about the things of the temporal life, what you shall eat, nor yet for your body, what you shall wear. The welfare of the soul is more than food and drink; the progress in the spirit is far above the need of raiment. When you are tempted to doubt the sureness of your bread, consider the ravens; they sow not neither reap, they have no storehouses or barns, and yet the Father provides food for every one of them that seeks it. And of how much more value are you than many birds! Besides, all of your anxiety or fretting doubts can do nothing to supply your material needs. Which of you by anxiety can add a handbreadth to your stature or a day to your life? Since such matters are not in your hands, why do you give anxious thought to any of these problems?

"Consider the lilies, how they grow; they toil not, neither do they spin; yet I say to you, even Solomon in all his glory was not arrayed like one of these. If God so clothes the grass of the field, which is alive today and tomorrow is cut down and cast into the fire, how much more shall he clothe you, the ambassadors of the heavenly kingdom. O you of little faith! When you wholeheartedly devote yourselves to the proclamation of the gospel of the kingdom, you should not be of doubtful minds concerning the support of yourselves or the families you have forsaken. If you give your lives truly to the gospel, you shall live by the gospel. If you are only believing disciples, you must earn your own bread and contribute to the sustenance of all who teach and preach and heal. If you are anxious about your bread and water, wherein are you different from the nations of the world who so diligently seek such necessities? Devote yourselves to your work, believing that both the Father and I know that you have need of all these things. Let me assure you, once and for all, that, if you dedicate your lives to the work of the kingdom, all your real needs shall be supplied. Seek the greater thing, and the lesser will be found therein; ask for the heavenly, and the earthly shall be included. The shadow is certain to follow the substance.

"You are only a small group, but if you have faith, if you will not stumble in fear, I declare that it is my Father's good pleasure to give you this kingdom. You have laid up your treasures where the purse waxes not old, where no thief can despoil, and where no moth can destroy. And as I told the people, where your treasure is, there will your heart be also.

"But in the work which is just ahead of us, and in that which remains for you after I go to the Father, you will be grievously tried. You must all be on your watch against fear and doubts. Every one of you, gird up the loins of your minds and let your lamps be kept burning. Keep yourselves like men who are watching for their master to return from the marriage feast so that, when he comes and knocks, you may quickly open to him. Such watchful servants are blessed by the master who finds them faithful at such a great moment. Then will the master make his servants sit down while he himself serves them. Verily, verily, I say to you that a crisis is just ahead in your lives, and it behooves you to watch and be ready.

"You well understand that no man would suffer his house to be broken into if he knew what hour the thief was to come. Be you also on watch for yourselves, for in an hour that you least suspect and in a manner you think not, shall the Son of Man depart."

For some minutes the twelve sat in silence. Some of these warnings they had heard before but not in the setting presented to them at this time.

As they sat thinking, Simon Peter asked, "Do you speak this parable to us, your apostles, or is it for all the disciples?"

And Jesus answered, "In the time of testing, a man's soul is revealed; trial discloses what really is in the heart. When the servant is tested and proved, then may the lord of the house set such a servant over his household and safely trust this faithful steward to see that his children are fed and nurtured. Likewise, will I soon know who can be trusted with the welfare of my children when I shall have returned to the Father. As the lord of the household shall set the true and tried servant over the affairs of his family, so will I exalt those who endure the trials of this hour in the affairs of my kingdom.

"But if the servant is slothful and begins to say in his heart, 'My master delays his coming,' and begins to mistreat his fellow servants and to eat and drink with the drunken, then the lord of that servant will come at a time when he looks not for him and, finding him unfaithful, will cast him out in disgrace. Therefore you do well to prepare yourselves for that day when you will be visited suddenly and in an unexpected manner. Remember, much has been given to you; therefore will much be required of you. Fiery trials are drawing near you. I have a baptism to be baptized with, and I am on watch until this is accomplished. You preach peace on earth, but my mission will not bring peace in the material affairs of men - not for a time, at least. Division can only be the result where two members of a family believe in me and three members reject this gospel. Friends, relatives, and loved ones are destined to be set against each other by the gospel you preach. True, each of these believers shall have great and lasting peace in his own heart, but peace on earth will not come until all are willing to believe and enter into their glorious inheritance of membership in the family of God. Nevertheless, go into all the world proclaiming this gospel to all nations, to every man, woman, and child."

And this was the end of a full and busy Sabbath day. On the morrow Jesus and the twelve went into the cities of northern Perea to visit with the seventy, who were working in these regions under Abner's supervision.

# LAST VISIT TO NORTHERN PEREA

FROM FEBRUARY 11 to 20, Jesus and the twelve made a tour of all the cities and villages of northern Perea where the associates of Abner and the members of the women's corps were working. They found these messengers of the gospel meeting with success, and Jesus repeatedly called the attention of his apostles to the fact that the gospel of the kingdom could spread without the accompaniment of miracles and wonders.

This entire mission of three months in Perea was successfully carried on with little help from the twelve apostles, and the gospel from this time on reflected, not so much Jesus' personality, as his *teachings.* But his followers did not long follow his instructions, for soon after Jesus' death and resurrection they departed from his teachings and began to build the early church around the miraculous concepts and the glorified memories of his divine-human personality.

On Sabbath, February 18, Jesus was at Ragaba, where there lived a wealthy Pharisee named Nathaniel; and since quite a number of his fellow Pharisees were following Jesus and the twelve around the country, he made a breakfast on this Sabbath morning for all of them, about twenty in number, and invited Jesus as the guest of honor.

By the time Jesus arrived at this breakfast, most of the Pharisees, with two or three lawyers, were already there and seated at the table. The Master immediately took his seat at the left of Nathaniel without going to the water basins to wash his hands. Many of the Pharisees, especially those favorable to Jesus' teachings, knew that he washed his hands only for purposes of cleanliness, that he abhorred these purely ceremonial performances; so they were not surprised at his coming directly to the table without having twice washed his hands. But Nathaniel was shocked by this failure of the Master to comply with the strict requirements of

Pharisaic practice. Neither did Jesus wash his hands, as did the Pharisees, after each course of food nor at the end of the meal.

After considerable whispering between Nathaniel and an unfriendly Pharisee on his right and after much lifting of eyebrows and sneering curling of lips by those who sat opposite the Master, Jesus finally said, "I had thought that you invited me to this to this house to break bread with you and perchance to inquire of me concerning the proclamation of the new gospel of the kingdom of God; but I perceive that you have brought me here to witness an exhibition of ceremonial devotion to your own self-righteousness. That service you have now done me; what next will you honor me with as your guest on this occasion?"

When the Master had thus spoken, they cast their eyes upon the table and remained silent. And since no one spoke, Jesus continued. "Many of you Pharisees are here with me as friends, some are even my disciples, but the majority of the Pharisees are persistent in their refusal to see the light and acknowledge the truth, even when the work of the gospel is brought before them in great power. How carefully you cleanse the outside of the cups and the platters while the spiritual-food vessels are filthy and polluted! You make sure to present a pious and holy appearance to the people, but your inner souls are filled with self-righteousness, covetousness, extortion, and all manner of spiritual wickedness. Your leaders even dare to plot and plan the murder of the Son of Man. Do not you foolish men understand that the God of heaven looks at the inner motives of the soul as well as on your outer pretenses and your pious professions? Think not that the giving of alms and the paying of tithes will cleanse you from unrighteousness and enable you to stand clean in the presence of the Judge of all men. Woe upon you Pharisees who have persisted in rejecting the light of life! You are meticulous in tithing and ostentatious in almsgiving, but you knowingly spurn the visitation of God and reject the revelation of His love. Though it is alright for you to give attention to these minor duties, you should not have left these weightier requirements undone. Woe upon all who shun justice, spurn mercy, and reject truth! Woe upon all those who despise the revelation of the Father while they seek the chief seats in the synagogue and crave flattering salutations in the market places!"

When Jesus would have risen to depart, one of the lawyers who was at the table, addressing him, said, "But, Master, in some of your statements you reproach us also. Is there nothing good in the scribes, the Pharisees, or the lawyers?"

And Jesus, standing, replied to the lawyer, "You, like the Pharisees, delight in the first places at the feasts and in wearing long robes while you put heavy burdens, grievous to be borne, on men's shoulders. And when the souls of men stagger under these heavy burdens, you will not so much as lift with one of your fingers. Woe upon you who take your greatest delight in building tombs for the prophets your fathers killed! And that you consent to what your fathers did is made manifest when you now plan to kill those who come in this day doing what the prophets did in their day - proclaiming the righteousness of God and revealing the mercy of the heavenly Father. But of all the generations that are past, the blood of the prophets and the apostles shall be required of this perverse and self-righteous generation. Woe upon all of you lawyers who have taken away the key of knowledge from the common people! You yourselves refuse to enter into the way of truth, and at the same time you would hinder all others who seek to enter therein. But you cannot thus shut up the doors of the kingdom of heaven; these we have opened to all who have the faith to enter, and these portals of mercy shall not be closed by the prejudice and arrogance of false teachers and untrue shepherds who are like whited sepulchres which, while outwardly they appear beautiful, are inwardly full of dead men's bones and all manner of spiritual uncleanness."

And when Jesus had finished speaking at Nathaniel's table, he went out of the house without partaking of food. And of the Pharisees who heard these words, some became believers in his teaching and entered into the kingdom, but the larger number persisted in the way of darkness, becoming all the more determined to lie in wait for him that they might catch some of his words which could be used to bring him to trial and judgment before the Sanhedrin at Jerusalem.

There were just three things to which the Pharisees paid particular attention:
1. The practice of strict tithing.
2. Scrupulous observance of the laws of purification.
3. Avoidance of association with all non-Pharisees.

At this time Jesus sought to expose the spiritual barrenness of the first two practices, while he reserved his remarks designed to rebuke the Pharisees' refusal to engage in social intercourse with non-Pharisees for another and subsequent occasion when he would again be dining with many of these same men.

The next day Jesus went with the twelve over to Amathus, near the border of Samaria, and as they approached the city, they encountered a group of ten lepers who sojourned near this place. Nine of this group were Jews, one a Samaritan. Ordinarily these Jews would have refrained from all association or contact with this Samaritan, but their common affliction was more than enough to overcome all religious prejudice. They had heard much of Jesus and his earlier miracles of healing, and since the seventy made a practice of announcing the time of Jesus' expected arrival when the Master was out with the twelve on these tours, the ten lepers had been made aware that he was expected to appear in this vicinity at about this time; and they were, accordingly, posted here on the outskirts of the city where they hoped to attract his attention and ask for healing. When the lepers saw Jesus drawing near them, not daring to approach him, they stood afar off and cried, "Master, have mercy on us; cleanse us from our affliction. Heal us as you have healed others."

Jesus had just been explaining to the twelve why the gentiles of Perea, together with the less orthodox Jews, were more willing to believe the gospel preached by the seventy than were the more orthodox and tradition-bound Jews of Judea. He had called their attention to the fact that their message had likewise been more readily received by the Galileans, and even by the Samaritans. But the twelve apostles were hardly yet willing to entertain kind feelings for the long-despised Samaritans.

Accordingly, when Simon Zelotes observed the Samaritan among the lepers, he sought to induce the Master to pass on into the city without even hesitating to exchange greetings with them.

Said Jesus to Simon, "But what if the Samaritan loves God as well as the Jews? Should we sit in judgment on our fellow men? Who can tell? If we make these ten men whole, perhaps the Samaritan will prove more grateful even than the Jews. Do you feel certain about your opinions, Simon?"

And Simon quickly replied, "If you cleanse them, you will soon find out."

And Jesus replied, "So shall it be, Simon, and you will soon know the truth regarding the gratitude of men and the loving mercy of God."

Jesus, going near the lepers, said, "If you would be made whole, go forthwith and show yourselves to the priests as required by the law of Moses."

And as they went, they were made whole. But when the Samaritan saw that he was being healed, he turned back and, going in quest of Jesus, began to glorify God with a loud voice. And when he had found the Master, he fell on his knees at his feet and gave thanks for his cleansing. The nine others, the Jews, had also discovered their healing, and while they also were grateful for their cleansing, they continued on their way to show themselves to the priests.

As the Samaritan remained kneeling at Jesus' feet, the Master, looking about at the twelve, especially at Simon Zelotes, said, "Were not ten cleansed? Where, then, are the other nine, the Jews? Only one, this alien, has returned to give glory to God." And then he said to the Samaritan, "Arise and go your way; your faith has made you whole."

Jesus looked again at his apostles as the stranger departed. And the apostles all looked at Jesus, save Simon Zelotes, whose eyes were downcast. The twelve said not a word. Neither did Jesus speak; it was not necessary that he should.

Though all ten of these men really believed they had leprosy, only four were thus afflicted. The other six were cured of a skin disease that had been mistaken for leprosy. But the Samaritan really had leprosy.

Jesus enjoined the twelve to say nothing about the cleansing of the lepers, and as they went on into Amathus, he remarked, "You see how it is that the children of the house, even when they are insubordinate to their Father's will, take their blessings for granted. They think it a small matter if they neglect to give thanks when the Father bestows healing upon them, but the strangers, when they receive gifts from the head of the house, are filled with wonder and are constrained to give thanks in recognition of the good things bestowed upon them." And still the apostles said nothing in reply to the Master's words.

As Jesus and the twelve visited with the messengers of the kingdom at Gerasa, one of the Pharisees who believed in him asked this question: "Lord, will there be few or many really saved?"

And Jesus, answering, said, "You have been taught that only the children of Abraham will be saved; that only the gentiles of adoption can hope for salvation. Some of you have reasoned that, since the Scriptures record that only Caleb and Joshua from among all the hosts that went out of Egypt lived to enter the promised land, only a comparatively few of those who seek the kingdom of heaven shall find entrance thereto.

"You also have another saying among you, and one that contains much truth: That the way which leads to eternal life is straight and narrow, that the door which leads thereto is likewise narrow so that, of those who seek salvation, few can find entrance through this door. You also have a teaching that the way which leads to destruction is broad, that the entrance thereto is wide, and that there are many who choose to go this way. And this proverb is not without its meaning. But I declare that salvation is first a matter of your personal choosing. Even if the door to the way of life is narrow, it is wide enough to admit all who sincerely seek to enter, for I am that door. And the Son will never refuse entrance to any child of the universe who, by faith, seeks to find the Father through the Son.

"But herein is the danger to all who would postpone their entrance into the kingdom while they continue to pursue the pleasures of immaturity and indulge the satisfactions of selfishness: Having refused to enter the kingdom as a spiritual experience, they may subsequently seek entrance thereto when the glory of the better way becomes revealed in the age to come. And when, therefore, those who spurned the kingdom when I came in the likeness of humanity seek to find an entrance when it is revealed in the likeness of divinity, then will I say to all such selfish ones: I know not whence you are. You had your chance to prepare for this heavenly citizenship, but you refused all such proffers of mercy; you rejected all invitations to come while the door was open. Now, to you who have refused salvation, the door is shut. This door is not open to those who would enter the kingdom for selfish glory. Salvation is not for those who are unwilling to pay the price of wholehearted dedication to doing my Father's will. When in spirit and soul you have turned your backs upon the Father's kingdom, it is useless in mind and body to stand before this door and knock, saying, 'Lord, open to us; we would also be great in the kingdom.' Then will I declare that you are not of my fold. I will not receive you to be among those who have fought the good fight of faith and won the reward of unselfish service in the kingdom on earth. And when you say, 'Did we not eat and drink with you, and did you not teach in our streets?' then shall I again declare that you are spiritual strangers; that we were not fellow servants in the Father's ministry of mercy on earth; that I do not know you; and then shall the Judge of all the earth say to you: 'Depart from us, all you who have taken delight in the works of iniquity.'

"But fear not; every one who sincerely desires to find eternal life by entrance into the kingdom of God shall certainly find such everlasting salvation. But you who refuse this salvation will some day see the prophets of the seed of Abraham sit down with the believers of the gentile nations in this glorified kingdom to partake of the bread of life and to refresh themselves with the water thereof. And they who shall thus take the kingdom in spiritual power and by the persistent assaults of living faith will come from the north and the south and from the east and the west. And, behold, many who are first will be last, and those who are last will many times be first."

This was indeed a new and strange version of the old and familiar proverb of the straight and narrow way.

Slowly the apostles and many of the disciples were learning the meaning of Jesus' early declaration: "Unless you are born again, born of the spirit, you cannot enter the kingdom of God." Nevertheless, to all who are honest of heart and sincere in faith, it remains eternally true: "Behold, I stand at the doors of men's hearts and knock, and if any man will open to me, I will come in and sup with him and will feed him with the bread of life; we shall be one in spirit and purpose, and so shall we ever be brethren in the long and fruitful service of the search for the Paradise Father." And so, whether few or many are to be saved altogether depends on whether few or many will heed the invitation: "I am the door, I am the new and living way, and whosoever wills may enter to embark upon the endless truth-search for eternal life."

Even the apostles were unable fully to comprehend his teaching as to the necessity for using spiritual force for the purpose of breaking through all material resistance and for surmounting every earthly obstacle which might chance to stand in the way of grasping the all-important spiritual values of the new life in the spirit as the liberated sons of God.

While most Palestinians ate only two meals a day, it was the custom of Jesus and the apostles, when on a journey, to pause at midday for rest and refreshment. And it was at such a noontide stop on the way to Philadelphia that Thomas asked Jesus, "Master, from hearing your remarks as we journeyed this morning, I would like to inquire whether spiritual beings are concerned in the production of strange and extraordinary events in the material world and, further, to ask whether the angels and other spirit beings are able to prevent accidents."

In answer to Thomas's inquiry, Jesus said, "Have I been so long with you, and yet you continue to ask me such questions? Have you failed to observe how the Son of Man lives as one with you and consistently refuses to employ the forces of heaven for his personal sustenance? Do we not all live by the same means whereby all men exist? Do you see the power of the spiritual world manifested in the material life of this world, save for the revelation of the Father and the sometime healing of his afflicted children?

"All too long have your fathers believed that prosperity was the token of divine approval; that adversity was the proof of God's displeasure. I declare that such beliefs are superstitions. Do you not observe that far greater numbers of the poor joyfully receive the gospel and immediately enter the kingdom? If riches evidence divine favor, why do the rich so many times refuse to believe this good news from heaven?

"The Father causes his rain to fall on the just and the unjust; the sun likewise shines on the righteous and the unrighteous. You know about those Galileans whose blood Pilate mingled with the sacrifices, but I tell you these Galileans were not in any manner sinners above all their fellows just because this happened to them. You also know about the eighteen men upon whom the tower of Siloam fell, killing them. Think not that these men who were thus destroyed were offenders above all their brethren in Jerusalem. These folks were simply innocent victims of one of the accidents of time.

"There are three groups of events which may occur in your lives:

"1. You may share in those normal happenings which are a part of the life you and your fellows live on the face of the earth.

"2. You may chance to fall victim to one of the accidents of nature, one of the mischances of men, knowing full well that such occurrences are in no way prearranged or otherwise produced by the spiritual forces of the realm.

"3. You may reap the harvest of your direct efforts to comply with the natural laws governing the world.

"There was a certain man who planted a fig tree in his yard, and when he had many times sought fruit thereon and found none, he called the vinedressers before him and said, 'Here have I come these three seasons looking for fruit on this fig tree and have found none. Cut down this barren tree; why should it encumber the ground?' But the head gardener answered his master: 'Let it alone for one more year so that I may dig around it and put on fertilizer, and then, next year, if it bears no fruit, it shall be cut down.' And when they had thus complied with the laws of fruitfulness, since the tree was living and good, they were rewarded with an abundant yield.

"In the matter of sickness and health, you should know that these bodily states are the result of material causes; health is not the smile of heaven, neither is affliction the frown of God.

"The Father's human children have equal capacity for the reception of material blessings; therefore does he bestow things physical upon the children of men without discrimination. When it comes to the bestowal of spiritual gifts, the Father is limited by man's capacity for receiving these divine endowments. Although the Father is no respecter of persons, in the bestowal of spiritual gifts he is limited by man's faith and by his willingness always to abide by the Father's will."

As they journeyed on toward Philadelphia, Jesus continued to teach them and to answer their questions having to do with accidents, sickness, and miracles, but they were not able fully to comprehend this instruction. One hour of teaching will not wholly change the beliefs of a lifetime, and so Jesus found it necessary to reiterate his message, to tell again and again that which he wished them to understand; and even then they failed to grasp the meaning of his earth mission until after his death and resurrection.

Jesus and the twelve were on their way to visit Abner and his associates, who were preaching and teaching in Philadelphia. Of all the cities of Perea, in Philadelphia the largest group of Jews and gentiles, rich and poor, learned and unlearned, embraced the teachings of the seventy, thereby entering into the kingdom of heaven. The synagogue of Philadelphia had never been subject to the supervision of the Sanhedrin at Jerusalem and therefore had never been closed to the teachings of Jesus and his associates. At this very time, Abner was teaching three times a day in the Philadelphia synagogue.

This very synagogue later on became a Christian church and was the missionary headquarters for the promulgation of the gospel through the regions to the east. It was long a stronghold of the Master's teachings and stood alone in this region as a center of Christian learning for centuries.

The Jews at Jerusalem had always had trouble with the Jews of Philadelphia. And after the death and resurrection of Jesus the Jerusalem church, of which James the Lord's brother was head, began to have serious difficulties with the Philadelphia congregation of believers. Abner became the head of the Philadelphia church, continuing as such until his death. And this estrangement with Jerusalem explains why nothing is heard of Abner and his work in the Gospel records of the New Testament. This feud between Jerusalem and Philadelphia lasted throughout the lifetimes of James and Abner and continued for some time after the destruction of Jerusalem. Philadelphia was really the headquarters of the early church in the south and east as Antioch was in the north and west.

It was the apparent misfortune of Abner to be at variance with all of the leaders of the early Christian church. He fell out with Peter and James (Jesus' brother) over questions of administration and the jurisdiction of the Jerusalem church; he parted company with Paul over differences of philosophy and theology. Abner was more Babylonian than Hellenic in his philosophy, and he stubbornly resisted all attempts of Paul to remake the teachings of Jesus so as to present less that was objectionable, first to the Jews, then to the Greco-Roman believers in the mysteries.

Thus was Abner compelled to live a life of isolation. He was head of a church that was without standing at Jerusalem. He had dared to defy James the Lord's brother, who was subsequently supported by Peter. Such conduct effectively separated him from all his former associates. Then he dared to withstand Paul. Although he was wholly sympathetic with Paul in his mission to the gentiles, and though he supported him in his contentions with the church at Jerusalem, he bitterly opposed the version of Jesus' teachings that Paul elected to preach. In his last years Abner denounced Paul as the "clever corrupter of the life teachings of Jesus of Nazareth, the Son of the living God."

During the later years of Abner and for some time thereafter, the believers at Philadelphia held more strictly to the religion of Jesus, as he lived and taught, than any other group on earth.

Abner lived to be 89 years old, dying at Philadelphia on the 21st day of November, A.D. 74. And to the very end he was a faithful believer in, and teacher of, the gospel of the heavenly kingdom.

# THE VISIT TO PHILADELPHIA

**T**HROUGHOUT this period of the Perean ministry, when mention is made of Jesus and the apostles visiting the various localities where the seventy were at work, it should be recalled that, as a rule, only ten were with him since it was the practice to leave at least two of the apostles at Pella to instruct the multitude. As Jesus prepared to go on to Philadelphia, Simon Peter and his brother, Andrew, returned to the Pella encampment to teach the crowds there assembled. When the Master left the camp at Pella to visit about Perea, it was not uncommon for from three to five hundred of the campers to follow him. When he arrived at Philadelphia, he was accompanied by over six hundred followers.

No miracles had attended the recent preaching tour through the Decapolis, and, excepting the cleansing of the ten lepers, thus far there had been no miracles on this Perean mission. This was a period when the gospel was proclaimed with power, without miracles, and most of the time without the personal presence of Jesus or even of his apostles.

Jesus and the ten apostles arrived at Philadelphia on Wednesday, February 22, and spent Thursday and Friday resting from their recent travels and labors. That Friday night James spoke in the synagogue, and a general council was called for the following evening. They were much rejoiced over the progress of the gospel at Philadelphia and among the near-by villages. The messengers of David also brought word of the further advancement of the kingdom throughout Palestine, as well as good news from Alexandria and Damascus.

**T**here lived in Philadelphia a very wealthy and influential Pharisee who had accepted the teachings of Abner, and who invited Jesus to his house Sabbath morning for breakfast. It was known that Jesus was expected in Philadelphia at this time; so a large number of visitors, among them many Pharisees, had come over from Jerusalem and from elsewhere. Accordingly, about forty of these leading men and a few lawyers were bidden to this breakfast, which had been arranged in honor of the Master.

As Jesus lingered by the door, speaking with Abner, and after the host had seated himself, there came into the room one of the leading Pharisees of Jerusalem, a member of the Sanhedrin, and as was his habit, he made straight for the seat of honor at the left of the host. But since this place had been reserved for the Master and that on the right for Abner, the host beckoned the Jerusalem Pharisee to sit four seats to the left, and this dignitary was much offended because he did not receive the seat of honor.

Soon they were all seated and enjoying the visiting among themselves since the majority of those present were disciples of Jesus or else were friendly to the gospel. Only his enemies took notice of the fact that he did not observe the ceremonial washing of his hands before he sat down to eat. Abner washed his hands at the beginning of the meal but not during the serving.

Near the end of the meal there came in from the street a man long afflicted with a chronic disease and now in a dropsical condition. This man was a believer, having recently been baptized by Abner's associates. He made no request of Jesus for healing, but the Master knew full well that this afflicted man came to this breakfast hoping thereby to escape the crowds which thronged him and thus be more likely to engage his attention. This man knew that few miracles were then being performed; however, he had reasoned in his heart that his sorry plight might possibly appeal to the Master's compassion. And he was not mistaken, for, when he entered the room, both Jesus and the self-righteous Pharisee from Jerusalem took notice of him. The Pharisee was not slow to voice his resentment that such a one should be permitted to enter the room. But Jesus looked upon the sick man and smiled so benignly that he drew near and sat down upon the floor. As the meal was ending, the Master looked over his fellow guests and then, after glancing significantly at the man with dropsy, said, "My friends, teachers in Israel and learned lawyers, I would like to ask you a question: Is it lawful to heal the sick and afflicted on the Sabbath day, or not?" But those who were there present knew Jesus too well; they held their peace; they answered not his question.

Then went Jesus over to where the sick man sat and, taking him by the hand, said, "Arise and go your way. You have not asked to be healed, but I know the desire of your heart and the faith of your soul." Before the man left the room, Jesus returned to his seat and, addressing those at the table, said, "Such works my Father does, not to tempt you into the kingdom, but to reveal Himself to those who are already in the kingdom. You can perceive that it would be like the Father to do just such things because which one of you, having a favorite animal that fell in the well on the Sabbath day, would not go right out and draw him up?"

And since no one would answer him, and inasmuch as his host evidently approved of what was going on, Jesus stood up and spoke to all present. "My brethren, when you are bidden to a marriage feast, sit not down in the chief seat, lest, perchance, a more honored man than you has been invited, and the host will have to come to you and request that you give your place to this other and honored guest. In this event, with shame you will be required to take a lower place at the table. When you are bidden to a feast, it would be the part of wisdom, on arriving at the festive table, to seek for the lowest place and take your seat therein, so that, when the host looks over the guests, he may say to you, 'My friend, why sit in the seat of the least? Come up higher'; and thus will such a one have glory in the presence of his fellow guests. Forget not, every one who exalts himself shall be humbled, while he who truly humbles himself shall be exalted. Therefore, when you entertain at dinner or give a supper, invite not always your friends, your brethren, your kinsmen, or your rich neighbors that they in return may bid you to their feasts, and thus will you be recompensed. When you give a banquet, sometimes bid the poor, the maimed, and the blind. In this way you shall be blessed in your heart, for you well know that the lame and the halt cannot repay you for your loving ministry."

As Jesus finished speaking at the breakfast table of the Pharisee, one of the lawyers present, desiring to relieve the silence, thoughtlessly said, "Blessed is he who shall eat bread in the kingdom of God" —that being a common saying of those days.

And then Jesus spoke a parable, which even his friendly host was compelled to take to heart. He said, "A certain ruler gave a great supper, and having bidden many guests, he dispatched his servants at suppertime to say to those who were invited, 'Come, for everything is now ready.' And they all with one accord began to make excuses. The first said, 'I have just bought a farm, and I must needs go prove it; I pray you have me excused.' Another said, 'I have bought five yoke of oxen, and I must go to receive them; I pray you have me excused.' And another said, 'I have just married a wife, and therefore I cannot come.' So the servants went back and reported this to their master. When the master of the house heard this, he was very angry, and turning to his servants, he said: 'I have made ready this marriage feast; the fatlings are killed, and all is in readiness for my guests, but they have spurned my invitation; they have gone every man after his lands and his merchandise, and they even show disrespect to my servants who bid them come to my feast. Go out quickly, therefore, into the streets and lanes of the city, out into the highways and the byways, and bring hither the poor and the outcast, the blind and the lame, that the marriage feast may have guests.' And the servants did as their lord commanded, and even then there was room for more guests. Then said the lord to his servants: 'Go now out into the roads and the countryside and constrain those who are there to come in that my house may be filled. I declare that none of those who were first bidden shall taste of my supper.' And the servants did as their master commanded, and the house was filled."

And when they heard these words, they departed; every man went to his own place. At least one of the sneering Pharisees present that morning comprehended the meaning of this parable, for he was baptized that day and made public confession of his faith in the gospel of the kingdom. Abner preached on this parable that night at the general council of believers.

The next day all of the apostles engaged in the philosophic exercise of endeavoring to interpret the meaning of this parable of the great supper. Though Jesus listened with interest to all of these differing interpretations, he steadfastly refused to offer them further help in understanding the parable. He would only say, "Let every man find out the meaning for himself and in his own soul."

Abner had arranged for the Master to teach in the synagogue on this Sabbath day, the first time Jesus had appeared in a synagogue since they had all been closed to his teachings by order of the Sanhedrin. At the conclusion of the service Jesus looked down before him upon an elderly woman who wore a downcast expression, and who was much bent in form. This woman had long been fear-ridden, and all joy had passed out of her life.

As Jesus stepped down from the pulpit, he went over to her and, touching her bowed-over form on the shoulder, said, "Woman, if you would only believe, you could be wholly loosed from your spirit of infirmity." And this woman, who had been bowed down and bound up by the depressions of fear for more than eighteen years, believed the words of the Master and by faith straightened up immediately. When this woman saw that she had been made straight, she lifted up her voice and glorified God.

Notwithstanding that this woman's affliction was wholly mental, her bowed-over form being the result of her depressed mind, the people thought that Jesus had healed a real physical disorder.

Although the congregation of the synagogue at Philadelphia was friendly toward the teachings of Jesus, the chief ruler of the synagogue was an unfriendly Pharisee. And as he shared the opinion of the congregation that Jesus had healed a physical disorder, and being indignant because Jesus had presumed to do such a thing on the Sabbath, he stood up before the congregation and said, "Are there not six days in which men should do all their work? In these working days come, therefore, and be healed, but not on the Sabbath day."

When the unfriendly ruler had thus spoken, Jesus returned to the speaker's platform and said, "Why play the part of hypocrites? Does not every one of you, on the Sabbath, loose his ox from the stall and lead him forth for watering? If such a service is permissible on the Sabbath day, should not this woman, a daughter of Abraham who has been bound down by evil these eighteen years, be loosed from this bondage and led forth to partake of the waters of liberty and life, even on this Sabbath day?"

And as the woman continued to glorify God, his critic was put to shame, and the congregation rejoiced with her that she had been healed.

As a result of his public criticism of Jesus on this Sabbath the chief ruler of the synagogue was deposed, and a follower of Jesus was put in his place.

Jesus frequently delivered such victims of fear from their spirit of infirmity, from their depression of mind, and from their bondage of fear. But the people thought that all such afflictions were either physical disorders or possession of evil spirits.

Jesus taught again in the synagogue on Sunday, and many were baptized by Abner at noon on that day in the river which flowed south of the city. On the morrow Jesus and the ten apostles would have started back to the Pella encampment but for the arrival of one of David's messengers, who brought an urgent message to Jesus from his friends at Bethany, near Jerusalem.


Very late on Sunday night, February 26, a runner from Bethany arrived at Philadelphia, bringing a message from Martha and Mary which said, "Lord, he whom you love is very sick." This message reached Jesus at the close of the evening conference and just as he was taking leave of the apostles for the night. At first Jesus made no reply. There occurred one of those strange interludes, a time when he appeared to be in communication with something outside of, and beyond, himself. And then, looking up, he addressed the messenger in the hearing of the apostles, saying, "This sickness is really not to the death. Doubt not that it may be used to glorify God and exalt the Son."

Jesus was very fond of Martha, Mary, and their brother, Lazarus; he loved them with a fervent affection. His first and human thought was to go to their assistance at once, but another idea came into his combined mind. He had almost given up hope that the Jewish leaders at Jerusalem would ever accept the kingdom, but he still loved his people, and there now occurred to him a plan whereby the scribes and Pharisees of Jerusalem might have one more chance to accept his teachings; and he decided, his Father willing, to make this last appeal to Jerusalem the most profound and stupendous outward working of his entire earth career. The Jews clung to the idea of a wonder-working deliverer. And though he refused to stoop to the performance of material wonders or to the enactment of temporal exhibitions of political power, he did now ask the Father's consent for the manifestation of his hitherto unexhibited power over life and death.

The Jews were in the habit of burying their dead on the day of their demise; this was a necessary practice in such a warm climate. It often happened that they put in the tomb one who was merely comatose, so that on the second or even the third day, such a one would come forth from the tomb. But it was the belief of the Jews that, while the spirit or soul might linger near the body for two or three days, it never tarried after the third day; that decay was well advanced by the fourth day, and that no one ever returned from the tomb after the lapse of such a period. And it was for these reasons that Jesus tarried yet two full days in Philadelphia before he made ready to start for Bethany.

Accordingly, early on Wednesday morning he said to his apostles, "Let us prepare at once to go into Judea again." And when the apostles heard their Master say this, they drew off by themselves for a time to take counsel of one another. James assumed the direction of the conference, and they all agreed that it was only folly to allow Jesus to go again into Judea, and they came back as one man and so informed him. Said James, "Master, you were in Jerusalem a few weeks back, and the leaders sought your death, while the people were minded to stone you. At that time you gave these men their chance to receive the truth, and we will not permit you to go again into Judea."

Then said Jesus, "But do you not understand that there are twelve hours of the day in which work may safely be done? If a man walks in the day, he does not stumble inasmuch as he has light. If a man walks in the night, he is liable to stumble since he is without light. As long as my day lasts, I fear not to enter Judea. I would do one more mighty work for these Jews; I would give them one more chance to believe, even on their own terms - conditions of outward glory and the visible manifestation of the power of the Father and the love of the Son. Besides, do you not realize that our friend Lazarus has fallen asleep, and I would go to awake him out of this sleep!"

Then said one of the apostles, "Master, if Lazarus has fallen asleep, then will he the more surely recover."

It was the custom of the Jews at that time to speak of death as a form of sleep, but as the apostles did not understand that Jesus meant that Lazarus had departed from this world, he now said plainly, "Lazarus is dead. And I am glad for your sakes, even if the others are not thereby saved, that I was not there, to the end that you shall now have new cause to believe in me; and by that which you will witness, you should all be strengthened in preparation for that day when I shall take leave of you and go to the Father."

When they could not persuade him to refrain from going into Judea, and when some of the apostles were loath even to accompany him, Thomas addressed his fellows, saying, "We have told the Master our fears, but he is determined to go to Bethany. I am satisfied it means the end; they will surely kill him, but if that is the Master's choice, then let us acquit ourselves like men of courage; let us go also that we may die with him." And it was ever so; in matters requiring deliberate and sustained courage, Thomas was always the mainstay of the twelve apostles.

On the way to Judea Jesus was followed by a company of almost fifty of his friends and enemies. At their noon lunchtime, on Wednesday, he talked to his apostles and this group of followers on the "Terms of Salvation," and at the end of this lesson told the parable of the Pharisee and the publican (a tax collector). Said Jesus, "You see, then, that the Father gives salvation to His children of earth, and this salvation is a free gift to all who have the faith to receive membership in the divine family. There is nothing you can do to earn this salvation. Works of self-righteousness cannot buy the favor of God, and much praying in public will not atone for lack of living faith in the heart. Men you may deceive by your outward service, but God looks into your souls. What I am telling you is well illustrated by two men who went into the temple to pray, the one a Pharisee and the other a publican. The Pharisee stood and prayed to himself, 'Oh God, I thank you that I am not like the rest of men, extortioners, unlearned, unjust, adulterers, or even like this publican. I fast twice a week; I give tithes of all that I get.' But the publican, standing afar off, would not so much as lift his eyes to heaven but smote his breast, saying, 'God be merciful to me a sinner.' I tell you that the publican went home with God's approval rather than the Pharisee, for every one who exalts himself shall be humbled, but he who humbles himself shall be exalted."

That night, in Jericho, the unfriendly Pharisees sought to entrap the Master by inducing him to discuss marriage and divorce, as did their fellows one time in Galilee, but Jesus artfully avoided their efforts to bring him into conflict with their laws concerning divorce. As the publican and the Pharisee illustrated good and bad religion, their divorce practices served to contrast the better marriage laws of the Jewish code with the disgraceful laxity of the Pharisaic interpretations of these Mosaic divorce statutes. The Pharisee judged himself by the lowest standard; the publican squared himself by the highest ideal. Devotion, to the Pharisee, was a means of inducing self-righteous inactivity and the assurance of false spiritual security; devotion, to the publican, was a means of stirring up his soul to the realization of the need for repentance, confession, and the acceptance, by faith, of merciful forgiveness. The Pharisee sought justice; the publican sought mercy. The law of the universe is: Ask and you shall receive; seek and you shall find.

Though Jesus refused to be drawn into a controversy with the Pharisees concerning divorce, he did proclaim a positive teaching of the highest ideals regarding marriage. He exalted marriage as the most ideal and highest of all human relationships. Likewise, he intimated strong disapproval of the lax and unfair divorce practices of the Jerusalem Jews, who at that time permitted a man to divorce his wife for the most trifling of reasons, such as being a poor cook, a faulty housekeeper, or for no better reason than that he had become enamored of a better-looking woman.

The Pharisees had even gone so far as to teach that divorce of this easy variety was a special dispensation granted the Jewish people, particularly the Pharisees. And so, while Jesus refused to make pronouncements dealing with marriage and divorce, he did most bitterly denounce these shameful floutings of the marriage relationship and pointed out their injustice to women and children. He never sanctioned any divorce practice that gave man any advantage over woman; the Master countenanced only those teachings which accorded women equality with men.

Although Jesus did not offer new mandates governing marriage and divorce, he did urge the Jews to live up to their own laws and higher teachings. He constantly appealed to the written Scriptures in his effort to improve their practices along these social lines. While thus upholding the high and ideal concepts of marriage, Jesus skillfully avoided clashing with his questioners about the social practices represented by either their written laws or their much-cherished divorce privileges.

It was very difficult for the apostles to understand the Master's reluctance to make positive pronouncements relative to scientific, social, economic, and political problems. They did not fully realize that his earth mission was exclusively concerned with revelations of spiritual and religious truths.

After Jesus had talked about marriage and divorce, later on that evening his apostles privately asked many additional questions, and his answers to these inquiries relieved their minds of many misconceptions. At the conclusion of this conference Jesus said, "Marriage is honorable and is to be desired by all men. The fact that the Son of Man pursues his earth mission alone is in no way a reflection on the desirability of marriage. That I should so work is the Father's will, but this same Father has directed the creation of male and female, and it is the divine will that men and women should find their highest service and consequent joy in the establishment of homes for the reception and training of children, in the creation of whom these parents become copartners with the Makers of heaven and earth. And for this cause shall a man leave his father and mother and shall cleave to his wife, and they two shall become as one."

And in this way Jesus relieved the minds of the apostles of many worries about marriage and cleared up many misunderstandings regarding divorce; at the same time he did much to exalt their ideals of social union and to augment their respect for women and children and for the home.

That evening Jesus' message regarding marriage and the blessedness of children spread all over Jericho, so that the next morning, long before Jesus and the apostles prepared to leave, even before breakfast time, scores of mothers came to where Jesus lodged, bringing their children in their arms and leading them by their hands, and desired that he bless the little ones. When the apostles went out to view this assemblage of mothers with their children, they endeavored to send them away, but these women refused to depart until the Master laid his hands on their children and blessed them. And when the apostles loudly rebuked these mothers, Jesus, hearing the tumult, came out and indignantly reproved them, saying, "Suffer little children to come to me; forbid them not, for of such is the kingdom of heaven. Verily, verily, I say to you, whosoever receives not the kingdom of God as a little child shall hardly enter therein to grow up to the full stature of spiritual adulthood."

And when the Master had spoken to his apostles, he received all of the children, laying his hands on them, while he spoke words of courage and hope to their mothers.

Jesus often talked to his apostles about the celestial mansions and taught that the advancing children of God must there grow up spiritually as children grow up physically on this world. And so does the sacred oftentimes appear to be the common, as on this day these children and their mothers little realized that the onlooking intelligences of Michael's local creation beheld the children of Jericho playing with the Creator of a universe.

Woman's status in Palestine was much improved by Jesus' teaching; and so it would have been throughout the world if his followers had not departed so far from that which he painstakingly taught them.

It was also at Jericho, in connection with the discussion of the early religious training of children in habits of divine worship, that Jesus impressed upon his apostles the great value of beauty as an influence leading to the urge to worship, especially with children. The Master by precept and example taught the value of worshiping the Creator in the midst of the natural surroundings of creation. He preferred to commune with the heavenly Father amidst the trees and among the lowly creatures of the natural world. He rejoiced to contemplate the Father through the inspiring spectacle of the starry realms of the Creator Sons.

When it is not possible to worship God in the tabernacles of nature, men should do their best to provide houses of beauty, sanctuaries of appealing simplicity and artistic embellishment, so that the highest of human emotions may be aroused in association with the intellectual approach to spiritual communion with God. Truth, beauty, and holiness are powerful and effective aids to true worship. But spirit communion is not promoted by mere massive ornateness and overmuch embellishment with man's elaborate and ostentatious art. Beauty is most religious when it is most simple and naturelike. How unfortunate that little children should have their first introduction to concepts of public worship in cold and barren rooms so devoid of the beauty appeal and so empty of all suggestion of good cheer and inspiring holiness! The child should be introduced to worship in nature's outdoors and later accompany his parents to public houses of religious assembly which are at least as materially attractive and artistically beautiful as the home in which he is daily domiciled.

As they journeyed up the hills from Jericho to Bethany, Nathaniel walked most of the way by the side of Jesus, and their discussion of children in relation to the kingdom of heaven led indirectly to the consideration of the ministry of angels. Nathaniel finally asked the Master this question: "Seeing that the high priest is a Sadducee, and since the Sadducees do not believe in angels, what shall we teach the people regarding the heavenly ministers?"

Then, among other things, Jesus said, "The angelic hosts are a separate order of created beings; they are entirely different from the material order of mortal creatures, and they function as a distinct group of universe intelligences. Angels are not of that group of creatures called 'the Sons of God' in the Scriptures; neither are they the glorified spirits of mortal men who have gone on to progress through the mansions on high. Angels are a direct creation, and they do not reproduce themselves. The angelic hosts have only a spiritual kinship with the human race. As man progresses in the journey to the Father in Paradise, he does traverse a state of being at one time analogous to the state of the angels, but mortal man never becomes an angel.

"The angels never die, as man does. The angels are immortal unless, perchance, they become involved in sin as did some of them with the deceptions of Lucifer. The angels are the spirit servants in heaven, and they are neither all-wise nor all-powerful. But all of the loyal angels are truly pure and holy.

"And do you not remember that I said to you once before that, if you had your spiritual eyes anointed, you would then see the heavens opened and behold the angels of God ascending and descending? It is by the ministry of the angels that one world may be kept in touch with other worlds, for have I not repeatedly told you that I have other sheep not of this fold? And these angels are not the spies of the spirit world who watch upon you and then go forth to tell the Father the thoughts of your heart and to report on the deeds of the flesh. The Father has no need of such service inasmuch as his own spirit lives within you. But these angelic spirits do function to keep one part of the heavenly creation informed concerning the doings of other and remote parts of the universe. And many of the angels, while functioning in the government of the Father and the universes of the Sons, are assigned to the service of the human races. When I taught you that many of these seraphim are ministering spirits, I spoke not in figurative language nor in poetic strains. And all this is true, regardless of your difficulty in comprehending such matters.

"Many of these angels are engaged in the work of saving men and women, for have I not told you of the seraphic joy when one soul elects to forsake sin and begin the search for God? I did even tell you of the joy in the *presence of the angels* of heaven over one sinner who repents, thereby indicating the existence of other and higher orders of celestial beings who are likewise concerned in the spiritual welfare and with the divine progress of mortals.

"Also are these angels very much concerned with the means whereby man's spirit is released from the tabernacles of the flesh and his soul escorted to the mansions in heaven. Angels are the sure and heavenly guides of the soul of man during that uncharted and indefinite period of time which intervenes between the death of the flesh and the new life in the spirit abodes."

And he would have spoken further with Nathaniel regarding the ministry of angels, but he was interrupted by the approach of Martha, who had been informed that the Master was drawing near to Bethany by friends who had observed him ascending the hills to the east. And she now hastened to greet him.

# THE RESURRECTION OF LAZARUS

IT WAS shortly after noon when Martha started out to meet Jesus as he came over the brow of the hill near Bethany. Her brother, Lazarus, had been dead four days and had been laid away in their private tomb at the far end of the garden late on Sunday afternoon. The stone at the entrance of the tomb had been rolled in place on the morning of this day, Thursday.

When Martha and Mary sent word to Jesus concerning Lazarus's illness, they were confident the Master would do something about it. They knew that their brother was desperately sick, and though they hardly dared hope that Jesus would leave his work of teaching and preaching to come to their assistance, they had such confidence in his power to heal disease that they thought he would just speak the curative words, and Lazarus would immediately be made whole. And when Lazarus died a few hours after the messenger left Bethany for Philadelphia, they reasoned that it was because the Master did not learn of their brother's illness until it was too late, until he had already been dead for several hours.

But they, with all of their believing friends, were greatly puzzled by the message which the runner brought back Tuesday forenoon when he reached Bethany. The messenger insisted that he heard Jesus say, "...this sickness is really not to the death." Neither could they understand why he sent no word to them nor otherwise proffered assistance.

Many friends from nearby hamlets and others from Jerusalem came over to comfort the sorrow-stricken sisters. Lazarus and his sisters were the children of a well-to-do and honorable Jew, one who had been the leading resident of the little village of Bethany. And notwithstanding that all three had long been ardent followers of Jesus, they were highly respected by all who knew them. They had inherited extensive vineyards and olive orchards in this vicinity, and that they were wealthy was further attested by the fact that they could afford a private burial tomb on their own premises. Both of their parents had already been laid away in this tomb.

Mary had given up the thought of Jesus' coming and was abandoned to her grief, but Martha clung to the hope that Jesus would come, even up to the time on that very morning when they rolled the stone in front of the tomb and sealed the entrance. Even then she instructed a neighbor lad to keep watch down the Jericho road from the brow of the hill to the east of Bethany; and it was this lad who brought tidings to Martha that Jesus and his friends were approaching.

When Martha met Jesus, she fell at his feet, exclaiming, "Master, if you had been here, my brother would not have died!" Many fears were passing through Martha's mind, but she gave expression to no doubt, nor did she venture to criticize or question the Master's conduct as related to Lazarus's death. When she had spoken, Jesus reached down and, lifting her upon her feet, said, "Only have faith, Martha, and your brother shall rise again."

Then answered Martha, "I know that he will rise again in the resurrection of the last day; and even now I believe that whatever you shall ask of God, our Father will give you."

Then, looking straight into the eyes of Martha, Jesus said, "I am the resurrection and the life; he who believes in me, though he dies, yet shall he live. In truth, whosoever lives and believes in me shall never really die. Martha, do you believe this?"

And Martha answered the Master, "Yes, I have long believed that you are the Deliverer, the Son of the living God, even he who should come to this world."

Jesus having inquired for Mary, Martha went at once into the house and, whispering to her sister, said, "The Master is here and has asked for you." And when Mary heard this, she rose up quickly and hastened out to meet Jesus, who still tarried at the place, some distance from the house, where Martha had first met him. The friends who were with Mary, seeking to comfort her, when they saw that she rose up quickly and went out, followed her, supposing that she was going to the tomb to weep.

Many of those present were Jesus' bitter enemies. That is why Martha had come out to meet him alone, and also why she went in secretly to inform Mary that he had asked for her. Martha, while craving to see Jesus, desired to avoid any possible unpleasantness which might be caused by his coming suddenly into the midst of a large group of his Jerusalem enemies. It had been Martha's intention to remain in the house with their friends while Mary went to greet Jesus, but in this she failed, for they all followed Mary and so found themselves unexpectedly in the presence of the Master.

Martha led Mary to Jesus, and when she saw him, she fell at his feet, exclaiming, "If you had only been here, my brother would not have died!" And when Jesus saw how they all grieved over the death of Lazarus, his soul was moved with compassion.

When the mourners saw that Mary had gone to greet Jesus, they withdrew for a short distance while both Martha and Mary talked with the Master and received further words of comfort and exhortation to maintain strong faith in the Father and complete resignation to the divine will.

The human mind of Jesus was mightily moved by the contention between his love for Lazarus and the bereaved sisters and his disdain and contempt for the outward show of affection manifested by some of these unbelieving and murderously intentioned people. Jesus indignantly resented the show of forced and outward mourning for Lazarus by some of these professed friends inasmuch as such false sorrow was associated in their hearts with so much bitter enmity toward himself. Some of those present, however, were sincere in their mourning, for they were real friends of the family.

After Jesus had spent a few moments in comforting Martha and Mary, apart from the mourners, he asked them, "Where have you laid him?"

Then Martha said, "Come and see."

And as the Master followed on in silence with the two sorrowing sisters, he wept. When the friendly Jews who followed after them saw his tears, one of them said, "Behold how he loved him. Could not he who opened the eyes of the blind have kept this man from dying?" By this time they were standing before the family tomb, a small natural cave, or declivity, in the ledge of rock which rose up some thirty feet at the far end of the garden plot.

It is difficult to explain to human minds just why Jesus wept. While we have access to the registration of the combined human emotions and divine thoughts, as of record in the mind of the Personalized Adjuster, we are not altogether certain about the real cause of these emotional manifestations. We are inclined to believe that Jesus wept because of a number of thoughts and feelings which were going through his mind at this time, such as:

1. He felt a genuine and sorrowful sympathy for Martha and Mary; he had a real and deep human affection for these sisters who had lost their brother.

2. He was perturbed in his mind by the presence of the crowd of mourners, some sincere and some merely pretenders. He always resented these outward exhibitions of mourning. He knew the sisters loved their brother and had faith in the survival of believers. These conflicting emotions may possibly explain why he groaned as they came near the tomb.

3. He truly hesitated about bringing Lazarus back to the mortal life. His sisters really needed him, but Jesus regretted having to summon his friend back to experience the bitter persecution which he well knew Lazarus would have to endure as a result of being the subject of the greatest of all demonstrations of the divine power of the Son of Man.

And now we may relate an interesting and instructive fact: Although this narrative unfolds as an apparently natural and normal event in human affairs, it has some very interesting sidelights. While the messenger went to Jesus on Sunday, telling him of Lazarus's illness, and while Jesus sent word that it was "not to the death," at the same time he went in person up to Bethany and even asked the sisters, "Where have you laid him?" Even though all of this seems to indicate that the Master was proceeding after the manner of this life and in accordance with the limited knowledge of the human mind, nevertheless, the records of the universe reveal that Jesus' Personalized Adjuster issued orders for the indefinite detention of Lazarus's Thought Adjuster on the planet subsequent to Lazarus's death, and that this order was made of record just fifteen minutes before Lazarus breathed his last.

Did the divine mind of Jesus know, even before Lazarus died, that he would raise him from the dead? We do not know. We know only what we are herewith placing on record.

Many of Jesus' enemies were inclined to sneer at his manifestations of affection, and they said among themselves, "If he thought so much of this man, why did he tarry so long before coming to Bethany? If he is what they claim, why did he not save his dear friend? What is the good of healing strangers in Galilee if he cannot save those whom he loves?" And in many other ways they mocked and made light of the teachings and works of Jesus.

And so, on this Thursday afternoon at about half past two o'clock, was the stage all set in this little hamlet of Bethany for the enactment of the greatest of all works connected with the earth ministry of Michael of Nebadon, the greatest manifestation of divine power during his incarnation in the flesh, since his own resurrection occurred after he had been liberated from the bonds of mortal habitation.

The small group assembled before Lazarus's tomb little realized the presence near at hand of a vast concourse of all orders of celestial beings assembled under the leadership of Gabriel and now in waiting, by direction of the Personalized Adjuster of Jesus, vibrating with expectancy and ready to execute the bidding of their beloved Sovereign.

When Jesus spoke those words of command, "Take away the stone," the assembled celestial hosts made ready to enact the drama of the resurrection of Lazarus in the likeness of his mortal flesh. Such a form of resurrection involves difficulties of execution which far transcend the usual technique of the resurrection of mortal creatures in semi-spirit form on the Mansion Worlds and requires far more celestial personalities and a far greater organization of universe facilities.

When Martha and Mary heard this command of Jesus directing that the stone in front of the tomb be rolled away, they were filled with conflicting emotions. Mary hoped that Lazarus was to be raised from the dead, but Martha, while to some extent sharing her sister's faith, was more exercised by the fear that Lazarus would not be presentable, in his appearance, to Jesus, the apostles, and their friends. Said Martha, "Must we roll away the stone? My brother has now been dead four days, so that by this time decay of the body has begun." Martha also said this because she was not certain as to why the Master had requested that the stone be removed; she thought maybe Jesus wanted only to take one last look at Lazarus. She was not settled and constant in her attitude.

As they hesitated to roll away the stone, Jesus said, "Did I not tell you at the first that this sickness was not to the death? Have I not come to fulfill my promise? And after I came to you, did I not say that, if you would only believe, you should see the glory of God? Wherefore do you doubt? How long before you will believe and obey?"

When Jesus had finished speaking, his apostles, with the assistance of willing neighbors, laid hold upon the stone and rolled it away from the entrance to the tomb.

It was the common belief of the Jews that the drop of gall on the point of the sword of the angel of death began to work by the end of the third day, so that it was taking full effect on the fourth day. They allowed that the soul of man might linger about the tomb until the end of the third day, seeking to reanimate the dead body; but they firmly believed that such a soul had gone on to the abode of departed spirits ere the fourth day had dawned.

These beliefs and opinions regarding the dead and the departure of the spirits of the dead served to make sure, in the minds of all who were now present at Lazarus's tomb and subsequently to all who might hear of what was about to occur, that this was really and truly a case of the raising of the dead by the personal working of one who declared he was "the resurrection and the life."

As this company of some forty-five mortals stood before the tomb, they could dimly see the form of Lazarus, wrapped in linen bandages, resting on the right lower niche of the burial cave. While these earth creatures stood there in almost breathless silence, a vast host of celestial beings had swung into their places preparatory to answering the signal for action when it should be given by Gabriel, their commander.

Jesus lifted up his eyes and said, "Father, I am thankful that you heard and granted my request. I know that you always hear me, but because of those who stand here with me, I thus speak with you, that they may believe that you have sent me into the world, and that they may know that you are working with me in that which we are about to do." And when he had prayed, he cried with a loud voice, "Lazarus, come forth!"

Though these human observers remained motionless, the vast celestial host was all astir in unified action in obedience to the Creator's word. In just twelve seconds of earth time the hitherto lifeless form of Lazarus began to move and presently sat up on the edge of the stone shelf whereon it had rested. His body was bound about with grave cloths, and his face was covered with a napkin. And as he stood up before them - alive - Jesus said, "Loose him and let him go."

All, save the apostles, with Martha and Mary, fled to the house. They were pale with fright and overcome with astonishment. While some tarried, many hastened to their homes.

Lazarus greeted Jesus and the apostles and asked the meaning of the grave cloths and why he had awakened in the garden. Jesus and the apostles drew to one side while Martha told Lazarus of his death, burial, and resurrection. She had to explain to him that he had died on Sunday and was now brought back to life on Thursday, inasmuch as he had had no consciousness of time since falling asleep in death.

As Lazarus came out of the tomb, the Personalized Adjuster of Jesus, now chief of his kind in this local universe, gave command to the former Adjuster of Lazarus, now in waiting, to resume abode in the mind and soul of the resurrected man.

Then went Lazarus over to Jesus and, with his sisters, knelt at the Master's feet to give thanks and offer praise to God. Jesus, taking Lazarus by the hand, lifted him up, saying, "My son, what has happened to you will also be experienced by all who believe this gospel except that they shall be resurrected in a more glorious form. You shall be a living witness of the truth which I spoke - I am the resurrection and the life. But let us all now go into the house and partake of nourishment for these physical bodies."

As they walked toward the house, Gabriel dismissed the extra groups of the assembled heavenly host while he made record of the first instance on Earth, and the last, where a mortal creature had been resurrected in the likeness of the physical body of death.

Lazarus could hardly comprehend what had occurred. He knew he had been very sick, but he could recall only that he had fallen asleep and been awakened. He was never able to tell anything about these four days in the tomb because he was wholly unconscious. Time is nonexistent to those who sleep the sleep of death.

Though many believed in Jesus as a result of this mighty work, others only hardened their hearts the more to reject him. By noon the next day this story had spread over all Jerusalem. Scores of men and women went to Bethany to look upon Lazarus and talk with him, and the alarmed and disconcerted Pharisees hastily called a meeting of the Sanhedrin that they might determine what should be done about these new developments.

Even though the testimony of this man raised from the dead did much to consolidate the faith of the mass of believers in the gospel of the kingdom, it had little or no influence on the attitude of the religious leaders and rulers at Jerusalem except to hasten their decision to destroy Jesus and stop his work.

At one o'clock the next day, Friday, the Sanhedrin met to deliberate further on the question, "What shall we do with Jesus of Nazareth?" After more than two hours of discussion and acrimonious debate, a certain Pharisee presented a resolution calling for Jesus' immediate death, proclaiming that he was a menace to all Israel and formally committing the Sanhedrin to the decision of death, without trial and in defiance of all precedent.

Time and again had this august body of Jewish leaders decreed that Jesus be apprehended and brought to trial on charges of blasphemy and numerous other accusations of flouting the Jewish sacred law. They had once before even gone so far as to declare he should die, but this was the first time the Sanhedrin had gone on record as desiring to decree his death in advance of a trial. But this resolution did not come to a vote since fourteen members of the Sanhedrin resigned in a body when such an unheard-of action was proposed. While these resignations were not formally acted upon for almost two weeks, this group of fourteen withdrew from the Sanhedrin on that day, never again to sit in the council. When these resignations were subsequently acted upon, five other members were thrown out because their associates believed they entertained friendly feelings toward Jesus. With the ejection of these nineteen men the Sanhedrin was in a position to try and to condemn Jesus with a solidarity bordering on unanimity.

The following week Lazarus and his sisters were summoned to appear before the Sanhedrin. When their testimony had been heard, no doubt could be entertained that Lazarus had been raised from the dead. Though the transactions of the Sanhedrin virtually admitted the resurrection of Lazarus, the record carried a resolution attributing this and all other wonders worked by Jesus to the power of the prince of devils, with whom Jesus was declared to be in league.

No matter what the source of his wonder-working power, these Jewish leaders were persuaded that, if he were not immediately stopped, very soon all the common people would believe in him; and further, that serious complications with the Roman authorities would arise since so many of his believers regarded him as the Messiah, Israel's deliverer.

It was at this same meeting of the Sanhedrin that Caiaphas the high priest first gave expression to that old Jewish adage, which he so many times repeated: "It is better that one man die, than that the community perish."

Although Jesus had received warning of the doings of the Sanhedrin on this dark Friday afternoon, he was not in the least perturbed and continued resting over the Sabbath with friends in Bethphage, a hamlet near Bethany. Early Sunday morning Jesus and the apostles assembled, by prearrangement, at the home of Lazarus, and taking leave of the Bethany family, they started on their journey back to the Pella encampment.

⭐ ⭐ ⭐

On the way from Bethany to Pella the apostles asked Jesus many questions, all of which the Master freely answered except those involving the details of the resurrection of the dead. Such problems were beyond the comprehension capacity of his apostles; therefore did the Master decline to discuss these questions with them. Since they had departed from Bethany in secret, they were alone. Jesus therefore embraced the opportunity to say many things to the ten which he thought would prepare them for the trying days just ahead.

The apostles were much stirred up in their minds and spent considerable time discussing their recent experiences as they were related to prayer and its answering. They all recalled Jesus' statement to the Bethany messenger at Philadelphia, when he said plainly, "This sickness is not really to the death." And yet, in spite of this promise, Lazarus actually died. All that day, again and again, they reverted to the discussion of this question of the answer to prayer.

Jesus' answers to their many questions may be summarized as follows:

1. Prayer is an expression of the finite mind in an effort to approach the Infinite. The making of a prayer must, therefore, be limited by the knowledge, wisdom, and attributes of the finite; likewise must the answer be conditioned by the vision, aims, ideals, and prerogatives of the Infinite. There never can be observed an unbroken continuity of material phenomena between the making of a prayer and the reception of the full spiritual answer thereto.

2. When a prayer is apparently unanswered, the delay often betokens a better answer, although one which is for some good reason greatly delayed. When Jesus said that Lazarus's sickness was really not to the death, he had already been dead eleven hours. No sincere prayer is denied an answer except when the superior viewpoint of the spiritual world has devised a better answer, an answer that meets the petition of the spirit of man as contrasted with the prayer of the mere mind of man.

3. The prayers of time, when indited by the spirit and expressed in faith, are often so vast and all-encompassing that they can be answered only in eternity; the finite petition is sometimes so fraught with the grasp of the Infinite that the answer must long be postponed to await the creation of adequate capacity for receptivity; the prayer of faith may be so all-embracing that the answer can be received only on Paradise.

4. The answers to the prayer of the mortal mind are often of such a nature that they can be received and recognized only after that same praying mind has attained the immortal state. The prayer of the material being can many times be answered only when such an individual has progressed to the spirit level.

5. The prayer of a God-knowing person may be so distorted by ignorance and so deformed by superstition that the answer thereto would be highly undesirable. Then must the intervening spirit beings so translate such a prayer that, when the answer arrives, the petitioner wholly fails to recognize it as the answer to his prayer.

6. All true prayers are addressed to spiritual beings, and all such petitions must be answered in spiritual terms, and all such answers must consist in spiritual realities. Spirit beings cannot bestow material answers to the spirit petitions of even material beings. Material beings can pray effectively only when they "pray in the spirit."

7. No prayer can hope for an answer unless it is born of the spirit and nurtured by faith. Your sincere faith implies that you have in advance virtually granted your prayer hearers the full right to answer your petitions in accordance with that supreme wisdom and that divine love which your faith depicts as always actuating those beings to whom you pray.

8. The child is always within his rights when he presumes to petition the parent; and the parent is always within his parental obligations to the immature child when his superior wisdom dictates that the answer to the child's prayer be delayed, modified, segregated, transcended, or postponed to another stage of spiritual ascension.

9. Do not hesitate to pray the prayers of spirit longing; doubt not that you shall receive the answer to your petitions. These answers will be on deposit, awaiting your achievement of those future spiritual levels of actual cosmic attainment, on this world or on others, whereon it will become possible for you to recognize and appropriate the long-waiting answers to your earlier but ill-timed petitions.

10. All genuine spirit-born petitions are certain of an answer. Ask and you shall receive. But you should remember that you are progressive creatures of time and space; therefore must you constantly reckon with the time-space factor in the experience of your personal reception of the full answers to your manifold prayers and petitions.

Lazarus remained at the Bethany home, being the center of great interest to many sincere believers and to numerous curious individuals, until the day of the crucifixion of Jesus, when he received warning that the Sanhedrin had decreed his death. The rulers of the Jews were determined to put a stop to the further spread of the teachings of Jesus, and they well judged that it would be useless to put Jesus to death if they permitted Lazarus, who represented the very peak of his wonder-working, to live and bear testimony to the fact that Jesus had raised him from the dead. Already had Lazarus suffered bitter persecution from them.

And so Lazarus took hasty leave of his sisters at Bethany, fleeing down through Jericho and across the Jordan, never permitting himself to rest long until he had reached Philadelphia. Lazarus knew Abner well, and here he felt safe from the murderous intrigues of the wicked Sanhedrin.

Soon after this Martha and Mary disposed of their lands at Bethany and joined their brother in Perea. Meantime, Lazarus had become the treasurer of the church at Philadelphia. He became a strong supporter of Abner in his controversy with Paul and the Jerusalem church and ultimately died, when 67 years old, of the same sickness that carried him off when he was a younger man at Bethany.

# LAST TEACHING AT PELLA

LATE ON Monday evening, March 6, Jesus and the ten apostles arrived at the Pella camp. This was the last week of Jesus' sojourn there, and he was very active in teaching the multitude and instructing the apostles. He preached every afternoon to the crowds and each night answered questions for the apostles and certain of the more advanced disciples residing at the camp.

Word regarding the resurrection of Lazarus had reached the encampment two days before the Master's arrival, and the entire assembly was agog. Not since the feeding of the five thousand had anything occurred which so aroused the imagination of the people. And thus it was at the very height of the second phase of the public ministry of the kingdom that Jesus planned to teach this one short week at Pella and then to begin the tour of southern Perea which led right up to the final and tragic experiences of the last week in Jerusalem.

The Pharisees and the chief priests had begun to formulate their charges and to crystallize their accusations. They objected to the Master's teachings on these grounds:

1. He is a friend of publicans and sinners; he receives the ungodly and even eats with them.

2. He is a blasphemer; he talks about God as being his Father and thinks he is equal with God.

3. He is a lawbreaker. He heals disease on the Sabbath and in many other ways flouts the sacred law of Israel.

4. He is in league with devils. He works wonders and does seeming miracles by the power of Beelzebub, the prince of devils.

On Thursday afternoon Jesus talked to the multitude about the "Grace of Salvation." In the course of this sermon he retold the story of the lost sheep and the lost coin and then added his favorite parable of the prodigal son.

Said Jesus, "You have been admonished by the prophets from Samuel to John that you should seek for God - search for truth. Always have they said, 'Seek the Lord while he may be found.' And all such teaching should be taken to heart. But I have come to show you that, while you are seeking to find God, God is likewise seeking to find you. Many times have I told you the story of the good shepherd who left the ninety and nine sheep in the fold while he went forth searching for the one that was lost, and how, when he had found the straying sheep, he laid it over his shoulder and tenderly carried it back to the fold. And when the lost sheep had been restored to the fold, you remember that the good shepherd called in his friends and bade them rejoice with him over the finding of the sheep that had been lost. Again I say there is more joy in heaven over one sinner who repents than over the ninety and nine just persons who need no repentance. The fact that souls are *lost* only increases the interest of the heavenly Father. I have come to this world to do my Father's bidding, and it has truly been said of the Son of Man that he is a friend of publicans and sinners.

"You have been taught that divine acceptance comes after your repentance and as a result of all your works of sacrifice and penitence, but I assure you that the Father accepts you even before you have repented and sends the Son and his associates to find you and bring you, with rejoicing, back to the fold, the kingdom of sonship and spiritual progress. You are all like sheep which have gone astray, and I have come to seek and to save those who are lost.

"And you should also remember the story of the woman who, having had ten pieces of silver made into a necklace of adornment, lost one piece, and how she lit the lamp and diligently swept the house and kept up the search until she found the lost piece of silver. And as soon as she found the coin that was lost, she called together her friends and neighbors, saying, 'Rejoice with me, for I have found the piece that was lost.' So again I say, there is always joy in the presence of the angels of heaven over one sinner who repents and returns to the Father's fold. And I tell you this story to impress upon you that the Father and His Son go forth to *search* for those who are lost, and in this search we employ all influences capable of rendering assistance in our diligent efforts to find those who are lost, those who stand in need of salvation. And so, while the Son of Man goes out in the wilderness to seek for the sheep gone astray, he also searches for the coin which is lost in the house. The sheep wanders away, unintentionally; the coin is covered by the dust of time and obscured by the accumulation of the things of men.

"And now I would like to tell you the story of a thoughtless son of a well-to-do farmer who *deliberately* left his father's house and went off into a foreign land, where he fell into much tribulation. You recall that the sheep strayed away without intention, but this youth left his home with premeditation. It was like this:

"A certain man had two sons; one, the younger, was lighthearted and carefree, always seeking for a good time and shirking responsibility, while his older brother was serious, sober, hard-working, and willing to bear responsibility. Now these two brothers did not get along well together; they were always quarreling and bickering. The younger lad was cheerful and vivacious, but indolent and unreliable; the older son was steady and industrious, at the same time self-centered, surly, and conceited. The younger son enjoyed play but shunned work; the older devoted himself to work but seldom played. This association became so disagreeable that the younger son came to his father and said, 'Father, give me the third portion of your possessions which would fall to me and allow me to go out into the world to seek my own fortune.' And when the father heard this request, knowing how unhappy the young man was at home and with his older brother, he divided his property, giving the youth his share.

"Within a few weeks the young man gathered together all his funds and set out upon a journey to a far country, and finding nothing profitable to do which was also pleasurable, he soon wasted all his inheritance in riotous living. And when he had spent all, there arose a prolonged famine in that country, and he found himself in want. And so, when he suffered hunger and his distress was great, he found employment with one of the citizens of that country, who sent him into the fields to feed swine. And the young man would fain have filled himself with the husks which the swine ate, but no one would give him anything.

"One day, when he was very hungry, he came to himself and said, 'How many hired servants of my father have bread enough and to spare while I perish with hunger, feeding swine off here in a foreign country! I will arise and go to my father, and I will say to him: Father, I have sinned against heaven and against you. I am no more worthy to be called your son; only be willing to make me one of your hired servants.' And when the young man had reached this decision, he arose and started out for his father's house.

"Now this father had grieved much for his son; he had missed the cheerful, though thoughtless, lad. This father loved this son and was always on the lookout for his return, so that on the day he approached his home, even while he was yet afar off, the father saw him and, being moved with loving compassion, ran out to meet him, and with affectionate greeting he embraced and kissed him. And after they had thus met, the son looked up into his father's tearful face and said, 'Father, I have sinned against heaven and in your sight; I am no more worthy to be called a son' - but the lad did not find opportunity to complete his confession because the overjoyed father said to the servants who had by this time come running up, 'Bring quickly his best robe, the one I have saved, and put it on him and put the son's ring on his hand and fetch sandals for his feet.'

"And then, after the happy father had led the footsore and weary lad into the house, he called to his servants, 'Bring on the fatted calf and kill it, and let us eat and make merry, for this my son was dead and is alive again; he was lost and is found.' And they all gathered about the father to rejoice with him over the restoration of his son.

"About this time, while they were celebrating, the elder son came in from his day's work in the field, and as he drew near the house, he heard the music and the dancing. And when he came up to the back door, he called out one of the servants and inquired as to the meaning of all this festivity. And then said the servant, 'Your long-lost brother has come home, and your father has killed the fatted calf to rejoice over his son's safe return. Come in that you also may greet your brother and receive him back into your father's house.'

"But when the older brother heard this, he was so hurt and angry he would not go into the house. When his father heard of his resentment of the welcome of his younger brother, he went out to entreat him. But the older son would not yield to his father's persuasion. He answered his father, saying, 'Here these many years have I served you, never transgressing the least of your commands, and yet you never gave me even a kid that I might make merry with my friends. I have remained here to care for you all these years, and you never made rejoicing over my faithful service, but when this your son returns, having squandered your substance with harlots, you make haste to kill the fatted calf and make merry over him.'

"Since this father truly loved both of his sons, he tried to reason with this older one: 'But, my son, you have all the while been with me, and all this which I have is yours. You could have had a kid at any time you had made friends to share your merriment. But it is only proper that you should now join with me in being glad and merry because of your brother's return. Think of it, my son, your brother was lost and is found; he has returned alive to us!'"

This was one of the most touching and effective of all the parables which Jesus ever presented to impress upon his hearers the Father's willingness to receive all who seek entrance into the kingdom of heaven.

Jesus was very partial to telling these three stories at the same time. He presented the story of the lost sheep to show that, when men unintentionally stray away from the path of life, the Father is mindful of such *lost* ones and goes out, with his Sons, the true shepherds of the flock, to seek the lost sheep. He then would recite the story of the coin lost in the house to illustrate how thorough is the divine *searching* for all who are confused, confounded, or otherwise spiritually blinded by the material cares and accumulations of life. And then he would launch forth into the telling of this parable of the lost son, the reception of the returning prodigal, to show how complete is the *restoration* of the lost son into his Father's house and heart.

Many, many times during his years of teaching, Jesus told and retold this story of the prodigal son. This parable and the story of the good Samaritan were his favorite means of teaching the love of the Father and the neighborliness of man.

✬ ✬ ✬

One evening Simon Zelotes, commenting on one of Jesus' statements, said, "Master, what did you mean when you said today that many of the children of the world are wiser in their generation than are the children of the kingdom since they are skillful in making friends with the mammon of unrighteousness?"

Jesus answered, "Some of you, before you entered the kingdom, were very shrewd in dealing with your business associates. If you were unjust and often unfair, you were nonetheless prudent and farseeing in that you transacted your business with an eye single to your present profit and future safety. Likewise should you now so order your lives in the kingdom as to provide for your present joy while you also make certain of your future enjoyment of treasures laid up in heaven. If you were so diligent in making gains for yourselves when in the service of self, why should you show less diligence in gaining souls for the kingdom since you are now servants of the brotherhood of man and stewards of God?

"You may all learn a lesson from the story of a certain rich man who had a shrewd but unjust steward. This steward had not only oppressed his master's clients for his own selfish gain, but he had also directly wasted and squandered his master's funds. When all this finally came to the ears of his master, he called the steward before him and asked the meaning of these rumors and required that he should give immediate accounting of his stewardship and prepare to turn his master's affairs over to another.

"Now this unfaithful steward began to say to himself, 'What shall I do since I am about to lose this stewardship? I have not the strength to dig; to beg I am ashamed. I know what I will do to make certain that, when I am put out of this stewardship, I will be welcomed into the houses of all who do business with my master.' And then, calling in each of his lord's debtors, he said to the first, 'How much do you owe my master?' He answered, 'A hundred measures of oil.' Then said the steward, 'Take your wax board bond, sit down quickly, and change it to fifty.' Then he said to another debtor, 'How much do you owe?' And he replied, 'A hundred measures of wheat.' Then said the steward, 'Take your bond and write fourscore.' And this he did with numerous other debtors. And so did this dishonest steward seek to make friends for himself after he would be discharged from his stewardship. Even his lord and master, when he subsequently found out about this, was compelled to admit that his unfaithful steward had at least shown sagacity in the manner in which he had sought to provide for future days of want and adversity.

"And it is in this way that the sons of this world sometimes show more wisdom in their preparation for the future than do the children of light. I say to you who profess to be acquiring treasure in heaven: Take lessons from those who make friends with the mammon of unrighteousness, and likewise so conduct your lives that you make eternal friendship with the forces of righteousness in order that, when all things earthly fail, you shall be joyfully received into the eternal habitations.

"I affirm that he who is faithful in little will also be faithful in much, while he who is unrighteous in little will also be unrighteous in much. If you have not shown foresight and integrity in the affairs of this world, how can you hope to be faithful and prudent when you are trusted with the stewardship of the true riches of the heavenly kingdom? If you are not good stewards and faithful bankers, if you have not been faithful in that which is another's, who will be foolish enough to give you great treasure in your own name?

"And again I assert that no man can serve two masters; either he will hate the one and love the other, or else he will hold to one while he despises the other. You cannot serve God and mammon."

When the Pharisees who were present heard this, they began to sneer and scoff since they were much given to the acquirement of riches. These unfriendly hearers sought to engage Jesus in unprofitable argumentation, but he refused to debate with his enemies. When the Pharisees fell to wrangling among themselves, their loud speaking attracted large numbers of the multitude encamped thereabouts; and when they began to dispute with each other, Jesus withdrew, going to his tent for the night.

When the meeting became too noisy, Simon Peter, standing up, took charge, saying, "Men and brethren, it is not seemly thus to dispute among yourselves. The Master has spoken, and you do well to ponder his words. And this is no new doctrine which he proclaimed to you. Have you not also heard the allegory of the Nazarites concerning the rich man and the beggar? Some of us heard John the Baptist thunder this parable of warning to those who love riches and covet dishonest wealth. And while this olden parable is not according to the gospel we preach, you would all do well to heed its lessons until such a time as you comprehend the new light of the kingdom of heaven. The story as John told it was like this:

"There was a certain rich man named Dives, who, being clothed in purple and fine linen, lived in mirth and splendor every day. And there was a certain beggar named Lazarus, who lay at this rich man's gate, covered with sores and desiring to be fed with the crumbs which fell from the rich man's table; yes, even the dogs came and licked his sores. And it came to pass that the beggar died and was carried away by the angels to rest in Abraham's bosom. And then, presently, this rich man also died and was buried with great pomp and regal splendor. When the rich man departed from this world, he waked up in Hades, and finding himself in torment, he lifted-up his eyes and beheld Abraham afar off and Lazarus in his bosom. And then Dives cried aloud, 'Father Abraham, have mercy on me and send over Lazarus that he may dip the tip of his finger in water to cool my tongue, for I am in great anguish because of my punishment.' And then Abraham replied, 'My son, you should remember that in your lifetime you enjoyed the good things while Lazarus in like manner suffered the evil. But now all this is changed, seeing that Lazarus is comforted while you are tormented. And besides, between us and you there is a great gulf so that we cannot go to you, neither can you come over to us.' Then said Dives to Abraham, 'I pray you send Lazarus back to my father's house, inasmuch as I have five brothers, that he may so testify as to prevent my brothers from coming to this place of torment.' But Abraham said, 'My son, they have Moses and the prophets; let them hear them.' And then answered Dives, 'No, No, Father Abraham! but if one go to them from the dead, they will repent.' And then said Abraham, 'If they hear not Moses and the prophets, neither will they be persuaded even if one were to rise from the dead.'"

After Peter had recited this ancient parable of the Nazarite brotherhood, and since the crowd had quieted down, Andrew arose and dismissed them for the night. Although both the apostles and his disciples frequently asked Jesus questions about the parable of Dives and Lazarus, he never consented to make comment thereon.


Jesus always had trouble trying to explain to the apostles that, while they proclaimed the establishment of the kingdom of God, the Father in heaven *was not a king.* At the time Jesus lived on earth and taught in the flesh, the people knew mostly of kings and emperors in the governments of the nations, and the Jews had long contemplated the coming of the kingdom of God. For these and other reasons, the Master thought best to designate the spiritual brotherhood of man as the kingdom of heaven and the spirit head of this brotherhood as the *Father in heaven.* Never did Jesus refer to his Father as a king. In his intimate talks with the apostles he always referred to himself as the Son of Man and as their elder brother. He depicted all his followers as servants of mankind and messengers of the gospel of the kingdom.

Jesus never gave his apostles a systematic lesson concerning the personality and attributes of the Father in heaven. He never asked men to believe in his Father; he took it for granted they did. Jesus never belittled himself by offering arguments in proof of the reality of the Father. His teaching regarding the Father all centered in the declaration that he and the Father are one; that he who has seen the Son has seen the Father; that the Father, like the Son, knows all things; that only the Son really knows the Father, and he to whom the Son will reveal Him; that he who knows the Son knows also the Father; and that the Father sent him into the world to reveal their combined natures and to show forth their conjoint work. He never made other pronouncements about his Father except to the woman of Samaria at Jacob's well, when he declared, "God is spirit."

You learn about God from Jesus by observing the divinity of his life, not by depending on his teachings. From the life of the Master you may each assimilate that concept of God which represents the measure of your capacity to perceive realities spiritual and divine, truths real and eternal. The finite can never hope to comprehend the Infinite except as the Infinite was focalized in the time-space personality of the finite experience of the human life of Jesus of Nazareth.

Jesus well knew that God can be known only by the realities of experience; never can He be understood by the mere teaching of the mind. Jesus taught his apostles that, while they never could fully understand God, they could most certainly *know H*im, even as they had known the Son of Man. You can know God, not by understanding what Jesus said, but by knowing what Jesus was. Jesus *was* a revelation of God.

Except when quoting the Hebrew scriptures, Jesus referred to Deity by only two names: God and Father. And when the Master made reference to his Father as God, he usually employed the Hebrew word signifying the plural God (the Trinity) and not the word Yahweh, which stood for the progressive conception of the tribal God of the Jews.

Jesus never called the Father a king, and he very much regretted that the Jewish hope for a restored kingdom and John's proclamation of a coming kingdom made it necessary for him to denominate his proposed spiritual brotherhood the kingdom of heaven. With the one exception - the declaration that "God is spirit" - Jesus never referred to Deity in any manner other than in terms descriptive of his own personal relationship with the First Source and Center of Paradise.

Jesus employed the word God to designate the *idea* of Deity and the word Father to designate the *experience* of knowing God. When the word Father is employed to denote God, it should be understood in its largest possible meaning. The word God cannot be defined and therefore stands for the infinite concept of the Father, while the term Father, being capable of partial definition, may be employed to represent the human concept of the divine Father as he is associated with man during the course of mortal existence.

To the Jews, Elohim was the God of gods, while Yahweh was the God of Israel. Jesus accepted the concept of Elohim and called this supreme group of beings God. In the place of the concept of Yahweh, the racial deity, he introduced the idea of the fatherhood of God and the worldwide brotherhood of man. He exalted the Yahweh concept of a deified racial Father to the idea of a Father of all the children of men, a divine Father of the individual believer. And he further taught that this God of universes and this Father of humanity were one and the same Paradise Deity.

Jesus never claimed to be the manifestation of Elohim (God) in the flesh. He never declared that he was a revelation of Elohim (God) to the worlds. He never taught that he who had seen him had seen Elohim (God). But he did proclaim himself as the revelation of the Father in the flesh, and he did say that whoso had seen him had seen the Father. As the divine Son he claimed to represent only the Father.

He was, indeed, the Son of even the Elohim God; but in the likeness of mortal flesh and to the mortal children of God, he chose to limit his life revelation to the portrayal of his Father's character in so far as such a revelation might be comprehensible to mortal man. As regards the character of the other persons of the Paradise Trinity, we shall have to be content with the teaching that they are altogether like the Father, who has been revealed in personal portraiture in the life of His incarnated Son, Jesus of Nazareth.

Although Jesus revealed the true nature of the heavenly Father in his earth life, he taught little about him. In fact, he taught only two things: that God in Himself is spirit, and that, in all matters of relationship with His creatures, He is a Father. On this evening Jesus made the final pronouncement of his relationship with God when he declared, "I have come out from the Father, and I have come into the world; again, I will leave the world and go to the Father."

But mark you! Never did Jesus say, "Whoso has heard me has heard God." But he did say, "He who has *seen* me has seen the Father." To hear Jesus' teaching is not equivalent to knowing God, but to *see* Jesus is an experience which in itself is a revelation of the Father to the soul. The God of universes rules the far-flung creation, but it is the Father in heaven who sends forth His spirit to dwell within your minds.

Jesus is the spiritual lens in human likeness that makes visible to the material creature Him who is invisible. He is your elder brother who, in the flesh, makes *known* to you a Being of infinite attributes whom not even the celestial hosts can presume fully to understand. But all of this must consist in the personal experience of the *individual believer.* God who is spirit can be known only as a spiritual experience. God can be revealed to the finite sons of the material worlds, by the divine Son of the spiritual realms, only as a *Father.* You can know the Eternal as a Father; you can worship Him as the God of universes, the infinite Creator of all existences.

# THE KINGDOM OF HEAVEN

SATURDAY afternoon, March 11, Jesus preached his last sermon at Pella. This was among the notable addresses of his public ministry, embracing a full and complete discussion of the kingdom of heaven. He was aware of the confusion which existed in the minds of his apostles and disciples regarding the meaning and significance of the terms "kingdom of heaven" and "kingdom of God," which he used as interchangeable designations of his bestowal mission. Although the very term kingdom of *heaven* should have been enough to separate what it stood for from all connection with *earthly* kingdoms and temporal governments, it was not. The idea of a temporal king was too deep-rooted in the Jewish mind thus to be dislodged in a single generation. Therefore Jesus did not at first openly oppose this long-nourished concept of the kingdom.

This Sabbath afternoon the Master sought to clarify the teaching about the kingdom of heaven; he discussed the subject from every viewpoint and endeavored to make clear the many different senses in which the term had been used. In this narrative we will amplify the address by adding numerous statements made by Jesus on previous occasions and by including some remarks made only to the apostles during the evening discussions of this same day. We will also make certain comments dealing with the subsequent outworking of the kingdom idea as it is related to the later Christian church.

In connection with the recital of Jesus' sermon it should be noted that throughout the Hebrew scriptures there was a dual concept of the kingdom of heaven. The prophets presented the kingdom of God as:

    1. A present reality; and as

    2. A future hope - when the kingdom would be realized in fullness upon the appearance of the Messiah. This is the kingdom concept which John the Baptist taught.

From the very first Jesus and the apostles taught both of these concepts. There were two other ideas of the kingdom which should be borne in mind:

3. The later Jewish concept of a worldwide and transcendental kingdom of supernatural origin and miraculous inauguration.

4. The Persian teachings portraying the establishment of a divine kingdom as the achievement of the triumph of good over evil at the end of the world.

Just before the advent of Jesus on earth, the Jews combined and confused all of these ideas of the kingdom into their apocalyptic concept of the Messiah's coming to establish the age of the Jewish triumph, the eternal age of God's supreme rule on earth, the new world, the era in which all mankind would worship Yahweh. In choosing to utilize this concept of the kingdom of heaven, Jesus elected to appropriate the most vital and culminating heritage of both the Jewish and Persian religions.

The kingdom of heaven, as it has been understood and misunderstood down through the centuries of the Christian era, embraced four distinct groups of ideas:

1. The concept of the Jews.

2. The concept of the Persians.

3. The personal-experience concept of Jesus - "the kingdom of heaven within you."

4. The composite and confused concepts which the founders and promulgators of Christianity have sought to impress upon the world.

At different times and in varying circumstances it appears that Jesus may have presented numerous concepts of the "kingdom" in his public teachings, but to his apostles he always taught the kingdom as embracing man's personal experience in relation to his fellows on earth and to the Father in heaven. Concerning the kingdom, his last word always was, "The kingdom is within you."

Centuries of confusion regarding the meaning of the term "kingdom of heaven" have been due to three factors:

1. The confusion occasioned by observing the idea of the "kingdom" as it passed through the various progressive phases of its recasting by Jesus and his apostles.

2. The confusion which was inevitably associated with the transplantation of early Christianity from a Jewish to a gentile soil.

3. The confusion which was inherent in the fact that Christianity became a religion which was organized about the central idea of Jesus' person; the gospel of the kingdom became more and more a religion *about* him.

★ ★ ★

The Master made it clear that the kingdom of heaven must begin with, and be centered in, the dual concept of the truth of the fatherhood of God and the correlated fact of the brotherhood of man. The acceptance of such a teaching, Jesus declared, would liberate men and women from the age-long bondage of animal fear and at the same time enrich human living with the following endowments of the new life of spiritual liberty:

1. The possession of new courage and augmented spiritual power. The gospel of the kingdom was to set men and women free and inspire them to dare to hope for eternal life.

2. The gospel carried a message of new confidence and true consolation for all men and women, even for the poor.

3. It was in itself a new standard of moral values, a new ethical yardstick wherewith to measure human conduct. It portrayed the ideal of a resultant new order of human society.

4. It taught the pre-eminence of the spiritual compared with the material; it glorified spiritual realities and exalted superhuman ideals.

5. This new gospel held up spiritual attainment as the true goal of living. Human life received a new endowment of moral value and divine dignity.

6. Jesus taught that eternal realities were the result (reward) of righteous earthly striving. Man's mortal sojourn on earth acquired new meanings consequent upon the recognition of a noble destiny.

7. The new gospel affirmed that human salvation is the revelation of a far-reaching divine purpose to be fulfilled and realized in the future destiny of the endless service of the salvaged sons and daughters of God.

These teachings cover the expanded idea of the kingdom that was taught by Jesus. This great concept was hardly embraced in the elementary and confused kingdom teachings of John the Baptist.

The apostles were unable to grasp the real meaning of the Master's utterances regarding the kingdom. The subsequent distortion of Jesus' teachings, as they are recorded in the New Testament, is because the concept of the gospel writers was colored by the belief that Jesus was then absent from the world for only a short time; that he would soon return to establish the kingdom in power and glory - just such an idea as they held while he was with them in the flesh. But Jesus did not connect the establishment of the kingdom with the idea of his return to this world. That centuries have passed with no signs of the appearance of the "New Age" is in no way out of harmony with Jesus' teaching.

The great effort embodied in this sermon was the attempt to translate the concept of the kingdom of heaven into the ideal of the idea of doing the will of God.

Long had the Master taught his followers to pray: "Your kingdom come; your will be done"; and at this time he earnestly sought to induce them to abandon the use of the term *kingdom of God* in favor of the more practical equivalent, *the will of God*. But he did not succeed.

Jesus desired to substitute for the idea of the kingdom, king, and subjects, the concept of the heavenly family, the heavenly Father, and the liberated children of God engaged in joyful and voluntary service for their fellows and in the sublime and intelligent worship of God the Father.

Up to this time the apostles had acquired a double viewpoint of the kingdom; they regarded it as:

1. A matter of personal experience then present in the hearts of true believers, and

2. A question of racial or world phenomena; that the kingdom was in the future, something to look forward to.

They looked upon the coming of the kingdom in the hearts of men as a gradual development, like the leaven in the dough or like the growing of the mustard seed. They believed that the coming of the kingdom in the racial or world sense would be both sudden and spectacular. Jesus never tired of telling them that the kingdom of heaven was their personal experience of realizing the higher qualities of spiritual living; that these realities of the spirit experience are progressively translated to new and higher levels of divine certainty and eternal grandeur.

On this afternoon the Master distinctly taught a new concept of the double nature of the kingdom in that he portrayed the following two phases:

"First. The kingdom of God in this world, the supreme desire to do the will of God, the unselfish love of man which yields the good fruits of improved ethical and moral conduct.

"Second. The kingdom of God in heaven, the goal of mortal believers, the estate wherein the love for God is perfected, and wherein the will of God is done more divinely."

Jesus taught that, by faith, the believer enters the kingdom *now*. In the various discourses he taught that two things are essential to faith-entrance into the kingdom:

1. *Faith, sincerity.* To come as a little child, to receive the bestowal of sonship as a gift; to submit to the doing of the Father's will without questioning and in the full confidence and genuine trustfulness of the Father's wisdom; to come into the kingdom free from prejudice and preconception; to be open-minded and teachable like an unspoiled child.

2. *Truth hunger.* The thirst for righteousness, a change of mind, the acquirement of the motive to be like God and to find God.

Jesus taught that sin is not the child of a defective nature but rather the off-spring of a knowing mind dominated by an unsubmissive will. Regarding sin, he taught that God *has* forgiven; that we make such forgiveness personally available by the act of forgiving our fellows. When you forgive your brother or sister in the flesh, you thereby create the capacity in your own soul for the reception of the reality of God's forgiveness of your own misdeeds.

By the time the Apostle John began to write the story of Jesus' life and teachings, the early Christians had experienced so much trouble with the kingdom-of-God idea as a breeder of persecution that they had largely abandoned the use of the term. John talks much about the "eternal life." Jesus often spoke of it as the "kingdom of life." He also frequently referred to "the kingdom of God within you." He once spoke of such an experience as "family fellowship with God the Father." Jesus sought to substitute many terms for the kingdom but always without success. Among others, he used: the family of God, the Father's will, the friends of God, the fellowship of believers, the brotherhood of man, the Father's fold, the children of God, the fellowship of the faithful, the Father's service, and the liberated sons and daughters of God.

But he could not escape the use of the kingdom idea. It was more than fifty years later, not until after the destruction of Jerusalem by the Roman armies, that this concept of the kingdom began to change into the cult of eternal life as its social and institutional aspects were taken over by the rapidly expanding and crystallizing Christian church.

Jesus was always trying to impress upon his apostles and disciples that they must acquire, by faith, a righteousness that would exceed the righteousness of slavish works which some of the scribes and Pharisees paraded so vaingloriously before the world.

Though Jesus taught that faith, simple childlike belief, is the key to the door of the kingdom, he also taught that, having entered the door, there are the progressive steps of righteousness which every believing child must ascend in order to grow up to the full stature of the robust children of God.

It is in the consideration of the technique of *receiving* God's forgiveness that the attainment of the righteousness of the kingdom is revealed. Faith is the price you pay for entrance into the family of God; but forgiveness is the act of God that accepts your faith as the price of admission. And the reception of the forgiveness of God by a kingdom believer involves a definite and actual experience and consists in the following four steps, the kingdom steps of inner righteousness:

1. God's forgiveness is made actually available and is personally experienced by men and women just in so far as they forgive their fellows.
2. Man will not truly forgive his fellows unless he loves them as himself.
3. To thus love your neighbor as yourself *is* the highest ethics.

4. Moral conduct, true righteousness, becomes, then, the natural result of such love.

It therefore is evident that the true and inner religion of the kingdom unfailingly and increasingly tends to manifest itself in practical avenues of social service. Jesus taught a living religion that impelled its believers to engage in the doing of loving service. But Jesus did not put ethics in the place of religion. He taught religion as a cause and ethics as a result.

The righteousness of any act must be measured by the motive; the highest forms of good are therefore unconscious. Jesus was never concerned with morals or ethics as such. He was wholly concerned with that inward and spiritual fellowship with God the Father which so certainly and directly manifests itself as outward and loving service for mankind. He taught that the religion of the kingdom is a genuine personal experience which none can contain within themselves; that the consciousness of being a member of the family of believers leads inevitably to the practice of the precepts of the family conduct, the service of one's brothers and sisters in the effort to enhance and enlarge the brotherhood.

The religion of the kingdom is personal, individual; the fruits, the results, are familial, social. Jesus never failed to exalt the sacredness of the individual as contrasted with the community. But he also recognized that men and women develop their characters by unselfish service; that they unfold their moral nature in loving relations with their fellows.

By teaching that the kingdom is within, by exalting the individual, Jesus struck the deathblow of the old society in that he ushered in the new dispensation of true social righteousness. This new order of society the world has little known because it has refused to practice the principles of the gospel of the kingdom of heaven. And when this kingdom of spiritual pre-eminence does come upon the earth, it will not be manifested in mere improved social and material conditions, but rather in the glories of those enhanced and enriched spiritual values which are characteristic of the approaching age of improved human relations and advancing spiritual attainments.

Jesus never gave a precise definition of the kingdom. At one time he would discourse on one phase of the kingdom, and at another time he would discuss a different aspect of the brotherhood of God's reign in the hearts of men and women. In the course of this Sabbath afternoon's sermon Jesus noted no less than five phases, or epochs, of the kingdom, and they were:

1. The personal and inward experience of the spiritual life of the fellowship of the individual believer with God the Father.

2. The enlarging brotherhood of gospel believers, the social aspects of the enhanced morals and quickened ethics resulting from the reign of God's spirit in the hearts of individual believers.

3. The supermortal brotherhood of invisible spiritual beings which prevails on earth and in heaven, the superhuman kingdom of God.

4. The prospect of the more perfect fulfillment of the will of God, the advance toward the dawn of a new social order in connection with improved spiritual living - the next age of man.

5. The kingdom in its fullness, the future spiritual age of light and life on earth.

Wherefore must we always examine the Master's teaching to ascertain which of these five phases he may have reference to when he makes use of the term kingdom of heaven. By this process of gradually changing man's will and thus affecting human decisions, Michael and his associates are likewise gradually but certainly changing the entire course of human evolution, social and otherwise.

The Master on this occasion placed emphasis on the following five points as representing the cardinal features of the gospel of the kingdom:

1. The pre-eminence of the individual.

2. The will as the determining factor in man's experience.

3. Spiritual fellowship with God the Father.

4. The supreme satisfactions of the loving service of humanity.

5. The transcendency of the spiritual over the material in human personality.

This world has never seriously or sincerely or honestly tried out these dynamic ideas and divine ideals of Jesus' doctrine of the kingdom of heaven. But you should not become discouraged by the apparently slow progress of the kingdom idea on Earth. Remember that the order of progressive evolution is subjected to sudden and unexpected periodical changes in both the material and the spiritual worlds. The bestowal of Jesus as an incarnated Son was just such a strange and unexpected event in the spiritual life of the world. Neither make the fatal mistake, in looking for the age manifestation of the kingdom, of failing to effect its establishment within your own souls.

Although Jesus referred one phase of the kingdom to the future and did, on numerous occasions, intimate that such an event might appear as a part of a world crisis; and though he did likewise most certainly, on several occasions, definitely promise sometime to return to Earth, it should be recorded that he never positively linked these two ideas together. He promised a new revelation of the kingdom on earth and at some future time; he also promised sometime to come back to this world in person; but he did not say that these two events were synonymous. From all we know these promises may, or may not, refer to the same event.

His apostles and disciples most certainly linked these two teachings together. When the kingdom failed to materialize as they had expected, recalling the

Master's teaching concerning a future kingdom and remembering his promise to come again, they jumped to the conclusion that these promises referred to an identical event; and therefore they lived in hope of his immediate second coming to establish the kingdom in its fullness and with power and glory. And so have successive believing generations lived on earth entertaining the same inspiring but disappointing hope.

Having summarized the teachings of Jesus about the kingdom of heaven, we are permitted to narrate certain later ideas which became attached to the concept of the kingdom and to engage in a prophetic forecast of the kingdom as it may evolve in the age to come.

Throughout the first centuries of the Christian propaganda, the idea of the kingdom of heaven was tremendously influenced by the then rapidly spreading notions of Greek idealism, the idea of the natural as the shadow of the spiritual - the temporal as the time shadow of the eternal.

But the great step which marked the transplantation of the teachings of Jesus from a Jewish to a gentile soil was taken when the Messiah of the kingdom became the Redeemer of the church, a religious and social organization growing out of the activities of Paul and his successors and based on the teachings of Jesus as they were supplemented by the ideas of Philo and the Persian doctrines of good and evil.

The ideas and ideals of Jesus, embodied in the teaching of the gospel of the kingdom, nearly failed of realization as his followers progressively distorted his pronouncements. The Master's concept of the kingdom was notably modified by two great tendencies:

1. The Jewish believers persisted in regarding him as the *Messiah*. They believed that Jesus would very soon return actually to establish the worldwide and more or less material kingdom.

2. The gentile Christians began very early to accept the doctrines of Paul, which led increasingly to the general belief that Jesus was the *Redeemer* of the children of the church, the new and institutional successor of the earlier concept of the purely spiritual brotherhood of the kingdom.

The church, as a social outgrowth of the kingdom, would have been wholly natural and even desirable. The evil of the church was not its existence, but rather that it almost completely supplanted the Jesus concept of the kingdom. Paul's institutionalized church became a virtual substitute for the kingdom of heaven which Jesus had proclaimed.

But doubt not, this same kingdom of heaven which the Master taught exists within the heart of the believer, will yet be proclaimed to this Christian church, even as to all other religions, races, and nations on earth - even to every individual.

The kingdom of Jesus' teaching, the spiritual ideal of individual righteousness and the concept of man's divine fellowship with God, became gradually submerged into the mystic conception of the person of Jesus as the Redeemer-Creator and spiritual head of a socialized religious community. In this way a formal and institutional church became the substitute for the individually spirit-led brotherhood of the kingdom.

The church was an inevitable and useful *social* result of Jesus' life and teachings; the tragedy consisted in the fact that this social reaction to the teachings of the kingdom so fully displaced the spiritual concept of the real kingdom as Jesus taught and lived it.

The kingdom, to the Jews, was the Israelite *community;* to the gentiles it became the Christian *church.* To Jesus the kingdom was the sum of those *individuals* who had confessed their faith in the fatherhood of God, thereby declaring their wholehearted dedication to the doing of the will of God, thus becoming members of the spiritual brotherhood of man and women.

The Master fully realized that certain social results would appear in the world as a consequence of the spread of the gospel of the kingdom; but he intended that all such desirable social manifestations should appear as unconscious and inevitable outgrowths, or natural fruits, of this inner personal experience of individual believers, this purely spiritual fellowship and communion with the divine spirit which indwells and activates all such believers.

Jesus foresaw that a social organization, or church, would follow the progress of the true spiritual kingdom, and that is why he never opposed the apostles' practicing the rite of John's baptism. He taught that the truth-loving soul, the one who hungers and thirsts for righteousness, for God, is admitted by faith to the spiritual kingdom; at the same time the apostles taught that such a believer is admitted to the social organization of disciples by the outward rite of baptism.

When Jesus' immediate followers recognized their partial failure to realize his ideal of the establishment of the kingdom in the hearts of men by the spirit's domination and guidance of the individual believer, they set about to save his teaching from being wholly lost by substituting for the Master's ideal of the kingdom the gradual creation of a visible social organization, the Christian church. And when they had accomplished this program of substitution, in order to maintain consistency and to provide for the recognition of the Master's teaching regarding the fact of the kingdom, they proceeded to set the kingdom off into the future. The church, just as soon as it was well established, began to teach that the kingdom was in reality to appear at the culmination of the Christian age, at the second coming of Christ.

In this manner the kingdom became the concept of an age, the idea of a future visitation, and the ideal of the final redemption of the saints of the Most High. The early Christians (and all too many of the later ones) generally lost sight of the

Father-and-son idea embodied in Jesus' teaching of the kingdom, while they substituted therefor the well-organized social fellowship of the church. The church thus became in the main a *social* brotherhood that effectively displaced Jesus' concept and ideal of a *spiritual* brotherhood.

Jesus' ideal concept largely failed, but upon the foundation of the Master's personal life and teachings, supplemented by the Greek and Persian concepts of eternal life and augmented by Philo's doctrine of the temporal contrasted with the spiritual, Paul went forth to build up one of the most progressive human societies that has ever existed on Earth.

The concept of Jesus is still alive in the advanced religions of the world. Paul's Christian church is the socialized and humanized shadow of what Jesus intended the kingdom of heaven to be - and what it most certainly will yet become. Paul and his successors partly transferred the issues of eternal life from the individual to the church. Christ thus became the head of the church rather than the elder brother of each individual believer in the Father's family of the kingdom. Paul and his contemporaries applied all of Jesus' spiritual implications regarding himself and the individual believer to the *church* as a group of believers; and in doing this, they struck a deathblow to Jesus' concept of the divine kingdom in the heart of the individual believer.

And so, for centuries, the Christian church has labored under great embarrassment because it dared to lay claim to those mysterious powers and privileges of the kingdom, powers and privileges which can be exercised and experienced only between Jesus and his spiritual believer brothers and sisters. And thus it becomes apparent that membership in the church does not necessarily mean fellowship in the kingdom; one is spiritual, the other mainly social.

Sooner or later another and greater John the Baptist is due to arise proclaiming "the kingdom of God is at hand" - meaning a return to the high spiritual concept of Jesus, who proclaimed that the kingdom is the will of his heavenly Father dominant and transcendent in the heart of the believer - and doing all this without in any way referring either to the visible church on earth or to the anticipated second coming of Christ. There must come a revival of the *actual* teachings of Jesus, such a restatement as will undo the work of his early followers who went about to create a socio-philosophical system of belief regarding the *fact* of Michael's sojourn on earth. In a short time the teaching of this story *about* Jesus nearly supplanted the preaching of Jesus' gospel of the kingdom. In this way a historical religion displaced that teaching in which Jesus had blended man's highest moral ideas and spiritual ideals with man's most sublime hope for the future - eternal life. And that was the gospel of the kingdom.

It is just because the gospel of Jesus was so many-sided that within a few centuries students of the records of his teachings became divided up into so many cults and sects. This pitiful subdivision of Christian believers results from failure to discern in the Master's manifold teachings the divine oneness of his matchless life. But someday the true believers in Jesus will not be thus spiritually divided in their attitude before unbelievers. Always we may have diversity of intellectual comprehension and interpretation, even varying degrees of socialization, but lack of spiritual brotherhood is both inexcusable and reprehensible.

Mistake not! There is in the teachings of Jesus an eternal nature that will not permit them forever to remain unfruitful in the hearts of thinking men. The kingdom as Jesus conceived it has to a large extent failed on earth; for the time being, an outward church has taken its place; but you should comprehend that this church is only the larval stage of the thwarted spiritual kingdom, which will carry it through this material age and over into a more spiritual dispensation where the Master's teachings may enjoy a fuller opportunity for development. Thus does the so-called Christian church become the cocoon in which the kingdom of Jesus' concept now slumbers. The kingdom of the divine brotherhood is still alive and will eventually and certainly come forth from this long submergence, just as surely as the butterfly eventually emerges as the beautiful unfolding of its less attractive creature of metamorphic development.

# ON THE WAY TO JERUSALEM

THE DAY after the memorable sermon on "The Kingdom of Heaven," Jesus announced that on the following day he and the apostles would depart for the Passover at Jerusalem, visiting numerous cities in southern Perea on the way.

The address on the kingdom and the announcement that he was going to the Passover set all his followers to thinking that he was going up to Jerusalem to inaugurate the temporal kingdom of Jewish supremacy. No matter what Jesus said about the nonmaterial character of the kingdom, he could not wholly remove from the minds of his Jewish hearers the idea that the Messiah was to establish some kind of nationalistic government with headquarters at Jerusalem.

What Jesus said in his Sabbath sermon only tended to confuse the majority of his followers; very few were enlightened by the Master's discourse. The leaders understood something of his teachings regarding the inner kingdom, "the kingdom of heaven within you," but they also knew that he had spoken about another and future kingdom, and it was this kingdom they believed he was now going up to Jerusalem to establish. When they were disappointed in this expectation, when he was rejected by the Jewish leaders, and later on, when Jerusalem was literally destroyed, they still clung to this hope, sincerely believing that the Master would soon return to the world in great power and majestic glory to establish the kingdom.

It was on this Sunday afternoon that Salome the mother of James and John Zebedee came to Jesus with her two apostle sons and, in the manner of approaching an Oriental potentate, sought to have Jesus promise in advance to grant whatever request she might make. But the Master would not promise; instead, he asked her, "What do you want me to do for you?"

Then answered Salome, "Master, now that you are going up to Jerusalem to establish the kingdom, I would ask you in advance to promise me that these my sons shall have honor with you, the one to sit on your right hand and the other to sit on your left hand in your kingdom."

When Jesus heard Salome's request, he said, "Woman, you know not what you ask." And then, looking straight into the eyes of the two honor-seeking apostles, he said, "Because I have long known and loved you; because I have even lived in your mother's house; because Andrew has assigned you to be with me at all times; therefore do you permit your mother to come to me secretly, making this unseemly request. But let me ask you, are you able to drink the cup I am about to drink?"

And without a moment for thought, James and John answered, "Yes, Master, we are able."

Said Jesus, "I am saddened that you know not why we go up to Jerusalem; I am grieved that you understand not the nature of my kingdom; I am disappointed that you bring your mother to make this request of me; but I know you love me in your hearts; therefore I declare that you shall indeed drink of my cup of bitterness and share in my humiliation, but to sit on my right hand and on my left hand is not mine to give. Such honors are reserved for those who have been designated by my Father."

By this time someone had carried word of this conference to Peter and the other apostles, and they were highly indignant that James and John would seek to be preferred before them, and that they would secretly go with their mother to make such a request. When they fell to arguing among themselves, Jesus called them all together and said, "You well understand how the rulers of the gentiles lord it over their subjects, and how those who are great exercise authority. But it shall not be so in the kingdom of heaven. Whosoever would be great among you, let him first become your servant. He who would be first in the kingdom, let him become your minister. I declare to you that the Son of Man came not to be ministered to but to minister; and I now go up to Jerusalem to lay down my life in the doing of the Father's will and in the service of my brethren."

When the apostles heard these words, they withdrew by themselves to pray. That evening, in response to the labors of Peter, James and John made suitable apologies to the ten and were restored to the good graces of their brethren.

In asking for places on the right hand and on the left hand of Jesus at Jerusalem, the sons of Zebedee little realized that in less than one month their beloved teacher would be hanging on a Roman cross with a dying thief on one side and another transgressor on the other side. And their mother, who was present at the crucifixion, well remembered the foolish request she had made of Jesus at Pella regarding the honors she so unwisely sought for her apostle sons.

On the forenoon of Monday, March 13, Jesus and his twelve apostles took final leave of the Pella encampment, starting south on their tour of the cities of southern Perea, where Abner's associates were at work. They spent more than two weeks visiting among the seventy and then went directly to Jerusalem for the Passover.

When the Master left Pella, the disciples encamped with the apostles, about one thousand in number, followed after him. About one half of this group left him at the Jordan ford on the road to Jericho when they learned he was going over to Heshbon, and after he had preached the sermon on "Counting the Cost." They went on up to Jerusalem, while the other half followed him for two weeks, visiting the towns in southern Perea.

In a general way, most of Jesus' immediate followers understood that the camp at Pella had been abandoned, but they really thought this indicated that their Master at last intended to go to Jerusalem and lay claim to David's throne. A large majority of his followers never were able to grasp any other concept of the kingdom of heaven; no matter what he taught them, they would not give up this Jewish idea of the kingdom.

Acting on the instructions of the Apostle Andrew, David Zebedee closed the visitors' camp at Pella on Wednesday, March 15. At this time almost four thousand visitors were in residence, and this does not include the one thousand and more persons who sojourned with the apostles at what was known as the teachers' camp, and who went south with Jesus and the twelve. Much as David disliked to do it, he sold the entire equipment to numerous buyers and proceeded with the funds to Jerusalem, subsequently turning the money over to Judas Iscariot.

David was present in Jerusalem during the tragic last week, taking his mother back with him to Bethsaida after the crucifixion. While awaiting Jesus and the apostles, David stopped with Lazarus at Bethany and became tremendously agitated by the manner in which the Pharisees had begun to persecute and harass him since his resurrection. Andrew had directed David to discontinue the messenger service; and this was construed by all as an indication of the early establishment of the kingdom at Jerusalem. David found himself without a job, and he had about decided to become the self-appointed defender of Lazarus when presently the object of his indignant solicitude fled in haste to Philadelphia. Accordingly, sometime after the resurrection and also after the death of his mother, David betook himself to Philadelphia, having first assisted Martha and Mary in disposing of their real estate; and there, in association with Abner and Lazarus, he spent the remainder of his life, becoming the financial overseer of all those large interests of the kingdom which had their center at Philadelphia during the lifetime of Abner.

Within a short time after the destruction of Jerusalem, Antioch became the headquarters of *Pauline Christianity,* while Philadelphia remained the center of the *Abnerian kingdom of heaven.* From Antioch the Pauline version of the teachings of Jesus and about Jesus spread to all the Western world; from Philadelphia the missionaries of the Abnerian version of the kingdom of heaven spread throughout Mesopotamia and Arabia until the later times when these uncompromising emissaries of the teachings of Jesus were overwhelmed by the sudden rise of Islam.

When Jesus and the company of almost one thousand followers arrived at the Bethany ford of the Jordan sometimes called Bethabara, his disciples began to realize that he was not going directly to Jerusalem. While they hesitated and debated among themselves, Jesus climbed upon a huge stone and delivered that discourse which has become known as "Counting the Cost."

The Master said, "You who would follow after me from this time on, must be willing to pay the price of wholehearted dedication to the doing of my Father's will. If you would be my disciples, you must be willing to forsake father, mother, wife, children, brothers, and sisters. If any one of you would now be my disciple, you must be willing to give up even your life just as the Son of Man is about to offer up his life for the completion of the mission of doing the Father's will on earth and in the flesh.

"If you are not willing to pay the full price, you can hardly be my disciple. Before you go further, you should each sit down and count the cost of being my disciple. Which one of you would undertake to build a watchtower on your lands without first sitting down to count up the cost to see whether you had money enough to complete it? If you fail thus to reckon the cost, after you have laid the foundation, you may discover that you are unable to finish that which you have begun, and therefore will all your neighbors mock you, saying, 'Behold, this man began to build but was unable to finish his work.' Again, what king, when he prepares to make war upon another king, does not first sit down and take counsel as to whether he will be able, with ten thousand men, to meet him who comes against him with twenty thousand? If the king cannot afford to meet his enemy because he is unprepared, he sends an embassy to this other king, even when he is yet a great way off, asking for terms of peace.

"Now, then, must each of you sit down and count the cost of being my disciple. From now on you will not be able to follow after us, listening to the teaching and beholding the works; you will be required to face bitter persecutions and to bear witness for this gospel in the face of crushing disappointment. If you are unwilling to renounce all that you are and to dedicate all that you have, then are you unworthy to be my disciple. If you have already conquered yourself within your own heart, you need have no fear of that outward victory which you must presently gain when the Son of Man is rejected by the chief priests and the Sadducees and is given into the hands of mocking unbelievers.

"Now should you examine yourself to find out your motive for being my disciple. If you seek honor and glory, if you are worldly minded, you are like the salt when it has lost its savor. And when that which is valued for its saltiness has lost its savor, wherewith shall it be seasoned? Such a condiment is useless; it is fit only to be cast out among the refuse. Now have I warned you to turn back to your homes in peace if you are not willing to drink with me the cup which is being prepared. Again and again have I told you that my kingdom is not of this world, but you will not believe me. He who has ears to hear let him hear what I say."

Immediately after speaking these words, Jesus, leading the twelve, started off on the way to Heshbon, followed by about five hundred. After a brief delay the other half of the multitude went on up to Jerusalem. His apostles, together with the leading disciples, thought much about these words, but still they clung to the belief that, after this brief period of adversity and trial, the kingdom would certainly be set up somewhat in accordance with their long-cherished hopes.

For more than two weeks Jesus and the twelve, followed by a crowd of several hundred disciples, journeyed about in southern Perea, visiting all of the towns wherein the seventy labored. Many gentiles lived in this region, and since few were going up to the Passover feast at Jerusalem, the messengers of the kingdom went right on with their work of teaching and preaching.

Jesus met Abner at Heshbon, and Andrew directed that the labors of the seventy should not be interrupted by the Passover feast; Jesus advised that the messengers should go forward with their work in complete disregard of what was about to happen at Jerusalem. He also counseled Abner to permit the women's corps, at least such as desired, to go to Jerusalem for the Passover. And this was the last time Abner ever saw Jesus in the flesh. His farewell to Abner was: "My son, I know you will be true to the kingdom, and I pray the Father to grant you wisdom that you may love and understand your brethren."

As they traveled from city to city, large numbers of their followers deserted to go on to Jerusalem so that, by the time Jesus started for the Passover, the number of those who followed along with him day by day had dwindled to less than two hundred.

The apostles understood that Jesus was going to Jerusalem for the Passover. They knew that the Sanhedrin had broadcast a message to all Israel that he had been condemned to die and directing that anyone knowing his whereabouts should inform the Sanhedrin; and yet, despite all this, they were not so alarmed as they had been when he had announced to them in Philadelphia that he was going to Bethany to see Lazarus. This change of attitude from that of intense fear to a state of hushed expectancy was mostly because of Lazarus's resurrection. They had reached the conclusion that Jesus might, in an emergency, assert his divine power and put to shame his enemies. This hope, coupled with their more profound and mature faith in the spiritual supremacy of their Master, accounted for the outward courage displayed by his immediate followers, who now made ready to follow him into Jerusalem in the very face of the open declaration of the Sanhedrin that he must die.

The majority of the apostles and many of his inner disciples did not believe it possible for Jesus to die; they, believing that he was "the resurrection and the life," regarded him as immortal and already triumphant over death.

On Wednesday evening, March 29, Jesus and his followers encamped at Livias on their way to Jerusalem, after having completed their tour of the cities of southern Perea. It was during this night at Livias that Simon Zelotes and Simon Peter, having conspired to have delivered into their hands at this place more than one hundred swords, received and distributed these arms to all who would accept them and wear them concealed beneath their cloaks. Simon Peter was still wearing his sword on the night of the Master's betrayal in the garden.

Early on Thursday morning before the others were awake, Jesus called Andrew and said, "Awaken your brethren! I have something to say to them." Jesus knew about the swords and which of his apostles had received and were wearing these weapons, but he never disclosed to them that he knew such things.

When Andrew had aroused his associates, and they had assembled off by themselves, Jesus said, "My children, you have been with me a long while, and I have taught you much that is needful for this time, but I would now warn you not to put your trust in the uncertainties of the flesh nor in the frailties of man's defense against the trials and testing which lie ahead of us. I have called you apart here by yourselves that I may once more plainly tell you that we are going up to Jerusalem, where you know the Son of Man has already been condemned to death. Again am I telling you that the Son of Man will be delivered into the hands of the chief priests and the religious rulers; that they will condemn him and then deliver him into the hands of the gentiles. And so will they mock the Son of Man, even spit upon him and scourge him, and they will deliver him up to death. And when they kill the Son of Man, be not dismayed, for I declare that on the third day he shall rise. Take heed to yourselves and remember that I have forewarned you."

Again were the apostles amazed, stunned; but they could not bring themselves to regard his words as literal; they could not comprehend that the Master meant just what he said. They were so blinded by their persistent belief in the temporal kingdom on earth, with headquarters at Jerusalem, that they simply could not - would not - permit themselves to accept Jesus' words as literal. They pondered all that day as to what the Master could mean by such strange pronouncements. But none of them dared to ask him a question concerning these statements. Not until after his death did these bewildered apostles wake up to the realization that the Master had spoken to them plainly and directly in anticipation of his crucifixion.

It was here at Livias, just after breakfast, that certain friendly Pharisees came to Jesus and said, "Flee in haste from these parts, for Herod, just as he sought John, now seeks to kill you. He fears an uprising of the people and has decided to kill you. We bring you this warning that you may escape."

And this was partly true. The resurrection of Lazarus had frightened and alarmed Herod, and knowing that the Sanhedrin had dared to condemn Jesus, even in advance of a trial, Herod made up his mind either to kill Jesus or to drive him out of his domains. He really desired to do the latter since he so feared him that he hoped he would not be compelled to execute him.

When Jesus heard what the Pharisees had to say, he replied, "I well know about Herod and his fear of this gospel of the kingdom. But, mistake not, he would much prefer that the Son of Man go up to Jerusalem to suffer and die at the hands of the chief priests; he is not anxious, having stained his hands with the blood of John, to become responsible for the death of the Son of Man. Go you and tell that fox that the Son of Man preaches in Perea today, tomorrow goes into Judea, and after a few days, will be perfected in his mission on earth and prepared to ascend to the Father."

Then turning to his apostles, Jesus said, "From olden times the prophets have perished in Jerusalem, and it is only befitting that the Son of Man should go up to the city of the Father's house to be offered up as the price of human bigotry and as the result of religious prejudice and spiritual blindness. Oh Jerusalem, Jerusalem, which kills the prophets and stones the teachers of truth! How often would I have gathered your children together even as a hen gathers her own brood under her wings, but you would not let me do it! Behold, your house is about to be left to you desolate! You will many times desire to see me, but you shall not. You will then seek but not find me." And when he had spoken, he turned to those around him and said, "Nevertheless, let us go up to Jerusalem to attend the Passover and do that which becomes us in fulfilling the will of the Father in heaven."

It was a confused and bewildered group of believers who this day followed Jesus into Jericho. The apostles could discern only the certain note of final triumph in Jesus' declarations regarding the kingdom; they just could not bring themselves to that place where they were willing to grasp the warnings of the impending setback. When Jesus spoke of "rising on the third day," they seized upon this statement as signifying a sure triumph of the kingdom immediately following an unpleasant preliminary skirmish with the Jewish religious leaders. The "third day" was a common Jewish expression signifying "presently" or "soon thereafter." When Jesus spoke of "rising," they thought he referred to the "rising of the kingdom."

Jesus had been accepted by these believers as the Messiah, and the Jews knew little or nothing about a suffering Messiah. They did not understand that Jesus was to accomplish many things by his death that could never have been achieved by his life. While it was the resurrection of Lazarus that nerved the apostles to enter Jerusalem, it was the memory of the transfiguration that sustained the Master at this trying period of his bestowal.

★ ★ ★

Late on the afternoon of Thursday, March 30, Jesus and his apostles, at the head of a band of about two hundred followers, approached the walls of Jericho. As they came near the gate of the city, they encountered a throng of beggars, among them one Bartimeus, an elderly man who had been blind from his youth. This blind beggar had heard much about Jesus and knew all about his healing of the blind Josiah at Jerusalem. He had not known of Jesus' last visit to Jericho until he had gone on to Bethany. Bartimeus had resolved that he would never again allow Jesus to visit Jericho without appealing to him for the restoration of his sight.

News of Jesus' approach had been heralded throughout Jericho, and hundreds of the inhabitants flocked forth to meet him. When this great crowd came back escorting the Master into the city, Bartimeus, hearing the heavy tramping of the multitude, knew that something unusual was happening, and so he asked those standing near him what was going on. And one of the beggars replied, "Jesus of Nazareth is passing by."

When Bartimeus heard that Jesus was near, he lifted up his voice and began to cry aloud, "Jesus, Jesus, have mercy upon me!" And as he continued to cry louder and louder, some of those near to Jesus went over and rebuked him, requesting him to hold his peace; but it was of no avail; he cried only the more and the louder.

When Jesus heard the blind man crying out, he stood still. And when he saw him, he said to his friends, "Bring the man to me."

And then they went over to Bartimeus, saying, "Be of good cheer; come with us, for the Master calls for you."

When Bartimeus heard these words, he threw aside his cloak, springing forward toward the center of the road, while those near by guided him to Jesus.

Addressing Bartimeus, Jesus said, "What do you want me to do for you?"

Then answered the blind man, "I would have my sight restored."

And when Jesus heard this request and saw his faith, he said, "You shall receive your sight; go your way; your faith has made you whole."

Immediately he received his sight, and he remained near Jesus, glorifying God, until the Master started on the next day for Jerusalem, and then he went before the multitude declaring to all how his sight had been restored in Jericho.

When the Master's procession entered Jericho, it was nearing sundown, and he was minded to abide there for the night. As Jesus passed by the customs house, Zaccheus the chief publican, or tax collector, happened to be present, and he much desired to see Jesus. This chief publican was very rich and had heard much about this prophet of Galilee. He had resolved that he would see what sort of a man Jesus was the next time he chanced to visit Jericho; accordingly, Zaccheus sought to press through the crowd, but it was too great, and being short of stature, he could not see over their heads. And so the chief publican followed on with the crowd until they came near the center of the city and not far from where he lived.

When he saw that he would be unable to penetrate the crowd, and thinking that Jesus might be going right on through the city without stopping, he ran on ahead and climbed up into a sycamore tree whose spreading branches overhung the roadway. He knew that in this way he could obtain a good view of the Master as he passed by. And he was not disappointed.

As Jesus passed by, he stopped and, looking up at Zaccheus, said, "Make haste, Zaccheus, and come down, for tonight I must abide at your house."

And when Zaccheus heard these astonishing words, he almost fell out of the tree in his haste to get down, and going up to Jesus, he expressed great joy that the Master should be willing to stop at his house.

They went at once to the home of Zaccheus, and those who lived in Jericho were much surprised that Jesus would consent to abide with the chief publican.

Even while the Master and his apostles lingered with Zaccheus before the door of his house, one of the Jericho Pharisees, standing nearby, said, "You see how this man has gone to lodge with a sinner, an apostate son of Abraham who is an extortioner and a robber of his own people."

And when Jesus heard this, he looked down at Zaccheus and smiled.

Then Zaccheus stood upon a stool and said, "Men of Jericho, hear me! I may be a publican and a sinner, but the great Teacher has come to abide in my house; and before he goes in, I tell you that I am going to bestow one half of all my goods upon the poor, and beginning tomorrow, if I have wrongfully exacted aught from any man, I will restore fourfold. I am going to seek salvation with all my heart and learn to do righteousness in the sight of God."

When Zaccheus had ceased speaking, Jesus said, "Today has salvation come to this home, and you have become indeed a son of Abraham." And turning to the crowd assembled about them, Jesus said, "And marvel not at what I say nor take offense at what we do, for I have all along declared that the Son of Man has come to seek and to save that which is lost."

They lodged with Zaccheus for the night. On the morrow they arose and made their way up the "road of robbers" to Bethany on their way to the Passover at Jerusalem.

Jesus spread good cheer everywhere he went. He was full of grace and truth. His associates never ceased to wonder at the gracious words that proceeded out of his mouth. You can cultivate gracefulness, but graciousness is the aroma of friendliness that emanates from a love-saturated soul.

Goodness always compels respect, but when it is devoid of grace, it often repels affection. Goodness is universally attractive only when it is gracious. Goodness is effective only when it is attractive.

Jesus really understood men; therefore could he manifest genuine sympathy and show sincere compassion. But he seldom indulged in pity. While his compassion was boundless, his sympathy was practical, personal, and constructive. Never did his familiarity with suffering breed indifference, and he was able to minister to distressed souls without increasing their self-pity.

Jesus could help men and women so much because he loved them so sincerely. He truly loved each man, each woman, and each child. He could be such a true friend because of his remarkable insight - he knew so fully what was in the heart and in the mind of man. He was an interested and keen observer. He was an expert in the comprehension of human need, clever in detecting human longings.

Jesus was never in a hurry. He had time to comfort his fellow men "as he passed by." And he always made his friends feel at ease. He was a charming listener. He never engaged in the meddlesome probing of the souls of his associates. As he comforted hungry minds and ministered to thirsty souls, the recipients of his mercy did not so much feel that they were confessing *to* him as that they were conferring *with* him. They had unbounded confidence in him because they saw he had so much faith in them.

He never seemed to be curious about people, and he never manifested a desire to direct, manage, or follow them up. He inspired profound self-confidence and robust courage in all who enjoyed his association. When he smiled on a man, that mortal experienced increased capacity for solving his manifold problems.

Jesus loved men and women so much and so wisely that he never hesitated to be severe with them when the occasion demanded such discipline. He frequently set out to help a person by asking for help. In this way he elicited interest, appealed to the better things in human nature.

The Master could discern saving faith in the gross superstition of the woman who sought healing by touching the hem of his garment. He was always ready and willing to stop a sermon or detain a multitude while he ministered to the needs of a single person, even to a little child. Great things happened not only because people had faith in Jesus, but also because Jesus had so much faith in them.

Most of the really important things which Jesus said or did seemed to happen casually, "as he passed by." There was so little of the professional, the well-planned, or the premeditated in the Master's earthly ministry. He dispensed health and scattered happiness naturally and gracefully as he journeyed through life. It was literally true, "He went about doing good."

And it behooves the Master's followers in all ages to learn to minister as "they pass by" - to do unselfish good as they go about their daily duties.

They did not start from Jericho until near noon since they sat up late the night before while Jesus taught Zaccheus and his family the gospel of the kingdom. About halfway up the ascending road to Bethany the party paused for lunch while the multitude passed on to Jerusalem, not knowing that Jesus and the apostles were going to abide that night on the Mount of Olives.

The parable of the pounds, unlike the parable of the talents, which was intended for all the disciples, was spoken more exclusively to the apostles and was largely based on the experience of Archelaus and his futile attempt to gain the rule of the kingdom of Judea. This is one of the few parables of the Master to be founded on an actual historic character. It was not strange that they should have had Archelaus in mind inasmuch as the house of Zaccheus in Jericho was very near the ornate palace of Archelaus, and his aqueduct ran along the road by which they had departed from Jericho.

Said Jesus, "You think that the Son of Man goes up to Jerusalem to receive a kingdom, but I declare that you are doomed to disappointment. Do you not remember about a certain prince who went into a far country to receive for himself a kingdom, but even before he could return, the citizens of his province, who in their hearts had already rejected him, sent an embassy after him, saying, 'We will not have this man to reign over us'? As this king was rejected in the temporal rule, so is the Son of Man to be rejected in the spiritual rule. Again I declare that my kingdom is not of this world; but if the Son of Man had been accorded the spiritual rule of his people, he would have accepted such a kingdom of men's souls and would have reigned over such a dominion of human hearts. Notwithstanding that they reject my spiritual rule over them, I will return again to receive from others such a kingdom of spirit as is now denied me. You will see the Son of Man rejected now, but in another age that which the children of Abraham now reject will be received and exalted.

"And now, as the rejected nobleman of this parable, I would call before me my twelve servants, special stewards, and giving into each of your hands the sum of one pound, I would admonish each to heed well my instructions that you trade diligently with your trust fund while I am away that you may have wherewith to justify your stewardship when I return, when a reckoning shall be required of you.

"And even if this rejected Son should not return, another Son will be sent to receive this kingdom, and this Son will then send for all of you to receive your report of stewardship and to be made glad by your gains.

"And when these stewards were subsequently called together for an accounting, the first came forward, saying, 'Lord, with your pound I have made ten pounds more.' And his master said to him: 'Well done; you are a good servant; because you have proved faithful in this matter, I will give you authority over ten cities.' And the second came, saying, 'Your pound left with me, Lord, has made five pounds.' And the master said, 'I will accordingly make you ruler over five cities.' And so on down through the others until the last of the servants, on being called to account, reported: 'Lord, behold, here is your pound, which I have kept safely done up in this napkin. And this I did because I feared you; I believed that you were unreasonable, seeing that you take up where you have not laid down, and that you seek to reap where you have not sown.' Then said his lord: 'You negligent and unfaithful servant, I will judge you out of your own mouth. You knew that I reap where I have apparently not sown; therefore you knew this reckoning would be required of you. Knowing this, you should have at least given my money to the banker that at my coming I might have had it with proper interest.'

"And then said this ruler to those who stood by, 'Take the money from this slothful servant and give it to him who has ten pounds.' And when they reminded the master that such a one already had ten pounds, he said, 'To every one who has shall be given more, but from him who has not, even that which he has shall be taken away from him.'"

And then the apostles sought to know the difference between the meaning of this parable and that of the former parable of the talents, but Jesus would only say, in answer to their many questions, "Ponder well these words in your hearts while each of you finds out their true meaning."

It was Nathaniel who so well taught the meaning of these two parables in the after years, summing up his teachings in these conclusions:

1. Ability is the practical measure of life's opportunities. You will never be held responsible for the accomplishment of that which is beyond your abilities.

2. Faithfulness is the unerring measure of human trustworthiness. He who is faithful in little things is also likely to exhibit faithfulness in everything consistent with his endowments.

3. The Master grants the lesser reward for lesser faithfulness when there is like opportunity.

4. He grants a like reward for like faithfulness when there is lesser opportunity.

When they had finished their lunch, and after the multitude of followers had gone on toward Jerusalem, Jesus, standing there before the apostles in the shade of an overhanging rock by the roadside, with cheerful dignity and a gracious majesty pointed his finger westward, saying, "Come, my brethren, let us go on into Jerusalem, there to receive that which awaits us; thus shall we fulfill the will of the heavenly Father in all things."

And so Jesus and his apostles resumed this, the Master's last journey to Jerusalem in the likeness of the flesh of mortal man.

# End Part Two

# Give a Gift to Loved Ones, Friends, and Colleagues That Can Change Their Lives.

CHECK YOUR LEADING BOOKSTORE OR ORDER HERE

Yes I want additional copies of The Greatest Story Ever Revealed. Please send the following number of copies:

\_\_ Part One @ $12.99 each
\_\_ Part Two @ $16.99 each
\_\_ Part Three @ $12.99 each
\_\_ Boxed Set @ $39.99 each

Shipping and handling $4.00 for first book or set plus $2.00 for each additional book or set.

My check or Money Order for $_____ is enclosed.

Please charge my \_Visa \_MC \_Discover \_ AMEX Credit card.

Name _____

Organization _____

Address _____

City/State/Zip _____

Card#_____exp_____

Signature_____

Please make your check payable and mail to:
Hart-Burn Press
PO Box 99
Newton Jct, NH 03859-0099
Fax: 603-382-8794 Email: info@stevehartbooks.com

Coming in the Spring of 2004

The Garden of Eden;
The Book of Genesis According to Andrew

Edited by Steve Hart

ISBN 0-9740318-6-0

Approx 250 pgs.
US $13.99

Excerpts on Following 4 Pages

Excerpts from, The Garden of Eden; The Book of Genesis According to Andrew:

On the naming of the garden...

When Material Sons, the biologic uplifters, begin their sojourn on an evolutionary world, their place of abode is often called the Garden of Eden because it is characterized by the floral beauty and the botanic grandeur of Edentia, the constellation capital. Van well knew of these customs and accordingly provided that the entire peninsula be given over to the Garden. Pasturage and animal husbandry were projected for the adjoining mainland. Of animal life, only the birds and the various domesticated species were to be found in the park. Van's instructions were that Eden was to be a garden, and only a garden. No animals were ever slaughtered within its precincts.

On the layout of the garden...

At the center of the Edenic peninsula was the exquisite stone temple of the Universal Father, the sacred shrine of the Garden. To the north the administrative headquarters was established; to the south were built the homes for the workers and their families; to the west was provided the allotment of ground for the proposed schools of the educational system of the expected Son, while in the "east of Eden" were built the domiciles intended for the promised Son and his immediate offspring. The architectural plans for Eden provided homes and abundant land for one million human beings.

On the Tree of Life...

The "tree of the knowledge of good and evil" may be a figure of speech, a symbolic designation covering a multitude of human experiences, but the "tree of life" was not a myth; it was real and for a long time was present on your world. When the Most Highs of Edentia approved the commission of Caligastia as Planetary Prince of Earth and those of the one hundred Jerusem citizens as his administrative staff, they sent to the planet, by the Melchizedeks, a shrub of Edentia, and this plant grew to be the tree of life on Earth.

On the fate of the First Garden...

After the first garden was vacated by Adam, it was occupied variously by the
Nodites, Cutites, and the Suntites. It later became the dwelling place of the northern Nodites who opposed co-operation with the Adamites. The peninsula had been
overrun by these lower-grade Nodites for almost four thousand years after Adam
left the Garden when, in connection with the violent activity of the surrounding vol-
canoes and the submergence of the Sicilian land bridge to Africa, the eastern floor
of the Mediterranean Sea sank, carrying down beneath the waters the whole of the
Edenic peninsula. Concomitant with this vast submergence the coast line of the
eastern Mediterranean was greatly elevated